HOLMAN Old Testament Commentary

Deuteronomy

GENERAL EDITOR
Max Anders

AUTHOR
Doug McIntosh

HOLMAN REFERENCE

Nashville, Tennessee

Holman Old Testament Commentary
© 2002 Broadman & Holman Publishers
Nashville, Tennessee
All rights reserved

Bible versions used in this book:

Unless otherwise stated all Scripture citation is from the HOLY BIBLE, NEW INTERNATIONAL VERSION®. Copyright © 1973, 1978, 1984 by International Bible Society. Used by permission of Zondervan Publishing House. All Rights Reserved. The "NIV" and "New International Version" trademarks are registered in the United States Patent and Trademark Office by International Bible Society. Use of either trademark requires the permission of International Bible Society.

The King James Version

Scripture passages marked NASB are taken from Scripture taken from the NEW AMERICAN STANDARD BIBLE, © Copyright The Lockman Foundation, 1960, 1962, 1963, 1968, 1971, 1972, 1973, 1975, 1977, 1995 Used by permission.

From the New King James Version. Copyright © 1979, 1980, 1982, Thomas Nelson, Inc., Publishers.

ISBN-13: 978-0-8054-9463-1
Dewey Decimal Classification: 222.15
Subject Heading: BIBLE. OT. Deuteronomy—Study
McIntosh, Doug
    Deuteronomy/Doug McIntosh
        p.   cm. — (Holman Old Testament commentary)
    Includes bibliographical references. (p.).
    ISBN 0–8054–9463–4
    1. Bible. O.T. Deuteronomy—Commentaries.   I. Title.   II. Series.

—dc21

2 3 4 5 6 7 8 • 11 10 09 08 07

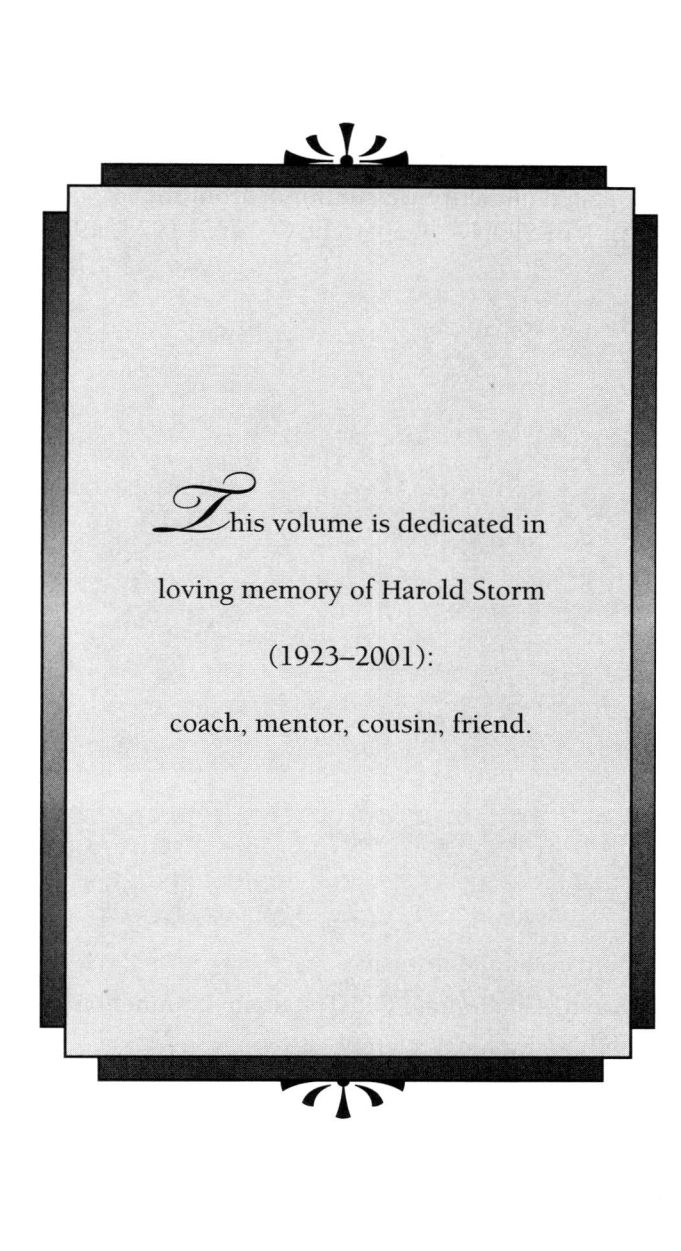

This volume is dedicated in loving memory of Harold Storm (1923–2001): coach, mentor, cousin, friend.

Contents

Editorial Preface ix
Acknowledgements x
Holman Old Testament Commentary Contributors xi
Holman New Testament Commentary Contributors xii
Holman Old Testament Commentary xiii
Introduction to Deuteronomy 1

Deuteronomy 1
   Celebrate His Faithfulness 7
Deuteronomy 2
   Facing the Enemy 23
Deuteronomy 3
   The Ministry of Courage 37
Deuteronomy 4
   A Call to Faithfulness 49
Deuteronomy 5
   The Authority of the Word 65
Deuteronomy 6
   The First and Greatest Commandment 81
Deuteronomy 7
   Holy War 93
Deuteronomy 8
   Man the Verbivore 105
Deuteronomy 9
   The Power of a Godly Intercessor 117
Deuteronomy 10
   What God Wants 131
Deuteronomy 11
   The Choice Is Ours 143
Deuteronomy 12
   Only One Way 155
Deuteronomy 13
   Confronting Error 167

Contents

Deuteronomy 14
    Distinctive Lord, Distinctive Life 177

Deuteronomy 15
    Developing a Generous Heart 187

Deuteronomy 16
    Seeking the Center 199

Deuteronomy 17
    The Great Society 209

Deuteronomy 18
    A Prophet like Moses 219

Deuteronomy 19
    God Our Refuge 229

Deuteronomy 20
    The Qualities of a Christian Warrior 239

Deuteronomy 21
    Matters of Life and Death 247

Deuteronomy 22
    Preserve and Protect 257

Deuteronomy 23
    The Cutting Edge 269

Deuteronomy 24
    Portrait of a Caring Society 279

Deuteronomy 25
    No Muzzled Oxen 289

Deuteronomy 26
    His Persistent Presence 297

Deuteronomy 27
    Coated Stones and Curses 307

Deuteronomy 28
    Decisions of Life and Death 317

Deuteronomy 29
    Eyes to See 327

Deuteronomy 30
    Choose Life 337

Deuteronomy 31
    Prelude to a Sad Song 347

Deuteronomy 32
>   What's Your Song? 357
Deuteronomy 33
>   The Riches of His Grace 365
Deuteronomy 34
>   Epitaph for a Giant 373
>   Bibliography 381
>   Glossary 383

Editorial Preface

Today's church hungers for Bible teaching, and Bible teachers hunger for resources to guide them in teaching God's Word. The Holman Old Testament Commentary provides the church with the food to feed the spiritually hungry in an easily digestible format. The result: new spiritual vitality that the church can readily use.

Bible teaching should result in new interest in the Scriptures, expanded Bible knowledge, discovery of specific scriptural principles, relevant applications, and exciting living. The unique format of the Holman Old Testament Commentary includes sections to achieve these results for every Old Testament book.

Opening quotations stimulate thinking and lead to an introductory illustration and discussion that draw individuals and study groups into the Word of God. "In a Nutshell" summarizes the content and teaching of the chapter. Verse-by-verse commentary answers the church's questions rather than raising issues scholars usually admit they cannot adequately solve. Bible principles and specific contemporary applications encourage students to move from Bible to contemporary times. A specific modern illustration then ties application vividly to present life. A brief prayer aids the student to commit his or her daily life to the principles and applications found in the Bible chapter being studied. For those still hungry for more, "Deeper Discoveries" take the student into a more personal, deeper study of the words, phrases, and themes of God's Word. Finally, a teaching outline provides transitional statements and conclusions along with an outline to assist the teacher in group Bible studies.

It is the editors' prayer that this new resource for local church Bible teaching will enrich the ministry of group, as well as individual, Bible study, and that it will lead God's people truly to be people of the Book, living out what God calls us to be.

Acknowledgements

My special thanks go to the staff at Cornerstone Bible Church, Lilburn, Georgia, for sharing the challenges of ministry with me: associate pastor Chuck Taylor, youth pastor Everett Bracken, and Kathy Berkstresser, Kay Himmel, Susan Bracken, and Jo Ann Jones. As always, loving thanks go also to my wife Cheryl, who shared me with my word processor for many months without complaining.

Holman Old Testament Commentary Contributors

Vol. 1, Genesis
ISBN 0-8054-9461-8
Kenneth O. Gangel and
Stephen J. Bramer

Vol. 2, Exodus, Leviticus, Numbers
ISBN 0-8054-9462-6
Glen Martin

Vol. 3, Deuteronomy
ISBN 0-8054-9463-4
Doug McIntosh

Vol. 4, Joshua
ISBN 0-8054-9464-2
Kenneth O. Gangel

Vol. 5, Judges, Ruth
ISBN 0-8054-9465-0
W. Gary Phillips

Vol. 6, 1 & 2 Samuel
ISBN 0-8054-9466-9
Stephen Andrews

Vol. 7, 1 & 2 Kings
ISBN 0-8054-9467-7
Gary Inrig

Vol. 8, 1 & 2 Chronicles
ISBN 0-8054-9468-5
Winfried Corduan

Vol. 9, Ezra, Nehemiah, Esther
ISBN 0-8054-9469-3
Knute Larson and Kathy Dahlen

Vol. 10, Job
ISBN 0-8054-9470-7
Steven J. Lawson

Vol. 11, Psalms 1–75
ISBN 0-8054-9471-5
Steven J. Lawson

Vol. 12, Psalms 76–150
ISBN 0-8054-9481-2
Steven J. Lawson

Vol. 13, Proverbs
ISBN 0-8054-9472-3
Max Anders

Vol. 14, Ecclesiastes, Song of Songs
ISBN 0-8054-9482-0
David George Moore and Daniel L. Akin

Vol. 15, Isaiah
ISBN 0-8054-9473-1
Trent C. Butler

Vol. 16, Jeremiah, Lamentations
ISBN 0-8054-9474-X
Fred M. Wood and Ross McLaren

Vol. 17, Ezekiel
ISBN 0-8054-9475-8
Mark F. Rooker

Vol. 18, Daniel
ISBN 0-8054-9476-6
Kenneth O. Gangel

Vol. 19, Hosea, Joel, Amos, Obadiah, Jonah, Micah
ISBN 0-8054-9477-4
Trent C. Butler

Vol. 20, Nahum, Habakkuk, Zephaniah, Haggai, Zechariah, Malachi
ISBN 0-8054-9478-2
Stephen R. Miller

Holman New Testament Commentary Contributors

Vol. 1, Matthew
ISBN 0-8054-0201-2
Stuart K. Weber

Vol. 2, Mark
ISBN 0-8054-0202-0
Rodney L. Cooper

Vol. 3, Luke
ISBN 0-8054-0203-9
Trent C. Butler

Vol. 4, John
ISBN 0-8054-0204-7
Kenneth O. Gangel

Vol. 5, Acts
ISBN 0-8054-0205-5
Kenneth O. Gangel

Vol. 6, Romans
ISBN 0-8054-0206-3
Kenneth Boa and William Kruidenier

Vol. 7, 1 & 2 Corinthians
ISBN 0-8054-0207-1
Richard L. Pratt Jr.

Vol. 8, Galatians, Ephesians, Philippians, Colossians
ISBN 0-8054-0208-X
Max Anders

Vol. 9, 1 & 2 Thessalonians, 1 & 2 Timothy, Titus, Philemon
ISBN 0-8054-0209-8
Knute Larson

Vol. 10, Hebrews, James
ISBN 0-8054-0211-X
Thomas D. Lea

Vol. 11, 1 & 2 Peter, 1, 2, 3 John, Jude
ISBN 0-8054-0210-1
David Walls and Max Anders

Vol. 12, Revelation
ISBN 0-8054-0212-8
Kendell H. Easley

Holman Old Testament Commentary

Twenty volumes designed for Bible study and teaching to enrich the local church and God's people.

Series Editor	Max Anders
Managing Editor	Steve Bond
Project Editor	Dean Richardson
Product Development Manager	Ricky D. King
Marketing Manager	Stephanie Huffman
Executive Editor	David Shepherd
Page Composition	TF Designs, Mt. Juliet, TN

Introduction to Deuteronomy

On a remote and rocky hillside in territory assigned to the tribe of his ancestor Judah, the Son of God once engaged in a fierce spiritual struggle against Satan. Three times the enemy of souls encouraged him to declare his independence from heaven in order to alleviate his suffering. Although physically weakened by forty days of fasting, the Savior refused to yield. As each temptation was offered, Jesus denied the tempter's urgings, in each case citing as his reason a passage from the Book of Deuteronomy. Three times the enemy attacked, and three times he was beaten off when Jesus took refuge in the words of God found in this great book.

Although many of his followers confess their lack of familiarity with Deuteronomy, Jesus knew it well and referred to it often. Repeatedly during his ministry the Lord quoted or alluded to the book in the resolution of personal attacks or theological disputes. The apostles, taking their cue from the Master, also frequently appealed to it and quoted from it in their letters. The New Testament writers either quote or allude to Deuteronomy nearly two hundred times, making it one of the most referenced volumes of Hebrew Scripture.

AUTHORSHIP

Until the eighteenth century, virtually all students of Deuteronomy were content to accept its own claims—that it came from the mouth and pen of Moses, the Hebrew lawgiver. The very first verse of the book, in fact, claims that Deuteronomy is the work of Moses, speaking under divine inspiration. The authorship of no other book of the Old Testament is so particularly emphasized.

References to both Moses' speaking and writing appear often throughout the book (see, e.g., 1:6,9; 5:1; 27:1,9; 29:2; 31:1,9,24,30; 33:1). One of these texts provides explicitly for the preservation of Moses' words:

> Moses wrote down this law and gave it to the priests, the sons of Levi, who carried the ark of the covenant of the LORD, and to all the elders of Israel. . . . After Moses finished writing in a book the words of this law from beginning to end, he gave this command to the Levites who carried the ark of the covenant of the LORD: "Take this Book of the Law and place it beside the ark of the covenant of the LORD

Deuteronomy

your God. There it will remain as a witness against you" (Deut. 31:9,24–26).

The "Book of the Law" described in this passage may be more, but it cannot be less, than the Book of Deuteronomy.

Nor does the testimony end inside the book itself. The rest of the Old Testament affirms and reaffirms that the human author of Deuteronomy (and the preceding four books of the Pentateuch) is Moses (see Josh. 1:7–8; Judg. 1:20; 3:4; 1 Kgs. 2:3; 2 Kgs. 14:6; 2 Chr. 25:4; Ezra 3:2). Likewise, the New Testament acknowledges that Deuteronomy is Mosaic in origin (Matt. 19:7; Mark 12:19; Luke 20:28; Acts 3:22; Rom. 10:19; 1 Cor. 9:9; Heb. 9:19; 10:28).

Most telling of all, Jesus explicitly attributed portions of Deuteronomy to Moses. On one occasion, local teachers asked Jesus to settle a dispute about the propriety of divorce in the life of the people of God. Jesus noted that Moses had allowed divorce as a concession to human weakness, alluding to a text in Deuteronomy as his authority (Matt. 19:3–9; see Deut. 24:1–4). After his resurrection, the Lord Jesus, "beginning with Moses and all the Prophets . . . explained to them what was said in all the Scriptures concerning himself" (Luke 24:27; see also v. 44). "Moses and all the Prophets" was an alternate way of referring to "the Law and the Prophets," or the Old Testament.

Mosaic authorship of Deuteronomy, however, has been vigorously challenged since the eighteenth century. In some circles, the Book of Deuteronomy is regarded as a seventh-century B.C. work, in fact the very "Book of the Law" discovered during the days of King Josiah (see 2 Kgs. 22:8–13). Cynical doubters of Mosaic authorship now regard that volume as a well-intentioned fraud intended to support Josiah's spiritual reforms in Judah. Among other things (so the view holds), Josiah wanted to centralize all spiritual authority in Jerusalem, so he had the Mosaic impersonator include a reference to a coming central sanctuary:

> You are to seek the place the LORD your God will choose from among all your tribes to put his Name there for his dwelling. To that place you must go; there bring your burnt offerings and sacrifices, your tithes and special gifts, what you have vowed to give and your freewill offerings, and the firstborn of your herds and flocks. There, in the presence of the LORD your God, you and your families shall eat and shall rejoice in everything you have put your hand to, because the LORD your God has blessed you (Deut. 12:5–7).

The view that Deuteronomy came into existence as part of an effort to support the Josianic reforms constitutes part of what has been called the "Documentary Hypothesis" of the authorship of the Pentateuch. According to

Introduction to Deuteronomy

this theory, the Pentateuch is a kind of patchwork quilt assembled from many literary remnants of Israel's old polytheistic religions. The assembler or "redactor" cleverly disguised the end product and gave it credibility by insisting that Moses was the original author. Placing in Moses' mouth words of condemnation of local Canaanite shrines, the redactor was able to gather all religious authority into the hands of the Jerusalem priesthood and to authenticate the Jerusalem temple long after it was built.

Virtually every thesis upon which the Documentary Hypothesis is based has now been shown to be faulty, but the antisupernaturalistic bias that spawned it remains too strong for critics simply to accept the simple declarations of the text. It continues to be taught in many theological seminaries.

READER PROFILE

By derivation from its Greek roots, the word *Deuteronomy* means "a second [giving of the] law," an expression that connects the book with its original hearers/readers. In Numbers 14, the Israelites who emerged from Egyptian bondage rebelled against the Lord. Consequently they were consigned to wander in the wilderness until they died. Their children (who were less than twenty years of age at the time of the rebellion) were the addressees of Deuteronomy, which was originally given as a series of addresses to them just before they entered the promised land.

These texts make it clear that the binding nature of Deuteronomy's covenant transcends the generation to which it was addressed. The people who were about to enter the land, in fact, had to take steps to ensure that succeeding generations would come to know Yahweh, the God of Israel, and to love him supremely:

> Hear, O Israel: The LORD our God, the LORD is one. Love the LORD your God with all your heart and with all your soul and with all your strength. These commandments that I give you today are to be upon your hearts. Impress them on your children. Talk about them when you sit at home and when you walk along the road, when you lie down and when you get up. Tie them as symbols on your hands and bind them on your foreheads (Deut. 6:4–8).

By extension (and based on testimony found in the New Testament), those same concerns belong on the spiritual priority list of every believer in Jesus Christ. Indeed, Jesus himself, when asked to state the greatest commandment in God's Law, quoted Deuteronomy 6:5 and explained that these words (together with Lev. 19:18) form a summary of all of Hebrew Scripture.

Deuteronomy

DATE OF WRITING

The Book of 1 Kings specifies that the building of Solomon's temple began in the fourth year of that ruler. Since this date can be fixed with confidence as 967/966 B.C., and since the same writer explains that the exodus was 480 years before this event (1 Kgs. 6:1), the date of the exodus must have been about 1446 B.C. Since Moses and the Israelites took forty years to arrive on the eastern bank of the Jordan River, Moses must have issued what we call Deuteronomy about 1406 B.C.

This date coincides closely with the evidence given by Jephthah when he reminded the Ammonites, "For three hundred years Israel occupied Heshbon, Aroer, the surrounding settlements and all the towns along the Arnon. Why didn't you retake them during that time?" (Judg. 11:26). Since Jephthah's judgeship can be placed at some point between 1106 and 1100 B.C., the internal biblical evidence for a date of about 1406 B.C. for the Book of Deuteronomy is quite strong.

Recent scholarship has buttressed the biblical date (and the claims of Moses' authorship of Deuteronomy) by an examination of the literary form of the book. Several researchers have observed how Deuteronomy follows the pattern of the suzerain-vassal treaties that were typical of the second millennium B.C. when Moses was living (but not those of the first millennium B.C.) Taken together, these considerations argue strongly for a date for Deuteronomy near the end of the fifteenth century B.C.

CHARACTERISTICS AND THEME

The most noteworthy feature of Deuteronomy is its call for total devotion to Yahweh, the God of Israel. The descendants of Abraham, Isaac, and Jacob appear, as the book opens, on the edge of that land promised long before to the three patriarchs. God had moved the hearts of mighty rulers and opened the Red Sea to bring them to such a condition. In Deuteronomy, he promises again to remain faithful to the covenant he had made with Israel's forebears and insists that Israel's happiness lies in a wholehearted commitment to him.

Although much of Deuteronomy is a recapitulation of commandments and decrees that had already been given years before to the older generation, the book is not simply a review of legal precepts. It also consists of exhortations to the descendants of Abraham to make sound spiritual choices based on what they know of God personally. As such, Deuteronomy is deeply pastoral, profoundly theological, and intensely personal: "Take to heart all the words I have solemnly declared to you this day, so that you may command your children to obey carefully all the words of this law. They are not just idle words for you—they are your life" (Deut. 32:46–47).

Introduction to Deuteronomy

Deuteronomy is a wellspring of rich theology. Moses both describes and assumes a God of wondrous capacities and virtues. He is omnipotent while caring for individuals, eternal while never losing touch with earthly matters, and personal even though transcendent. He may be known by his acts in history, but those acts are properly understood through the propositions and interpretive statements of his word.

As such, he is a God who expects and requires from his people a total and unqualified devotion to him. He has proven himself faithful through many generations and as such expects and requires that Israel will turn away from any other deities. It is not enough that they regard him as the supreme God of the universe. For their own good, he will not allow his people to make room in their lives for other gods. The only acceptable worship is exclusive worship.

Deuteronomy is a book for believers who are living on the edge of a hostile culture. Just as Israel was about to face the challenge of living in a land occupied by idolatrous and pagan peoples, modern Christians in the West must learn to live in cultures that are hostile toward their faith. Whether those forces are modern and claim that all religions are false, or postmodern and claim that all of them are true, the process is the same. By giving exclusive loyalty to the God of Abraham, Isaac, and Jacob, the believer can maintain a distinctive identity in a culture that seems determined to destroy or reshape his convictions.

Israel brought a strict monotheism into a land glutted by a thousand deities. Israel's point of view was utterly rejected by their contemporaries, but the people of the land did not stop with resistance. They intended to convert the Israelites and to bring them into conformity with the local culture.

In the same way, postmodern visions of political correctness not only resist any proclamation of an exclusive gospel, but they seek to enlighten and convert those who propagate such a narrow perspective. It has been said that postmodernism is elitist about people and egalitarian with respect to ideas. Biblical faith is precisely the opposite. Yahweh is unique (Deut. 6:4), and he tolerates no rivals. Jesus is the way, the truth, and the life (John 14:6). Only a consistent, wholehearted dedication to remain faithful to the true God will enable the people of God to maintain a vibrant relationship with God and a powerful testimony for him.

The Book of Deuteronomy is organized as a covenant document. It falls into six essential sections: (1) the preamble (1:1–5), where the words of the book are defined as those of Israel's great king, Yahweh, conveyed through a covenant mediator, Moses; (2) the historical prologue (1:6–4:49), reviewing the faithfulness of the Lord even in the face of the disloyalty of the previous generation; (3) the general stipulations (5:1–11:32), describing the general principles of the relationship between Israel and Yahweh; (4) the specific

Deuteronomy

stipulations (chs. 12–26), following roughly the summary of the covenant contained in the Ten Commandments; (5) the covenant sanctions or blessings and curses (chs. 27–28), describing the benefits of adherence to the covenant and the penalties of breaking it; and (6) the witnesses (chs. 29–32) to the entire transaction. Chapter 33 contains Moses' farewell blessings on the tribes, and chapter 34 records his death.

Deuteronomy 1

Celebrate His Faithfulness

I. **INTRODUCTION**
   Checking the Chimney

II. **COMMENTARY**
   A verse-by-verse explanation of the chapter.

III. **CONCLUSION**
   Unnecessary Pillars

   An overview of the principles and applications from the chapter.

IV. **LIFE APPLICATION**
   The Limitations of a Knapsack

   Melding the chapter to life.

V. **PRAYER**
   Tying the chapter to life with God.

VI. **DEEPER DISCOVERIES**
   Historical, geographical, and grammatical enrichment of the commentary.

VII. **TEACHING OUTLINE**
   Suggested step-by-step group study of the chapter.

VIII. **ISSUES FOR DISCUSSION**
   Zeroing the chapter in on daily life.

Deuteronomy 1

Quote

"Our office is a ministry of grace and salvation. It subjects us to great burdens and labors, dangers and temptations, with little reward or gratitude from the world. But Christ himself will be our reward if we labor faithfully."

Martin Luther

BIOGRAPHICAL PROFILE: CALEB

- Son of Jephunneh the Kenizzite of the tribe of Judah
- His name means "dog" in the sense of "servant"
- A member of the team of spies who investigated the promised land
- One of two spies who insisted that the land could be conquered
- Later appointed with others by Joshua to assign tribal allotments in the land

BIOGRAPHICAL PROFILE: JOSHUA

- Designated successor of Moses; also called Hoshea
- His name means something akin to "Yahweh is salvation"
- Son of Nun and a member of the tribe of Ephraim
- Also a member of the company of spies, and, like Caleb, one who insisted on fighting
- Servant of Moses during the exodus and wilderness wanderings
- Appointed general by Moses at the time of the Amalekite attack

Deuteronomy 1

IN A NUTSHELL

*G*od's purpose in history is to draw to himself a family of people who are bound to him and to one another by cords of love. In gaining this purpose, he takes the initiative by expressing his love first. Deuteronomy 1 is the record of his past blessings, intended to provoke Israel to love him in return.

Celebrate His Faithfulness

I. INTRODUCTION

Checking the Chimney

In the early hours of a wet Evansville morning, a driver lost control of his vehicle and smashed through the porch into the front of Lee Roy Book's home. When a utility crew came to the house and began to check for gas leaks, they found that the home's chimney and gas pipes were plugged by debris. Because of this, carbon monoxide fumes had been backing up into the house for some time.

The poisonous and odorless gas had been creating health problems for Book for a while. Some two years before, he had begun experiencing flu-like symptoms, including unexplained trembling, headaches, chills, and nausea. He would also black out intermittently and undergo periods of forgetfulness. "I'd come to when I got in the fresh air," he said, "but every day it was getting worse and worse. It was awful." Had the utility vehicle not made its unauthorized entry, he might well have died from the poisonous effects of the gas.

The ironic twist to the story, however, came when it was discovered that Lee Roy Book once made his living as a building contractor. As such, he knew the perils of badly vented furnaces and chimneys. In fact, he regularly urged his customers to check their flues every two to three years to keep just such a problem from occurring. Yet it never dawned on him to check his own chimney.

A lot of people make the same mistake spiritually. They rarely consider the many ways that God has blessed them in the past and the implications of those blessings for the way they should live their lives.

The opening chapter of Deuteronomy describes an entire nation that failed to check its chimney. Israel had repeatedly been the recipient of God's faithful acts of kindness, but they had neglected drawing the proper implications from such blessings. In Deuteronomy 1, Moses called on the people to remember God's faithfulness as a spur to their own spiritual lives.

II. COMMENTARY

Celebrate His Faithfulness

MAIN IDEA: *Unbelief can rob God's people of joys that he intends them to have.*

🅐 The Discourse of Moses (1:1–5)

SUPPORTING IDEA: *God's faithfulness commends his word to us.*

1:1. The **words** of Deuteronomy constitute a series of addresses that **Moses** issued **to all Israel** to renew the covenant between the Lord and the nation. The original generation (those twenty or more years old) that had left Egypt had died in the wilderness because of their unbelief. The younger generation now stood poised on the **east** side of the **Jordan** River, ready to invade the land of promise. More precisely, they were camped **in the Arabah**, the broad, deep, and arid valley that runs between the Sea of Galilee and the Dead Sea. Although the term *Arabah* commonly describes that portion of the Great Rift Valley between the southern tip of the Dead Sea and the northern end of the Gulf of Aqaba, on occasion it refers to the area north of the Dead Sea. That such is the intent here is made clear by Numbers 35:1, which explains that God spoke to Moses "on the plains of Moab by the Jordan across from Jericho" (see also Num. 36:13).

Most of the other place names in this verse refer to locations that are today unknown. Three of them (**Tophel, Laban**, and **Dizahab**) appear only here in Scripture. The location is significant, for the Israelite army stayed in camp and did not move during the entire Book of Deuteronomy. It was a time for reflection and dedication, a time to prepare people who were about to do battle. As such, it provides help for those who are preparing to engage in spiritual battle.

1:2. Although the distance from **Horeb** (the desolate area that includes Mount Sinai) **to Kadesh Barnea** in the edge of the Holy Land (about 150 miles in a straight line) normally requires only **eleven days** to cross, it had taken Israel forty years to arrive in the Arabah. Rebellion and unbelief had led to terrible delays and judgments, including the death of an entire generation. Deuteronomy contains exhortations and appeals designed to prevent the recurrence of such folly. Although the somewhat parenthetical statement of verse 2 seems tame enough on its surface, it conveys a wistful reminder of what might have been had Israel followed the Lord faithfully from the outset.

1:3. **Moses** and the people were now in their **fortieth year** of travel since leaving Egypt. Since the exodus from Egypt is specified as occurring 480 years before the construction of Solomon's temple (see 1 Kgs. 6:1), the exodus date can be placed at about 1446 B.C., and the conquest forty years later in 1406 B.C. Although it is commonly asserted, on the basis of archeological evidence, that the exodus took place around 1290 B.C., the internal biblical evidence for the earlier date is quite consistent. For example, Jephthah the judge later explained how Israel had been in the region east of the Jordan River for three hundred years (Judg. 11:26). Since by common consent the judgeship of Jephthah took place about 1106–1100, the information in Judges fits perfectly with that of 1 Kings 6:1, confirming a date of about 1406 for the beginning of the conquest.

Instead of the more direct route from the south, Israel had wandered hundreds of additional miles and had arrived at the eastern boundary of the Holy

Land proper. On the first day of the eleventh month (January or February on the modern calendar), **Moses proclaimed to the Israelites** what God **had commanded him concerning** their behavior during the invasion of their new homeland and in the years to follow.

They had been redeemed from slavery in Egypt, but they did not know how to behave as free people. The application to Christian living seems clear enough: extrication from a life of enslavement is only the beginning of God's purpose in the believer. Spiritual living requires an awareness of God's commandments and his ways. Before undertaking any significant new venture, the thoughtful person will assess the state of his spiritual life and consider what God expects from him in the days to come.

1:4. The address of Moses (essentially the rest of the Book of Deuteronomy) followed the nation's defeat of **Sihon** and **Og**, Amorite kings who ruled territory east of the Jordan River. Although these territories were not a part of the original land grant to Abraham, God gave them as a homeland to Reuben, Gad, and the half-tribe of Manasseh. The allotments were added to the land of promise because Sihon and Og had refused a request for Israel's passage through their lands on their approach to Canaan. In response to Moses' promise to pass peacefully through their region, the two kings had attacked the Israelite army (see Num. 21:21–24; 32:33). Those fresh victories must have proved a great encouragement to an army soon to do battle with much larger nations.

1:5. The newly conquered territory lay east of the Jordan River in the land that had long been inhabited by the descendants of **Moab**, one of the incestuously conceived children of Abraham's nephew Lot (see Gen. 19:37). The Moabites were thus distant cousins of the Israelites, although they did not serve the God of Israel, choosing to worship Chemosh instead (see, e.g., Jer. 48:13). It was in this formerly Moabite territory that **Moses began to expound** God's law. The word *expound* is related to the Hebrew word for a "well" of water. Moses in effect "draws out" the content and the intent of God's actions in history and his commandments for Israel's conduct.

B The Declaration to the Nation (1:6–8)

SUPPORTING IDEA: *Once God has offered his people life, it must be grasped by faith.*

1:6. Many Bible scholars have noted that Deuteronomy follows the outline of an Ancient Near Eastern suzerain-vassal treaty. After the preamble (corresponding to 1:1–5 in Deuteronomy), the standard procedure in such treaties was to include a section reviewing the relationships between the master and his covenant partner. This so-called historical prologue gave the basis upon which the suzerain issued stipulations for the peaceful and prosperous continuation of the relationship. The historical prologue in Deuteronomy begins with this verse and continues through 4:49.

Moses did not begin his review with the exodus but with the events that many of his hearers had been alive to experience. That history began at **Horeb**, where God first established his covenant with the newly redeemed nation. There Yahweh ordered his people to take their first steps on the road to the promised land, since they had **stayed long enough** at Mount Sinai. It was time to advance.

1:7. God used a series of expressions to define the promised land. It included **the hill country of the Amorites**, an expression that describes the central mountain ridge that forms the bulk of the Holy Land. The **Arabah** corresponds roughly to what is sometimes described as the Jordan Valley, lying to the east of the hill country. The **western foothills** are often called the Shephelah, and they form the connection between the central hill country of Palestine and the land **along the coast**. The latter expression is apparently intended to cover what is now often called the coastal plain that runs from the Gaza Strip to Lebanon. The **Negev** ("South") includes the triangular area from Gaza on the coast to the Dead Sea and then southward to the Gulf of Aqaba. Both Beersheba and Kadesh Barnea lie within this area. The northern boundary of the promised land was to be along **the great River, the Euphrates**.

1:8. God commanded his people to **take possession** of what he had **given** them. It is characteristic of the God of heaven to place a worthy objective before his people in such a fashion. He had already **given** the land to Israel, although at the time God spoke these words Israel had yet to control a square foot of it. He deeded the land to them by virtue of an oath sworn to **Abraham, Isaac and Jacob**, their forefathers.

C The Designation of the Leaders (1:9–18)

SUPPORTING IDEA: *Divinely given success generally brings new problems in the life of faith.*

1:9–11. Moses recalled his own relationship with the people of Israel. The staggering increase in the size of the nation provided living proof that they were renewing a covenant with a faithful God. They had, however, become a burden **too heavy** for Moses **to carry alone**. Moses had already divided Israel into manageable units at the advice of his father-in-law Jethro (Exod. 18:13–27). Yahweh had increased the numbers of the nation so greatly that they had become **as many as the stars in the sky**. Moses' simile in verse 10 recalls the language of God's ancient promise to Abraham: "I will surely bless you and make your descendants as numerous as the stars in the sky" (Gen. 22:17; see also 15:5; 26:4; Exod. 32:13).

Although an entire generation had died, their children had been fruitful in spite of their disagreeable surroundings. The army that had gathered in the Arabah numbered 601,730 men twenty years old and above. Assuming a comparable number of women, the total population of the nation (including children) must have approached **two million**. Although the nation had caused Moses considerable pain, he desired nothing but prosperity for them, and asked that Yahweh **increase** them **a thousand times** more and continue to bless them according to his promise (v. 11).

1:12. Nonetheless, the enormous size of the nation created an impossible leadership task for Moses. He could not **bear** their **problems**, . . . **burdens and** . . . **disputes** alone, so he appealed to them for help.

1:13–14. Their assistance, Moses explained, should be offered in the form of **wise, understanding and respected men** from each tribe who could serve as leaders. The word *respected* translates a Hebrew term suggesting that the leaders of Israel should be people who were well-known to those they would lead. The leaders of Israel needed both insight and the respect of their community in order to function well. The nation as a whole could see the virtues of dividing the workload, and they endorsed Moses' proposal.

1:15–18. Moses appointed these **leading men** of each tribe into a hierarchy of **tribal officials**. The ablest leaders within each tribe were made commanders of thousands; the next ablest, commanders of hundreds; and so on, according to the needs of the people and the ability of the leaders. Apparently the greatest needs concerned the resolution of disputes, since Moses refers to these men as judges. By calling these leaders both **commanders** and **judges**, Moses gave them both a military/executive function and a judicial task.

In his instructions to the leaders, he charged them at the time of their appointment to hear disputes and judge them fairly. At the Israelite bar of justice, the alien would be able to plead his case as well as the native, and the judges were to weigh the cases without partiality.

D The Design of the Spies (1:19–25)

SUPPORTING IDEA: *Recalling God's faithfulness in the past should build the believer's resolve to trust him for the future.*

1:19–20. The original intent was that Israel should enter the promised land from the south. Thus, in accord with divine instructions, the nation set out from **Horeb**, taking the most direct northerly route **toward the hill country of the Amorites**. Although this was typically an eleven-day journey, the trip was a hazardous one through a **vast and dreadful desert**. The last word is probably better translated "wilderness." The Sinai peninsula is characterized less by sand than by rocks, mountains, and ravines. The Hebrew word describes places that are arid but have enough vegetation to support herds and flocks (cp. Gen. 16:7; 21:20; 1 Sam. 17:28) at least seasonally.

Israel managed, by God's help, to get to the southwestern entry point of the land, **Kadesh Barnea**. That location, which was to have been only a brief stop along a triumphant journey, turned out to be a name that would live in biblical infamy. It was at the edge of **the hill country of the Amorites**. The last word often serves as a description of ethnic groups who lived in mountainous areas: "The Amalekites live in the Negev; the Hittites, Jebusites and Amorites live in the hill country; and the Canaanites live near the sea and along the Jordan" (Num. 13:29).

1:21. God placed the land before Israel as both a blessing and a challenge. As a blessing, he had already **given** them **the land**. As a challenge, they still had to **go up and take possession of it**. That meant engaging in battle and refusing to give in to their fears. Like many of God's gifts, the process was important as well as the end result. Israel would emerge from their battles with a track record. They would know that God could be trusted to protect them in the hardest circumstances. Moses insisted that Israel not be afraid or discouraged, exhortations that he would use again and again throughout Deuteronomy (cp. 1:29; 3:22; 20:1,3; 31:6,8).

1:22–23. The congregation suggested that before the invasion they gain some basic knowledge of the land by sending a small delegation to spy it out. Moses emphasized in his statement that support for this suggestion was virtually unanimous (**all of you came to me**). The report of the spies would help determine the best approach to the land and how rapidly they would encounter settled areas as they moved inland. Moses followed this counsel and selected one man from each tribe to serve on this reconnaissance task force.

It is worth noting that the Numbers account of this same episode points out that Moses sent the spies under God's direction: "The LORD said to Moses, 'Send some men to explore the land of Canaan, which I am giving to the Israelites. From each ancestral tribe send one of its leaders'" (Num. 13:1–2). Apparently the suggestion originated with the people, but when the **idea seemed good** to Moses, he consulted the Lord about it. The Numbers account merely omits the steps leading up to the Lord's direction. Although the original idea may have been prompted by fear and uncertainty on the congregation's part, its value was apparent to Moses and endorsed by the Lord. Military prudence would dictate that an army should know the **route . . . to take** and the obstacles that would lie in its path in the form of fortified **towns**.

1:24–25. The scouting expedition correctly assumed that the hill country would prove the most challenging part of the invasion, so they explored that region first. In the process, they discovered the **Valley of Eshcol**, the fertile region near Hebron known even now for its choice vineyards.

The full account of the spies' journey, which covered the length and breadth of the promised land, is given in Numbers 13:3–33. The fruit of the land was so excellent that the intelligence team properly concluded, **It is a good land that the LORD our God is giving us**. At least to this point, the scouts would have had to confess that what God had said had proven reliable in every detail. It should have seemed a small inference at that point to

Deuteronomy 1:26-28

conclude that God's presence with the army in its coming battles would also prove reliable.

E The Disbelief of the People (1:26–40)

SUPPORTING IDEA: God finds stubbornness and unbelief intolerable, especially among those who ought to know better.

1:26–28. Unfortunately, the spies' report continued beyond their positive estimate of the goodness of the land. They (with the exception of Caleb and Joshua) were discouraged by the opposition waiting for them, and their pessimism infected the whole nation. When Moses said, **you were unwilling to go up**, he was referring to the nation as such. The generation he was now addressing on the plains of Moab was younger than twenty years of age when their parents refused to take the land. As a result, they escaped God's judgment on their parents. Still, there were many in their late teens at the time who had imbibed deeply of their parent's negativism and unbelief.

1:29–31. Moses urged the people not to yield to their fears, since the Lord they served was the same one who had fought for them in Egypt, a fact they could not deny, since it took place **before** their **very eyes**.

And there was more. God had also fought for them **in the desert**. The reference may be to the events at Rephidim that had transpired before the encampment at Sinai. At that time, the Amalekites had attacked Israel in an altogether unprovoked way. Moses put Joshua in charge of Israel's defense and went up to a nearby hill to pray. God heard his prayers and granted Israel a victory. Moses had even immortalized the place by dedicating an altar there, and calling it Yahweh Nissi ("The Lord my banner"). Although Israel was not trained for battle, God had fought for them, and they should have been spiritually sensitive to what he did there.

God's paternal faithfulness was undeniable and had been demonstrated all the way to **this place** (Kadesh Barnea). Fear of the right type can be beneficial to the people of God (see Prov. 1:7), but the fear of man's hostile intentions seldom fits that category. Indeed, the fear of God was missing from the hearts of Israel at Kadesh Barnea. Believers should be more concerned for God's opinion of them than for what human opponents might do to their bodies: "Do not be afraid of those who kill the body but cannot kill the soul. Rather, be afraid of the One who can destroy both soul and body in hell" (Matt. 10:28).

1:32–33. In spite of all the evidence that should have forestalled such unbelief, Israel refused to **trust in the LORD** and go forward. Moses repudiated his countrymen's timidity, reminding them that the Lord had faithfully blazed a trail for them on the journey and had signified his presence with them **in fire by night and in a cloud by day**. The cloud typically rested over the tabernacle of meeting, the center of Israel's existence as they traveled. It also enabled the nation to know precisely when to break camp and the direction they should take (see Num. 10:33–34).

The thoughtful believer recalls God's faithfulness in the past when confronted by any new threat. Part of spiritual maturity is a strong sense of one's own history. Believers forget what God has done at their own peril. The central worship event for Christians is concerned with remembering what God has done: "This is my body, which is for you; do this in remembrance of me. . . . This cup is the new covenant in my blood; do this, whenever you drink it, in remembrance of me" (1 Cor. 11:24–25).

1:34–36. The seriousness of Israel's unbelief was proven by the Lord's reaction to the groaning and unbelief in the tents of Israel. He **was angry and solemnly swore** that no one of the generation that had disbelieved him would see **the good land** that he had promised. The exception was **Caleb son of Jephunneh**, who had followed the Lord wholeheartedly. (Joshua was another exception, a self-evident one since he had already been designated as the new leader of the nation after Moses' death; cp. Deut. 1:37–40 and Num. 27:18–22.)

1:37–40. While Moses was severely tested at Kadesh Barnea, his loss of control came somewhat later in the Wilderness of Zin (see Num. 20:1–12), when the people again provoked him and he failed to carry out God's commands. As a result, he forfeited the joy of leading the nation into the land, and designated Joshua as his successor.

The people had justified their unbelief by cloaking it in concern for their **little ones**, but God, in a just and fitting twist, decreed that those very children would **enter the land** and **take possession of it**. He commanded that the parents of those youngsters begin their sentence of wandering by turning their backs on the promised land and moving along the Red Sea highway. In this context the **Red Sea** referred to is its eastern arm, known today as the Gulf of Elath or the Gulf of Aqaba. The Hebrew expression translated by Red Sea (*yam suf*, "Sea of Reeds") includes this eastern gulf as well as its western counterpart, today called the Gulf of Suez.

F The Defeat of the Army (1:41–46)

SUPPORTING IDEA: *God resists those who display presumption and arrogance even when their objective is valid.*

1:41–42. The sin and rebellion of the senior generation of Israelites reached its apex following Moses' solemn announcement that they would not enter the land because of their unbelief. They suddenly recovered their military ardor. Tossing off a quick declaration of their repentance, they announced their determination **to go up into the hill country**. Moses warned them that they would be going without God, who had withdrawn his presence from them. This made their defeat certain.

Deuteronomy 1:43–44

1:43–44. In spite of Moses' warnings, the people in their arrogance determined to do battle, and the outcome was just as the Lord had predicted. The Amorites put them to flight much as a **swarm of bees** might do to an incautious honey-hunter. They were soundly defeated from **Seir** in the west **to Hormah** in the east, a distance of about fifty miles.

1:45–46. At the end of this disgraceful episode, the people returned to Kadesh Barnea and **wept before the LORD**, but he did not retract his determination to have that generation die in the wilderness. They were consigned to roam aimlessly around the Kadesh encampment for **many days**.

> **MAIN IDEA REVIEW:** Unbelief can rob God's people of joys that he intends them to have.

III. CONCLUSION

Unnecessary Pillars

After the great fire of 1666, the greater part of London was rebuilt under the masterful eye of Sir Christopher Wren. As the centerpiece of his efforts, the great architect designed and rebuilt St. Paul's Cathedral. Once his work on the nation's capital was finished, he was asked to design a new town hall for Windsor. One prominent member of the city council found fault with the plans Wren submitted and insisted that the roof of the proposed building needed additional support in the form of extra pillars. Wren argued that the building was quite safe and the roof would need no additional support. The council member carried the day, however, by suggesting to people in the community that they would be risking their lives to enter the new town hall. The local citizens complained, and the council insisted that the pillars be added.

Wren succumbed to the local pressure—or so it was thought—and the extra pillars were constructed. It was many years afterward, when both the architect and his opponent were long dead, that the rest of the story was uncovered. Workmen were ordered to climb into the roof area to do repairs and cleaning. They found that the pillars that Wren had added to the plan were two inches short of touching the roof (the gap was not visible from the floor). The architect was so certain that his building would stand that he added pillars, but only in a decorative way.

God's word needs no support. The fact that it is his word ought to be enough. Although history has borne it out repeatedly, those episodes are merely decorative. The cutting edge of every Christian life comes when we apply the truth of that word to our next challenge. God is waiting to see whether or not we will believe him. In the words of the hymn writer,

What more can he say,
Than to you he hath said,
To you who for refuge,
To Jesus have fled?

PRINCIPLES

- God's promises form strong encouragement toward godly conduct.
- A leader needs both internal credentials and the respect of the community.
- Fear is the enemy of spiritual progress.
- The person who follows Christ can always do more than he thinks he can.

APPLICATIONS

- Reflect often on God's faithfulness in your life.
- Determine that you will fight the spiritual battle that God lays out for you.
- Do not be reluctant to ask for help from others.
- Seek to develop a wise and understanding character that commands respect from others.

IV. LIFE APPLICATION

The Limitations of a Knapsack

Once there were four people on an airplane that began having engine trouble. The passengers included a pilot, a preacher, a Boy Scout, and a professor from MIT. The airplane began to lose altitude, and the pilot left the cockpit to tell the passengers what was happening. He explained, "I hate to say this, but we are going to crash. Our problem is that there are four of us, but only three parachutes. Somebody is not going to be able to get out. Now I have a family, and they are going to be in trouble if I don't make it, so I'm going to leave." He grabbed a parachute and jumped out.

The professor said, "I think you should both know that I am the smartest man in the world. It would be an incalculable loss to society if I were to die, so I'm leaving." He grabbed a parachute and jumped out of the plane.

The preacher turned to the Boy Scout and said, "Son, I know the Lord, and I'm ready to be with him. You've got your whole life in front of you, so you go ahead and take the last parachute."

Deuteronomy 1

The Boy Scout said, "No problem, preacher; the smartest man in the world just grabbed my knapsack and jumped out the door. Here, have a parachute."

The world is full of intelligent people who are falling through space headed for a horrible end with only a knapsack to protect them. God wants us to be his messengers to point out that there is a means of escape. We can't do it unless we think the job is worth doing; and we won't do it if we think, as Israel did at Kadesh Barnea, that the job is too big for us. God grant that we see the world's peril, that the good news of Jesus Christ might be offered to a generation that so desperately needs him.

V. PRAYER

O God, keep us from being so foolish that we see you only as the solution to our next problem; help us revel in your past faithfulness and tell others of it, that we and they can live our lives in a way that honors you. Amen.

VI. DEEPER DISCOVERIES

A. All Israel (1:1)

The audience of Moses' address on the banks of the Jordan River is specified as "all Israel" in Deuteronomy 1:1. This does not mean, of course, that the entire nation was within hearing distance of him as he spoke but only that the nation at large heard (or read) his words eventually. After the death of the exodus generation, Moses ordered that a census be taken of those eligible for military service (males twenty years old and above) as they stood poised on the edge of the land (Num. 26:4). The count showed that Israel had an army of 601,730 men. Since most were married and there were many children, the total population of Israel must have approached two million or more. Since Deuteronomy would shortly be reduced to writing, the words of Moses would have been disseminated quickly throughout the tribes.

B. The Extent of the Land (1:7–8)

God promised Israel possession of "the hill country of the Amorites . . . the Arabah . . . the mountains . . . the western foothills . . . the Negev and along the coast . . . the land of the Canaanites and . . . Lebanon, as far as the great river, the Euphrates" (Deut. 1:7). It is doubtful that Israel has laid claim to this entire expanse at any time except for a brief period under Solomon (1 Kgs. 4:21). The territory approaching the Euphrates River lies under the control today of two of Israel's bitterest enemies, the Syrians and the Iraqis. Nonetheless, God has promised that in time the full extent of the promise will become a reality. Ezekiel prophesied of its ultimate extent (see Ezek. 47:15–20).

C. The Anakites (1:28)

The reconnaissance party was terrified at the sight of the Anakites as they scouted the land. They were apparently extraordinarily tall: "We saw the Nephilim there (the descendants of Anak come from the Nephilim). We seemed like grasshoppers in our own eyes, and we looked the same to them" (Num. 13:33). The patriarch, Anak, founded the city of Hebron: "They gave them Kiriath Arba (that is, Hebron), with its surrounding pastureland, in the hill country of Judah. (Arba was the forefather of Anak.)" (Josh 21:11; see also 14:15). When Israel had penetrated the land, Caleb and Joshua eventually engaged in battle with the Anakites and drove them out of the hill country into the coastal region around Gaza, Gath, and Ashdod. It seems probable that Goliath and the other oversized Philistines descended from Anak and his children.

D. A Knowledge of Good and Evil (1:39)

Israel accused God of intending to have their children killed at Kadesh Barnea: "The little ones that you said would be taken captive, your children who do not yet know good from bad—they will enter the land" (Deut. 1:39). Since God decreed that those twenty years old and above would die for their unbelief, it would seem that Israelites were held accountable as adults beginning on their twentieth birthday. The conclusion is supported by God's decree that only people who were twenty and above could offer sacrifices (Exod. 30:14) and serve in the military (Num. 1:3,18). Only Levites who were twenty years old could serve in the temple (1 Chr. 23:24,27). Many of those who were under twenty, of course, knew what they were doing when they rebelled against God. In mercy, however, he drew the line of death higher than it had to be in the hopes that the younger generation would come to repentance for their unbelief.

E. The Amorites (1:44)

The term *Amorite* appears in a variety of ways in Old Testament narratives. Sometimes it designates in a general way the pre-Israelite ethnic occupants of Palestine (see Gen. 15:16). In other places, it describes the people groups that lived on the east side of the Jordan River, including the two kings, Sihon and Og, who were conquered by Israel on their approach from the east (Num. 21:21; Deut. 31:4). The Gibeonites, the people with whom Israel was tricked into establishing a covenant, are designated by Joshua as Amorites (2 Sam. 21:2). The term commonly describes in general the inhabitants that Israel expelled from the land, although the individual people groups within the larger expression are often specified by different terms. The deities of Canaan are described as "the gods of the Amorites" (Josh. 24:15).

VII. TEACHING OUTLINE

A. INTRODUCTION

1. Lead Story: Checking the Chimney

2. Context: Moses reviews with the nation the history of their relationship with Yahweh. The chapter portrays the startling contrast between the inconsistent behavior of the Israelites and the constant and faithful actions of the Lord. Moses places before the new generation their twin legacies of a faithful God and a less-than-faithful national tradition.

3. Transition: The history of Israel forms a capsule summary of the history of God's people through the ages. We are often less than consistent in the way we follow his word, yet he remains faithful to us and to our welfare. Although the constancy of his love remains, we forfeit many of life's greatest joys when our behavior is inconsistent and unfaithful.

B. COMMENTARY

1. The Discourse of Moses (1:1–5)
2. The Declaration to the Nation (1:6–8)
3. The Designation of the Leaders (1:9–18)
4. The Design of the Spies (1:19–25)
5. The Disbelief of the People (1:26–40)
6. The Defeat of the Army (1:41–46)

C. CONCLUSION: THE LIMITATIONS OF A KNAPSACK

VIII. ISSUES FOR DISCUSSION

1. Can you think of times when God has proven faithful in your life even as you were indifferent or hostile toward him?

2. What spiritual insights can you gain from Deuteronomy 1 that can help improve your faithfulness to him?

3. How have your fears kept you from obedience in the past?

4. Can thoughtful reflection on your spiritual history prevent such episodes from happening again?

Deuteronomy 2

Facing the Enemy

I. **INTRODUCTION**
   The Other Side of the Unknown

II. **COMMENTARY**
   A verse-by-verse explanation of the chapter.

III. **CONCLUSION**
   Moody's Harp

   An overview of the principles and applications from the chapter.

IV. **LIFE APPLICATION**
   Resigning the Commission

   Melding the chapter to life.

V. **PRAYER**
   Tying the chapter to life with God.

VI. **DEEPER DISCOVERIES**
   Historical, geographical, and grammatical enrichment of the commentary.

VII. **TEACHING OUTLINE**
   Suggested step-by-step group study of the chapter.

VIII. **ISSUES FOR DISCUSSION**
   Zeroing the chapter in on daily life.

Deuteronomy 2

> **Quote**
>
> "I am now about to take Orders and my degree, and go into the world. What will become of me I know not. All I can say is I look for perpetual conflicts and struggles in that life and hope for no other peace, but only a cross, while on this side of eternity."
>
> George Whitefield

ETHNIC PROFILE: THE ANAKITES

- A tribe inhabiting the area around the Jordan River at the time of the Israelite conquest
- A Hebrew plural form (literally, *Anakim*) meaning "those of Anak," the name of the original male ancestor of the group
- Originated in the area of Hebron, called before the conquest Kiriath Arba ("the city of Arba")
- The most commonly mentioned group of people of exceptional size in the Hebrew Scriptures

IN A NUTSHELL

God desires that his people face the uncertainties of the future courageously, drawing their strength from a thoughtful reflection on his faithfulness.

Facing the Enemy

I. INTRODUCTION

The Other Side of the Unknown

On October 14, 1947, Chuck Yeager broke the sound barrier in Bell Laboratories' experimental rocket plane, the Bell X-1. The plane, painted a bright orange, was essentially a large engine with a couple of stubby wings attached, and it was notoriously hard to control. In order to conserve fuel, it was taken aloft by a specially designed B-29 bomber and dropped before firing its engine.

The penetration of the sound barrier wasn't supposed to happen that October day. The program was set up to approach the speed of sound very gradually, and Yeager's goal on the occasion was to fly at .97 Mach, 97 percent of the speed of sound. Yeager, like the other test pilots in the program, knew that unpredictable things happened the closer one flew to the sound barrier. The plane would typically begin to vibrate. The X-1 was not a particularly stable plane to begin with, and Yeager began the flight with an arm that had been injured earlier in the week. It took several seconds simply to get control of things once he had been dropped from the mother plane.

When the X-1 had only 30 percent of its fuel remaining, Yeager put the plane into a shallow dive and began to increase speed. As he approached his target velocity, the vibrating increased to the point that it was difficult even to read the instruments on what people in the program had come to call the "orange beast." Those strange vibrations had caused some experts to conclude that penetration of the sound barrier was impossible. They felt that unknown forces would simply tear apart any plane that got too close to breaking through the speed of sound.

Then, just when it seemed that the plane could take no more, the vibrating stopped. Yeager glanced at his air speed gauge and noted that he had just passed 1.0 Mach. For about twenty seconds, he flew at supersonic speed for the first time in human history, and he described it as though gliding on glass. All the fears and uncertainties had given way to victory over the sound barrier.

Any worthy objective has a way of generating fear. When Israel set out to conquer the promised land, their fears were evident. They didn't know what would happen once they crossed the Jordan River and entered the land. They knew that aggressive peoples lived within the area that God had promised to give them, and they knew that those peoples would resist their invasion.

They had to overcome their fears if they were to conquer the land and begin to live in it.

In the same way, Christians must move past their fears when dealing with each challenge to spiritual growth. They dare not shrink away from dealing with temptation and bad habits because they are afraid of the turbulence that will be a part of their lives when they go to war with them.

II. COMMENTARY

Facing the Enemy

MAIN IDEA: *Believers engaged in spiritual warfare must reflect on the faithfulness of God and face the future with courage.*

A Instructions Concerning the Edomites (2:1–8)

SUPPORTING IDEA: *Being prepared to do spiritual battle requires a thoughtful consideration of God's kindnesses in the past.*

2:1. Chapter 2 of Deuteronomy fits into that portion of the book that looks backward at the historic relationship between Yahweh and his covenant people. After Moses recounted Israel's catastrophic failure at Kadesh Barnea, he recalled for the people their dealings with several people groups on the way to their staging area east of the Jordan River.

For Israel to enter the promised land from the east required that they turn back to the south and east from Kadesh Barnea **toward the desert**. Moses had received such directions directly from the Lord shortly after the Kadesh Barnea and Hormah debacles of the previous chapter. Moses omitted from his narrative the events described in Numbers 20:22, which describes how the nation was denied access to the main northern route by the Edomites. Following this, they turned southward toward the route that approached the eastern arm of the Red Sea, the body of water known today as the Gulf of Aqaba or the Gulf of Elath.

The hill country of Seir is the mountain ridge that parallels the Arabah. It runs southward from the southern end of the Dead Sea to near the Gulf of Aqaba and generally forms the western boundary of the territory of the Edomites. In Hebrew Scripture, *Seir* often becomes a virtual synonym for "Edom." The travels of Israel were carefully designed not to invade Edomite territory, since the Edomites were descendants of Esau, Jacob's brother. Although the Edomites were not worshipers of Yahweh, their land was not part of the region that God had promised to the patriarchs. Israel's behavior was not to be provocative but gentle in dealing with their kinsmen.

2:2–3. God explained to Moses at some point that Israel had gone far enough south to avoid encroachment into Edom. He told Moses that the nation had made its **way around this hill country long enough**. They could **turn north** without being seen as a threat to Edom's territorial integrity, and so move into the staging area east of the Jordan River before their invasion of the Holy Land.

2:4. The Lord made his intentions explicit when he told Moses to **give the people** the **orders** to avoid conflict with the Edomites. They were only to **pass through** Edomite territory. The region was filled with their cousins, **the descendants of Esau**, and blood ties were to be respected even when those cousins would later prove to be bitter enemies of Israel.

When Israel had approached the promised land during the Book of Numbers, they had congregated not far from Edom's borders, creating discomfort among the descendants of Esau. In the absence of knowledge, the Edomites could only guess at Israel's intentions. The Lord warned Israel that Edom's fear of them was dangerous. As a result, the army of Israel should **be very careful** not to engage in actions that might incite an attack.

2:5–6. Israel had nothing to gain by provoking Edom **to war**. God had already determined that he would **not give** them **any of Edom's land, not even enough to put** their **foot on**. Edom's possession of **the hill country of Seir** came directly from Isaac's decision to bless Esau and his descendants (see Gen. 27:39–40). Although God had determined to give Israel the land of promise, he also had not forgotten Esau. The latter was shortsighted and impetuous (see Heb. 12:16–17), but he was still a child of Isaac and a grandson of Abraham. God determined to bless him for their sakes.

As a result of the place that God had given the Edomites, Israel would regard themselves as guests in a neighboring country, not as invaders. If they consumed anything from Edom's territory, they were to reimburse the local people **in silver** for that **food** and **water**.

2:7. If they needed any other reasons to pay for what they consumed, Israel only had to remember that **the LORD** had **blessed** them during their long travels **in all the work** of their **hands**. It was pointless to covet anything that they might see in the territory of Edom, since God had **watched over** their travels for **forty years** and had seen to it that they had **lacked** for nothing. If he could care for them as they walked through a **vast desert**, he could certainly provide for them during the brief portion that still remained of their trip and during the invasion itself.

2:8. Instead of taking **the Arabah road** that wound through Edomite territory, Israel took the longer route to the east, **the desert road**. The former proceeds north **from Elath and Ezion Geber** toward **Moab**. The two towns were located at the northern extremity of the eastern arm of the Red Sea. Elath (modern Eilat) was a seaport community a mile or so east of Ezion Geber, which became in time the main site of Solomon's international trade (1 Kgs. 9:26).

B Instructions Concerning the Moabites and Ammonites (2:9–23)

SUPPORTING IDEA: *Those who undertake ministry for God can maintain their humility by remembering his work on behalf of others and their own failures.*

2:9. God gave strict instructions to Israel not to **harass the Moabites** or to use some unethical pretext to **provoke them** into battle. Even if they should defeat the Moabite army, God had determined **not to give** Israel **any part of their land**. He reminded the Israelites that the Moabites were cousins, since they were the **descendants of Lot**, Abraham's nephew. The kinship applied to both the Moabites and the Ammonites, in fact, because Moab and Ammon were Lot's sons, incestuously conceived by Lot's daughters following the destruction of Sodom and Gomorrah (see Gen. 19:36–38).

2:10–12. These verses form a lengthy parenthesis recalling how the Moabites had come into possession of the land that they inhabited. At one time, the territory had been occupied by the **Emites**. This term appears elsewhere only in Genesis 14:5.

The original ethnic inhabitants of Moab were **strong and numerous** and physically resembled **the Anakites**, known for being **tall** and strong. Anak originally settled in the region of Hebron or Kiriath Arba south of Jerusalem and was himself part of a larger ethnic group known as the **Rephaites**. The latter group lived also in Ammon (see v. 20) as well as in Moab and Bashan—essentially the entire area east of the Jordan River.

As for the highland plateau of **Seir** (part of Edom), Deuteronomy explains that the original indigenous peoples were **Horites**, a group known in secular history as the Hurrians. The Edomites, **the descendants of Esau**, drove the Horites out of the area and took possession, a process similar to what **Israel** was about to do **in the land** that God was giving them.

2:13–15. With God's instructions in mind, the nation was ordered to **get up and cross the Zered Valley**, the southern boundary of the Moabites. They would need to remember what they had been told. The Moabites were entitled to their land in the same way that Israel was entitled to theirs. In each case, God had provided a homeland. Israel needed to remember that they were in no position to take a superior attitude toward the peoples east of the Jordan River. For one thing, they were all the descendants of a common grandparent. For another, Israel's behavior on the way to the land of Ammon was far from exemplary.

In fact, it had taken the Israelites **thirty-eight years** to arrive at the Zered Valley **from the time** they left **Kadesh Barnea**. The extraordinary slowness of their journey had been required because a whole **generation of fighting men** had rebelled against God's command to take the land. As a result, **the LORD**

Deuteronomy 2:20–23

had sworn that none of them would enter the promised land. Over that thirty-eight years, the Lord had **completely eliminated** the offenders **from the camp**. Humility and dependence, therefore, would be the order of the day.

2:16–19. True to his word, God waited for **the last** of the rebellious fighting men to die and then issued instructions for Israel to **pass by the region of Moab at Ar**. While under God's judgment, the nation moved toward the promised land with incredible slowness. In a sense, they were people merely waiting for other people to die for thirty-eight years. When the last rebel had perished, however, the pace quickened. They moved through Moab and found themselves quickly on the doorstep of **the Ammonites**.

Just as he had with the Moabites, God issued instructions to respect the place that the Ammonites held in his affections. Although they were idolaters and not worshipers of the true God, he still loved them and had given them their land **as a possession**.

Israel was thus not to **harass them or provoke them to war** in the hopes of capturing their property. God had decided already that their land would lie outside the confines of the promise made to the patriarchs. As **descendants of Lot** like the Moabites, the Ammonites were to be respected as recipients of blessings from God and as cousins.

2:20–23. Like the Moabites and Israel, the Ammonites were once outsiders. The **Rephaites** once inhabited the territory that was occupied by Ammon as Israel approached its own homeland. The Ammonites preferred to use their own nomenclature for the people **who used to live there**, referring to them by the more localized name, **Zamzummites** (this group may well be the Zuzites referred to in Gen. 14:5).

The Ammonites, like the Moabites, were small in numbers and normal in stature. Although the Zamzummites were **strong and numerous, and as tall as the Anakites**, they succeeded in capturing their land because **the Lord** was fighting for them. As a result, the Ammonites **drove them out** and occupied the land. The application to Israel's hearts seems clear. What God had already done for the Moabites and the Ammonites, he could and would do for Israel.

If Israel needed any other encouragement, the historian recalls again that God **had** already **done the same** for the Edomites, **the descendants of Esau**. They, too, had faced a challenge, not only in **the Horites** who occupied the land that God had decided to give them, but in the mountainous topography of **Seir** itself. Edom also succeeded and **drove** out the Horites.

While he was encouraging Israel with an account of what God had done for other peoples, Moses invoked the similar example of **the Avvites**. These are apparently to be regarded as another Anakite subgroup, living **in villages as far** away from their normal regions **as Gaza**. Although they, too, would have been of superior size, **the Caphtorites** dislodged them and **settled in** their place. Caphtor is apparently to be identified with the Mediterranean island of Crete. The Caphtorites are mentioned in Genesis 10:14, and those mentioned here were apparently a second migration of the people known as the Philistines.

Moses' point seems to be that these very groups had already been defeated in battle because of divine influence—and would be again once Israel entered the land.

Ⓒ Encountering Sihon (2:24–37)

SUPPORTING IDEA: God fashions the tests that believers face and supplies the resources to gain victory for his people and glory for himself.

2:24–25. As Moses stood near the Jordan River and addressed the army of Israel, he recalled for them not only the way God had provided for them in their travels but how he showed himself able to lead them to victory. Even before they crossed the Jordan River to enter the land of Canaan, Israel had been victorious in encounters with two Amorite kings, Sihon and Og. The first of these is now described.

God instructed the people to **cross the Arnon Gorge**, the northern boundary of Moab, and move into the country controlled by **Sihon the Amorite, king of Heshbon**. For the first time in the experience of the new generation, Israel would face a potential enemy that was not related by blood. The Amorites were to be removed so that Israel could **take possession** of the country. The term *Amorites* describes territory, not a political entity. Sihon ruled a city-state, receiving tribute from the territory that lay around him. Heshbon was situated about ten miles east-northeast of the northern tip of the Dead Sea.

To assist in Israel's success against Sihon and other groups, God promised to bring **terror and fear** of Israel upon the nations that Israel would fight against. **Reports** of Israel's great victory over Egypt at the Red Sea would cause their opponents to **tremble and be in anguish**.

2:26–27. Moses then recalled for his people the strategy used in the defeat of **Sihon king of Heshbon**. Rather than simply invading Amorite territory, Moses sent **messengers** who offered **peace** to Sihon. Moses explained that Israel only wanted to **pass through** Amorite territory on their way to the Jordan River crossing opposite Jericho. The Israelites vowed to **stay on the main road** and not send raiding parties into the countryside. In this way, the nation would make an effort to respect settled international boundaries and not become a threat to the welfare of Sihon's kingdom.

The point was a tender one, given the historical context. The area just north of the Arnon River had been for many years property claimed by the Moabites. Only recently had Sihon invaded the area, destroyed Heshbon, and then rebuilt the same city to serve as his capital. Sihon's reluctance to allow Israel passage may have arisen from insecurities about the stability of his own borders.

2:28–29. Moses had appealed to Sihon on the basis of the fact that—at least as Moses told the story—he had received the same courtesy from **the descendants of Esau** (the Edomites) and from **the Moabites**. Moses reasoned in his message to Sihon that since the other local people groups had been so hospitable, Sihon should also extend Israel a like kindness.

2:30–31. Moses' approach, however, did not work. Sihon **refused to let Israel pass through** his territory. His stubborn attitude was at the same time freely chosen by him and the product of divine intervention. God had made Sihon's **spirit stubborn and his heart obstinate** in order to gain glory for himself. God dealt with Sihon in much the same manner as he had with Pharaoh, allowing the monarch's pride and willfulness to lead him into danger, and thus to **give him into** Israel's **hands**. For Sihon, stubbornness became the axe that would cut him down to size. Indeed, God announced to Moses that he had **begun to deliver Sihon and his country** over to Israel. As a result, the Israelite army should **begin to conquer and possess his land**. From the biblical point of view, no conflict exists between God's work and man's work. God delivered, but Israel was still required to conquer.

2:32–33. When Israel showed no signs of retiring southward from Amorite territory, **Sihon** mustered **his army** and **came out to meet** Israel **in battle**. The result was a total rout of the Amorite force. Sihon perished along **with his sons and his whole army**.

2:34–36. Israel annihilated the population of Sihon's kingdom and **left no survivors**. They did not destroy the property of the land (in the form of gardens, vineyards, buildings, and livestock), however, but only the people. Whatever could be carried along with them as they approached the Jordan River they carried off for themselves. In time, the land east of the river would be occupied by the tribes of Reuben, Gad, and one-half of the tribe of Manasseh; but for the moment, Israel continued north toward a rendezvous with other enemies.

Moses defined Sihon's territory in verse 36 as extending from **Aroer** northward to **Gilead**. Since the southern boundary of Gilead is the Jabbok River, the territory included everything between the Arnon and the Jabbok. The description in verse 36 suggests that the southern boundary point was comprised of two different towns: **From Aroer on the rim of the Arnon Gorge, and from the town in the gorge**. However, it is likely that the second phrase merely elucidates the first and should be translated, "From Aroer on the rim of the Arnon Gorge, namely, from the town in the gorge." The purpose of the careful geographical descriptions is to bear testimony to the faithfulness of God. Between the Arnon and the Jabbok, **not one town was too**

strong for the Israelite army because **the LORD gave** Israel **all of them**. The experience of Israel in facing their Amorite enemy proved to be a great encouragement to them, because they had many enemies still to fight.

2:37. Israel was careful, however, not to **encroach** upon the territory of the **Ammonites**, which lay to the east of the Amorite kingdoms of Sihon and Og. The Ammonite lands were not part of the promises made to the patriarchs; and besides, the Ammonites were relatives of Israel. Most importantly, however, the Lord had given his own protection to the Ammonites and placed their land off limits to Israel.

> **MAIN IDEA REVIEW:** *Believers engaged in spiritual warfare must reflect on the faithfulness of God and face the future with courage.*

III. CONCLUSION

Moody's Harp

Today Dwight Moody's name is well-known and honored because of his legacies: Moody Bible Institute in Chicago, Moody Press, and the Moody Broadcasting Network, to name a few. Like all godly men, however, from time to time he experienced hard times in his ministry.

Moody had preached on one Sunday with great earnestness but with little visible fruit. On Monday morning, he awoke feeling discouraged and downcast. While he was sitting in his study and feeling sad, a young friend who taught a Bible class each Sunday came to visit. Moody could tell in an instant that the young man had had an experience very unlike his own on the previous Lord's day. The young teacher was in a state of considerable elation.

Moody's visitor asked, "What kind of day did you have yesterday?"

The great evangelist admitted that he had not seen much in the way of results from his preaching. "And what about you?" he asked his young friend.

"It went very well indeed. I never had a better day."

"What was your subject?"

"I taught on the life and character of Noah. Did you ever preach on Noah? Did you ever study his life? You had better do it now. It will do you good."

Instead of resenting the young teacher's advice, Moody took it to heart and reached for his Bible. He began to explore the experiences and efforts of the man who was directed by God to save the ancient world from God's judgment. As he read and thought, it occurred to him that Noah was a man who preached for 120 years to his own generation and did not see a single convert outside his own family. But through all those terrible years, it appeared that he never became discouraged.

Moody reflected, "I closed my Bible. The cloud had gone; I have never hung my harp on the willows since that day."

Discouragement has caused the defection of more Christian workers than the devil ever has. It is good to remember when we are depressed or fearful that other Christians have faced daunting tasks greater than our own. The same God who sustained them is waiting to encourage us and remind us of who he is.

PRINCIPLES

- Timidity in dealing with one's internal enemies (sins) constitutes cowardice.
- God's promises sometimes come to fruition slower than we would like, but they are fulfilled in his timing.
- The temptations and bad habits which believers face sometimes look like giants, but they must be confronted and overcome by his strength.

APPLICATIONS

- Consider what areas of your life need to be overcome.
- Take some time today to recall how God has worked in your life.
- Give God glory by sharing your recollections with another believer.

IV. LIFE APPLICATION

Resigning the Commission

One of the most poignant scenes in American history took place in 1787 when George Washington resigned his commission as head of the Continental Army. For eight harsh and challenging years, Washington and his fellow officers had put themselves in danger and suffered with their men as they led the army against the British. They had gone through a brutal winter at Valley Forge, sleeping in the cold and watching their barefoot men leave bloody footprints in the snow. They had seen Washington write appeal after appeal to the Continental Congress, pleading for money for arms, ammunition, and clothing for the troops, only to be turned down or ignored. For many months they had suffered one devastating defeat after another. Desertions had

Deuteronomy 2

multiplied, and even those sympathetic to the patriot cause expected the Continental Army to be defeated.

Slowly, events began to turn their way. Washington led his ragtag army to a famous victory at Trenton and again at Princeton. People began to revise their thinking, and spirits lifted.

Finally, victory was theirs. The officers and General Washington met for one last time at an inn where they enjoyed dinner together and reflected on the hardships of the eight years of conflict. Finally, Washington extended them his thanks and the thanks of the newborn nation. He then rose and went to each of them in turn, thanking him personally for his faithful service in their campaigns together. Soon every eye was shedding tears as they acknowledged the conclusion of their years together. Then Washington went to the Congress and tendered his resignation, since the objective for which he and his men had fought had been attained.

Many Christians have resigned their commissions in the spiritual struggle, too. Unlike Washington's, however, their war is not over. Christ calls believers to endure in the work of ministry and self-conquest until the time that he declares all enemies vanquished at his feet.

V. PRAYER

Lord, grant that we may realize the gravity of even the small choices we make. Keep us conscious that others are watching our actions and drawing conclusions about the validity of our convictions—even when we are not aware of their scrutiny. Help us to live with eternity's values in view at all times. Amen.

VI. DEEPER DISCOVERIES

A. Universal Sovereignty (2:10–12)

This parenthetical section interrupts the flow of Moses' story somewhat but contains important theology. Israel was made by these words to understand that God was sovereign over other ethnic groups just as he was over them. The Edomites were enabled by God to drive out the Horites "just as Israel did in the land the LORD gave them as their possession" (Deut. 2:12). Every land belongs to God, and he proposes and disposes as he sees fit (Ps. 50:12).

These words have an ethical purpose. Later in the Book of Deuteronomy, God would emphasize that Israel's favored position was due not to their numerical superiority (which didn't exist) and still less to their moral superiority (which likewise didn't exist; see Deut. 7:7–8). They would soon possess the land of promise because of God's faithful commitment to the patriarchs.

Whether they were in the land or out of it, Israel was always to recognize God's personal involvement with all of human experience. No expression of human pride escapes him, and no cry of despair eludes his notice. He is the God of all that is.

B. A Land of Giants (2:20)

The Rephaim and their related groups were apparently enormous in physical stature. One of their descendants, Goliath of Gath, is the Bible's best-known giant. He is described in Scripture as "a champion named Goliath, who was from Gath . . . out of the Philistine camp. He was over nine feet tall" (1 Sam. 17:4). The Hebrew text reads literally, "His height was six cubits and a span." Since the standard cubit measured about seventeen and one-half inches and the span half as much, Goliath would have been about nine feet five inches tall.

The Amorite king Og of Bashan also came from the same stock. Deuteronomy 3:11 describes his bed this way: "His bed was made of iron and was more than thirteen feet long and six feet wide. It is still in Rabbah of the Ammonites." The defeat of these men of impressive physical stature and warrior credentials appears in Scripture as a caution against spiritual timidity and a warning against unmerited pride.

VII. TEACHING OUTLINE

A. INTRODUCTION

1. Lead Story: The Other Side of the Unknown
2. Context: Before entering the land promised to the patriarchs, God challenged Israel to remember the way he had provided for their welfare and protected them through many difficulties. As a result, they should strengthen themselves and prepare to engage in the conflict to which he had called them.
3. Transition: This passage reveals the sovereign way that God fashions the footsteps of his children and encourages those who are his to follow him completely and fearlessly.

B. COMMENTARY

1. Instructions Concerning the Edomites (2:1–8)
2. Instructions Concerning the Moabites and Ammonites (2:9–23)
3. Encountering Sihon (2:24–37)

C. CONCLUSION: RESIGNING THE COMMISSION

VIII. ISSUES FOR DISCUSSION

1. Explain how this chapter forms an illustration of the principle enunciated by Paul: "If it is possible, as far as it depends on you, live at peace with everyone" (Rom. 12:18).
2. Do you think that God's action in hardening the spirit of Sihon was contrary to Sihon's own inclinations?
3. Why do you think the people of God need exhortations to overcome their timidity?

Deuteronomy 3

The Ministry of Courage

I. **INTRODUCTION**
Two-a-Day McCabe

II. **COMMENTARY**
A verse-by-verse explanation of the chapter.

III. **CONCLUSION**
The Indispensable Virtue
An overview of the principles and applications from the chapter.

IV. **LIFE APPLICATION**
Powers and Tasks
Melding the chapter to life.

V. **PRAYER**
Tying the chapter to life with God.

VI. **DEEPER DISCOVERIES**
Historical, geographical, and grammatical enrichment of the commentary.

VII. **TEACHING OUTLINE**
Suggested step-by-step group study of the chapter.

VIII. **ISSUES FOR DISCUSSION**
Zeroing the chapter in on daily life.

Deuteronomy 3

> **Quote**
>
> "This ministry of consolation and encouragement is not to be regarded as inferior and of secondary importance. ... Did we but discern it, we are daily surrounded by lonely, aching and sometimes broken hearts."
>
> J. Oswald Sanders

GEOGRAPHICAL PROFILE: BASHAN

- The fertile area adjacent to and east of the Sea of Galilee
- Assigned after its conquest to half the tribe of Manasseh
- Well suited for raising cattle, sheep, and goats (Ps. 22:12; Deut. 32:14)
- Appears in the Hebrew Bible always with the definite article, "the Bashan"
- The term means "fertile, fruitful"
- The modern Golan Heights

IN A NUTSHELL

In Deuteronomy 3, God demonstrates that what he promises, he is able to perform, often giving even more than what was promised. His largesse is a function of his grace, power, and love, and is designed to encourage his people to an ever-expanding confidence in his faithfulness and goodness.

The Ministry of Courage

I. INTRODUCTION

Two-a-Day McCabe

Charles Cardwell McCabe was a man of considerable talents. People began to notice him during the Civil War when he served as regimental chaplain of the 122nd Ohio Infantry. Among other things McCabe possessed a remarkable singing voice, and his contemporaries declared that he, more than any other, was responsible for the popularity of the "Battle Hymn of the Republic." Captured with his regiment during the war, McCabe was confined with many of his regiment at Libby Prison in Richmond, where he waited out the conclusion of the war.

After Appomattox, he became a church planter in the Methodist Episcopal denomination. McCabe rode trains all over the land in a tireless attempt to start new churches and raise money so others could join the effort.

On one such trip in the spring of 1881, he was reading the newspaper while traveling in the Pacific Northwest. An article that described the deliberations of the national convention of the Freethinkers of America caught his eye. The report included the text of a speech by the nation's most famous atheist, the notorious Robert Ingersoll. Ingersoll was quoted as saying, "The churches are dying out all across America. They are struck with death. By the dawn of the twentieth century, churches will be but relics of a bygone day."

McCabe knew better, of course. He had been traveling the breadth of the land planting churches with great success, but the article infused him with new energy. He left the train at the next station just long enough to fire off a telegram to Robert Ingersoll (whom he knew) at the convention of Freethinkers. It read: "Dear Bob. We are building more than one Methodist church for every day in the year and propose to make it two a day! Signed, Charles Cardwell McCabe. P.S. All hail the power of Jesus' name!"

Somehow the episode became public knowledge and found its way into several leading newspapers. McCabe and Ingersoll began an ongoing series of public debates on the future of Christian faith. Auditoriums would be filled whenever a debate between them was announced. In the middle of these encounters, some unknown believer composed a song based on the McCabe telegram. It went, "The infidels, a motley band, in counsel met and said, 'Churches are dying across the land and soon they'll all be dead.' When suddenly a message came, that left them in dismay. (Chorus:) All hail the power of Jesus' name, we're building two a day. We're building two a day, dear Bob,

Deuteronomy 3:1–2

we're building two a day. All hail the power of Jesus' name, we're building two a day."

C. C. McCabe became known as "Two-a-Day McCabe." For many years he and his associates made good on their stated goal, and the words of Robert Ingersoll now seem only a historical curiosity. God was pleased to honor the bold faith of a man who refused to be intimidated by the boastfulness of unbelief. C. C. McCabe knew he was on the winning side, and he declined to give in to his fears. His is the spirit that God calls on believers to exhibit as they engage in the spiritual conflicts of Christian living.

II. COMMENTARY

The Ministry of Courage

MAIN IDEA: When his people trust him, God demonstrates his power and glory by giving them victories.

A The Defeat of Bashan (3:1–11)

SUPPORTING IDEA: Even large opponents fall before God's power.

3:1–2. Following the defeat of Sihon, king of Heshbon, Israel moved, going **along the road toward Bashan**, the area east of the Sea of Galilee, roughly corresponding to the region that is today called the Golan Heights. Although Israel now controlled the region east of Jericho and could have invaded Canaan at that point, such a maneuver was made impractical by having an enemy, Og and his army, lurking in their rear. As a result, they moved past the fords of the Jordan River into the region controlled by Og.

The latter recognized the threat that Israel posed to his own security and **with his whole army marched out to meet** Israel **at Edrei**. Edrei was located about thirty miles southeast of the Sea of Galilee (called in Hebrew Scripture the Sea of Kinnereth; Num. 34:11). The Amorite army's approach might easily have rattled the people, but God anticipated that possibility and issued words of encouragement to Moses: **Do not be afraid**. These words, which constitute the most common imperative in Scripture, recognize the tendency of the fallen heart to panic at the sight of any threat and to forget the living reality of the God of heaven. Since Og was, like Sihon, an Amorite king (see Deut. 3:8), he was to be destroyed utterly, and his cities were to be taken over by Israel.

The divine encouragement to Moses came in terms that were familiar by now: **I have handed him over to you**. God expressed his determination to crush Og and **his whole army** by describing the deed as already done, although the battle had yet to be fought. In this case the divine encouragement was supported by a recent precedent: what the nation had done **to Sihon king of the Amorites**.

3:3–5. The description of the defeat of **Og king of Bashan** is given in terms much like those used to describe Sihon's downfall, although the account is briefer. Moses explained to Israel how the Lord had given into Israel's hands **Og** and **all his army**, a force that was so soundly routed that Israel left **no survivors**. As with Sihon's defeat, the destruction of Bashan provided Israel with new wealth and living space, since the Israelite army **took all his cities**.

There were **sixty** of these **cities**, and Israel captured them all. These cities constituted the district known as **Argob**, the heart of **Og's kingdom** in the larger area known as **Bashan**. It should be noted that the word *city* does not suggest an area of exceptional size or population. Archaeologists have discovered that the typical fortified settlement of the time enclosed an area of five to fifteen acres and would have housed no more than a few thousand people.

The cities were not pushovers, however. Indeed, they were **all . . . fortified with high walls** and barred **gates**. In addition to these sixty conquests, an even larger number of **unwalled villages** were conquered.

3:6–7. Along with conquering Og and his army, the Israelites **completely destroyed** the inhabitants of these communities. As with the territory of Sihon, these words do not apply to the property involved but to the people who inhabited the towns of the Amorites. The phrase *completely destroyed* translates a single Hebrew verb, a term with a technical meaning, "to devote to destruction" as a religious act. It suggests that in putting the inhabitants of Bashan to the sword, Israel acted directly under divine instruction. As God will point out later (see 20:16) and as Israel had already discovered to their shame, the nation would not prove resistant to the blandishments of an idolatrous native population. Had they left that population intact and simply moved in alongside them, Israel's spiritual history would have been even worse than it was. The destruction of the population left **all the livestock** and other wealth to be **carried off** by Israel.

3:8–10. These verses constitute a summary of Israel's victories in the Transjordan area. Moses describes the conquered area as being the territory **east of the Jordan** and bounded on the south by **the Arnon Gorge** and on the north by **Mount Hermon**, a distance of about 140 miles. Apparently the name *Hermon* was not a commonly accepted designation for this northernmost peak, as the text is careful to point out that it was designated **Sirion by the Sidonians** (Phoenecians) and had been called **Senir** by the **Amorites**.

The region described by Moses is a long plateau that drops on the west into the Jordan Valley. **All** the population centers **on the plateau**, including **Gilead** (south of Bashan) and **Bashan** itself, were captured by Israel.

Deuteronomy 3:11

3:11. The defeat of **Og** was especially significant in that he had been the last remaining Rephaite king east of the Jordan River. That gigantic race, which had so intimidated the parents of those who were listening to Moses' words, was now no longer a threat to those who would make their home in the area of Transjordan. That he had been a formidable opponent found testimony in the size of **his bed**, which **was more than thirteen feet long and six feet wide**. (Some scholars think that the Hebrew word translated *bed* means "sarcophagus" here. Either way, the structure, which in time became a museum piece, gave eloquent testimony to the intimidating size of this Amorite king.) **Rabbah** of the people of Ammon occupied the ancient site of the modern city of Amman, Jordan.

B The Division of the Land (3:12–22)

SUPPORTING IDEA: *God often delivers even more than he promises.*

3:12. God's original promise to Abraham specified that his descendants would in time possess the land of Canaan, a term that in general use describes the land west of the Jordan River. However, because the Amorites had resisted the progress of Israel, God had determined to add their territory to the original land grant to the patriarchs. **Of the land** that Israel conquered east of the Jordan River, Moses gave the southern portion to **the Reubenites and the Gadites**. That southern portion began at **the Arnon**, the northern boundary of Moab, and extended to **half the hill country of Gilead**. The original account of this land distribution notes that it was originally requested by the Reubenites and Gadites (Num. 32:1–5).

3:13–15. The northern half of Israelite Transjordan Moses **gave to the half tribe of Manasseh**. It included the northern portion of **Gilead** and all the region of **Bashan**—essentially, **the kingdom of Og**, including its power base, **the whole region of Argob**. The latter was known at the time as **a land of the Rephaites**, or, as some translations have it, "a land of the giants."

Why Moses distributed the choice lands of Bashan to the Manassites becomes clear in verse 14. **Jair, a descendant of Manasseh**, led the battle against Og's army and **took the whole region of Argob**, with its royal cities of Ashtaroth and Edrei. Jair renamed the region in his own honor, calling it **Havvoth Jair**, "the villages of Jair." To another prominent leader of Manasseh by the name of **Makir** Moses gave the region of **Gilead**.

3:16–17. The Reubenites and the Gadites received the land between **Gilead** (with its southern boundary on the **Jabbok River**) and **the Arnon Gorge**, eventually with Gad occupying the northern half and Reuben the southern half. The **western border** of both territories was the Jordan River, and the eastern border was the Ammonite frontier. (**Kinnereth** is the Old Testament name for the Sea of Galilee, and the **Sea of the Arabah** is today known as the Dead Sea.)

3:18–20. The rapid conquest of the Transjordan region carried with it a particular danger. Two and one-half tribes of Israel now had homes waiting for them. The foes were exterminated, the land was fertile, and they had been waiting for an entire generation for just those conditions. Moses moved quickly to set aside premature celebration and the jealousy that could have attended it. He **commanded** the Transjordanian tribes at that time to leave their **wives**, . . . **children**, and **livestock** to occupy the towns they had conquered. The army, however, would have to participate in the battles west of the Jordan River. The largest part of the work remained to be done, and justice dictated that they view their countrymen's needs as their own. There were to be no exceptions.

All their **able-bodied men, armed for battle**, would need to **cross over ahead** of their **brother Israelites**. Moses insisted that even the mere suspicion of hesitation should be removed from the Transjordanian tribes. They were to fight as enthusiastically in their brothers' interests as in their own.

In time, however, the western nine and one-half tribes would also be victorious and gain the promised **rest** of having their own **land** free of enemies. Only after that could Reuben, Gad, and the half tribe of Manasseh return east of the Jordan River **to the possession** that Moses had **given** them. The Transjordanian tribes honored their commitment and were in time commended by Joshua for their faithfulness (see Josh. 22:1–6).

3:21–22. The victories east of the Jordan River had a particular value not only for the tribes who would live there but also for the commander who would lead in the remainder of the conquest. As a result, Moses **commanded Joshua** that he should **not be afraid** of the peoples of Canaan. God had already shown his power and strength by defeating the two powerful Amorite kingdoms, and he would **do the same to all the kingdoms** that Joshua and Israel would face.

C The Disappointment of Moses (3:23–29)

SUPPORTING IDEA: *God holds leaders to a strict accountability.*

3:23–24. Moses, however, had already been told by the Lord that he would not be able to cross the Jordan River and enter the land of promise. Earlier in Israel's travels he had disobeyed God's instructions while dealing with a group of Israelite malcontents. Told to speak to a rock in the wilderness so that God might draw water from it for the people, Moses instead vented his frustrations: "He and Aaron gathered the assembly together in front of the rock and Moses said to them, 'Listen, you rebels, must we bring you water out of this rock?'" (Num. 20:10).

Deuteronomy 3:25–26

After years of dealing with a spiritually obtuse nation, Moses had reached the limits of his patience. However, his error was grave, since as the leader of God's people and God's personal representative on earth he bore a special responsibility. God's judgment was severe: "The LORD said to Moses and Aaron, 'Because you did not trust in me enough to honor me as holy in the sight of the Israelites, you will not bring this community into the land I give them'" (Num. 20:12).

Moses found this punishment grievous and as a result **pleaded with the LORD** at that time to have the sentence set aside. Having learned his lesson well, he began with a solemn recognition of God's sanctity and unique position: **What god is there in heaven or on earth who can do the deeds and mighty works you do?**

3:25–26. Hard on the heels of this beautiful sentiment came the meat of Moses' request: **Let me go over and see the good land beyond the Jordan.** It is clear from the Lord's answer that Moses had mentioned this petition a number of times, for he was told not to speak to God **anymore** about the matter. This episode forms one of the rare occasions in Scripture where God instructed a believer to stop praying. Moses was also involved in another such occasion (Exod. 14:15; see also Josh. 7:10).

Moses, still feeling the pain of his lost privileges, blamed his situation on the misbehavior of the people: **Because of you the LORD was angry with me**. As far as it goes, this statement is true. Had not Israel proven to be such a disagreeable and rebellious nation, the events of Numbers 20 would not have transpired. However, godly leadership functions according to the needs of those who are led. Being stronger, the godly person must assume more of the spiritual responsibility and expect to be judged by a stricter standard (see Jas. 3:1).

3:27–29. Having set aside Moses' request, the Lord gave instructions to Moses to undertake his last ministry for God. He was to go up **to the top of Pisgah and look** over into the land from the Transjordanian plateau. He could see what he would be missing, although he would not cross the Jordan River himself. Instead, he was to **commission Joshua**, at the same time encouraging him and strengthening him for the work he would undertake. Joshua rather than Moses would cause Israel **to inherit the land** that Moses would view from Pisgah (apparently a part of or at least associated with Mount Nebo; see Deut. 34:1).

> **MAIN IDEA REVIEW:** When his people trust him, God demonstrates his power and glory by giving them victories.

III. CONCLUSION

The Indispensable Virtue

Courage is the virtue that makes all other virtues possible. Fear causes the timid to stay away from risks and avoid change. Standing firm in one's convictions about the necessity of growth is essential if spiritual reality is to find a voice in human experience.

The world saw an illustration of this principle in the political realm during the days of the Cold War. Americans insisted that democracy was a better form of human government and that communism would in the end prove to be a disaster. That claim was valid, and there was nothing wrong with making it.

After making such claims, however, the Western democracies proceeded to act as though democracy was doomed unless they did unprincipled things to buttress it. So, democratic governments spent countless billions on intelligence and arms for other countries, even assassinating rulers and presidents in the process. They behaved as though they were sure that the people in totalitarian countries could never see what they had seen. They could have saved themselves lots of worry and money if they had simply had the courage to live out their convictions.

We can make the same mistake in the spiritual realm. We can profess the sufficiency of Jesus Christ to make us right with God and then become compulsively busy while showing people that we are not really sure that Jesus Christ is adequate to justify us before the Father.

PRINCIPLES

- The victories of today are granted to us so we might fight the battles of tomorrow well.
- God sometimes allows us to face large enemies so that he might gain greater glory when the victory comes.
- A leader who loses control of himself cannot hope to influence the people he leads.

APPLICATIONS

- Reflect today on possible areas in which steadfastness and courage are lacking in your life.
- Ask God to help you take a stand in an area of your life where courage has been lacking in the past.
- Share the story of a victory that you have experienced so that another person can be encouraged.

IV. LIFE APPLICATION

Powers and Tasks

God does not offer the Christian life as an escape from tribulations. It does include an escape from the wrong kind of tribulations (the kind caused by sin); but it does not exempt believers from pressures. It is in the way we face these pressures that we have the greatest opportunities to influence the people around us. God wants us to trust him and let him give us a quiet confidence that the tribulations of the moment will pass and that it is in the deep waters that we experience his presence with us.

Many Christians dread facing their daily lives because they feel pressured and stressful; and yet they never avail themselves of prayer, one of God's key provisions for such burdens. Often they behave like people who are not Christians and simply look for the quickest way out. Sometimes they pray that God will remove the problems and relieve them of the challenges. They hope for escape, somehow, and spend their time worrying or exhibiting a murmuring, complaining spirit. Phillips Brooks gave more biblical counsel: "Do not pray for tasks equal to your powers, but for powers equal to your tasks." Today's pains not only affect today. They are God's training ground for our tomorrows.

V. PRAYER

Father, grant us the courage to stand with you in the storms we face and to be forthright in giving you the credit when others praise us for our courage. Amen.

VI. DEEPER DISCOVERIES

A. Gilead (3:10)

The term *Gilead* is used to describe the region east of the Jordan River and west of Ammonite territory. Although used sometimes of the small land grant given to Makir, son of Manasseh, the term generally describes the larger area that lies between the Sea of Galilee and the Dead Sea. Gilead was the home of Elijah (1 Kgs. 17:1), and by the time of the New Testament it was called Perea. Gilead is well watered, hilly, and thickly wooded and is well-known for its production of olives, grapes, and citrus fruit.

The Israelites who settled there were generally from the tribes of Manasseh and Gad. After the period of the judges, the settlers of Gilead were often under harassment from the neighboring Ammonites, who were seeking to expand their own territory.

B. Cubit (3:11)

This verse notes that Og's bed "was more than thirteen feet long and six feet wide." The Hebrew text states, more technically, that "nine cubits [was] its length and four cubits its width, according to the standard cubit" (NKJV). The last phrase is literally, "according to the cubit of a man." This form of measurement, the most common biblical linear standard, came from a measurement available to everyone: the distance between the elbow and the tip of the middle finger, approximately eighteen inches. A cubit is also twice the distance of the space between the thumb and the tip of the little finger, what the Bible calls "a span."

The measurement of the "cubit of a man" received confirmation some years ago when the Siloam inscription was discovered in Jerusalem. It describes the length of Hezekiah's Tunnel as 1,200 cubits long. Its length in modern terms is 1,749 feet, yielding a measurement for the standard cubit of 17.49 inches.

C. Rest (3:20)

Moses refers to Israel obtaining "rest" once the nation's enemies were overcome: "Until the LORD gives rest to your brothers as he has to you, and they too have taken over the land that the LORD your God is giving them, across the Jordan" (Deut. 3:20). The concept of "rest" used extensively in the Epistle to the Hebrews finds its roots in this portion of Deuteronomy. To obtain rest is to conquer the land. In Deuteronomy literal land is in view; in Hebrews spiritual victories and rewards are the focus.

Although in popular Christian hymnody Canaan is a picture of heaven, in Deuteronomy it describes instead the believer's spiritual challenges. Instead of an idyllic existence, Israelites entering Canaan were just starting to do battle against countless enemies—a scene hardly suggestive of Paradise.

VII. TEACHING OUTLINE

A. INTRODUCTION
1. Lead Story: Two-a-Day McCabe
2. Context: Moses continues his description of Israel's victories east of the Jordan River, explaining how Reuben, Gad, and one of the half-tribes of Manasseh obtained their homeland, and how he secured from them a commitment to support their brother tribes during the remainder of the conquest.

Deuteronomy 3

3. Transition: The first river that has to be crossed in any life is the barrier of fear. Whether the objective is the securing of a homeland or the building of character, courage is the indispensable commodity that makes possible any conquest.

B. COMMENTARY
1. The Defeat of Bashan (3:1–11)
2. The Division of the Land (3:12–22)
3. The Disappointment of Moses (3:23–29)

C. CONCLUSION: POWERS AND TASKS

VIII. ISSUES FOR DISCUSSION
1. Can you recall occasions when you did battle with your own apprehensions and won?
2. What are some values that this chapter suggests for the keeping of a journal?
3. What is the single greatest fear that inhibits you in your journey of spiritual growth?

Deuteronomy 4

A Call to Faithfulness

I. INTRODUCTION
A Colony of Heaven

II. COMMENTARY
A verse-by-verse explanation of the chapter.

III. CONCLUSION
Closing the Door on the Wrong Person

An overview of the principles and applications from the chapter.

IV. LIFE APPLICATION
The Logistics of the Conquest

Melding the chapter to life.

V. PRAYER
Tying the chapter to life with God.

VI. DEEPER DISCOVERIES
Historical, geographical, and grammatical enrichment of the commentary.

VII. TEACHING OUTLINE
Suggested step-by-step group study of the chapter.

VIII. ISSUES FOR DISCUSSION
Zeroing the chapter in on daily life.

Quote

"The humble heart is [God's] throne in regard to his gracious presence, and heaven is his throne in regard to his glorious presence, and yet neither of these thrones will hold him, for the heaven of heavens cannot contain him."

Thomas Watson

IN A NUTSHELL

God appeals to Israel to recognize his uniqueness, to respond in loyal love on the basis of that uniqueness, and to serve him faithfully and exclusively because of it. It is in the interests of those who know him well to cleave to him only and exclude all other deities from their affections.

A Call to Faithfulness

I. INTRODUCTION

A Colony of Heaven

In the years between the writing of the Old Testament and the New Testament, the Roman Empire came into existence. Built out of the disappointments of the old republic and its continuing civil wars, the Empire struggled to recruit troops to defend and expand its far-flung borders. Eventually the Roman emperors, beginning with Augustus Caesar, offered special incentives to join the legions. Those who served a full term would receive full Roman citizenship with all its rights and privileges.

In order to receive these privileges, however, the veterans were expected to settle into special cities called colonies. By their presence on the Empire's frontier, the retired citizen-soldiers would become a "little Rome" and represent the great city and its culture before the distant masses. The purpose of such colonies was twofold: to preserve order on the frontiers and to extol the virtues of the homeland.

By the time of the New Testament, the city of Philippi had become such a Roman colony. There the apostle Paul founded a church during his second missionary journey. Eventually, the apostle would write to the little group of Christians there and describe their role in Philippi in terms they could appreciate: "Our citizenship is in heaven. And we eagerly await a Savior from there, the Lord Jesus Christ" (Phil. 3:20).

The veterans must have nodded their heads at those words, because they had come to Philippi for a similar purpose. Paul was calling them to a still-higher end, to represent their real homeland, heaven itself. As one translator rendered Philippians 3:20, "We are a colony of heaven."

As Israel drew near the promised land, Moses reminded them that their real purpose in that land was to serve as representatives of their God. They could, by their behavior and devotion, appeal to the hearts of their neighbors; or, by their spiritual laxity and disobedience, they could abandon such a noble purpose and be drawn into useless and destructive pursuits.

Christian believers are to form, in effect, a little colony of heaven where they live. By their godly conduct, they are to disarm critics and win friends and new citizens for their true homeland. That process starts with the realization of the immense privileges and standing that they possess at the moment of their conversion.

Deuteronomy 4:1–2

II. COMMENTARY

A Call to Faithfulness

> **MAIN IDEA:** God blesses his people richly and reveals himself to them in the expectation that they will become fully his in affections and behavior.

A The Privileges of Israel's Citizens (4:1–14)

> **SUPPORTING IDEA:** High privilege creates high responsibility. Israel, which had seen great actions on God's part, was to cleave to him in steadfast love.

4:1–2. As Israel waited near the Jordan River across from the city of Jericho, the moment of truth was about to arrive. One might suppose that God would brief the nation on military tactics and strategy, since they were about to begin a protracted military conflict. Instead, he addressed the people's spiritual condition. Israel needed, if it was to **live** and **go in and take possession of the land**, to **hear** what God had to say. His **decrees and laws** were about to be taught (the teaching will begin in ch. 5), and the people would be well advised to **follow them**. Since their future success (either in battle or elsewhere) would depend upon his blessing, they must pay close attention.

Moses admonished Israel very sternly that they should avoid the standard blunders about divine instruction. On the one hand, they must **not add to what** he **commanded** by augmenting God's law with human additions. Legalism first adds to God's law and in time invalidates it (see Mark 7:13).

On the other hand, Israel must avoid the equally critical mistake that is made when people **subtract from** God's imperatives. Choosing not to obey what is valid in effect removes biblical teaching from its lofty status of divine authority. The believer's authority is God's Word—nothing less, nothing more, nothing else (see also Rev. 22:18–19).

4:3–4. If anyone on earth had reasons to take God's law seriously, Israel certainly did. They **saw** with their **own eyes what the LORD did at Baal Peor**. The reference is to the events described in Numbers 25, when Israel was caught up in a frenzy of local paganism and immorality: "[The women of Moab] invited [Israel] to the sacrifices to their gods. The people ate and bowed down before these gods" (Num. 25:2). The result of this rebellion was a plague among the people, a judgment that was terminated only when the leaders of the moral revolt were executed. Twenty-four thousand people died in the divine discipline that came from the rebellion, as Moses' listeners knew. It was likely that most of Moses' hearers had lost close relatives in the debacle.

The people who did not bow down before the pagan deity **Baal of Peor**, but who instead **held fast to the LORD**, remained **alive** to hear Moses' words and to experience the bright prospect of a homeland. (For more on *Baal*, see

"Deeper Discoveries.") Although God in grace often does not place disobedience in judgment in so close a relationship, he did at Peor, and all those who heard him could not fail to recognize that God had acted just as Moses described. In fact, as Moses spoke, Israel was standing in the very spot where God had acted (see Deut. 3:29).

4:5–6. The things that Moses had already **taught** Israel (as well as the formal restatement of the covenant that would follow in ch. 5) were not the products of human invention but the very **decrees and laws** that the Lord **had commanded** him. They were not experimental but authoritative. Israel was not to speculate about them but instead to **follow them** once they were inside the land that would soon be their home.

God's laws, in fact, had a still wider application than their values in giving Israel an ordered society. If God's people would **observe them carefully**, his laws would display to the surrounding nations Israel's own **wisdom and understanding**. God's moral principles were so distinctive that reports would soon surface among the pagans in that part of the world and cause them to reflect about Israel's special status.

This external focus was built in to the original covenant with Abraham, whom God promised, "I will bless those who bless you, and whoever curses you I will curse; and all peoples on earth will be blessed through you" (Gen. 12:3). Israel was to be a light to the nations (see Isa. 49:6), and part of its luminescence would become apparent through its own faithfulness to God's laws.

4:7–8. The benefits of obedience and faithfulness to God would set Israel apart and give them a platform from which to speak his law outside their borders, for God's **righteous decrees and laws** were built around a personal relationship with him. Other nations knew nothing of this. Pagan peoples engaged in the appeasement of remote and angry deities, but Yahweh was **near** to his people **whenever** they prayed **to him**.

4:9. The great danger that Israel would have to overcome was forgetfulness. They would have to **be careful**, and watch **closely**, and see to it that they not **forget** the events that brought them into their homeland.

The forgetfulness of which Moses spoke is not primarily a problem of mental alertness but spiritual laxity. When Israel later began a large-scale defection to the idolatry of Canaan, it was not because they had forgotten Yahweh's name, still less because they no longer felt he deserved their devotion. He had simply receded from the consciousness at the moment that their defection began. Once it was under way, they were so distracted with the passing pleasures of sin that they did not give him a moment's thought. Godly living is a process that must be renewed each day.

4:10. Merely abhorring the tendency to forgetfulness, however, is not enough. If spiritual reality is to be passed from one generation to the next, it must be positively remembered. To underscore this point, Moses called on the nation to **remember the day** they **stood before the** LORD at Mount Sinai.

Deuteronomy 4:11-12

They were there at God's behest, to **hear** his **words** and as a result to **revere him as long as they live in the land**. Without personal copies of God's Word, Israel had to recall the solemn event when God drew especially near and to allow it to impress upon them the uniqueness of the God they served. Reverence for God and faith in him begin with a regular exposure to his words: "So then faith comes by hearing, and hearing by the word of God" (Rom. 10:17 NKJV).

4:11–12. That special day at Horeb had begun when the people drew **near to the foot of the mountain**. They observed the sharp and frightening contrasts between the light of God's **fire** and the **black clouds and deep darkness** that surrounded it. In this sobering context, they saw **no form**, but **only a voice**—the voice of God himself. Clearly, God intended that this dramatic scene should make an impression on them, and it did. For many years afterward, the leaders of Israel reminded them of these events: "The earth shook, the heavens poured down rain, before God, the One of Sinai, before God, the God of Israel" (Ps. 68:8; see also Deut. 33:2; Judg. 5:5; Hab. 3:3).

The absence of a visible representation of God was designed to teach his people that he could not be legitimately represented in the shape of an idol. No visual symbol could possibly do justice to his character and his majesty, and they were to rid themselves of this practice at the outset.

4:13–14. God used the spectacular scene at Horeb to declare to Israel **his covenant**, summarized in **the Ten Commandments**. Moses was about to restate this covenant beginning in chapter 5. Here he reminded them that God **commanded** them **to follow** the covenantal stipulations and then **wrote them on two stone tablets**.

The best and most useful location for God's commandments, however, is in the hearts of his people. As a result, **the Lord directed** Moses to **teach** the people **the decrees and laws** they needed.

B The Portrayal of Israel's God (4:15–43)

SUPPORTING IDEA: *Yahweh, God of Israel, is unlike any man-made deity, and he expects loyalty on the part of Israel. At the same time, he extends mercy to sinners.*

4:15–18. Moses applied the crucial lesson of **Horeb** directly to the people as he continued. Since they **saw no form of any kind the day the LORD spoke** to them, they needed to **watch** themselves **very carefully** and shun any form of idolatry. To construct **an image of any shape** whatever, whether it represents a **man or a woman** or **any animal**, would have a dehumanizing effect on them; they would **become corrupt**. When man worships anything less than his Creator, he loses touch with that which provides him with dignity and purpose. Since God created humanity to have fellowship with him, to pretend satisfaction in a relationship with a creature robs both man and God of the majesty that they ought to possess. Israel was not to become like the nations, because their God was greater than the gods of those nations.

4:19–20. Neither, however, should Israel **look up to the sky** and conclude that since **the sun, the moon and the stars** were remote that they were worthy of devotion. There is an element in man that concludes that whatever is distant and unattainable must be worthy of adoration. Moses warned Israel that they were to resist this tendency and **not be enticed into bowing down** to the stellar heavens. The night sky, although beautiful, is a testimony of God's common grace; the stars are things that **the Lord . . . has apportioned to all the nations**. The heavens testify of his order and goodness (cp. Ps. 19:1–6).

Israel, by contrast, was a nation that knew more than the common experience of all the nations. In fact, the Lord showed his personal interest in them, since he had rescued them from **the iron-smelting furnace** (a metaphor for Egypt), a place of misery, destruction, and purification. He had delivered them from the common corruptions and indignities that lost people bring on themselves and had made them into **the people of his inheritance**. The last phrase emphasizes God's delight in Israel, since in the experience of humanity, inheritances are given to children and grandchildren. God had decided to invest himself in the people of Israel to transform them as a people, a privilege that they dared not take for granted.

4:21–22. Moses used himself as an example of what happens when people trifle with the Almighty. Referring to the episode of Numbers 20, the lawgiver reminded Israel that the Lord was angry with him because of their unbelief. Because of Moses' irreverence, God **solemnly swore** that he would not be able to **cross the Jordan and enter the good land** that they were about to inherit. Instead, he would **die** in Transjordan, while the nation took **possession of that good land**.

Moses thus became a picture of privileges lost by compromise. His relationship with God was fully functional. His sins were forgiven, and he was being used by God in worthwhile ministry. Still, his experience shows that our choices have enduring consequences that cannot be overcome even by godly sorrow and repentance.

4:23–24. The leader of God's nation quickly brought his hearers to the application he wanted to make. They were **not to forget the covenant** that God had made with their fathers and was about to renew with them. The primary way they could violate that covenant was through the making of idols. God's uniqueness cannot be duplicated or even approximated by imitating it in some visible form. Nothing that is created can picture the Creator, although everything that is created testifies in some way to his greatness. As a result, God had **forbidden** visual metaphors for himself, even if the person who worshiped somehow could recognize that the true God was not present in the artifact itself. Such failure to recognize Yahweh's uniqueness would

Deuteronomy 4:25–26

provoke him to a just anger and a determination to punish such evil, since the true **God is a consuming fire** and **a jealous God**.

4:25–26. God's warnings against idolatry would have to be repeated to future generations. Although the generation that came out of Egypt had seen his wonders there, they would have to declare their knowledge of such things to their **children** and see that they were transmitted still further, to their **grandchildren**. If Israel did not go to the trouble to do this, after the nation had **lived in the land a long time**, they stood to lose by becoming **corrupt**. The evidence of their corruption would appear when they constructed an **idol**, thus **doing evil in the eyes of the LORD**. They would repeat the same mistake that Israel had made in its brush with idolatry at Baal Peor (see Num. 25) when they had provoked God to anger.

The ancient suzerain-vassal treaties made provisions for the violation of the covenant by either participant in it, and so did God's covenant. He promised Israel that if they should violate his covenant by turning their hearts toward false gods, he would **call heaven and earth as witnesses** against them. Later, God used this formula in explaining why he found it essential to send them into captivity in Babylon (see Isa. 1:2–4).

4:27–28. Defection from the Lord and his covenant would result in the loss of the very land that Israel now stood to possess. The Lord would **scatter** them **among** the Gentile **peoples** where they would be used and cast aside. **Few** of the people so dispossessed would **survive** while living among the Gentiles. Their affection for pagan deities would become complete in those circumstances, and they would **worship man-made gods of wood and stone**. When God's people lose their uniqueness, they forfeit the very rationale for their existence among the nations. The reality of which these verses were the predictions took place beginning in 606 B.C. when Judah was taken captive and marched into captivity in Babylon.

4:29. Although Israel's defection would carry with it a host of painful consequences, it would not be final or irreversible. If from the scene of their sorrowful discipline they should decide to **seek the LORD**, they would **find him** even in their misery—provided they looked for him intensely, **with all** their **heart** and **with all** their **soul**. God's loyalty to them would not be diminished, although their loyalty to him might be lacking. Even in their darkest hour, he would be there with forgiveness and acceptance (although they might still be required to live under his rod). The penitential prayers of Daniel 9 and Nehemiah 9 revolve around this promise of national forgiveness and spiritual rehabilitation.

4:30–31. Israel's national captivity would, in fact, have an end. When they found themselves **in distress** because **all these things have happened**, **then in later days** they would **return to the LORD**. In his grace, he would permit a reconciliation when the people returned and began to **obey him**. God's people may become disobedient and unfaithful to his covenant, but he remains unchanged. As a **merciful God**, he swore not to **abandon or destroy**

those who were his. His attachment to Israel did not exist because of their superior behavior but because of God's **covenant** made long ago with their **forefathers**. That covenant had been **confirmed** to those patriarchs, Abraham, Isaac, and Jacob, by a solemn **oath** on God's part.

4:32–34. In rescuing Israel from Egyptian slavery and in granting them the privileges of seeing him reveal himself, God had done something unprecedented. **From one end of the heavens to the other**, no one had seen anything **so great as this** act of redemption in the history of humanity. God had taken **for himself one nation**, Israel, **out of another nation**, Egypt. He had done so by using remarkable methods, including **signs and wonders**, by giving them victory in **war**, and various other **great and awesome deeds**. All these **things** God had done for them in ways that could not be ignored, since they happened **before** their **very eyes**.

4:35–36. Moses then gave the rationale for this line of argument. Israel was **shown these things** so they might appreciate the uniqueness of their God. Yahweh alone **is God**, and **besides him there is no other**. God went to unusual lengths to reveal himself to Israel, and he did so for a significant reason—**to discipline** them. The expression suggests not punishment or retribution but profound instruction. God's intent was didactic not judicial. He made them **hear his voice** . . . **from out of the fire** so they might understand that he tolerates no rivals.

4:37–38. The ties that bound the Lord to Israel originated with him. **He loved** the nation's **forefathers**, although their behavior was not always praiseworthy. Because he loved them, he **chose their descendants after them** and rescued them from the bondage of Egypt. He did not stop with such a miraculous deliverance, however; God intended, additionally, **to drive out** of the promised land **nations greater and stronger** than Israel.

The term *nations* in this context refers to ethnic groupings, not to political units. At the time of the invasion, such ethnic groupings were typically united by geographical proximity and often, although not always, by a central city-state. When God specified for Abraham the nations that he would in time expel, he listed "the Kenites, Kenizzites, Kadmonites, Hittites, Perizzites, Rephaites, Amorites, Canaanites, Girgashites and Jebusites" (Gen. 15:19–21). The Jebusites are well-known in biblical history as the inhabitants of Jebus, the city later to be known as Jerusalem. Although the later city would grow far beyond the boundaries of Jebus, the latter's surface area amounted to only about eight acres and would have contained only about three thousand inhabitants. Although other Jebusites would have lived in the surrounding hills, those together with the city dwellers could not have outnumbered Israel by themselves.

The reference, therefore, to **nations greater and stronger than you** (v. 38) must include the combined numbers of all the nations inside Canaan's boundaries. The property of these peoples would become Israel's **inheritance**.

Deuteronomy 4:39–40

The order of the events of verse 37 is significant. God demonstrates his love, then looks for a response. His choice and unilateral determination to bless the nation precede anything that they do. The order is reminiscent of 1 John 4:10, "This is love: not that we loved God, but that he loved us and sent his Son as an atoning sacrifice for our sins."

4:39–40. Israel's wisdom lay in a frank recognition that they had received more than they could have asked for, and in a constant awareness of the power of their God. They were to **acknowledge and take to heart** the uniqueness of Yahweh and to behave accordingly. They were to recognize that **the LORD is God in heaven above and on the earth below** and that **there is no other**. They could do this by observing **his decrees and commands**. If they did so, it would **go well** with them and their succeeding generations; they would know the benefits of living harmoniously under the authority of the God who made all things. Among those benefits would be **long life**.

4:41–42. Moses could not proceed with an enumeration of the decrees and commands of the covenant without resolving one bit of unfinished business. He had earlier ordered in a general way the designation of six cities of refuge (cp. Num. 35:9–34) once the land had been conquered. Now that the region **east of the Jordan** had been subdued, Moses specified the **three cities** that were to be so designated in that conquered area. These refuge cities were to serve, in effect, as jails (of which Israel had none). Their function was to preserve the life of the **person** who had **killed** another **unintentionally, . . . without malice aforethought**. These words carefully enunciate a recognition of the difference between murder in the usual sense, which is planned, and manslaughter, a death that can be caused by a rapid, unthinking response or by an accident.

The provision of these cities recognizes the need for careful investigation and clear-eyed weighing of evidence and motivation. God is concerned for justice not only for the victim of an accidental death but for the proper disposition of the case with respect to the one who unintentionally took a life. The cities of refuge were to provide a forum for investigation, a place into which the manslayer could **flee** and **save his life**.

4:43. The Transjordanian cities of refuge included **Bezer** in the south, **Ramoth** in the center of the land, and **Golan** in the north. The distribution of these cities was intentional, ensuring that no one in need of refuge would be too far away from such a city.

C The Preamble to Israel's Covenant (4:44–49)

SUPPORTING IDEA: *In view of Israel's unique position among the nations, they are to take his law to heart.*

4:44. Everything in Deuteronomy to this point is prologue. **Moses** has spent four chapters preparing the hearts of his listeners to consider why they should take seriously **the law** that he is now about to **set before** them. This refers to the contents of chapters 5–26.

4:45–46. God's law is to be stated in the form of **stipulations, decrees and laws**. The differences between these terms are minor. The first emphasizes that the items that follow are part of a covenant, a binding agreement. The second, *decrees,* calls attention to God as the majestic source of the obligations. *Laws* emphasizes that there are penalties attached for violation of the covenant's terms.

The setting in which the covenant's details were enumerated provided the critical backdrop for its being taken seriously. The covenant's laws were specified at the time when the reality of God's blessing of Israel could not be challenged. They had just come **out of Egypt** according to God's promise. They were poised **in the valley . . . of the Jordan** to invade the territory of Canaan, again according to God's promise. They were dwelling **in the land of Sihon king of the Amorites**, territory that God had given them even beyond his original promise to the patriarchs. In every way, God had delivered. His goodness toward them was incontestable.

4:47–49. Israel had also come into possession of **the land of Og king of Bashan**, the two tracts together extending from **the Arnon Gorge** to **Mount Hermon** and enveloping **the Arabah east of the Jordan, as far as the Sea of the Arabah** (i.e., the Dead Sea). God had nothing left to prove to Israel. It remained to be seen whether they would take his covenant to heart and obey it.

> **MAIN IDEA REVIEW:** *God blesses his people richly and reveals himself to them in the expectation that they will become fully his in affections and behavior.*

III. CONCLUSION

Closing the Door on the Wrong Person

A general practitioner called a specialist in a town fifty miles away for advice. He explained to the specialist how a young boy was being slowly killed by an infection that was causing him to hemorrhage internally.

"I don't know how to deal with this infection," said the first doctor, "but you do. This is your area of specialty. Can you come at once?"

The specialist said, "I'm on my way."

He jumped in his car and headed toward the distant hospital where the young boy lay. Reaching the outskirts of his own town, the specialist stopped at a traffic light. Suddenly his car door was yanked open and a man wearing a gray cap, a brown leather jacket, and brandishing a revolver shouted at him, "Get out of the car!"

The doctor said, "But I can't get out. You see, I'm trying . . ."

Deuteronomy 4

The man with the revolver cut him off in mid-sentence. "I don't care what you are trying to do. Get out of that car, or I will kill you right now!"

The doctor left the car and watched the man drive off. The carjacked doctor tried desperately to find a telephone. After trying four or five houses only to find no one home, he finally discovered someone who would allow him to call a taxi. The taxi took him to the bus station. He boarded a bus and finally arrived at his intended destination. However, his confrontation with the car thief caused him to be two hours later than he had planned.

The general practitioner met him at the door. "I'm glad you came," he said, "but you're too late. My patient died nearly twenty minutes ago. Maybe if you had not been delayed, you could have saved him. I would like for you to come with me to meet his mother and father. His father is nearly hysterical with grief. Maybe you can say something to comfort him."

As they entered the family waiting room, the doctor saw the father. He was wearing a gray cap and a brown leather jacket. In his hurry to get to the hospital, the father had shut out the one person who could save his son.

We see the tragedy in that, and yet we have difficulty seeing the calamity in shutting out of our lives the God whose grace we can't live without. In time, Israel would abandon the God whose kindness and power they could not survive without. Christians often behave in a similar fashion.

My wife has a little plaque mounted in her kitchen window that contains a large measure of wisdom. It says, "Be kind, because the next person you meet is carrying a burden." That is sound counsel. It is equally true that burdened people are invited to roll their burdens onto the God whose shoulders are adequate for the heaviest weight: "Cast all your anxiety on him because he cares for you" (1 Pet. 5:7). Don't make the mistake in a moment of panic of excluding the one whose history demonstrates the reality of his care.

PRINCIPLES

- The shortest route to being admired by people is to understand and obey God's revelation.
- The church of Jesus Christ is always one generation away from disappearing.
- Forgiveness does not erase the historical consequences of bad moral choices.
- In forgetting God's Word, we neglect our own well-being and ignore the one who can bring our grandest dreams to fruition.

APPLICATIONS

- Ponder the ways that you may have neglected portions of God's truth in your own life.

- Confess your sins before God and ask for his help in moving in a new direction.
- Share with someone how God has given you a spiritual victory in the past.
- Ask a confidant to pray with you about personal concerns.

IV. LIFE APPLICATION

The Logistics of the Conquest

By the time Israel arrived in the Jordan Valley, they had accumulated a significant history of experience with God's sufficiency. The Book of Numbers explains that there were in Israel at the time of the departure from Egypt a total of 603,550 fighting men twenty years of age and upward. If we assume an equal number of adult women and a conservative number of children, the total population of Israel must have exceeded two million people while they were in the wilderness. All these people had to be fed and provided with water—no small challenge for the most skilled generals and quartermasters.

Even assuming a minimal diet of one hatful of manna per meal, the people would have needed about one thousand tons of food per day—the equivalent of a freight train load one and one-half miles long, every day for forty years. If the people used only two gallons of water per day (for drinking and washing) per person, God had to supply the equivalent of a train of tank cars hundreds of miles long every day. Every time Israel stopped at night, they required a camping area covering dozens of square miles.

God called Israel out of Egypt into the Sinai with only the promise that he would provide for them, and they responded (at least at first). Whether their faith was strong or weak, he provided all these needs as a demonstration of his faithfulness. He even led them away from the main roads so they would not have to fight too soon. In everything he showed them his power and consistency, and he expected them to conclude that what he had done yesterday he could do again today if it was required.

Although we are not called to the same immediate objective as Israel, we are called to recognize his faithfulness for our personal needs. The God who supplied Israel with miraculous food each morning can provide for our needs. To deny his goodness by exhibiting a nervous and worrisome temperament is to expose his reputation to criticism and shame. He is the same God today that he was during Israel's wilderness wanderings.

V. PRAYER

Father, keep us from thinking we can gain our goals by simply applying our superior intelligence and insights. Help us to see that true Christian living

Deuteronomy 4

results in a humble dependence upon your enablement, which is so much greater than depending on our own limited strength. Amen.

VI. DEEPER DISCOVERIES

A. Baal (4:3)

Baal was the name that described the supreme deity among the Canaanite population of the promised land at the time of the conquest. The Hebrew word *baal* is a neutral term, meaning simply "lord" or "possessor," and it was used in ancient times originally as a title for the God of Israel. Jonathan had a son named Merib-Baal, "The Lord is my Advocate," and David fathered a son whom he named Beeliada, "The Lord knows."

However, the region of Phoenecia/Sidon in what is now called Lebanon contained an aggressive pagan cult that advocated the worship of a Baal quite unlike the God of Israel. The Baal of the Sidonians was a sun god who was worshiped in various forms, depending on the location of the people who were doing the worshiping. As such, Baal of Peor appears prominently in the Old Testament narrative, in both Numbers 25, where the full account of Israel's folly occurs, and in the briefer mention in Deuteronomy: "The LORD your God destroyed from among you everyone who followed the Baal of Peor" (4:3). References also appear in Scripture to Baal-Gad, Baal-Hermon, Baal-Hamon, and the like. Sometimes, Baals were named for attributes of the deity. An example is Baal-Zebub, a Philistine deity whose name in time became identified with the devil himself (cp. Matt. 10:25).

In some cults, Baal expected an offering of a living sacrifice—specifically, the firstborn child of the person who was bringing the sacrifice. Hebrew Scripture describes this grisly process as "causing [someone] to pass through the fire" and roundly condemns it. Ahaz, king of Judah, for example, received the following negative review by the biblical writer: "He walked in the ways of the kings of Israel and even sacrificed his son in the fire, following the detestable ways of the nations the LORD had driven out before the Israelites" (2 Kgs. 16:3).

Israel found its most profound danger from Baalism during the rule of King Ahab, who married Jezebel, daughter of Ethbaal, king of the Sidonians and priest in the Baal cult. Ahab thus took into his nation a woman who was committed to the exclusive worship of Baal, the sad results of which are well-known.

In the Baal cults, the deity had a female consort, Asherah or Ashtarte, a fertility goddess. Worshipers believed that the renewal of nature each spring represented the fruits of cohabitation between Baal and Ashtarte. She was worshiped by means of a wooden pillar or totem, references to which appear in Scripture: "[Asa] deposed his grandmother Maacah from her position as queen mother, because she had made a repulsive Asherah pole. Asa cut the pole down and burned it in the Kidron Valley" (1 Kgs. 15:13).

B. Covenant (4:13)

Deuteronomy represents the renewal of a covenant: "He declared to you his covenant, the Ten Commandments, which he commanded you to follow and then wrote them on two stone tablets" (Deut. 4:13). The Ten Commandments constitute the distilled essence of the covenant, which is fully described in Deuteronomy 5–26.

The word *covenant* (Heb. *berith*) appears 265 times in the Old Testament, with about 10 percent of the references appearing in Deuteronomy. The word refers to a legal disposition of property, generally between two parties or groups. A covenant includes promises made in the expectation of certain behavior on the part of the recipients. Consequently, a covenant usually describes the penalties that ensue if the beneficiary of the covenant promises should fail to honor his own obligations.

In the case of a divine covenant, no person could possibly hold God to account for his faithfulness to the covenant, so the Lord took an unusual step in giving assurances of his faithfulness with respect to the covenant he initiated. The Epistle to the Hebrews explains: "When God made his promise to Abraham, since there was no one greater for him to swear by, he swore by himself, saying, 'I will surely bless you and give you many descendants'" (Heb. 6:13–14).

C. Inheritance (4:21)

In the Book of Deuteronomy, the inheritance of Israel is the land of promise. Moses' use of the term is typical: "The LORD . . . swore that I would not cross the Jordan and enter the good land the LORD your God is giving you as your inheritance" (4:21). As such, the inheritance represents far more than new birth, which is often pictured in the events at the Red Sea. The inheritance was a reward that was promised for faithfulness at the end of many battles. As such, the notion of inheritance is picked up by the New Testament writers and made a synonym for the rewards of the Christian believer who serves Christ: "You know that you will receive an inheritance from the Lord as a reward. It is the Lord Christ you are serving" (Col. 3:24; cp. Acts 20:32; Heb. 6:12; Rev. 21:7). The word presupposes not simply that the reward will be gained but that it will prove to be the bequest of a generous parent.

D. Miraculous Signs and Wonders (4:34)

The words of Moses in Deuteronomy make it clear that signs and wonders were never commonplace in human history: "Has any god ever tried to take for himself one nation out of another nation . . . by miraculous signs and

Deuteronomy 4

wonders?" (Deut. 4:34). The exodus/wanderings/conquest period was a time of remarkable involvement on God's part in the affairs of his people. Aside from a brief time during the ministries of Elijah and Elisha, the next protracted period of signs and wonders took place fourteen centuries later during the New Testament era.

The purpose of signs and wonders is to provoke people to faith and godly living (John 2:11; 6:2). In the case of the signs and wonders of the exodus and conquest, they also testified to the reality of and divine approval of a new epoch in biblical history (cp. Heb. 2:1–4), just as they did at the time of the New Testament.

VII. TEACHING OUTLINE

A. INTRODUCTION
1. Lead Story: A Colony of Heaven
2. Context: Moses calls on his countrymen to recognize their privileged role as recipients of God's blessings. They are to acknowledge his goodness and remain faithful to him.
3. Transition: God always takes the initiative in bringing people to himself. His love is freely given, and it creates no obligations on his part. The obligations belong to those who have been the recipients of his love.

B. COMMENTARY
1. The Privileges of Israel's Citizens (4:1–14)
2. The Portrayal of Israel's God (4:15–43)
3. The Preamble to Israel's Covenant (4:44–49)

C. CONCLUSION: THE LOGISTICS OF THE CONQUEST

VIII. ISSUES FOR DISCUSSION

1. Can you think of times when you witnessed unmistakable evidences of God's work in your life? What conclusions did you draw from these about your future relationship with him?
2. If you had seen the signs and wonders that Israel saw at the time of the exodus and conquest, would you have behaved differently than them? Why or why not?
3. How is the importance of being a person of your word emphasized in this chapter?
4. What are some ways you can testify to God's uniqueness in your life today?

Deuteronomy 5

The Authority of the Word

I. **INTRODUCTION**
   Nearly Forgotten Beginnings

II. **COMMENTARY**
   A verse-by-verse explanation of the chapter.

III. **CONCLUSION**
   The Perils and Power of Alexander Duff
   An overview of the principles and applications from the chapter.

IV. **LIFE APPLICATION**
   The (Un)Chicken Lady
   Melding the chapter to life.

V. **PRAYER**
   Tying the chapter to life with God.

VI. **DEEPER DISCOVERIES**
   Historical, geographical, and grammatical enrichment of the commentary.

VII. **TEACHING OUTLINE**
   Suggested step-by-step group study of the chapter.

VIII. **ISSUES FOR DISCUSSION**
   Zeroing the chapter in on daily life.

Deuteronomy 5

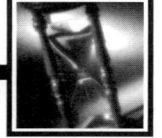

Quote

"The remarkable thing about fearing God is that when you fear God you fear nothing else, whereas if you do not fear God you fear everything else."

Oswald Chambers

In a Nutshell

Both at Sinai and in the Jordan Valley, God called attention to the solemnity of his covenant and to his revelation of himself by signs and wonders. In doing so, he showed that he expects his people to hear and obey and to honor him supremely in all they do and say.

The Authority of the Word

I. INTRODUCTION

Nearly Forgotten Beginnings

On a December day in 1891 in Springfield, Massachusetts, Dr. James Naismith became the inventor of the game of basketball. Today his name is honored in the Naismith Award, given annually to the nation's best college basketball player, but his purpose in inventing the game has been largely forgotten. According to another James Naismith (the grandson and namesake of the inventor), basketball came into existence because of the spiritual concerns of its inventor. He invented basketball "to lead other young men to Christ."

Dr. Naismith was an ordained minister as well as a physician. He noticed that during the winter the young men who came to the YMCA Training School in Springfield tended to be bored, since outdoor games like baseball and football were no longer so inviting due to the Massachusetts winters. He decided to invent something new to give the young men some constructive and wholesome activity during the winter months.

His original idea was for a game of "boxball," played by tossing a soccer ball into a cardboard box mounted on the wall. The gym's janitor was unable to locate two suitable boxes for the purpose at the time, but he did find an alternative: two peach baskets. Dr. Naismith quickly came up with thirteen rules, and basketball came into existence.

Sixty years later, in a development that Dr. Naismith would have approved, missionary Dick Hillis saw how the game could be used to advantage in ministry. Dick had recently been expelled from mainland China due to the communist takeover. He was ministering to the Nationalist Chinese troops who were living in Taiwan when he noticed that many of them went for long stretches with little to do and that they tended to choose basketball as their preferred leisure activity. The idea came to him to recruit teams in the United States to visit Taiwan and play some of the local service teams. At the same time, they would give their testimonies (through translators) and share the gospel of Christ.

Since that time, Hillis's dream has become a wonderful reality. Hundreds of teams have gone to Asia and other continents serving as sports ambassadors for Jesus Christ. These teams often hold basketball clinics for young players and play local teams, giving a brief gospel presentation at halftime. In many cases, applications are distributed that allow spectators to sign up for a free Bible correspondence course in their native language. Tens of thousands of people have completed these courses, and many have turned to faith in Jesus Christ.

The basic ministry approach has been expanded to include baseball, soccer, volleyball, and even drama teams. Thousands of people will attend an athletic event and pay attention to the gospel there, but they would never darken the door of a church. The first business of evangelism is to gain a hearing for the word, and basketball has proven to be effective to that end. Dr. Naismith would have been proud.

II. COMMENTARY

Authority of the Word

MAIN IDEA: God presents his word to humanity in ways that are intended to give it credibility and to encourage fidelity to it.

A Introduction to the Covenant Summary (5:1–5)

SUPPORTING IDEA: God expects his Word to be learned and obeyed and as a result provides a credible mediator for it.

5:1. God's primary desire in establishing his covenant with Israel was to have them delight in him and **follow** his commandments with a joyful heart. Before that could happen, they would first have to **hear** those commandments. *Hear* thus became a loaded word in the context of covenant renewal, meaning, "Hear, take to heart, and obey." Israel would have not only to hear what Moses was declaring but also to **learn them** and to **follow them**. Godly living involves both the immaterial and the material parts of man. The mind becomes the reservoir of virtues that are then carried out in obedience.

5:2–3. Moses called Israel to participate not in a new **covenant** but in one that was established **at Horeb**. It was thus to be distinguished from the Abrahamic covenant, made with Israel's forebears long before. Thus, **fathers** refers not to the generation that had died in the wilderness because of unbelief but to the patriarchs: Abraham, Isaac, and Jacob. The covenant that God made with them was unconditional, and it consisted of promises that God would give the land of promise to their offspring. Since the fulfillment of those promises was an immediate prospect, the Horeb covenant, being renewed in the Jordan River valley, was designed to tell Israel how to behave in the land and what to do to ensure their blessing.

God's Horeb covenant (sometimes called the Mosaic covenant for obvious reasons) was enacted in perpetuity with Israel. It would apply to succeeding generations, just as it had applied to the previous generation. **All** of Israel was bound by its terms.

5:4–5. Moses recalled the circumstances in which God transmitted the covenant, describing it as a **face to face** encounter. The original giving of the

Ten Commandments **on the mountain** was accompanied by **fire**, thunder, and a variety of impressive circumstances so that Israel would take it seriously. His design produced the desired result. Israel was **afraid of the fire and did not go up the mountain**, asking Moses to serve as mediator between God and themselves. Moses assumed this role and **stood between the LORD** and Israel so that they would be able to receive his commandments in a form that would not terrify them.

B The Covenant Summary: The Ten Commandments (5:6–21)

SUPPORTING IDEA: *God's Word calls his people to adore him exclusively and completely and to love people as themselves.*

5:6–7. The first commandment of the Lord called on Israel to have **no other gods** before him. It was not uncommon in the Ancient Near East for people groups to "adopt" new deities that their neighbors worshiped. At the very top of God's list of decrees lay the insistence that the worship of Yahweh should be exclusive as well as earnest. The true God of heaven would tolerate no rivals in his efforts to win the hearts of his people.

Israel's dedication was not called for, however, in a merely arbitrary way. Yahweh was their **God**, who brought them **out of Egypt** and its miseries. God had already demonstrated his commitment to them in an unmistakable and powerful way. Their allegiance and devotion to him should emerge from an appreciation of what he had already done in setting them free from **slavery**. It should be noted that the concept of freedom in Scripture differs from modern notions. Freedom is not a life lived free of restraints but a life that recognizes healthy limits, those that are certain to produce prosperity and order for the person who observes them.

5:8–10. God's second commandment prohibited the construction or formation of any **idol**. God did not specify for Israel that only idols representing other gods were prohibited, but all idols—even those that claimed to be a representation of the true God—were ruled out. Israel had already attempted the latter and with disastrous results (see Exod. 32:4–5). God had expressed his contempt for such a representation of himself and had insisted that those involved suffer the consequences (cp. Exod. 32:7–10,27).

When humanity invents some physical representation of the true God, it is always cast in the form of **anything in heaven above or on the earth beneath or in the waters below**, representations that could not approach the virtues of Yahweh. As a result, the people of God were not to **bow down to them or worship them**. God warned in advance that such actions would provoke him to anger, because he was **a jealous God** who demanded exclusive loyalty, and on his own terms (for more on God's jealousy, see "Deeper Discoveries").

God's insistence on owning the hearts of his people would produce hurtful results for Israel that would be felt even to **the third and fourth generation** of those who **hate** him. Whether people are willing to face it or not, their spiritual choices will have repercussions in the experience of their **children**. Israel was privileged to know this explicitly from God's own mouth so they would abhor any affections or behavior that would offend the Lord.

At the same time, they worshiped a God who extended his grace much further than his judgment, showing **love to a thousand generations** of the descendants of those who **love** him. That love would be exhibited in the keeping of his **commandments** (cp. John 14:15).

5:11. The third stipulation of God's covenant involved the **misuse** of the divine **name**. God had granted to Israel the knowledge of his covenant name Yahweh. Ancient tradition has, in the name of obedience to this very command, robbed the world of familiarity with it, whether for good or ill: *Yahweh* has become "the Lord." The substitution at least fails from the point of view of category. *The Lord* is a title; *Yahweh* is a name. The commandment does not prohibit its use but its abuse. Later in this same book, God insisted that oaths be affirmed by using the divine name: "You shall fear [Yahweh] your God; you shall serve Him, and to Him you shall hold fast, and take oaths in His name" (Deut. 10:20 NKJV; cp. 6:13).

The point of the third commandment was not simply to prohibit blasphemy or profanity, although it certainly does that. The names of deities were often used in incantations in attempts to manipulate the deity and to use his power for personal ends. A New Testament example is seen in the Book of Acts: "Some of the itinerant Jewish exorcists took it upon themselves to call the name of the Lord Jesus over those who had evil spirits, saying, 'We exorcise you by the Jesus whom Paul preaches'" (Acts 19:13 NKJV). They felt that simply invoking the name of Jesus would result in the exorcism of demons.

Yahweh would not be manipulated, however, either by those who professed an allegiance to him or by outsiders. His name was to be treasured and honored, and one means of doing so was through respecting it as the name of the unique God of heaven; doing otherwise would result in guilt before God: Yahweh **will not hold anyone guiltless who misuses his name**.

5:12–15. The fourth commandment of the covenant summary specified the observance of a special day of the week. The NIV rendering, **Observe the Sabbath day by keeping it holy**, suggests that Israel was already engaged in such observance, but the Hebrew text carries no such implication. The grammatical construction here should be regarded as gerundive, yielding a translation such as, "Observe the Sabbath day by setting it apart." Israelites were to refrain from letting a Saturday be regarded as ordinary. The seventh day was to be a special day of the week.

The original command about the Sabbath in Exodus 20:8 used the verb *zakar*, "remember." In Deuteronomy 5:12, the word is changed to *shamar*, "keep, observe." The reference to **as the LORD your God has commanded you** recalls the original occasion at Horeb.

The Sabbath commandment is the first of the Decalogue to be stated positively instead of as a prohibition. The text actually contains two commands: (1) observe the Sabbath and (2) work the other six days. The command apparently was given to Israel for three purposes. First, it recalled the week of creation and the pattern established by God in working for six days and resting on the seventh (cp. Gen. 2:2–3). Second, it met the need of humanity for a regular periodic day of rest. Third, Sabbath observance set Israel apart as a special nation to God (see Exod. 31:13).

No tradition of Sabbath observance is found in any other ancient culture at this time. Israel needed to recall each Sabbath day how they were **slaves in Egypt** and were required to work constantly. Then God **brought** them out **with a mighty hand and an outstretched arm** and made them his own people. Such a mighty act of creation recalled his original creative work and emphasized their dependence on the Lord for everything.

The Sabbath was to be a time of rest for the entire household. The master of the house, sons, daughters, servants, and even aliens were to know the privilege of one day set apart for rest. It has been observed that the wife of the household is not mentioned. It may be that the omission is intentional to avoid the suggestion that this law applied to routine domestic activities.

5:16. The fifth commandment of the covenant summary marks a significant break in the context. The first four commandments deal with a person's relationship to God. The last six circumscribe his relationship to his neighbor. Many interpreters have noted how in this the Ten Commandments are summarized in the two greatest commandments as related by Jesus: "'Love the Lord your God with all your heart and with all your soul and with all your mind.' This is the first and greatest commandment. And the second is like it: 'Love your neighbor as yourself'" (Matt. 22:37–39).

The people-oriented portion of the Decalogue begins with a command to **honor your father and your mother.** Parents hold a unique position with respect to their function as life-givers to their children and as those upon whom continuation of the covenant begins. A godly society would require that those who were given the stewardship of making God known to the next generation should receive deference and respect. The word *honor,* in fact, translates a Hebrew word that is rendered "glorify" when used with respect to God. Obeying parents is only part of the process of honoring them.

Two benefits will accrue to those who observe the fifth commandment. First, they will **live long**. Second, the events of that long life will **go well**. No other commandment of the Decalogue gives such specific blessings.

5:17. The sixth and following commandments are again couched in terms of prohibitions, beginning with **You shall not murder**. The Hebrew imperative uses a verb that is far more specific than the generic English term "kill," generally used in the older translations. The prohibition does not rule out any and every form of the taking of human life. It does not prohibit, for example, the homicide committed by a police officer in the course of saving innocent lives. Nor does it preclude capital punishment, a practice which is specifically authorized, with certain safeguards, in Scripture: "Whoever sheds the blood of man, by man shall his blood be shed; for in the image of God has God made man" (Gen. 9:6; cp. Lev. 24:17).

Murder would not be included in such things as accidental death, or even spontaneous retaliations in anger for some wrong done, either real or perceived. The content of the sixth commandment is elaborated in Deuteronomy 19:11–13: "If a man hates his neighbor and lies in wait for him, assaults and kills him, and then flees to one of these cities [of refuge], the elders of his town shall send for him, bring him back from the city, and hand him over to the avenger of blood to die. Show him no pity. You must purge from Israel the guilt of shedding innocent blood, so that it may go well with you." Murder is, among other things, the usurping of a prerogative that is reserved for God alone. He gives life and takes it. For a person to murder another is to set himself up as a rival to God himself.

5:18. The seventh commandment prohibits the practice of **adultery**, which is the violation of the marriage covenant (see Mal. 2:14). Adultery involves a sexual relationship between people when one or both of them are married to another. As such, it constitutes unfaithfulness in a relationship of commitment. Those who would be unfaithful in such basic commitments are unlikely to be faithful in other matters that are less easily observed, such as one's commitment to God.

Adultery differs from *fornication* in that the latter is a broader term. It includes adultery as well as sex outside marriage in which neither party is married; it also includes all other extramarital sexual unchastity, such as prostitution and homosexuality (see Jude 1:7).

5:19. The eighth commandment, **You shall not steal**, prohibits the confiscation, either through forcible or surreptitious means, of the property of others. The prohibition against murder ruled out the removal of another's life. The command against adultery, similarly, prohibited the removal of the sanctity of the marriage covenant. The eighth command extends such violations to personal property.

Theft also betrays an attitude that is incompatible with the covenant in general. God promised to bless and sustain Israel if the people would be faithful to him. Deciding to steal the goods of another suggests a fundamental unbelief in the truthfulness and reliability of God or dissatisfaction with the level of his provision for a member of the covenant community.

5:20. The ninth commandment prohibits perjury, the bearing of **false testimony against** one's **neighbor**. The last term is not restricted in its application to other Israelites and can mean either a native (Lev. 19:18) or a resident alien (Lev. 19:34) or even a pagan (Exod. 11:2). Character assassination and false accusations are totally out of bounds for the people of God.

5:21. The tenth and final stipulation of the covenant summary prohibited coveting. Students of Deuteronomy have long been aware that this last command differs significantly from the previous nine in that it addresses an inner condition or state of desire rather than the actions taken in pursuit of such desires.

An obvious implication of this difference is that the final commandment is the only one of the ten that can be broken without the knowledge of anyone in the community. In a sense, therefore, **You shall not covet** seems to be a prohibition that can be violated without civil penalty.

The wisdom of God, however, lies embedded in the tenth commandment. Yahweh insisted that genuine righteousness lies not at the level of visible actions but inside the individual soul. Jesus later in the Sermon on the Mount took precisely such an interpretive direction, insisting that both murder in the heart as well as the overt act were sinful (see Matt. 5:21–22). God thus declared to his people that they should never be satisfied with challenging evil at the level of the visible and overt; rather, they are to meet it at the outer gate of the spirit.

In the course of attempting to obey the tenth commandment (and the first nine, but less obviously), the individual Israelite would come face-to-face with the divine purpose of the law: to make him conscious that there was a moral chasm between himself and his God. As Paul would later explain (Rom. 3:19–20), the central purpose of God's law was to show the universality of sin and to put humanity in touch with its guilt. That guilt, in turn, was designed to encourage the guilty person to exercise faith in the God who alone can impute righteousness.

The Attesting Circumstances of the Covenant Summary (5:22–33)

SUPPORTING IDEA: *God is delighted when his people take him seriously and incline their hearts to him in loving obedience.*

5:22–23. These **commandments** refers to the immediately preceding section (vv. 6–21), making reference again to the original giving of the Ten

Commandments at Sinai. At that time, **the LORD proclaimed** these stipulations to the **whole assembly** on the mountain. To ensure that his words received the proper attention, God gave supporting evidences of their supernatural character. His voice was accompanied by **fire**, a **cloud**, and a **deep darkness**. So that there would be a tangible token of what he had said, **he wrote them on two stone tablets and gave them** to Moses. There were people alive as Moses spoke who had **heard the voice out of the darkness**. The experience proved so frightening to the nation that the **leading men** of the tribes and the **elders** sought to exempt them from any further direct exposure to the voice of God.

5:24–25. Israel recognized by its awesome presentation the great authority of the Word of God and the power of its originator. The nation's representatives explained to Moses that they recognized God's goodness in letting them survive the experience. God had **shown** them **his glory and his majesty** as they **heard his voice from the** midst of the fire. In spite of their recognition of God's holiness and their sinfulness, they had **seen that a man** could **live even if God speaks with him**.

At the same time, they were not anxious to repeat the experience, recognizing that they might indeed **die** if they should hear God's voice a second time. The **fire** that they saw testified to the moral purity of God, and their recognition that they were guilty sinners led them to conclude that such a fire might **consume** them if they heard **the voice of the LORD our God any longer**.

5:26–27. Only two possibilities were open to Israel. They could flee in a vain attempt to escape from responsibility to obey God's authoritative word, or they could find a mediator who could listen and report to them what he had said. The content of the message was powerful all by itself, but the form in which God had delivered it inspired terror in the people. A mediator might be able to get past the method of delivery and bring God's word back to them.

As a result, the leaders asked Moses to **go near and listen to all** God would say, then **tell** them **whatever the LORD** said. The people recognized (at this time at least) the supreme value of God's word. They wanted to hear it, but in a form that did not terrify them, recognizing that **mortal man** had never **heard the voice of the living God speaking out of fire** and **survived**. The nation committed itself, once the message was delivered, to **obey** what God said.

5:28–29. Israel has on occasion been criticized for their request for a mediator. A superficial reading of the original account in Exodus 20:18–21 might yield the erroneous conclusion that the people were to be faulted for wanting to receive God's revelation by the hands of another human being. "If only," their critics explain, "they had had the courage to hear God's voice directly instead of receiving his truth secondhand."

God did not share this viewpoint. Instead, he commended the people for their recognition that they were ill equipped to encounter the word of God through direct revelation. Instead of revealing a substandard spirituality, the people's request for a mediator was on target: **I have heard what this people said to you. Everything they said was good.** It seems sensible to request a mediator when God shakes the earth in his self-revelation.

The request for a mediator, in addition to being wise, also indicated a humility that was commendable. God saw that (for once) the people's **hearts were inclined to fear** him and to **keep** his **commands**. He only wished that such an attitude might routinely characterize them.

5:30–31. God gave instructions to Moses to have the people **return to their tents** instead of remaining at the foot of the mountain. Moses, however, was to remain **with** God and hear his **commands, decrees and laws**. The mediator would then **teach** Israel to follow those laws **in the land** they would soon **possess**.

5:32–33. Having recalled the dramatic events that took place at the base of Sinai, Moses applied the lesson to the new generation. Since the word of God possesses such authority, they were to **be careful to do what the LORD had commanded** them. If they did, they would live and prosper and prolong their **days in the land**.

> **MAIN IDEA REVIEW:** God presents his word to humanity in ways that are intended to give it credibility and to encourage fidelity to it.

III. CONCLUSION

The Perils and Power of Alexander Duff

Alexander Duff at age twenty-three became the first foreign missionary of the Church of Scotland in 1829. His intended ministry was to be in India, but nearing the coast of the subcontinent, Duff's ship, the *Lady Holland,* ran upon a reef. It quickly became apparent that the ship was doomed. The mariners could not dislodge her, and the waves began to break the ship apart. The greater portion of the vessel washed away, and the passengers, including Duff and his new wife, clung desperately to the part that remained lodged on the reef. All night they hung on, expecting to be washed away at any moment as the waves crashed around them.

The next day rescuers were able to bring the survivors ashore safely; but all the possessions that the Duffs had brought with them in anticipation of their ministry had been washed away by the sea. Among those possessions was Alexander Duff's library of some eight hundred volumes.

Deuteronomy 5

Grateful that their lives had been saved but at the same time sorrowful that they were beginning their ministry without so many essentials, the Duffs later stood on the shore looking out at the reef where they had nearly lost their lives. Duff noticed something floating on the surface of the water, gradually drifting ashore. He waded out in the surf to examine the item and discovered it to be his Bible. Out of the sizable library he had brought to India, it alone survived.

Duff was encouraged to see his worn and beloved Bible again. He squeezed out the worst of the salt water and carefully smoothed out its pages. Calling for his companions who had survived the wreck with him, he read some comforting passages to them. In the following weeks, he used the same Bible to begin a class with some local boys. That ministry eventually became a training school that equipped local Christians for leadership in the Indian church. Neither salt water nor shipwreck could diminish the spiritual power contained in the pages of Scripture.

PRINCIPLES

- The fear of the Lord is a reverential awe that comes from a commitment to avoid behavior that displeases him.
- Who God is lies at the root of all biblical commandments concerning what he wants from humankind.
- God's blessings always appear in greater numbers than his acts of judgment.
- When God unveils himself in all his holiness, people need a mediator, Jesus Christ, to stand in the gap between God and man.

APPLICATIONS

- Lift a prayer to God today for a heart that is inclined to hear and obey God's Word.
- Evaluate the state of your heart toward God. Is it warm toward him, or has your devotional time become a chore?
- Determine to avoid any use of the divine name in a frivolous way.
- The purpose of teaching God's revelation of himself is to produce people who love and obey him.

IV. LIFE APPLICATION

The (Un)Chicken Lady

The late Christian Herter was governor of Massachusetts in 1956 and was running for a second term. As he spent the day attempting to gather votes in the coming election, his schedule brought him to a church barbecue. The governor had had an early start that day, had missed lunch, and was famished. He passed down the lunch serving line piling his plate high with goodies until he came to the woman in charge of serving chicken. She placed a piece of chicken on his plate and turned to the next person.

Considering the growls coming from his stomach, Governor Herter said to her, "Excuse me—do you mind if I have another piece of chicken?"

"Sorry," she explained. "I'm supposed to give only one piece of chicken to each person."

"But I'm starved," Herter pleaded.

"Sorry," the woman said again. "Only one to a customer."

At that point, the governor thought it might be worthwhile to let this stubborn woman know of his office. "Do you know who I am?" he asked. "I am the governor of this state."

"Do you know who I am?" the woman said. "I'm the lady in charge of the chicken. Move along, Mister."

Obedience is easier when we keep our eyes on the authority of the one who gives us our commandments and the charge by which we live. When we take our stand on the majesty and glory of God, we know that nothing is more important in this life than our obedience of and trust in him. Our courage to do right will never be any greater than the clarity of our vision of God.

V. PRAYER

Father, help us never to take your truth for granted. Instead, let us see it for what it is—your gift to us to help make us like yourself through Jesus Christ our Lord. Amen.

VI. DEEPER DISCOVERIES

A. A Jealous God (5:9)

God declared to Israel that they should refrain from attachments to other gods because he was and is "a jealous God." Some people stumble at this connection, since jealousy and its close cousin, envy, are normally regarded as the products of the flesh (see Gal. 5:19–21).

There are exceptions to this general rule, however. When people are bound together by covenant (as in marriage or in the ties between Yahweh and Israel), and an intruder threatens to harm one of the parties, it is proper for the other to be jealous of the misplaced affections. A husband who is sworn to uphold the sanctity and welfare of his wife, and who is indifferent when she is drawn to another man, could not be considered worthy of

Deuteronomy 5

commendation. If he cares about her, he cannot take pleasure when he sees her taking steps that violate her vows and are likely to result in harm to her.

Among human beings, jealousy is often the product of offended pride or personal insecurity. With God, of course, no such motivations exist. He is concerned when those he loves are drawn away from what is supremely valuable—himself—to what is less so: "My people have committed two sins: They have forsaken me, the spring of living water, and have dug their own cisterns, broken cisterns that cannot hold water" (Jer. 2:13).

B. Showing Love (5:10)

When God described himself to Israel as "showing love to a thousand generations" (Deut. 5:10), he used a rich and profound word for love. The Hebrew word *hesed* describes God's unilaterally extended favor to the undeserving, and it comes into the New Testament (through the Septuagint) in the terms *grace* and *love* in varying combinations. *Hesed* is the motivation by which God chose Israel and brought the nation into a covenant with himself. In fact, *hesed* (translated *lovingkindness* in older translations) and *berith* (covenant) appear often as synonyms (see Deut. 7:9).

C. Inclined Hearts (5:29)

God recognized that Israel's request for a mediator came from hearts which were deeply affected by the power of his word, and he mused that he would always have it so: "Oh, that their hearts would be inclined to fear me and keep all my commands always, so that it might go well with them and their children forever!" (Deut. 5:29). An inclined heart is a predisposition to look in specific places for answers and appears often in Scripture. God recognized in Israel a predisposition to idolatry and prescribed a reminder of his own truth: "You shall have the tassel, that you may look upon it and remember all the commandments of the LORD and do them, and that you may not follow the harlotry to which your own heart and your own eyes are inclined" (Num. 15:39 NKJV).

Scripture recognizes that it is the responsibility of humanity to incline their hearts toward God (see Josh. 24:23 NKJV). David admitted that he needed help in inclining his own heart toward God (see Ps. 119:36 NKJV). God has the power to create a predisposition away from himself on the part of people who displease him (see Ps. 141:4 NKJV).

VII. TEACHING OUTLINE

A. INTRODUCTION

1. Lead Story: Nearly Forgotten Beginnings

2. Context: Moses delivers a summary of God's covenant with his people. The Ten Commandments serve as the core of what God expects of man—love for him and love for others.
3. Transition: God knows that we are spiritually wayward people. To accommodate our weaknesses, he provided in Moses a mediator so his word could be given in a form that would not terrify Israel. In a similar way, Jesus Christ became a mediator between God and humanity.

B. COMMENTARY

1. Introduction to the Covenant Summary (5:1–5)
2. The Covenant Summary: The Ten Commandments (5:6–21)
3. The Attesting Circumstances of the Covenant Summary (5:22–33)

C. CONCLUSION: THE (UN)CHICKEN LADY

VIII. ISSUES FOR DISCUSSION

1. Do you routinely give the Word of God the respect it deserves?
2. Do you allow your body a day each week to recover from its routine labors?
3. Can you recall times that you have escaped from more dangerous temptations by rebuking covetousness in yourself?
4. What are some useful ways that you can make the Word of God a more important part of your daily life?
5. What are some virtues of Bible memorization?

Deuteronomy 6

The First and Greatest Commandment

I. **INTRODUCTION**
Off the Hook

II. **COMMENTARY**
A verse-by-verse explanation of the chapter.

III. **CONCLUSION**
Transcending Her Limits
An overview of the principles and applications from the chapter.

IV. **LIFE APPLICATION**
The Untainted Gift
Melding the chapter to life.

V. **PRAYER**
Tying the chapter to life with God.

VI. **DEEPER DISCOVERIES**
Historical, geographical, and grammatical enrichment of the commentary.

VII. **TEACHING OUTLINE**
Suggested step-by-step group study of the chapter.

VIII. **ISSUES FOR DISCUSSION**
Zeroing the chapter in on daily life.

Deuteronomy 6

> Quote

"The labor of self-love is a heavy one indeed. Think whether much of your sorrow has not arisen from someone speaking slightingly of you. As long as you set yourself up as a little god to which you must be loyal, how can you hope to find inward peace?"

A. W. Tozer

Deuteronomy 6

IN A NUTSHELL

In Deuteronomy 6, Moses summarizes both the whole duty of man and his greatest privilege—to love God with all that he is and has—and describes the barriers to doing so. The chapter concludes with counsel on how this core truth can be transmitted to future generations.

The First and Greatest Commandment

I. INTRODUCTION

Off the Hook

Jack Eckerd's first exposure to the work and ministry of Chuck Colson's Prison Fellowship came when Colson appeared on William F. Buckley's television program. Colson was advocating restitution to victims as a feature of the national criminal justice picture, a proposal about which he was and is passionate. Several days later, he received a call from Jack Eckerd asking him to visit Florida and address what Eckerd considered to be a criminal justice crisis in that state. Together with the Florida attorney general and the president of the state senate, they began to visit cities throughout Florida, advocating reform in the criminal justice statutes and traveling on Jack Eckerd's business jet.

As they went from place to place, Eckerd would introduce Chuck Colson to the crowds by saying, "This is Chuck Colson, my friend; I met him on Bill Buckley's television program. He's born again; I'm not. I wish I were." Colson would speak of his concerns about the criminal justice system, and they would move to another location. When the group would return to the plane for their next trip, he would spend the entire trip talking to Jack Eckerd about the Lord Jesus. Then they would land, Eckerd would do his introduction again, and the process would be repeated.

When Colson left, he gave Eckerd several books by Christian authors, including C. S. Lewis's *Mere Christianity,* a book that had been instrumental in his own conversion. When Colson arrived at home, he then sent Eckerd several of his own books.

They corresponded for a year or so, and Eckerd kept reading. Eventually some of the things Colson had written in *Loving God* broke through, and Jack Eckerd decided that Jesus had indeed risen from the dead. He received Christ as his Savior.

Shortly after his conversion, Eckerd was walking through one of his drug stores and noticed copies of *Playboy* and *Penthouse* for sale. He had seen them before, but they had never bothered him; now they did. When he returned to his office, he called in the chief operating officer of his drugstores and said, "Take those magazines out of my stores."

The CEO responded, "You can't mean that, Mr. Eckerd. We make three million dollars a year on those books."

Eckerd stuck by his decision: "Take them out of my stores."

When the magazines had been removed, Chuck Colson called Jack Eckerd and asked, "Did you do that because of your commitment to Christ?"

Eckerd answered, "Why else would I give away three million dollars? The Lord wouldn't let me off the hook."

The drugstore retailer didn't stop there. He wrote the heads of other drugstore chains and challenged them to do likewise. At first, they ignored him. Then, as Eckerd's began to see significant sales increases coming from people who appreciated their stand, they began to follow suit. Eventually, eleven thousand retail outlets across America removed the objectionable magazines from their store shelves, and it all started when one Christian could not be comfortable with professing a love for God while ignoring moral principles. To use his own words, his love for God wouldn't let him off the hook.

II. COMMENTARY

The First and Greatest Commandment

MAIN IDEA: Moses simplifies the whole duty of Israel (and of humanity) by crystallizing the moral law into a single command to love God supremely.

A The Introduction to the Great Commandment (6:1–3)

SUPPORTING IDEA: The well-being of Israel and humanity at large both now and in perpetuity depends upon fidelity to the Great Commandment.

6:1. Although the reader is often struck by the enormity and complexity of the truths contained in Scripture, God's Word from time to time crystallizes vast concepts into brief, pithy summations. What Jesus called "the first and greatest commandment" (Matt. 22:38) is one of these. So lofty a statement deserves a worthy verbal fanfare, and Moses provides it in the first three verses of the chapter.

Although the NIV renders the words **these** and **commands** in the plural, in the Hebrew text both words are singular. Probably we should understand the word *command* in the generic sense of *legislation,* and the following terms as explanatory: "This is the legislation, the decrees and laws, the Lord your God directed."

6:2–3. The direction given to Israel through Moses was designed to produce four results. First, God gave his law so Israel would **fear the LORD**. Such an awe-filled respect should be expressed **by keeping all his decrees and commands**. The outcome of such behavior would be seen in the second purpose of the law, that Israel might **enjoy long life**. Israel was to understand that each successive breath was taken by the permission of the Creator and never to take a long life for granted.

The third purpose of the divine law was to allow the long lives of Israel's people to **go well**. Whether the nation prospered or struggled would be connected with their devotion to God. The final stated purpose of the law was that Israel would **increase greatly** in the land they were receiving. The land could support such an increase because it was a fertile place, **flowing with milk and honey**. The last expression, occurring twenty times in the Old Testament, is a poetic way of describing the land's rich potential.

B The Definition of the Great Commandment (6:4–9)

SUPPORTING IDEA: *God should be loved supremely, exclusively, and earnestly.*

6:4–5. These verses constitute the core statement of biblical faith. They are known in traditional Judaism as "the Shema," a transliteration of the first Hebrew word of verse 4, **Hear**. In this context, the command to *hear* implies "to heed, to listen closely for the purposes of obedience." The heart of biblical religion is a determination to know what God has said and to conform one's beliefs and behavior accordingly. As Jesus would later insist, "Whoever has my commands and obeys them, he is the one who loves me" (John 14:21). His disciples could hardly have missed the point of this statement, in which Jesus insisted on the same devotion that Israel had been commanded to give Yahweh.

Israel needed to hear, first of all, that **the LORD our God, the LORD is one**. This rendering is one of several possible translations of this text. Another is, "The Lord our God is one (Lord)." Still another option is, "The Lord is our God, the Lord alone." All these and a few others are permissible grammatically, and in the end all point in the same direction—to the uniqueness and supremacy of Yahweh, God of Israel. The NIV rendering, which reflects the most common approach to the Hebrew text, emphasizes the unity (and implied self-consistency) of Yahweh. The second and third translations emphasize God's distance from the invented deities of the nations and suggest that Israel's strength lies not only in the worship of Yahweh but in the exclusive worship of him. (For the trinitarian implications of Deuteronomy 6:4, see "Deeper Discoveries.")

Israel's recognition that God is unique in the universe was to bring them to **love** him **with all** their **heart, soul**, and **strength**. This statement Jesus would use later to summarize the whole duty of man and the essence of the Scriptures (Matt. 22:37; cp. Mark 12:29–30, Luke 10:27). In biblical Hebrew, the *heart* was less the seat of the emotions (as in modern parlance) than it was the locus of the intellect and will. In Hebrew Scripture, one *thinks* with the heart: "Let none of you think evil in your heart against your neighbor . . . says the LORD" (Zech. 8:17 NKJV; cp. also Deut. 9:4, 2 Sam. 13:33; Esth. 4:13; Isa. 10:7). Perhaps for this reason Jesus added an expression to his quotation of Deuteronomy

6:5, "Love the Lord your God with all your heart and with all your soul and *with all your mind* and with all your strength" (Mark 12:30, italics mine).

Strength describes not so much a person's physical power as his intensity. God wants earnestness in a person's religion; he desires not merely that we possess a faith but that our faith should possess us. A case in point was good king Josiah, who served God with consummate zeal after the Book of the Law was discovered in the temple. Second Kings 23:25 states that "neither before nor after Josiah was there a king like him who turned to the LORD as he did—with all his heart and with all his soul and with all his strength, in accordance with all the Law of Moses." (For the concept of *soul,* see "Deeper Discoveries.")

6:6. Spiritual zeal is above all to be personal. God's **commandments** are not to be treated as a listing of the acts we perform but as a description of who we are. His truth is to be placed upon the **hearts** of his people. Those who would regard the Old Testament as nothing but a collection of rules have missed the point of it. God's covenant with Israel was not to be merely enforced externally through the imposition of penalties for its violation; God insisted that Israel's faith be essentially a matter of the heart.

6:7. God's commands were not, in the Israelite economy, the property of royalty or the elite. They were true of everyone and for everyone, even the **children** of those who were entering into the covenant. Godly parents would **impress** God's commandments upon the inward parts of each successive generation. Here the text uses a word that is often used to describe the sharpening of a knife upon a whetstone. Children are to be sharpened as willing instruments for God as they grow old.

Deuteronomy knows nothing of the modern folly that suggests that religion be presented in an atmosphere of neutrality and that children be presented with all the options and left to decide for themselves the direction of their spiritual lives. The biblical perspective on the spiritual training of children insists that children already possess a direction when they are born. Unfortunately, that slant is sure to destroy them if left unchecked. Wise parents give their children the added benefit of hearing the truth from the very beginning, so that their wayward tendencies can be brought under control early on.

No opportunity to engage in spiritual training should be lost, whether formal (**talk about them**) or informal (**when you walk along the road**), whether late (**when you lie down**) or early (**when you get up**). The literary device of using two extremes (high, low; cold, hot; up, down) to represent everything in between (sometimes known as a *merism*) is a common convention in the Old Testament (cp., e.g., Ps. 139:2–5).

6:8–9. Israel was to take the law of God and to use it in every realm of life. It is clear from the context that the references to binding the law as **symbols** upon the **hands** and on the **foreheads** are intended to be understood figuratively, although these verses are taken in a physical sense in some expressions of Judaism. Moses' instruction to **write them on the doorframes of your houses and on your gates** forms the basis for the Jewish custom of placing a small Scripture portion inside a small box (a *mezuzah*) that is then attached to the entry door frame of the household.

The intent is too all-encompassing to be satisfied by mere adornments, however. The commandments were to be sovereign over individual Israelites, and they were to serve as constraints on their hands and as mental checks upon their thinking. The purpose of using such symbolism was to connect God's law with the everyday, routine matters of life. Nothing was to be considered outside the scope of his authority.

C The Threats to Its Near-Term Obedience (6:10–19)

SUPPORTING IDEA: *Forgetfulness, compromise, and incomplete obedience are severe threats to obedience to the Great Commandment.*

6:10–12. The nation that stood on the east bank of the Jordan River had seen God work in spectacular ways. Those who were nearing sixty years of age had been nineteen at the time of the troubles of Kadesh Barnea. They had been old enough to remember the events of Sinai, the crossing of the Red Sea, and the destruction of the Egyptian army. They had seen a whole generation of rebels die in the wilderness. If encounters with the miraculous could create godly people, they would have qualified.

In addition, they were soon to witness still more of God's work. They were about to enter **the land** God had sworn to give their **fathers, to Abraham, Isaac and Jacob**. Instead of inheriting a land of ruins and devastation, they were about to take possession of **cities** they **did not build**, **houses filled with** goods they **did not provide**, and **wells** they **did not dig**. In addition, they would inherit orchards and vineyards.

Moses warned them that the leading spiritual danger they would face on entering the land would be forgetting the Lord. What adversity would not do, prosperity and satisfaction could. They were to be on their guard against spiritual lethargy.

The life of the spirit is one that is cultivated. Human experience bears out the suggestion that the most critical threats to godly living come at the moment when we think we have life by the throat. Israel, said Moses, should **be careful** that they did **not forget the LORD** who had **brought** them such benefits. The absence of dangerous enemies would suggest that they could relax. They must, instead, cultivate the inner life and water the garden of devotion to God.

6:13–15. In the course of developing their relationship with God, it would not be enough simply to worship Yahweh. Israel would have to worship him exclusively. They were to **serve him only** and take **oaths in his**

Deuteronomy 6:16-19

name solely. They were to disregard the attractions of **other** deities who were worshiped by **the peoples** around them.

To do otherwise meant offending the LORD, who was dwelling daily **among** them. His **anger** would **burn against** them if they were so ungrateful and foolish as to join themselves to other gods. That mistake could prove fatal, leading to physical death or removal **from the face of the land** that God was giving them.

6:16-19. Forgetting the LORD would not simply mean the removal of the true **God** from their collective memory. Instead, Israel's forgetfulness would be demonstrated by a failure of devotion. That might be exhibited in their repeating the mistakes of their forefathers, who put God to the **test** at **Massah** (see Exod. 17:1-7). To test God involves forcing him, through overlooking his past faithfulness, to act in defense of his holiness. Israel at Massah had forgotten how God had provided for them through each step of their perilous journey. Israel could commit the same blunder if they forgot how God had given them such a fine homeland and stumbled into the clutches of false religion.

Instead, they were to **keep the commands of the** LORD and to do what was **right and good** in his sight. Such behavior would increase the likelihood and speed of their success in possessing **the good land that the** LORD **promised** to their **forefathers** and would enlist God's help in **thrusting out** their **enemies**.

D The Provision for Its Long-Term Obedience (6:20-25)

SUPPORTING IDEA: *The future glory and prosperity of Israel depends upon teaching the Great Commandment to future generations.*

6:20. Every generation is only twenty years away from barbarism. Those twenty years constitute the amount of time needed to transform a human being from a self-consumed infant into a responsible person who can make room in his life for God and for others. God instructed Israel that they should recognize their vulnerability to the loss of their faith in the form of the next generation and spare neither expense nor effort in training their children.

At the top of the agenda for every parent lies the opportune moment when a child **asks** for an explanation of **the meaning** of the truth that the Lord **has commanded**. Parents should be ready with an appropriate response for such a choice opportunity.

6:21-22. Israelite parents were to recall for their youngsters how they **were slaves of Pharaoh in Egypt**, and how **the** LORD **brought** them out **with a mighty hand**. Parents should recall their personal knowledge of God's redemption, telling children what took place **before** their own **eyes**. God's **signs and wonders** should be remembered and used to encourage the new generation to recognize that they worshiped a God of power, love, and faithfulness.

6:23-25. The purpose of God's redeeming work should be emphasized. God did not simply **bring** Israel **out** from Egypt, but he did so to **bring** them

in and give them **the land that he promised**. Conversion is essential, but it is a beginning, not an end. The believer in Jesus Christ is not simply rescued from the penalty of his sin; he is redeemed to love God and his neighbor so that others might come to know him.

The test of any parent's effectiveness as a teacher of youth would not be seen simply in the behavior of his children. Godly parents do not invest themselves only in the next generation. Their teaching work should be designed so that the people of God **might always prosper and be kept alive**. If the church cannot bring its own offspring into a relationship with God, they are not likely to have much of an impact on others. So believers might know what God expects of them, he **commanded** them **to obey all these decrees and to fear the** LORD. If Israel did so, they would enjoy a **righteousness** that was both personal and promising.

> **MAIN IDEA REVIEW:** Moses simplifies the whole duty of Israel (and of humanity) by crystallizing the moral law into a single command to love God supremely.

III. CONCLUSION

Transcending Her Limits

The days of the Cold War, when believers in the Soviet Union were suffering from terrible oppression, produced the remarkable story of an old woman who suffered from multiple sclerosis. She had been a victim of the disease for years, and her body was twisted and nearly useless. She could not speak or even turn her head. Only one part of her anatomy was functional—at least in part—and that was her right hand.

Given her condition, there seemed to be little she could do to advance the cause of Christ in her country. However, she decided to use the abilities she had. Each morning, her husband would raise her to a sitting position on her old sofa and place before her a well-used manual typewriter. She would then proceed to use her index finger to type out, one painstaking letter at a time, a translation of a Christian book into Russian. Some days, she only finished a page or two. Other days, she managed four or five.

She typed parts of the Russian Bible or books by Billy Graham or other teachers to spread the gospel and to show her love for God. Paradoxically, her illness served an important role in allowing her to perform this laborious task. She knew she could carry on her work without fear of arrest because the secret police had written her off as useless because of her illness. She multiplied her effectiveness by praying as she typed, offering up her requests that the books she was typing would bear fruit. A genuine love for God will always find a method of expression.

Deuteronomy 6

PRINCIPLES

- Teaching is most effective when it uses a combination of formal and informal methods.
- Believers often have more to fear from their successes than from their disappointments.
- Forgetfulness of God often issues from a failure to reflect on his past faithfulness.
- Making room for any influence that might compete with God for first place in one's life is always a blunder.

APPLICATIONS

- Ask God to help you determine whether he occupies the position of supreme affection in your life.
- Look for an opportunity to convey your spiritual passion to a child or young person.
- Write a letter to a friend or acquaintance, sharing with them something that Jesus Christ has done in your life recently.
- Take a spiritual inventory of the gifts that God has given you. Give him thanks for his goodness.

IV. LIFE APPLICATION

The Untainted Gift

An ancient legend tells the story of a man crossing the desert who found a wonderful spring filled with cold, clear water. He sampled it and found it so refreshing that he decided to offer a container of it to the king as a sign of his respect. He filled a leather bottle with fresh spring water and carried it across an arid desert for days before finally arriving at the king's palace.

Begging permission to present the king with his humble gift, he was admitted to the royal presence, where he explained his joy in the discovery of the desert spring. Unaware that the water he carried had been tainted by its aged container, he presented his spring water to the king. Impressed by the story, the king drank deeply and sent away his loyal subject with his commendation and gratitude.

When the king's servants sampled the remainder of the water, they were amazed that his majesty had enjoyed it. One of his servants commented, "It was not the water he enjoyed, but the love that brought it."

Believers may offer to God gifts that are marred by many imperfections, but the one who knows the heart measures the motives as well as the gifts. Any gift is sweetened by being mixed with love.

V. PRAYER

Father, our affections and devotion are often weak. In your strength, strengthen our desires for you until you are supreme in our hearts as well as in our behavior. Amen.

VI. DEEPER DISCOVERIES

A. The Lord Is One (6:4)

Christians from the beginning of the church have affirmed the tri-unity of God. Often this is expressed in the form of an equal recognition of the realities that God is one in essence while existing in three distinct and coequal persons. While the doctrine is drawn explicitly from the New Testament, the Hebrew Bible makes allowances for its later revelation.

Deuteronomy 6:4 insists that God is "one," translating the Hebrew word *echad*. The text avoids the use of another term, *yahidh*, which means "unique, the only one of its kind." *Echad* is found in passages like Genesis 2:24, which states, "For this reason a man will leave his father and mother and be united to his wife, and they will become one flesh." *Echad* can be used, as it is in the latter passage, to express a unity that is compound in nature.

The oneness of God in Christian theology is a oneness of essence. The persons of the Trinity always act in unison and with a common purpose in mind.

B. Soul (6:5)

Moses explained to the Israelites, "Love the LORD your God with all your heart and with all your soul and with all your strength" (Deut. 6:5). The *soul* forms a complex topic in biblical revelation. The Hebrew equivalent, *nephesh*, was a word that was originally related to a term that meant "breath," but in the Old Testament it is translated by no less than a dozen different English expressions. It appears in the Hebrew Bible over 750 times.

Its original connection is seen in one of its earliest appearances in Genesis: "The LORD God formed the man from the dust of the ground and breathed into his nostrils the breath of life, and the man became a living being" (Gen. 2:7). Thus man *is* a soul, as well as being in some sense constituted by a soul that forms part of his immaterial being: "May God himself, the God of peace, sanctify you through and through. May your whole spirit, soul and body be kept blameless at the coming of our Lord Jesus Christ" (1 Thess. 5:23).

Soul can be a synonym for *life* or *person*: "[Please] spare the *lives* of my father and mother, my brothers and sisters, and all who belong to them, and . . . save us from death" (Josh. 2:13, italics mine). The word sometimes conveys the notion of the source of the appetites, emotions, and intelligence. It is in this last realm that its use in Deuteronomy 6:5 finds a home. To love God with the

Deuteronomy 6

soul is to love him with everything that is important to us. Just as a person's appetite is intensely personal, so our decision to love God supremely must be a deeply felt personal decision.

The reasons for loving God are objective, grounded in his demonstrated love for us; but the decision to obey his word and love him intensely is an individual matter. Some twenty times in the Hebrew Bible, *nephesh* forms the subject of the Hebrew verb *awa*, "to desire, crave": "My soul craves." Believers are to crave knowledge of God so they can love him more completely.

VII. TEACHING OUTLINE

A. INTRODUCTION
1. Lead Story: Off the Hook
2. Context: Fresh from his elaboration of the Ten Commandments and the essential content of the covenant, Moses brings Israel face-to-face with the essential core of their relationship to God: they are to love him above all and to see to it that that conviction is passed on.
3. Transition: Man's highest purpose is found when he loves his maker with total devotion. Believers must understand the importance of the Great Commandment and the obstacles they will face in obeying this command.

B. COMMENTARY
1. The Introduction to the Great Commandment (6:1–3)
2. The Definition of the Great Commandment (6:4–9)
3. The Threats to Its Near-Term Obedience (6:10–19)
4. The Provision for Its Long-Term Obedience (6:20–25)

C. CONCLUSION: THE UNTAINTED GIFT

VIII. ISSUES FOR DISCUSSION

1. What are the most common barriers to loving God supremely that you face?
2. To what extent were your attitudes toward God formed when you were young?
3. Do you know of people whose spiritual development was arrested through poor parenting?
4. Do you know of people whose spiritual lives were enriched through sound parenting?
5. In what ways do you "forget the Lord"?

Deuteronomy 7

Holy War

- **I. INTRODUCTION**
  The Mighty Troll

- **II. COMMENTARY**
  A verse-by-verse explanation of the chapter.

- **III. CONCLUSION**
  How Firm a Foundation
  An overview of the principles and applications from the chapter.

- **IV. LIFE APPLICATION**
  War Is No Picnic
  Melding the chapter to life.

- **V. PRAYER**
  Tying the chapter to life with God.

- **VI. DEEPER DISCOVERIES**
  Historical, geographical, and grammatical enrichment of the commentary.

- **VII. TEACHING OUTLINE**
  Suggested step-by-step group study of the chapter.

- **VIII. ISSUES FOR DISCUSSION**
  Zeroing the chapter in on daily life.

Deuteronomy 7

Quote

"We can have no fellowship with the enemies of God within us or around us, but to our hurt; therefore our only wisdom is to maintain unceasing war against them."

Matthew Henry

Deuteronomy 7

IN A NUTSHELL

Moses gives God's directions for carrying on holy war against the inhabitants of the promised land. Just as Israel could not tolerate the evangelists of paganism within her territories, the believer in Jesus cannot compromise with his own sinful inclinations but must instead destroy them.

Holy War

I. INTRODUCTION

The Mighty Troll

A brave knight was riding through the countryside looking for adventure. As he stopped for refreshment at a village inn, one of the local citizens described how their community was being terrorized by a horrible monster that lived in a nearby cave. Since his chivalric code encouraged its constituents to help the weak and oppressed, the knight decided that he would do what he could to rescue them.

Once he had expressed this determination, the villagers warned him that others had attempted to rescue them as well. All those brave knights had entered the troll's cave never to be heard from again. The aspiring hero insisted that he would try as well, so the citizens of that community led him to the edge of town and the monster's cave.

He observed immediately that the cave in question was in reality a dark pit whose opening was too narrow to enter in his full battle regalia. So he discarded his helmet, body armor, and his chain mail, and stripped himself down to pants, shirt, and boots. He decided to enter the ogre's cave with only a long dagger tied to a cord around his neck.

Tying a strong rope to a nearby tree, the knight dropped its other end into the dark hole of the monster and began to lower himself into the cavity. Eventually, he reached the smooth floor of the ogre's cave and waited for his eyes to adjust to the darkness. He soon noticed a large mound, which turned out to be a pile of the bones and the weapons of his predecessors, those brave knights who had failed to return.

He soon noticed another pile of debris a few yards away. Because of the darkness, he couldn't make out exactly what this pile consisted of, so he began to approach the mound.

Just as he drew near, the monster appeared. To his amazement, the ogre turned out not to be a gargantuan figure of surpassing strength, but a tiny individual only a couple of hands high. This mini-monster waved his pencil-sized sword and shouted at the top of his small voice in several vain attempts to intimidate his much larger foe.

The knight grabbed a sword from the first mound he had seen and prepared to eliminate the tiny intruder, who immediately ran into a hole near the second mound. As the knight drew near, he noticed that the second mound was made up of great treasures—balls of gold larger than baseballs and diamonds the size of lemons.

He paused. Lying before him was wealth the likes of which he had never imagined. In an instant, the tiny troll was forgotten in the face of this new opportunity. Only one problem remained: how to carry his treasure out of the dark hole. His trousers contained no pockets, and he knew no one would believe him unless he returned with at least one piece of this newly discovered treasure-trove.

He decided to place one of the diamonds in his mouth until he had reached the opening of the cave. Selecting one that would fit his mouth comfortably, he began to climb his rope back to the surface. The effort, however, required great exertion, and soon he was suffering from lack of breath. He would have to breathe through his mouth or suffocate. As he sucked in a large breath, the diamond slipped into his airway, causing him to fall to his death on the mound of bones far below him. In the brief instant before his death, he realized that the real monster was not the tiny creature in the cave, but the mighty troll of greed that lay within his own heart.

Man's own longings are the worst tyrants that the world knows. Godly living begins when we recognize that we are our own worst enemy and we determine to do battle against the foes within us.

II. COMMENTARY

Holy War

MAIN IDEA: God wants believers to face their inner enemies courageously and to eliminate them one by one.

A Identifying the Enemy (7:1–5)

SUPPORTING IDEA: No mercy should be shown to anything with the potential to destroy the moral life of God's people.

7:1. Israel's primary task as they entered the land of promise was to rid it of its current inhabitants. They could not **possess** the land while its current inhabitants resided there. **Seven nations** are enumerated in the text; together, these were **larger and stronger** than Israel. The **Hittites** apparently were a fragment of a group with origins in Asia Minor. Individuals from this ethnic category resided in the Holy Land at least as early as the time of Abraham (cp. Gen. 23). The **Canaanites** and the **Amorites** (see "Deeper Discoveries," ch. 1) occupied the central mountain range of Palestine. The **Girgashites** appear elsewhere in Scripture, but little is known about them (cp. Gen. 10:16; 1 Chr. 1:14; Josh. 3:10; 24:11). The **Jebusites** (perhaps originally a subgroup of the Hittites) occupied the small mountain village of Jebus, which in time would come to be known as Jerusalem.

7:2. Moses took it as a given that the Lord would in time grant Israel military success over their enemies. It was afterward, when God's people had **defeated them**, that the true dangers became clear. The remnant of each people group was supposed to be expelled from the land (cp. v. 1) or destroyed totally. God expressly forbade the use of methods that were customarily used by victors; Israel must **make no treaty with them**. In fact, the nation must **show them no mercy**. (For a consideration of the moral and theological implications of this policy, see "Deeper Discoveries.")

7:3–4. Still another option had to be ruled out. Israelites were not to **intermarry** with those who survived, either during the lifetimes of the invading generation or in the succeeding generations. The risks of doctrinal pollution were too great. God did not simply say that they *might* attract Israelites into paganism, but instead insisted that they *would* do so. If this restriction were ignored, **the LORD's anger** would be turned toward Israel and would **quickly destroy** them.

God's policy was a generalization that did admit of exceptions. The most obvious one was Moses himself, who had married a Cushite woman (cp. Num. 12). Another was Rahab, a worshiper of Yahweh from Jericho (cp. Heb. 11:31). In time she married an Israelite named Salmon and became the mother of Boaz and an ancestor of King David (and of Jesus). Intermarriage with worshipers of the Lord was clearly not a problem. However, Israelites were normally safe in concluding that few such would remain in the land. To marry an idolater was to invite an advocate of idolatry into an Israelite home, an event that would be laced with peril.

7:5. Instead, Israelites were to destroy the surviving populations of the seven ethnic groups that occupied the land, and then take the process still further. They were to **break down** the remaining idolatrous **altars** and destroy **their sacred stones** or pillars, which may have been male fertility symbols.

Their **Asherah poles** should receive similar treatment. The term describes wooden poles used in the worship of Asherah or Ashtarte, the female consort of Baal. These items figure prominently in the prophetic books. Ahab, king of Israel, apparently due to the influence of his wife Jezebel, constructed an Asherah pole in Samaria (cp. 1 Kgs. 16:29–33).

B Assessing the Motives (7:6–16)

SUPPORTING IDEA: *Israel's unique position depended on fidelity to God. Therefore, the distasteful and difficult work of holy war must proceed.*

7:6. Perhaps more than any other chapter of Scripture, Deuteronomy 7 flies in the face of the modern passion for political correctness. In this chapter Israel is given property at the expense of a group of resident ethnic groups and told to eradicate them from the land. It was not because of their moral superiority, however, that they were chosen for such elevation. Israel was simply regarded as **a people holy** or separate by virtue of their relationship with God. It was God's choice, and not their superior behavior, that made them special in his sight, **his treasured possession**.

7:7. Lest they be infected with the bacteria of pride, God explained through Moses that he **did not set his affection** on Israel because they **were more numerous than other peoples.** On the contrary, they were the **fewest of all peoples.** Such an evaluation could hardly apply to Israel as it then stood east of the Jordan River, since, as Moses observed in Deuteronomy 1:10, "The LORD your God has multiplied you, and here you are today, as the stars of heaven in multitude" (NKJV) When God chose Israel, however, he really chose one man, Abraham, and set him apart together with his as-yet-unborn offspring (Gen. 12:1–3).

7:8. Since he had discarded the option that God chose Israel because of their numbers, Moses explained why God did place Israel first in his affections. **It was because the LORD loved** them; in other words, simply because he chose to do so. If there was any special reason for his choice, it had to do with **the oath** that God **swore to** Israel's **forefathers.** God loved them simply because he loved them; it was in his nature to do so. And because he loved them, he **brought** them **out** of Egypt **with a mighty hand and redeemed** them from a life **of slavery.** God's choice of Israel commended God's character, not Israel's. This distinction is especially important in view of the modern notion that God chose Israel because of their intrinsic religious fervor or moral superiority.

7:9–11. God's sovereign choice implies that he alone **is God.** Happily, his sovereignty is not his only attribute, nor even his leading one. He is **the faithful God,** demonstrating that faithfulness by honoring his loving commitments **to a thousand generations of those who love him.** As such, he makes a glorious ally and friend, but an especially formidable enemy; **he will not be slow to repay to their face those who hate him.** To *hate* in this context suggests repudiating the covenant connection that God was making with Israel. There were many reasons **therefore** why his people should **take care** to follow his ways.

7:12. God promised that he would **keep his covenant** with Israel on the condition that they **pay attention** to his **laws** and carefully **follow them.** Verse 12 provides the general statement of which the following three verses form the elaboration.

7:13–15. The blessings that would descend on Israel when they kept God's covenant included increasing **numbers** of people and livestock, prosperity of their fields and orchards, and freedom from the **diseases** that they **knew in Egypt.** These benefits would come because God would love Israel and bless them richly in the days ahead as they lived **in the land.** The barrenness of people and livestock that other peoples experienced Israel would be able to avoid. In addition to freedom from the illnesses of Egypt, Israel would instead see how God would inflict those **horrible diseases** on their enemies.

7:16. The first task of obedience, however, would be Israel's compliance with the unpleasant business of ridding the land of **all the peoples** who were currently living there. As he did in verse 2, God insisted that the native population be destroyed without **pity,** because they posed the strongest imaginable threat to all that God wanted to do for Israel. God's people must not **serve their gods** and allow them to become a **snare**.

C Pursuing the Victory (7:17–26)

SUPPORTING IDEA: *God will provide the victory if his people refuse to be intimidated by their enemies.*

7:17. In spite of his multiple encouragements that Israel would conquer, God knew that many of the soldiers lacked confidence that they could win such a war against a superior and well-entrenched group of foes. Even as Moses spoke, people in the ranks were wondering how they could overcome and drive out an enemy who was **stronger** than they were.

7:18–19. God's answer to this question was to call Israel to **remember well** what he had done **to Pharaoh and to all Egypt**, a much larger nation than any of the peoples in Canaan. Such memories should have been easy to recall, because Israel **saw with their own eyes** the challenges that were made to him by the Egyptians, and the **miraculous signs and wonders** that God performed in response. The God who called on them to trust him and to resist the Egyptians was now calling on them to fight the Canaanites. He had not lost his **mighty** character between the exodus and the time of Moses' speech, but he was ready to do **the same to all the peoples** who were waiting for them inside the land.

7:20–21. Instead of fleeing from their enemies, Israel would soon know the joys of seeing their enemies flee. To ensure his nation's success, God promised to **send the hornet** among their enemies. The exact nature of this threat is unspecified. God could have been describing an actual attack of large numbers of insects, but the likelihood is that the hornet serves as a figure of speech for some unnamed terror, possibly the Lord himself.

Instead of being **terrified** by the nations, Israel should recognize that God, who serves among his people as their chief **warrior** and defender, is a **great and awesome God**. They should put their trust in him, strap on their weapons, and move ahead from victory to victory.

7:22–23. However, God would not, as he did against the Egyptians, destroy all the armies of the nations in one brief encounter, **all at once**. Instead, he would **drive out those nations . . . little by little**. Israel would fight a war that it could win, but not a war that would be swift or uncomplicated. It was to Israel's benefit that they not enter a deserted land. Had they done so, **the wild animals** would **multiply around** them and place them in jeopardy.

The war that Christians must fight bears many similarities to the divine design for occupying the Holy Land. Christians must go to war every day, putting to death the deeds of the body so they can live victorious lives (cp. Rom. 6:13; 8:13; Col. 3:5; 1 Pet. 2:11). Although the greatest victory is already won (Rom. 6:6; Gal. 5:24), a life still waits to be carved out for each soldier, and progress generally comes little by little. Come it will, however, to the one who fights, just as it would for Israel. The Lord promised to **deliver** their enemies **over** if his people would fight faithfully.

7:24. Even the mightiest **kings** in Canaan would fall into the hand of the Israelite army. When that happened, Israel would be obliged to **wipe out their names from under heaven**. The strength of Israel's enemies was only apparent. Although they might possess some power, in the end they would not **be able to stand** against the army of God.

7:25. Once the battles were over, however, the work would just be started. Israel was to **burn** any **images** of Canaanite **gods** that survived the invasion. Some of these idols were adorned or covered with **silver and gold**, and in the natural course of things Israel would be tempted to **covet** such treasures (possibly after they had been melted down) for one's personal wealth. God warned his people to avoid such longings. Although such items were attractive, God found them **detestable**. They were strictly off limits for Israel's citizens. (For an example of a catastrophe caused by a violation of this principle, see Josh. 7.)

7:26. If Israelites violated the restrictions of verse 25, they would put themselves at risk. Instead of the idols, they themselves would be set apart for destruction. God wanted Israel, as he wants Christians, to learn to **utterly abhor and detest** anything that had the potential of coming between them and their God. The believer's enemies are typically internal rather than external, and they pose a powerful threat to spiritual health and progress.

MAIN IDEA REVIEW: *God wants believers to face their inner enemies courageously and to eliminate them one by one.*

III. CONCLUSION

How Firm a Foundation

No one knows who wrote it, but the hymn "How Firm a Foundation" expresses well the spirit of Deuteronomy 7. Its message has long been a favorite of the people of God. Teddy Roosevelt loved it. So did Andrew Jackson, who, as he lay dying, asked that it be sung at his bedside. Robert E. Lee requested that worshipers sing it at his funeral. Its words encourage believers to trust God when dangers lie on every side:

> When thru the deep waters I call thee to go,
> The rivers of woe shall not thee overflow.
> For I will be with thee thy troubles to bless
> And sanctify to thee thy deepest distress.
> When thru fiery trials thy pathway shall lie,
> My grace, all-sufficient, shall be thy supply.
> The flame shall not hurt thee, I only design
> Thy dross to consume and thy gold to refine.

Life Application

The words of this beloved hymn first appeared in Dr. John Rippon's *Selection of Hymns* in 1787. Its popularity lies in its connection with the reluctance to endure danger and hardship, and the comfort that comes from knowing that God has promised his presence for the person who takes spiritual risks in a divinely sanctioned cause.

Ultimately, that includes all Christians, since we are commanded to take up arms against those aspects of our character that need eliminating. When we do so, we have the encouragement of knowing that the Lord Jesus is alongside for the duration:

> The soul that on Jesus hath leaned for repose,
> I will not, I will not desert to his foes.
> That soul, though all hell should endeavor to shake,
> I'll never, no never, no never forsake.

PRINCIPLES

- Wisdom lies in recognizing the dangers that lie within us and doing battle with them daily.
- The choice of a mate is crucial because no one has a greater influence on our spiritual lives.
- Kindness that allows barriers to one's relationship with God to spring up is self-destructive.
- God chooses people not for what he can do for them but for the good they can do for others.

APPLICATIONS

- Take some time to recall the faithfulness of God in your past. Give him thanks for all his goodness.
- Do an honest appraisal of your own faithfulness: to God, to family, to your church and community.
- If your results are less than satisfactory, make a list of ways you will be different in the future.
- Assess areas of your life where you are fearful. How do these parallel the experience of Israel as they waited to enter the promised land?

IV. LIFE APPLICATION

War Is No Picnic

In 1861, as the Civil War began, the northern press was impatient to punish the impudent Confederates and to put a quick end to the war. Editors from Chicago to Boston urged fast action and encouraged moving against the rebel army entrenched southwest of Washington, D.C.

Union General Irvin McDowell decided to move against the Confederate lines around Manassas on Sunday afternoon, July 21. Unfortunately, the timing of the army's movement was no secret in the area around Washington. Thousands of curious people decided that watching the coming battle might prove an interesting way to spend a summer afternoon. They packed picnic baskets, donned their best clothes, and drove carriages into the Virginia countryside to have lunch and watch the battle.

They soon discovered, however, that armed conflict makes a poor spectator sport. Their heroes in blue were repelled by the Confederate army and began a frantic retreat into the District of Columbia. Soon the only road heading east was crowded with fleeing soldiers and panicked civilians attempting to dodge the exploding shells of Confederate artillery.

The attitude of those civilians contains some disturbing parallels with the viewpoint of many modern Christians. People do not always take seriously the intensity of the spiritual war that constitutes Christian living. Being a Christian carries with it immense challenges as well as profound joys. Recognizing the first is required for a full experience of the second.

V. PRAYER

Father, help us to learn what comes with such difficulty for us—that we are dependent and needy creatures. In our moral lives and in every other way we must call upon you for the strength and resources we need for the battle. Make good soldiers of us for Jesus' sake, and for our own sakes. Amen.

VI. DEEPER DISCOVERIES

A. No Mercy (7:2)

As Israel entered the land of promise, they were told, "When the LORD your God has delivered them over to you and you have defeated them, then you must destroy them totally. Make no treaty with them, and show them no mercy" (Deut. 7:2). Few statements of Scripture have received harsher criticism than this one. It seems to conflict with repeated biblical commands to show mercy to others (see Zech. 7:9; Mic. 6:8; Matt. 23:23). What are we to make of this divinely announced policy of extermination?

In part, the policy represents God's own justice at work through Israel's weapons of war. God waited until this period of time to bring Israel into the land, at the moment Canaanite culture was at its most depraved (cp. Gen. 15:16). The Canaanites needed to be judged, and Israel was God's instrument of judgment.

However, it should also be noted that extermination does not represent the standard policy that God commanded Israel to pursue. When describing Israel's behavior toward the inhabitants of Canaan, the normal imperative was not *exterminate* but *drive out*: "When you cross the Jordan into Canaan, drive out all the inhabitants of the land before you. Destroy all their carved images and their cast idols, and demolish all their high places" (Num. 33:51–52). Calls to *expel* or *drive out* far outnumber commands to kill the Canaanites.

The two commands are actually compatible when seen from God's perspective. He had two primary purposes in bringing Israel into Canaan. First, he wanted to give the land to Israel and fulfill his promises to the patriarchs. Second, he desired to provide Israel a homeland that was free of the temptations to moral depravity that were part of Canaanite religion. As a result, the culture had to be destroyed—an action as easily accomplished by expulsion as by extermination.

Israel's slow approach over a period of forty years was closely observed by the native peoples (cp. Josh. 2:9–11). Many of them must have left voluntarily as Israel drew near, particularly after the dramatic and early victory at Jericho. Those who held out and remained behind the walls of Canaanite cities would have been the people who had the most to lose by leaving: the civic and religious leaders most committed to the blasphemous and degraded Canaanite cult. God knew that if they survived they would prove enthusiastic evangelists for the twisted cult—and so they did.

Israel's greatest danger would come after the fighting was over, when they saw the survivors of the battles they fought. Their natural inclination would have been to bring those devotees to paganism into their own homes and to adopt their guests' immoral and destructive religious practices. Their most profound danger, in effect, came in showing mercy toward those who posed a lethal danger to them.

Regrettably, that danger became a reality. Because Israel refused to exterminate that hard core of survivors, God's people became infected with idolatry so deeply that they themselves eventually had to be driven from the land. Israel exhibited an incomplete dedication to an important task. They thought so little of God's commands and their own spiritual lives that they permitted small pockets of wickedness to infect their nation.

Believers can make a similar mistake. We are to have no mercy on the sins that lie resident within us. We are persistently and without hesitation to drive them out of our lives, or they will become causes for spiritual stumbling.

B. Set Apart for Destruction (7:26)

God warned Israel, "Do not bring a detestable thing into your house or you, like it, will be set apart for destruction. Utterly abhor and detest it, for it is set apart for destruction" (Deut. 7:26). The Hebrew word translated "set apart for destruction" is *herem*, a term that means "something that God has

Deuteronomy 7

asked to be destroyed as an act of devotion to him." It generally appears in contexts of war or violent conflict.

God asked Israel to ignore the apparent beauty of the idols they would encounter and commanded that they offer them up to him in an irretrievable act of worship. The penalty for ignoring this command would be severe: the disobedient Israelites themselves would become *herem,* and their own lives would be in danger of destruction.

VII. TEACHING OUTLINE

A. INTRODUCTION
1. Lead Story: The Mighty Troll
2. Context: After insisting that Israel should love and worship the Lord alone (Deut. 6), God gives the first testing ground for this devotion. Israel would have to do the uncomfortable work of either driving out or destroying the pagan populations that survived the invasion. The future and spiritual health of Israel depended on their obedience.
3. Transition: In a similar fashion, God calls on Christians to put to death the deeds of the old man with the help of the Holy Spirit (Rom. 8:13). We must identify the enemy, assess our own motives, and pursue complete victory.

B. COMMENTARY
1. Identifying the Enemy (7:1–5)
2. Assessing the Motives (7:6–16)
3. Pursuing the Victory (7:17–26)

C. CONCLUSION: WAR IS NO PICNIC

VIII. ISSUES FOR DISCUSSION

1. What are some of your most persistent "inner enemies"?
2. Few people are disturbed by divine judgment in contexts like the flood of Genesis or the destruction of Sodom, but many take issue with Israel's role in expelling the Canaanites. Why do you think the latter is viewed so differently?
3. Based on what you read in Deuteronomy 7, can you formulate a working definition of what it means to be a "holy people"?
4. What does it mean to be part of a nation that is "chosen" as one of God's own treasures?
5. In what ways can a believer be fearful about taking up the challenge of ridding his life of a sinful habit?

Deuteronomy 8

Man the Verbivore

I. **INTRODUCTION**
Polish Surprise

II. **COMMENTARY**
A verse-by-verse explanation of the chapter.

III. **CONCLUSION**
Divine Breakthrough
An overview of the principles and applications from the chapter.

IV. **LIFE APPLICATION**
Encounter with the Word
Melding the chapter to life.

V. **PRAYER**
Tying the chapter to life with God.

VI. **DEEPER DISCOVERIES**
Historical, geographical, and grammatical enrichment of the commentary.

VII. **TEACHING OUTLINE**
Suggested step-by-step group study of the chapter.

VIII. **ISSUES FOR DISCUSSION**
Zeroing the chapter in on daily life.

Deuteronomy 8

> ## Quote
>
> "My mother's influence in molding my character was conspicuous. She forced me to learn daily long chapters of the Bible by heart. To that discipline and patient, accurate resolve I owe not only much of my general power of taking pains, but of the best part of my taste for literature."
>
> John Ruskin

IN A NUTSHELL

Moses in Deuteronomy 8 summarizes the best and worst possibilities for Israel's future. Whether God's people would rise to heights of blessing or sink into destruction would depend upon their attitude toward his word. The chapter marshals strong arguments against the deceitfulness of pride and for a conscious, thankful reliance upon God.

Man the Verbivore

I. INTRODUCTION

Polish Surprise

E. Schuyler English, beloved Bible teacher of a previous generation, told the story of a small village in eastern Poland. The people were poor and not particularly well educated, and they lived some distance from the major cities of that country.

A man named Michael Billester visited the village on one of his trips as a colporteur (a traveling salesman specializing in Bibles and devotional literature) during the 1930s. Finding the population too poor to purchase even a single Bible, Billester gave one away to one of the village residents as he left.

He did not visit the small village again until 1940. While he was away, God was at work using that Bible he had left behind as a gift.

To begin with, the man who owned it read it and was converted through his reading. He was so filled with joy that he began to share the contents of his precious possession with others in the village. By the time Michael Billester came to the village again, others—some two hundred of them in fact, nearly the whole village—had been converted as well.

Upon his return, Billester was delighted to discover a transformed group of villagers. They, in turn, were thrilled to see the man who had by his generosity caused a revolution in their hometown. Since a Sunday was included in the time of his visit, Michael was asked to speak at the worship service.

Rather than bringing a prepared message, Billester suggested that the people recite verses of Scripture that had become particularly meaningful in their lives. Upon hearing this, one of the villagers stood up and asked, "Perhaps we misunderstood. Did you mean verses or chapters?"

Scarcely able to believe what he was hearing, Billester asked, "Do you mean that there are people here who can recite whole chapters of the Bible?"

That was indeed what the questioner had meant. It seems that the villagers had, entirely apart from any human guidance, come to recognize the immense value of the Scriptures. They had passed around the village's lone Bible, allowing each household to keep it for a month. As the time drew near when each family had to yield up the Bible to the next household, they could hardly bear the thought of losing it. As a result, they had begun to memorize long portions of the Scriptures so they could still "possess" it while others were enjoying the book itself. Some of them had memorized the Psalms; others had committed the Book of Genesis or Luke to memory. Between them, the two hundred people of the village had memorized nearly the entire Bible.

Those humble villagers had come to realize what others of greater "sophistication" sometimes overlook: that if God has spoken, his words are important. God intended man to be a *verbivore*, a "word eater," and to digest and personalize his revelation. Those Polish villagers had seen for themselves the wonderful power and virtue of personal interaction with Scripture. They could have declared the "amen" to Jeremiah's declaration: "Your words were found, and I ate them, and Your word was to me the joy and rejoicing of my heart" (Jer. 15:16 NKJV).

II. COMMENTARY

Man the Verbivore

> **MAIN IDEA:** *Even the wisest people learn little from their successes; God warns his people against allowing their victories (which he will grant) to lead them into pride and spiritual indifference. Instead, they should pay close attention to God's Word.*

A The Impact of Hindsight (8:1–5)

> **SUPPORTING IDEA:** *Although their parents died in the wilderness for their stubbornness, Israel could profit from the older generation's failure by remembering that God had used adversity to train them.*

8:1. Israel could truly hope to **live** if they would **follow every command** that Moses was issuing on God's behalf. Life without God at the center is a slow form of death; so Moses urged Israel to take God's commands seriously. In a similar spirit, Paul warned, "The widow who lives for pleasure is dead even while she lives" (1 Tim. 5:6). If Israel responded properly, the nation would not only really live; they would also **increase** in numbers and would **possess the land** that God had **promised** to Abraham, Isaac, and Jacob.

8:2. If the nation needed any encouragement to follow the Lord, they had only to **remember how the LORD** had **led** them for the past **forty years**. That leading had been focused on two purposes. First, God had sought to **humble** them. It may seem strange to think of a nation of slaves needing to be humbled, but they had needed precisely that. Pride is native to the human heart, and it knows no socioeconomic or ethnic boundaries. It was the first sin, and it forms the wellspring for all others. Solomon observed, "There are six things the LORD hates, seven that are detestable to him: haughty eyes" (Prov. 6:16–17).

Second, God in his leading of Israel had determined to **test** them in order to **know what was in** their **heart**—in particular, whether obedience to his **commands** was their intent. The older generation had failed on both counts and had been sentenced to roam meaninglessly until they died away. The imminent invasion of Canaan would show what was in the hearts of the younger generation. They would have to be tested about their own devotion to the words of the Lord.

8:3–4. Moses' hearers had themselves been **humbled**, of course, even though they were mere teenagers at the time when Israel sinned at Kadesh Barnea. They had, through experiencing **hunger** and having that longing satisfied by divinely given **manna** (mentioned here for the first time in Deuteronomy), learned a critical lesson: **man does not live on bread alone.** His spiritual needs are as profound as his physical needs, and they must be satisfied. That spiritual longing can only be met, however, by **every word that comes from the mouth of the LORD.** (For more on manna, see "Deeper Discoveries.") Here we find an explicit reference to divinely created longings that exist universally in the human heart. God made humanity with a spiritual nature that can find satisfaction in nothing less than the Creator.

Moses recalled how God's provision for Israel went further than providing their food. He miraculously provided for their clothing and their health as well: their **clothes did not wear out** and their **feet did not swell** during the four decades that Israel wandered in the wilderness.

8:5. Still, all God's disciplinary actions were paternal in nature. He dealt with Israel **as a man disciplines his son.** It was critical that the nation **know in their heart** that the painful experiences they underwent in the wilderness were the product of a loving as well as a sovereign God. The differences between punishment and discipline have to do with both the intent behind the actions and the affections which motivated them. People sometimes punish to exact judgment for past actions. God disciplines in order to teach and always in the interest of those whom he disciplines.

B The Implications of Foresight (8:6–10)

SUPPORTING IDEA: *God placed before his people enormous blessings and lavish benefits. If they were wise, his actions would result in thanksgiving and a renewed sense of devotion to him.*

8:6. Moses described the life God desires from his people in terms of three categories. The first is *behavioral*: they were to **observe the commands** he gave in what they did. The second category is *habitual* and goes deeper. Israel was to walk **in God's ways** whether a specific commandment addressed their behavior or not. They could always ask, "Is what I am about to do reflective of the character of God?" The third category is *motivational*: Israel was to revere God at all times. They were to possess a reverential fear that would motivate them to take no chances. Unless they were sure that what they were about to do was acceptable before God, they should refrain.

8:7–9. Such ethical care is not to be simply based on what God may do to them for violations of his covenant. Morality should be based as well on the recognition of God's generosity and faithfulness. In the case of Israel, their behavior was to be motivated by gratitude for the good land he was giving them. It was, after all, **a land with streams and pools of water** that could provide for them and for their animals and crops. Underground were **springs** that emerged in **the valleys and hills**, making it possible to grow **wheat and barley**. The land contained **vines** and **trees** that yielded useful and delicious fruit and places where caches of **honey** could be found. Because the land was fertile, **bread** would **not be scarce** there, and there would be such an abundance that Israel would **lack nothing**.

Israel's new land would contain mineral wealth as well as natural fertility. Its rocks contained **iron** that could be used for weapons and household implements. Israelites were familiar with iron smelting from their time in Egypt (Deut. 4:20). However, they did not possess the technology they would need to craft iron implements effectively. The native Canaanites, by contrast, had already learned to construct iron chariots (Josh. 17:18). **Copper** deposits were later found and mined from the region between the Dead Sea and the Gulf of Aqaba and exported through the harbor at Ezion-geber (cp. 1 Kgs. 9:26–28). Copper was used in a variety of alloys, including in combination with tin to produce bronze.

8:10. A land filled with such resources was designed to have a spiritual impact when it was received. When Israel had **eaten** and was **satisfied**, they were directed to **praise the LORD . . . for the good land** that they were enjoying. Combined with 8:1–5, this paragraph shows how God uses both positive reinforcement and painful adversity to achieve his purposes with his people. As a wise father, he understands how to apply these elements in precisely the proper proportions to accomplish his purpose, and his word is always productive: "My word that goes out from my mouth . . . will not return to me empty, but will accomplish what I desire and achieve the purpose for which I sent it" (Isa. 55:11).

C The Importance of Insight (8:11–20)

SUPPORTING IDEA: *If God's people were to dwell contentedly in the land, they would have to forsake their tendency to pride and spiritual forgetfulness and pay close attention to God's Word.*

8:11. Prosperity brings with it as many spiritual hazards as adversity. Although Israel was about to make the transition from a nation of homeless ex-slaves to a settled people, they would face many dangers. In particular, they would need to **be careful** and **not forget** the LORD. As they were about to invade the land, when life and death lay in the balance each day, they could hardly deny their need of God's favor and protection. Later, when their enemies were vanquished and life was less tense, they would find themselves lulled into a false sense of independence. That might lead to a pattern of **failing to observe his commands, his laws and his decrees.**

8:12–14. Israel would need to exercise spiritual alertness and recognize their natural tendency to forget the one who gave them everything. **Otherwise,** that inclination would cause them great sorrow and dismay. Once they began to **build fine houses and settle down** and to see their **herds and flocks** and personal wealth **increase,** they could fall victim to pride and spiritual arrogance.

The godly person is as much a student of himself as he is of God. The unguarded heart is always vulnerable to folly, and God extended his kindness to Israel not only in his gifts but also in his counsel. Becoming spiritually lax is not an option for a person who would be Christlike. The greatest test comes when the crisis is over and we seem to have won the battle. **Then the heart** tends to become **proud**; and with pride comes the lack of a sense of need.

8:15–16. In contrast to the rich land Israel was about to enter, God had **led** them **through the vast and dreadful desert, that thirsty and waterless land.** Making the land doubly inhospitable, it was inhabited by **venomous snakes and scorpions.** In order to provide for the basic necessities of survival, God **brought** Israel **water** out of the **hard rock** so common to that area.

Even in the midst of such hardships, however, the Lord provided for Israel's thousands. He **gave** them **manna to eat in the desert,** a food that their **fathers** knew nothing about (a sentiment that is repeated from v. 3). He forced them, as he led them through that forbidding land, into a position where they had to realize their dependence on him. The process was designed **to humble and to test** them so that **in the end** they might prosper physically and spiritually. God always has his eye on the end of the process of spiritual formation rather than its immediate or short-term results. Believers may not enjoy the process, but they can always praise him for the ultimate benefits of spiritual growth.

8:17–18. The most formidable barrier to the enjoyment of that prosperity lay not in the enemies who lived across the Jordan River but deep within the pride-stained heart of every Israelite. They had it within them to conclude that their own **power** and **strength** had **produced** the **wealth** they would enjoy.

God's antidote for this foolish conclusion was to encourage Israel to **remember the Lord** and recognize him as the source of the **ability to produce wealth.** The successes that Israel was soon to enjoy were nothing more than confirmations of the **covenant** that God had made with their **forefathers.**

8:19–20. A prideful independence could take Israel even further, however. If they should **forget the LORD** and engage in the worship of **other gods,** they would soon **be destroyed.** They need only remember that **the nations**

Deuteronomy 8

west of the Jordan River were themselves being driven from the land because of their failure to worship their Creator. The survival of Israel and its future testimony to the virtues of Yahweh hung in the balance.

> **MAIN IDEA REVIEW:** *Even the wisest people learn little from their successes; God warns his people against allowing their victories (which he will grant) to lead them into pride and spiritual indifference. Instead, they should pay close attention to God's Word.*

III. CONCLUSION

Divine Breakthrough

History records how the communist leaders of the old Soviet Union tried desperately to destroy all traces of Christian influence from Russia and her affiliated nations, all to no avail. Josef Stalin acted as a primary catalyst in attempting to eradicate Christian churches, Bibles, and Christians from public life. Stalin's henchmen went throughout the land during the 1930s, confiscating Bibles and arresting their owners. Many of those arrested were taken to prison camps and in many cases were never heard from again.

After the fall of the Iron Curtain in 1989, believers (and they were still there by the millions) came out from hiding again. In an effort to encourage many of the newly visible Russian Christians, one missionary organization sent a team of people to the city of Stavropol to engage in a series of ministry projects. The team had asked for a shipment of Russian Bibles from Moscow to facilitate their work, but those Bibles were delayed. While the team was awaiting the arrival of their Bibles, they heard that there was already a whole warehouse filled with confiscated Bibles right in Stavropol, a vestige of Stalinist policy. They inquired from the local authorities about obtaining these for use in their work. No one was sure if the Bibles were still there, but local officials gave the team permission to use them if they could be found—which they were.

The missionaries rented a truck to load the Bibles from the warehouse and recruited a number of locals to help them in their work. Among these helpers was a surly young man who told them that he would help them only for the money involved; he was not at all sympathetic with their mission.

During the time that the trucks were being loaded, this difficult young man was suddenly nowhere to be found. The missionaries finally found him sitting in the corner of the warehouse with an open Bible lying on his lap, weeping profusely. It seems that while the trucks were being loaded, he had decided to take a Bible for himself. Opening it, he discovered on the inside of the front cover his own grandmother's signature. She had been among the believers arrested during the Stalinist purges, and her Bible had been among those confiscated. That Bible had been used by God to penetrate the hard shell of her grandson in a way that she could never have guessed. Personal contact with the Word of God yields life-changing results.

PRINCIPLES

- God leads his people whether they are obedient or rebellious, but his leading is far more pleasant when they obey.
- God's loving discipline brings us face-to-face with our pride.
- Chastening is a mark of affection, not a sign of rejection.
- God delights in providing his people with material gain and comfort, although prosperity can pose a threat to spiritual well-being.

APPLICATIONS

- Ask God to reveal to you any point where pride has become a barrier to his best in your life.
- Pick a portion of God's Word—in Deuteronomy or elsewhere—and begin to commit it to memory. Lay out a few verses to learn each week.
- Once your passage has been memorized, take a verse with you through the day. Mull it over in free moments and apply it to your experience.
- Assess the ways (if any) that you have allowed a consciousness of your dependence on God to slip away from you. Determine to move in a new direction.

IV. LIFE APPLICATION

Encounter with the Word

Many people are familiar with the remarkable ministry of Amy Carmichael and her work with the downtrodden women of India (particularly temple prostitutes). In addition to her evangelism and social work, Amy wrote devotional books. When she died in 1951, thousands mourned her passing.

Her ministry began when one particular passage of Scripture came alive in her life. As a young girl in Belfast, she was walking home from church one damp Sunday morning with her family when she saw an old woman laboring under a load that was too heavy for her. Amy and her siblings came to the rescue of the unfortunate woman and helped by carrying her bundle and helping steady her uncertain gait.

Their act of kindness caused them some embarrassment, since the street was filled with their friends who found it amusing that Amy and her siblings

Deuteronomy 8

were occupied in so inglorious an endeavor. She drew immediate comfort, however, when she remembered a text that she had recently read in 1 Corinthians. Paul describes in chapter 3 of that epistle how the fires of God's judgment would put to the test the work of Christian believers. Every man's "work will be shown for what it is," Paul wrote, when that work would be put to the test. Only those whose work survived the searching scrutiny of the divine examination would receive a reward. Others would be saved, but lose their reward. At that moment, Amy determined that she would make her life count—that her works would pass the test and qualify her for eternal responsibility. "I said nothing to anyone," she wrote later, "but I knew that something had happened that had changed life's values. Nothing could ever matter again but the things that were eternal."

Such is the power of God's Word. For those who will make it their own, God will use that word to transform values and enrich their lives. In the case of Amy Carmichael, that meant in turn transforming and enriching the lives of others.

V. PRAYER

Father, keep us from the folly of thinking we are free agents. Help us acknowledge that apart from you we can do nothing, and give us a heart to delight in your victories more than our own. Amen.

VI. DEEPER DISCOVERIES

A. Manna (8:3)

Moses challenged Israel to remember that God had fed them "with manna which you did not know nor did your fathers know, that He might make you know that man shall not live by bread alone; but man lives by every word that proceeds from the mouth of the LORD" (Deut. 8:3 NKJV). As Moses acknowledged, Israel had never seen manna before the wilderness experience. The Bible strongly suggests that the reason for this lack of acquaintance with the food of the desert lay in the fact that it had not existed before; it was a supernaturally provided form of sustenance.

In the Numbers account, Moses noted that the "manna was like coriander seed, and its color like the color of bdellium" (Num. 11:7 NKJV). It tasted similar to wafers made with honey (Exod. 16:31). Although some modern commentators compare manna to substances that are currently found in and around the Sinai peninsula, manna was not a natural product. It disappeared as miraculously as it had first appeared (Josh. 5:12). Aaron put a small portion of it into an urn and laid it before the Lord in the tabernacle so Israel could see in later generations the food that had sustained their forefathers

(Exod. 16:32–33). The miraculous character of God's provision appears in Psalms 78:24, which notes, "[God] rained down manna for the people to eat, he gave them the grain of heaven."

Manna's supernatural character yielded an epoch-making lesson for Israel. If God could so easily supply the items they needed for survival, then they should trust him implicitly, recognizing that they needed to know and heed his word even above the food that sustained them.

VII. TEACHING OUTLINE

A. INTRODUCTION
1. Lead Story: Polish Surprise
2. Context: Divinely granted victories can be wonderful in our lives, but they inevitably lead to new problems. Can we stand the tests of prosperity?
3. Transition: What we need to cope with our successes is a strong consciousness of our dependence; and there is nothing that can equal the Word of God in providing that.

B. COMMENTARY
1. The Impact of Hindsight (8:1–5)
2. The Implications of Foresight (8:6–10)
3. The Importance of Insight (8:11–20)

C. CONCLUSION: ENCOUNTER WITH THE WORD

VIII. ISSUES FOR DISCUSSION

1. God led Israel into experiences of hunger and deprivation. What are the implications of this for believers?
2. What are the differences between a healthy and a pathological fear of God?
3. Does the Lord's desire for praise and blessing suggest some inner need for compliments? If not, why do you think we are commanded to praise him?
4. Believers often excuse acts of disobedience on the basis of a lack of ability to obey. How valid are such excuses?
5. Based on your own spiritual experience, do you tend to learn more about God in times of prosperity or in times of adversity? Why do you think this is so?

Deuteronomy 9

The Power of a Godly Intercessor

I. **INTRODUCTION**
Standing in the Gap

II. **COMMENTARY**
A verse-by-verse explanation of the chapter.

III. **CONCLUSION**
The Quiet Sister
An overview of the principles and applications from the chapter.

IV. **LIFE APPLICATION**
Praying Hyde
Melding the chapter to life.

V. **PRAYER**
Tying the chapter to life with God.

VI. **DEEPER DISCOVERIES**
Historical, geographical, and grammatical enrichment of the commentary.

VII. **TEACHING OUTLINE**
Suggested step-by-step group study of the chapter.

VIII. **ISSUES FOR DISCUSSION**
Zeroing the chapter in on daily life.

Deuteronomy 9

> ## Quote
>
> "It is a good thing to let prayer be the first business in the morning and the last in the evening. Guard yourself against such false and deceitful thoughts that keep whispering, 'Wait a while. In an hour or so I will pray. I must first finish this or that.' Thinking such thoughts we get away from prayer into other things that will hold us and involve us till the prayer of the day comes to naught."
>
> Martin Luther

IN A NUTSHELL

Deuteronomy 9 contains the record and example of Moses as intercessor before God. Taking on a ministry that would suggest the heavenly work of Jesus, his descendant, Moses describes how he stood in the gap between God in his righteous anger and Israel in rebellion, and preserved the lives of God's people.

The Power of a Godly Intercessor

I. INTRODUCTION

Standing in the Gap

In the early years of the eighteenth century, Protestant Christians, exiled by persecution from their homeland in Bohemia, fled over the border into Germany. One German nobleman, Count Nicholas Ludwig von Zinzendorf, who was himself a believer, proved sympathetic with these suffering people and offered them a place of refuge in his own territory. Count von Zinzendorf established a small village that became known as Herrnhut ("under the Lord's watch") so that these refugees would be able to survive.

Over the next few years, Herrnhut and its people became a center for the launching of international missions. The process began when twenty-four men and twenty-four women agreed to spend one hour each day in regularly scheduled prayer, the intent being to establish a constant "watch" of prayer around the clock. This perpetual prayer vigil lasted for over one hundred years!

As time passed, others joined them in the effort that eventually provoked the first great push of Protestant missions. As they prayed, von Zinzendorf asked for volunteers who would be willing to go out, representing this little Moravian community in the cause of the gospel. Twenty-six people stepped forward. Of these, twenty-two had died within two years, and two of the others were in prison. Nevertheless, from the little community of six hundred Moravians, eventually seventy missionaries were sent to places like the West Indies, Greenland, Turkey, and Lapland.

Count von Zinzendorf himself traveled to the American colonies to set up communities of Moravian brethren in the New World. He and his followers may have had their most profound impact on world history, however, by means of their influence on the Wesley brothers. John and Charles, who had come to Georgia as missionaries themselves, happened to be on a ship headed back to England when a storm overtook their little vessel in mid-Atlantic. John was terrified of what seemed to be his impending death, but he noticed through his fright that the Moravians who were on board were calm and hopeful. They seemed so much more settled internally than he was.

When the storm had passed, he asked them their secret. They explained how they had come to trust in the finished work of Jesus Christ for them, and so they knew that their destiny was secure regardless of what might happen to their bodies. The encounter was the initial link in a chain leading to the conversion of both John and Charles Wesley, who were among the leaders of an awakening that swept England in the middle of the eighteenth century.

Who can doubt that the powerhouse for that mid-century revival and for the missionary effort that led to it resided in the prayer efforts of Herrnhut? Intercessors constitute the greatest unseen group of spiritual heroes in world history. Their labors are not seen, but the results are. Those who pray for the spiritual needs of others do immeasurable good in the world, often preventing (at least for a time) divine judgment.

When Judah was guilty of moral degradation, God looked for someone to intercede for them, and he found no one: "I looked for a man among them who would build up the wall and stand before me in the gap on behalf of the land so that I would not have to destroy it, but I found none" (Ezek. 22:30). As a result of the missing intercessor, God expressed his displeasure: "So I will pour out my wrath on them and consume them with my fiery anger, bringing down on their own heads all they have done, declares the Sovereign LORD" (Ezek. 22:31).

Fortunately, in Israel's darkest days, they possessed as their intercessor the prophet Moses, who stood in the gap for them so they could survive and enter the promised land.

II. COMMENTARY

The Power of a Godly Intercessor

> **MAIN IDEA:** Although God's people find many successes in the world, they must not fall prey to a spirit of pride. We succeed not because of our moral superiority but because of the faithfulness of our divine intercessor and because of the great mercy of God.

A The Peril of Misunderstanding (9:1–6)

> **SUPPORTING IDEA:** God's man warned his people of drawing wrong conclusions about their successes. They would succeed not because they deserved to but because of God's grace.

9:1. Moses prefaced the new chapter by using (for the fourth time in Deuteronomy) the imperative, **Hear, O Israel** (cp. 4:1, 5:1, 6:4). These solemn words suggest that what follows deserves the most careful attention (cp. Jesus' use of the expression, "Most assuredly I say to you" [NKJV] some twenty-five times in John's Gospel). Israel was about **to cross the Jordan** and begin to **dispossess nations greater and stronger** than themselves. The cities they were soon to attack were heavily fortified. The expression **walls up to the sky** is a hyperbole that means something like "exceptionally well defended." Humanly speaking, Israel had no hope of successful siege operations against such well-prepared defenses.

9:2. To complicate matters still further, the local populations could not be considered pushovers. **The people** who opposed them were **strong and tall**. In fact, they included a group whose reputations were well-known even to Israel in its nomadic condition: the **Anakites** (see "Deeper Discoveries," ch. 1). These defenders were such fierce warriors that their reputation had become a proverb in the region. Israel had heard people say: **Who can stand up against the Anakites?** From a purely human point of view, Israel stood no chance against such a capable and determined group of people.

9:3. However, Israel could count on the fact that they were not limited to humanly constructed probabilities. Their success would not be a testimony to their military skill or their intelligence network. **The LORD would be the one who** went **across** the Jordan River **ahead** of the Israelite army; and he would proceed in a way that would prove most destructive to Israel's enemies, **like a devouring fire**. God would **destroy** some of those enemies and would **subdue** others. Israel would be left with two options regarding the latter: they could either **drive** the pagans **out** or they could **annihilate them quickly**.

9:4–5. Such a remarkable string of military successes could have an unfortunate effect **after** the fact. It would be possible for individual Israelites to draw wrong conclusions. If someone should say, **The LORD has brought me here to take possession of this land because of my righteousness**, they would be committing a terrible blunder. Israel (as Moses will explain beginning in v. 7) possessed a bad track record when it came to righteousness.

On the contrary, God would **drive** the Canaanites **out** primarily **on account of the wickedness of these nations**. Israel's military prosperity was a product of their God's determination to judge the wicked, not his desire to reward the righteous. In order to drive home the point, Moses said virtually the same thing in verse 5, adding that God's faithfulness also had something to do with Israel's military success. God was merely seeking **to accomplish what he swore to** Israel's **fathers, to Abraham, Isaac and Jacob**.

9:6. Far from commending their own outstanding spirituality, God's goodness in providing Israel a homeland would be seen in spite of the fact that Israel was **a stiff-necked people**. The last expression suggests an unwillingness to adjust to God's yoke and is a figurative way of describing stubbornness. It occurs eight times in Hebrew Scripture, in each case describing Israel corporately (cp. v. 13; 10:16; Exod. 32:9; 33:3,5; 34:9; 2 Chr. 30:8).

🅑 The Pattern of Rebellion (9:7–25)

SUPPORTING IDEA: *Israel built up a pattern of rebellion beginning in Egypt and continuing through the wilderness until it reached its zenith at Kadesh-Barnea.*

9:7. This verse constitutes a summary of verses 8–25, and begins with **remember this and never forget**. Spiritual insensitivity is often associated with a poor or selective memory. God wanted Israel to reflect soberly on their distressing record **from the day** they **left Egypt until** they **arrived** on the fringe of the promised land. God does not desire his people to spend their lives grieving over their sins, but neither does he want them to be unconcerned about their obedience. Israel's track record had been consistently **rebellious against the LORD** through Moses' long association with them.

9:8–9. Although Moses could have recalled the difficulties he had being accepted by their fathers, he did not do so, preferring to begin with the events that took place **at Horeb**. One incident in particular was worth noting—the time that the Lord was **angry enough to destroy** his people. The episode in question took place when Moses **went up on the mountain to receive** God's covenant summary. **The tablets of stone**, written with the finger of God (cp. v. 10; Exod. 31:18), formed a priceless link between the Lord and his people and would ordinarily have been preserved at all costs. These stone tablets were given to Moses at the end of a period of **forty days and forty nights** when he **ate no bread and drank no water**. He found from personal experience the reality that the presence of God is more satisfying than food (cp. Deut. 8:3).

9:10–11. The **two stone tablets** that Moses received contained a summary of the covenant between God and Israel. **On them** were written the **commandments**, those items that the Lord **proclaimed to** Israel audibly at Sinai. He had spoken **out of the fire, on the day of the assembly**. Although Israel had been in many assemblies, Moses did not need to specify which assembly; no one would ever forget that time. The reference to **the finger of God** is certainly an anthropomorphism (a description of God in human terms), but it conveys in an unmistakable way God's personal investment in the precious words of his **covenant**. Placing the words in **stone** suggested that they were to be treasured and passed down from generation to generation.

9:12. It was not to be, however. While Moses was involved in a glorious personal experience with God, the people of Israel had **turned away** from the covenant before the covenant's tokens (the tablets) could be delivered to them. God described Israel to Moses as **your people**. These words contained an implied test: would Moses be willing to shoulder the responsibility of being an intercessor? Would he, like his countryman Jesus, stand between his people and divine judgment? Those people had **quickly** engaged in the most basic form of wickedness, having **made a cast idol for themselves** even as that idol's antithesis, their living Lord, had been graciously reaching out to them through Moses.

9:13–14. God's reaction, played out in his conversation with Moses, was based on his people's miserable pattern of rebellion. He described Israel as **a stiff-necked people indeed** (cp. notes on v. 6), and he proposed that Moses leave him **alone** so he could carry out a just policy of destroying Israel. Instead of taking Israel into the promised land, God proposed that he **make** from Moses **a nation stronger and more numerous than** Israel.

The words **let me alone** resonate with meaning in this context. They contain the implicit notion that, if Moses should choose to press the case, God would abandon his proposal for the sake of Moses' intercession. So it is with all biblical warnings. If God had determined to destroy Israel, he would not have announced his displeasure with them to Moses; he simply would have executed his purpose. Prophetic warnings carry with them either an expressed or an implied condition: "unless you repent" (cp. Rev. 2:5 NKJV). God is someone to whom we can pray, and (from our point of view at least) our prayers make a difference. To Moses' credit, he donned the mantle of the intercessor and pleaded for "his" people.

9:15–17. Before praying, however, there was unpleasant work to be done. Moses **turned and went down from the mountain**, still **ablaze with** the **fire** of God's purity. He bore in his **hands** the **two tablets** expressive of that purity. What he saw vindicated the horrible description that he had heard on the mountain. Israel had indeed **sinned against the LORD** and had made **an idol**. The nation had **turned aside quickly** from the kind of life that God had outlined for them as a testimony of his grace.

Standing before Israel as God's representative, he acted on God's behalf: **I took the two tablets and threw them out of my hands, breaking them to pieces before your eyes**. As Israel had shattered the covenant, so Moses had broken the symbol and expression of the covenant.

9:18. Moses acted at Horeb in the role of a priest. Just as he had represented God before men at the base of the mountain, so he turned and **once again** represented men before God in prayer. He **fell prostrate before the LORD for forty days and forty nights**. Although he had not eaten for an identical period earlier, he endured a second sustained fast **because of** Israel's **sin**. Grieving over the sin of others is a mark of godly character.

9:19–20. Moses **feared** God's **anger** for two reasons. First, he knew that God was **angry enough** with the people **to destroy** them. He interceded for Israel as a nation, and again **the LORD listened** to him. Secondly, he was concerned for his own brother, Aaron, since God was also **angry enough** with him **to destroy him** as well. The lives of people he loved dearly were hanging in the balance when Moses retired to Sinai to intercede for them. Moses prayed for Israel at large, but he **prayed for Aaron too**.

Deuteronomy 9:21

Intercessors carry within them a set of conflicting impulses. On the one hand, because they love the Lord, they sense his righteous anger and the depth of his offended holiness. On the other hand, they love the very sinners who have provoked him, and who are so spiritually needy. These are rarely held in such tension as Moses held them. Most of us who pray feel intensely enough the dangers in which sinners find themselves; but few appreciate the painful nature of the offenses themselves. Moses' power in prayer was no doubt connected to his deep realization of both these matters.

9:21. That Moses understood the divine perspective is proven by his actions with respect to that terrible **calf** that Aaron **had made**. He took **that sinful thing** and **burned it**. Then he took the remains, **crushed** them, and **ground** the product into **powder**. To remove it—and to allow Israel to internalize it (cp. Exod. 32:20)—he cast the remnants of Israel's sin **into a stream that could carry it away down the mountain**.

9:22. Although dramatic, the events at Horeb hardly exhausted Israel's capacity for rebellion. They **also made the** LORD **angry at Taberah**, only three days away from Sinai, when they began to complain (Num. 11:1–3). Since God had provided so faithfully for them for so long, and since they had quickly put him to the test again, he acted in judgment and sent the fire of judgment into the outskirts of the camp.

Israel had also rebelled at **Massah** (Exod. 17:1–7) when they were thirsty. Moses, at God's direction, brought water out of a rock in the desert for the people, but it was recognized as an overt example of tempting the Lord; "He called the place Massah and Meribah because the Israelites quarreled and because they tested the LORD saying, 'Is the LORD among us or not?'" (Exod. 17:7).

Similarly, Israel had rebelled against the Lord at the place known to biblical history as **Kibroth Hattaavah** ("the graves of craving"). Although God had only shortly before dealt with Israel over the events at Taberah, they again put him to the test by their complaining. They craved meat, so he miraculously provided quail, and along with it a dose of severe discipline: "While the meat was still between their teeth and before it could be consumed, the anger of the LORD burned against the people, and he struck them with a severe plague. Therefore the place was named Kibroth Hattaavah, because there they buried the people who had craved other food" (Num. 11:33–34).

9:23–24. When it came to sheer disappointment, however, the events at **Kadesh Barnea** provided the pinnacle. Israel should have been ready to **take possession of the land** at that time. They had been redeemed from Egypt. They had been instructed at Sinai and through their wilderness experiences. Still, they rebelled against the command of the Lord by their refusal to go up confidently and do battle against the Canaanites. By adopting the pessimistic report of the spies (Num. 13:1–14:10), the people exhibited a determination not to **trust** or **obey** the Lord. Since the events described in verses 8–24 covered the history of that generation of adults, Moses could summarize their character by saying, **You have been rebellious against the LORD ever since I have known you.**

9:25. One can scarcely imagine the discomfort and weariness that Moses experienced as he **lay prostrate before the LORD** for **forty days and forty nights** at Sinai. Yet, as long as God had it in mind to **destroy** his people, Moses would not relent from his appeals to God's mercy. At the end of this period, God told Moses that he would accompany Israel into the promised land (Exod. 33:15–17).

The Prototype of Intercession (9:26–29)

SUPPORTING IDEA: *Moses intercedes for Israel by appealing to the highest goal of history, the glory of God, as expressed in his faithfulness to the patriarchs.*

9:26. Moses recalled in a highly condensed form the substance of his prayer of intercession. He addressed God as **O Sovereign LORD**. The English expression only approximates the content of the underlying Hebrew because of translation conventions. The Hebrew text here is literally, "O Lord Yahweh." The first term is a title that emphasizes divine prerogatives; the second word is the personal name of God, and one that has particular covenantal associations. (The Hebrew *Yahweh* is customarily translated "Lord" in English Bibles. In this combination, of course, it could hardly be used, since "O Lord Lord" is hardly coherent.) Moses recognized that God could do as he pleased as Lord of everything. At the same time, he approached him as the one who had used the name Yahweh in instituting his covenant with Israel.

Moses appealed to God as well on the strength of the personal investment that God had made in the people of his chosen nation. They were his **own inheritance**, people whom he personally had **redeemed** by expressions of **great power**.

9:27. Moreover, these wayward people were the children of God's **servants Abraham, Isaac and Jacob**. If God could not forgive them because of **their wickedness and their sin**, could he not do so for the sake of those beloved patriarchs? If God would only remember the promises he had made to those three men, he might forgive the many rebellions and the **stubbornness** of their offspring.

9:28–29. The trump card in Moses' prayer lay in his appeal to the glory of God. The Egyptians—**the country from which** God **brought** them—would gain a victory if God chose to destroy Israel. They would call into question his abilities: **the LORD was not able to take them into the land**. Likewise, they would cast doubts upon his faithfulness and integrity: which **he had promised them**. And they would find in Israel's destruction a total

Deuteronomy 9

misunderstanding of the divine motives: **because he hated them, he brought them out to put them to death.**

The glory of God is the purpose around which all history moves. There can be nothing greater than the expression of his glory, and nothing worse than calling it into question. All of human redemption is subsidiary to the glory of God (Eph. 1:14). Moses longed for it and recognized that there could be no higher appeal. The glory of God would be diminished if Israel were destroyed, for **they** were his **people**, his **inheritance**.

> **MAIN IDEA REVIEW:** *Although God's people find many successes in the world, they must not fall prey to a spirit of pride. We succeed not because of our moral superiority but because of the faithfulness of our divine intercessor and because of the great mercy of God.*

III. CONCLUSION

The Quiet Sister

William Carey was born in 1761 into a poor family in Northamptonshire, England. His father was a weaver and a schoolteacher, and Carey received the basics of an education at home. His formal schooling was finished when he was apprenticed to a shoemaker and cobbler at age fourteen.

Carey then showed his determination to learn by educating himself during slow moments at his cobbler's bench. By sheer diligence and application, he learned Latin, Greek, Hebrew, French, and Dutch. By the time he was twenty, he could read the Bible in six languages.

Carey posted a map of the world near his bench so he could pray for the evangelization of the nations. Shortly after his marriage at age twenty, he began preaching in the local Baptist church.

Although he now had a home to support, Carey had a heart for the lost peoples of the world. He read with great intensity the accounts of the explorations of Captain James Cook and in time called into question the lack of missionary vision of British Christians. He wrote an essay, "An Enquiry into the Obligations of Christians to use Means for the Conversion of the Heathen," that ruffled many a pastoral feather. He preached a notable sermon entitled, "Expect Great Things from God; Attempt Great Things for God."

Taking his own advice, Carey began the English Baptist Missionary Society and offered himself as a candidate. After many disappointments, Carey landed in Serampore, a Danish enclave near Calcutta, India, where he was to carry out his life's work. Carey began a publishing house that eventually, during his lifetime, published the Bible in forty-two languages and dialects, providing God's Word for more than three hundred million people.

All these accomplishments are public knowledge. What is not generally known is that William Carey had a sister. Her obscurity is easily attributable to the fact that she was an invalid who lived in England, far from the scene of his triumphs. She was nearly paralyzed, but that didn't keep her from supporting her brother's work through intercessory prayer. She read his many letters carefully and prayed for the difficulties he was facing from month to month. She could not translate the Bible, but she did what she could do in occupying her post in God's army—that of intercessor. Heaven will in time declare the enormousness of the contribution that she made, along with her more famous sibling, to the cause of Christ.

PRINCIPLES

- There is no limit to what God's people can expect their God to do if they are rightly related to him.
- In any spiritual undertaking, God's first order of business is to see to the spiritual health of his people.
- Believers are inclined to attribute their spiritual successes to their godliness when it would be more accurate to connect them with God's faithfulness.
- The believer who feels the agony caused by rebellion will grow to become the best intercessor.
- Persistence in prayer brings results that casual prayer does not.

APPLICATIONS

- Make a prayer list of the ten most important people in your life and begin to uphold them before God regularly.
- Pick someone in your circle of acquaintances who is not a believer and ask for God to give you an open door so you can share the gospel with him or her.
- Read a good biography of someone like George Mueller, Hudson Taylor, or John Hyde, and glean from it principles of effective praying.
- Ask a friend to join you in arriving early and in praying for your pastor for a few minutes before church each Sunday.
- Let your pastor know you're praying for him!

IV. LIFE APPLICATION

Praying Hyde

Not long ago a little book by Bruce Wilkinson captivated the attention of the world, landing atop not only the Christian bookstore list of best-sellers, but

Deuteronomy 9

that of the *New York Times* as well. *The Prayer of Jabez* explained how the petition of an obscure Old Testament figure had gained Bruce's attention many years ago. He read how Jabez prayed, "Oh, that you would bless me and enlarge my territory! Let your hand be with me, and keep me from harm so that I will be free from pain" (1 Chr. 4:10). Bruce began to offer this prayer to God each day and saw answers repeatedly, just as God had answered Jabez so long ago.

The prayer of Jabez in fact has borne fruit many times. A missionary by the name of John Hyde noticed it and was stimulated to pray more earnestly. He was so successful at it that during his life he became known as "Praying Hyde"; his prayers were much coveted by people around the world.

Dr. J. Wilburn Chapman once explained in a letter to a friend how Hyde and his prayers had impacted Chapman's life and ministry. He had been holding a series of evangelistic meetings in England, but his ministry was—at least to all appearances—bearing little fruit. Crowds were small, and there were few professions of faith.

Chapman then received word that John Hyde was coming to pray for him and his ministry. He wrote of Hyde: "He came to my room, turned the key in the door, and dropped to his knees, and waited five minutes without a single syllable coming from his lips. I could hear my own heart thumping, and his beating. I felt hot tears running down my face. I knew I was with God. Then with upturned face, down which the tears were streaming, he said, 'O God.' Then for five minutes at least he was still again; and then, when he knew that he was talking with God, there came from the depths of his heart such petitions for me as I had never heard before. I rose from my knees to know what real prayer was."

Hyde's prayer for Chapman's work bore dramatic fruit. In the next meeting, the crowd was much larger, and fifty people professed faith in Christ. God's blessing continued for many months, and Chapman attributed much of the results of these meetings to the intercession of Praying Hyde.

V. PRAYER

Father, how easy it is for us to attribute our successes to our own merits, and how that must grieve your heart! Help us to be realists in every way and to see that we are not here to glorify ourselves, but you. Thank you that you are faithful even when we are not. Amen.

VI. DEEPER DISCOVERIES

A. Like a Devouring Fire (9:3)

Moses encouraged Israel on the edge of the promised land by saying, "The LORD your God is the one who goes across ahead of you like a devouring fire. He will destroy [your enemies]; he will subdue them before you" (Deut. 9:3). The simile of a devouring or consuming fire often appears in Scripture as a picture of the judgment of God: "See, the Name of the LORD comes from afar, with burning anger and dense clouds of smoke; his lips are full of wrath, and his tongue is a consuming fire" (Isa. 30:27; cp. 30:30,33; 33:14; Nah. 1:5–6).

God's judgment may be temporal, in his present opposition to kings, nations, and individuals, or eternal at the great white throne (Rev. 20:11–15). The second coming of Christ is often spoken of in fiery terms: "This will happen when the Lord Jesus is revealed from heaven in blazing fire with his powerful angels. He will punish those who do not know God and do not obey the gospel of our Lord Jesus" (2 Thess. 1:7–8; cp. Isa. 66:15). The writer of Hebrews alludes to Deuteronomy 9:3 and 4:24 in exhorting Christians to live holy lives: "Therefore, since we are receiving a kingdom that cannot be shaken, let us be thankful, and so worship God acceptably with reverence and awe, for our 'God is a consuming fire'" (Heb. 12:28–29).

Many people who do not object to God judging Sodom and Gomorrah or the wickedness terminated by the flood of Noah still find fault with Israel's invasion of Canaan. The point of view of Deuteronomy, however, sees Israel as the divine instrument of wrath upon wickedness. That they had something to gain (a homeland) from the process is beside the point. There is no suggestion in Scripture that Israel was qualified morally to act in judgment against the Canaanites. In fact, Deuteronomy 9:4–6 expressly teaches that they were not. God sometimes uses dirty objects for his work simply because clean ones are not to be found.

B. Destruction (9:20)

Aaron, Moses' brother and the first high priest of Israel, acted unfaithfully and stupidly in fashioning the golden calf (see Exod. 32:1–6). In his defense, he may have considered the calf a vehicle for worshiping the true God (cp. Exod. 32:5), but he should have known better.

Discipline of believers to the point of death is not an uncommon subject in Scripture. The apostle John spoke of a category of sin that could lead to death: "If anyone sees his brother sinning a sin which does not lead to death, he will ask, and He will give him life for those who commit sin not leading to death. There is sin leading to death. I do not say that he should pray about that" (1 John 5:16 NKJV).

One believer at Corinth began an affair with his stepmother. When Paul heard of it, he determined to end this public embarrassment and "deliver such a one to Satan for the destruction of the flesh, that his spirit may be saved in the day of the Lord Jesus" (1 Cor. 5:5 NKJV).

When other Christians in Corinth began to drink excessively as part of their observance of the Lord's Supper, God was not amused. He began to afflict them bodily in various ways. Initially, the offending believers began to

Deuteronomy 9

experience weakness. When they still failed to repent, God sent sickness among them. Some were so obstinate in their participation in drunkenness at the Lord's Supper that he took their lives (1 Cor. 11:20–22,27–30).

The solution to this problem was and is repentance born of self-judgment: "If we judged ourselves, we would not come under judgment" (1 Cor. 11:31). Had Aaron considered what he was about to do, he would have resisted the will of the crowd and refused to cooperate in their idolatry. As it was, he narrowly escaped death, and then only by Moses' intercession. Christian intercessors can save the physical lives of disobedient believers.

VII. TEACHING OUTLINE

A. INTRODUCTION
1. Lead Story: Standing in the Gap
2. Context: God's promise to give Israel a homeland carried with it an implicit danger. They might easily conclude that God had given them the land of promise because they were so righteous.
3. Transition: All believers need to understand that God acts kindly toward us not because we are so good but because he is.

B. COMMENTARY
1. The Peril of Misunderstanding (9:1–6)
2. The Pattern of Rebellion (9:7–25)
3. The Prototype of Intercession (9:26–29)

C. CONCLUSION: PRAYING HYDE

VIII. ISSUES FOR DISCUSSION

1. Have you ever concluded that God was blessing you because of your goodness? Do you still think so?
2. Are there areas of your life now where you are behaving stubbornly? Could you benefit from intercessory prayer?
3. Do you think God was determined to destroy Israel and create a new nation from Moses' offspring? If he wasn't, why did he make such a suggestion to Moses?
4. In what ways did Moses fulfill the role of a faithful intercessor?
5. What are some of the barriers you find in your own prayer life to interceding for people in need?
6. How have you appealed to God on the basis of his reputation when interceding for others?

Deuteronomy 10

What God Wants

I. **INTRODUCTION**
Praying Hands

II. **COMMENTARY**
A verse-by-verse explanation of the chapter.

III. **CONCLUSION**
No Sacrifice

An overview of the principles and applications from the chapter.

IV. **LIFE APPLICATION**
Looking for Me

Melding the chapter to life.

V. **PRAYER**
Tying the chapter to life with God.

VI. **DEEPER DISCOVERIES**
Historical, geographical, and grammatical enrichment of the commentary.

VII. **TEACHING OUTLINE**
Suggested step-by-step group study of the chapter.

VIII. **ISSUES FOR DISCUSSION**
Zeroing the chapter in on daily life.

Deuteronomy 10

> **Quote**
>
> "If and when a horror turns up you will then be given Grace to help you. I don't think one is usually given it in advance. 'Give us our daily bread' (not an annuity for life) applies to spiritual gifts too; the little daily support for the daily trial. Life has to be taken day by day and hour by hour."
>
> C. S. Lewis

IN A NUTSHELL

Deuteronomy 10 finds Moses describing again for Israel the many expressions of God's grace they had enjoyed. His grace had been lavished upon them, and in return he sought a willing and constant allegiance and affection, expressed through obedience to his commandments.

What God Wants

I. INTRODUCTION

Praying Hands

Albrecht Dürer was named for his father and was one of a family of eighteen children that lived near Nürnberg, Germany, in the fifteenth century. Although the father of the family was a goldsmith, feeding a brood of so many children taxed his financial resources to the limit. Albrecht the elder was concerned especially about providing an education for his younger namesake and one of his brothers. The two boys had both given evidence of great artistic talent at a young age. Both wanted to become artists, but they also knew that their father would not be able to provide the needed training for both of them.

Finally it was decided that the two boys would toss a coin. The winner would go off to art school in Nürnberg for four years, and the other would go into the mines to help support his brother. At the end of four years, their roles would be reversed so that both could receive the training they needed. The newly trained artist could support his patient brother either by the sales of his art or by working in the mines.

Albrecht the younger won the toss and went off to school. His brother went into the mines and began the dangerous work that would support his brother's ambitions. To the family's delight, Albrecht's talent was immediately noticed at the academy. By the time he graduated, his artworks were already beginning to be sold for significant prices.

When he graduated, Albrecht returned home to a wonderful celebration. He received the praise of his family and friends and at the end of the meal lifted a glass to his brother, thanking him for the years of faithful support. Albrecht explained that he would now be glad to uphold his part of the bargain and work for four years to put his brother through the academy.

Sadly, his brother explained that it could never be. His artistic aspirations were finished. Four years in the mines and the onset of arthritis had made it impossible to him to hold a paintbrush easily. His hands were gnarled, painful, and unsteady. He would never become an artist.

Later, to pay homage to his brother, Albrecht Dürer drew his brother's mangled hands as they were raised in prayer. Those praying hands, so beautifully reproduced, remind the world that people rarely achieve their dreams alone, and that gratitude can and should produce beauty.

The Christian life is to be lived on the same principle. The standing we have before God is the product of the selfless work of another. The only

Deuteronomy 10:1–2

reasonable service of worship that we have is to live lives of beauty and offer ourselves to God daily as living sacrifices.

II. COMMENTARY

What God Wants

> **MAIN IDEA:** Moses recalls for Israel a long series of kindnesses that were the result of God's grace. These were designed to produce a wholehearted love of God and a life of obedience.

A What God Did: The Remembrance of God's Faithfulness (10:1–11)

> **SUPPORTING IDEA:** Israel had seen God provide for them and direct them for many years. They had benefited from the outpouring of his goodness.

10:1–2. Moses recalled for his people the results of his intercession for them after their disobedience at Mount Sinai. God accepted Moses' petitions to spare Israel and invited him to **chisel out two stone tablets** so God could renew the covenant with them. God's invitation to **come up to me on the mountain** makes it clear that he was no longer seeking Israel's destruction at the time this command was issued.

Moses was also told to **make a wooden chest**, a command not included in the original account in Exodus 34:1–9. Some critics have used this description to discredit the historical validity of the Deuteronomy account, but the easiest solution is simply to recognize that the accounts are supplementary. Moses at this stage of his ministry was not concerned to give a strict chronology, but he compressed his recollection of the events to single out the key point: God was renewing the broken covenant with Israel and insisting that the record of that covenant (at least in summary) should remain at the center of Israel's existence, **in the chest**, the ark of the covenant.

The Lord determined to **write on the tablets** of stone the original **words that were on the first tablets**, broken by Moses when he confronted the disobedient nation. God was not changing the terms of the covenant but reaffirming them as originally given, even to the point of personally rewriting them.

10:3. Although **the ark** was eventually refined and adorned by Bezalel (Exod. 37:1), Moses apparently originally crafted the box itself **out of acacia wood** so he could fulfill the Lord's command to deposit the **tablets** there. Contrary to Israel's lackluster adherence to divine commands, Moses was careful to do exactly what God had said. He **chiselled out** of **stone** tablets that were exactly **like the first ones**, and then **went up on the mountain** with those tablets ready to receive God's writing. (For more on the ark of the covenant, see "Deeper Discoveries.")

10:4–5. The LORD did as he had promised and **wrote** on the tablets **what he had written before**. Specifically, the Lord carved **the Ten Commandments**, the summary of what he wanted Israel to do as his people. Although the entire covenant included much of the last half of Exodus, all of Leviticus, and a good portion of Numbers, it could all be crystallized in these ten statements. These ten, in turn, were later summarized by Jesus in an even briefer fashion: "'Love the Lord your God with all your heart and with all your soul and with all your mind.' This is the first and greatest commandment. And the second is like it: 'Love your neighbour as yourself.' All the Law and the Prophets hang on these two commandments" (Matt. 22:37–40).

The Ten Commandments carried special weight with Israel because he **proclaimed** them to the nation **on the mountain, out of the fire**, on the day of that solemn assembly. When Moses received the newly rewritten tablets, he brought them **back down the mountain** and did **as the** LORD **had commanded**, placing the tablets into the ark that he had made. They had stayed there until the time that Moses was speaking, both as a testimony of God's grace, mercy, and faithfulness, and as a witness against Israel's rebellious behavior.

10:6–7. God's faithfulness went beyond the rewriting of the Ten Commandments and the renewal of the covenant. He also made provisions for the continuation and renewal of the Aaronic priesthood after **Aaron died**. God saw to it that **Eleazar his son succeeded him** in the priesthood.

As these events unfolded, the nation was provided for as well in its travels on the way to the staging area they now occupied. The exact locations mentioned in verses 6–7 are impossible to locate precisely, but at least some of them must have been located near the northern tip of the Gulf of Aqaba on the eastern arm of the Red Sea.

The Aaronic priesthood, as the Epistle to the Hebrews would later note, suffered from being carried out by men who were weak and sinful and who required replacement because of death. Later, the high priesthood of Christ would supersede that of Aaron (Heb. 5:1–10; 7:11–17). The Lord Jesus fulfilled the role of "one who has become a priest not on the basis of a regulation as to his ancestry but on the basis of the power of an indestructible life. For it is declared: 'You are a priest forever, in the order of Melchizedek'" (Heb. 7:16–17).

10:8. When Moses said **at that time** he leaped backward chronologically beyond the time of the death of Aaron to the episode of the golden calf. In the descriptions of that disgraceful event, the Levites were not mentioned until Moses came down from the mountain, and then they became the executioners of their kinsmen. Although they had been chosen for their role in worship long before (cp. Num. 3:5–4:49; 8:6–22; 18:1–7), their behavior at the base of Mount Sinai and their zeal for the Lord's purposes showed they were properly **set apart** to carry the symbol of God's holiness, **the ark of the covenant**. As Moses spoke, those same Levites were continuing **to stand before the LORD to minister and to pronounce blessings in his name** because of their faithfulness, which was all the more marked because their high priest, Aaron, had acted unfaithfully during this same episode.

10:9. The special position of **the Levites** appeared as well in their having **no share or inheritance** in the land of promise itself. Instead of material goods, **the LORD** himself was to be **their inheritance**.

By making their reward their closeness to God rather than material benefits, God declared to Israel and to us the highest of all values in his thinking. To know God and to find one's full satisfaction in that knowledge is the ultimate goal of Christian experience. The Lord's greatest delight comes when his people discover that ultimate value lies in the knowledge of God. Nothing in the material world can compete with the delights that are present in his person.

10:10–11. Moses had **stayed on the mountain** with the Lord for a second time, interceding for his rebellious and wayward countrymen. Perhaps to Moses' amazement, **the LORD listened to** his appeals on this occasion, since **it was not his will to destroy** Israel in spite of their unfaithful behavior. By way of assurance to Moses (and through him to the whole nation), he instructed the prophet to **lead the people on their way**. His avowals that they should **enter and possess the land** promised **to their fathers** were still in force.

B What God Wants: The Results of God's Faithfulness (10:12–22)

SUPPORTING IDEA: *In view of God's persistent grace, Israel should abandon their stubbornness and instead fear, love, and obey God at all times.*

10:12–13. Since God had provided for Israel's every need, it stood to reason that he expected something in return. Moses put the issue to his people in the form of a question: What was God asking of them as they stood across the Jordan River from the land he had promised to give them?

In this first summary of the proper response to grace, the Lord was asking Israel to place him at the core of their lives. They should **fear** him, **walk in all his ways**, . . . **love him**, **serve** him wholeheartedly, and **observe** his **commands**. In short, he was asking them for their hearts.

Since Israel owed Yahweh their very lives, his requests seemed little to ask, especially since the commands he was giving them were designed **for their good**. There is never a conflict of interest when it comes to godly living.

God asks nothing of anyone that would require them to act contrary to their best interests. Even those who are asked in the course of things to give their physical lives for their beliefs are trading transitory comforts for an eternity of joy.

10:14–15. Along with these general requests, Moses added a specific expectation—submission to God's ways. As a preface, he reminded Israel that Yahweh owned **the heavens, even the highest heavens, the earth and everything in it**. For unexplained reasons he **set his affection** on Israel's **forefathers and loved them**. Going even further, **he chose** the members of that generation, the **descendants** of those forefathers, **above all the nations**. He favored them with his personal attention, performing miracles and acts of power to rescue them from bondage and to give them a better life and an eternal hope.

10:16. Because of God's choice of Israel and his expressions of grace toward them, they should **circumcise** their **hearts** and **be stiff-necked no longer**. The first expression suggests inner rather than mere outer conformity to the terms of the covenant.

The second expression, being *stiff-necked,* appears throughout Scripture as a picture of stubbornness (cp. Job 9:4; 2 Chr. 30:8; 36:13; Neh. 9:16–17,29; Jer. 7:26; 17:23; 19:15). Thus Moses called for repentance from their present condition of spiritual stubbornness.

10:17–18. Moses added a second specific request for a change in Israel's behavior. Not only should Israel drop its stubborn and wayward attitudes; they should manifest their repentance in their treatment of the aliens that would soon be coming into their midst.

Setting the stage for this demand, Moses rebuked their spiritual indifference by describing God as the **God of gods and Lord of lords**. These words do not acknowledge the objective reality of other deities but their subjective reality in the minds and hearts of lost people. God takes the point of view in Scripture that no problem can be addressed adequately until it is first acknowledged. God must on occasion blast before he can rebuild.

Unlike these pagan deities, Moses explained, the God of Israel **shows no partiality and accepts no bribes**. He expects righteous behavior, and he has a right to see it among his people. Israel could not hope to please him unless they recognized that he defended **the cause of the fatherless and the widow**, those who had no other defender. He also loved **the alien** and provided his **food and clothing**.

10:19. As a result of God's affection for aliens, Israel was to follow suit. If God's own example should prove insufficient to motivate them, they need only remember their own plight when they were **aliens in Egypt**. Israel knew the empty feeling of being outsiders in a strange place. When others found

Deuteronomy 10:20–22

themselves in a similar predicament in Israel, the people of God should show compassion and **love**.

10:20–22. The chapter concludes with a second summary of God's expectations. Israel was to **fear the LORD** and **serve him**. His people were to **hold fast to him and take** their **oaths in his name**. His name was always to be held in reverence and should become the object of their **praise** since he had performed **great and awesome wonders** for them, miracles that they **saw** with their **own eyes**.

Not the least of his actions on their behalf was his multiplication of the nation. When Jacob took his family into Egypt to escape the famine, they numbered only **seventy** people, and by the time Moses spoke, they had become like **the stars in the sky**. In the divine frame of reference, what God has done for his people is always the basis of what they do for him. Grace is always given freely by God, but grace received should always issue in a joyous delight in him.

> **MAIN IDEA REVIEW:** Moses recalls for Israel a long series of kindnesses that were the result of God's grace. These were designed to produce a wholehearted love of God and a life of obedience.

III. CONCLUSION

No Sacrifice

The average person in the Western world knows the name of David Livingstone only because of Henry Stanley's famous statement, "Dr. Livingstone, I presume." During his lifetime, however, Livingstone was arguably the world's best-known missionary. By the time Stanley caught up with Livingstone, he had been in Africa for many years and had known a life filled with hardship. A lion had attacked him, leaving his left arm virtually useless. He had been through countless confrontations with hostile tribes and had lost his wife to a fever. In fact, he had lost almost everything that a man can lose while serving Christ.

While on a brief visit to England, he was once asked by a group of students to reflect on his losses. He answered:

> For my own part, I have never ceased to rejoice that God has appointed me to such an office. People talk of the sacrifice I have made in spending so much of my life in Africa. . . . Is that a sacrifice which brings its own blest reward in healthful activity, the consciousness of doing good, peace of mind, and a bright hope of glorious destiny hereafter? Away with the word in such a view, and with such a

thought! It is emphatically no sacrifice. Say rather it is a privilege. Anxiety, sickness, suffering, or danger, now and then, with a foregoing of the common conveniences and charities of this life, may make us pause, and cause the spirit to waver, and the soul to sink; but let this only be for a moment. All these are nothing when compared with the glory which shall be revealed in and for us. I never made a sacrifice.

The heart that delights in God and longs only to see his glory advance will seldom be conscious of sacrifice. God in his wisdom asks that we first love him and then live in keeping with that core value. He does not want his people to think of what they do as sacrificial, even though from the world's point of view it may be just that. Gratitude for the grace of God will always be found near the center of the biblical Christian's most powerful motivations.

PRINCIPLES

- Just as the ark rested in the center of Israel's camp, God wants his Word to form the center of the believer's life.
- The most blessed gift that God can give any person is a knowledge of himself.
- Fear of God and love for God coexist happily in the heart of people who are rightly related to him.
- God's commandments not only reflect his holiness; they promote our happiness.

APPLICATIONS

- Make a list of five ways God has demonstrated his faithfulness in your life.
- Ask God to help you open a conversation with someone who doesn't know him. Share one or two points of the list you made with that person.
- Write a letter (or an E-mail) to someone important to you and share one or two points of your list.
- Do a frank assessment of your attitude about a point of recurring disobedience in your life. Do you believe that God gave you that troublesome commandment for your good?

Deuteronomy 10

IV. LIFE APPLICATION

Looking for Me

An evangelist once described his mother as a woman characterized by great love for people. As an example he recalled the childhood memory of finding her serving a meal to an old tramp. She had gone shopping and encountered the unfortunate man and invited him home for a warm meal.

As he was enjoying his lunch, her guest looked at his hostess and said, "I wish there were more people like you in the world."

The evangelist's mother answered, "Oh, there are; you just have to look for them."

The man shook his head at her remark: "But, lady, I didn't need to look for you. You looked for me."

The people of God ought to be characterized by their initiative in moving in the direction of the unlovely. Jesus sought out the sick, the maimed, the lame, the bruised, the brokenhearted, the wretched wanderer, the poor, and the forgotten. We are supposed to be imitators of him. Even if all we have to offer is a warm meal, we can do it in his name.

V. PRAYER

Father, make us people who declare through our lives and words that knowing you is the supreme value. Help us be lovers of the unlovely and people who remember when we were lost and separated from you. Help us exhibit the grace of gratitude. Amen.

VI. DEEPER DISCOVERIES

A. Ark of the Covenant (10:3)

God instructed Moses to place the two tablets of stone with the Ten Commandments inscribed in the ark of the covenant. The ark was a small chest forty-five inches long by twenty-seven inches wide and high. Today we would call it a "chest," and at the time the first English translations were done in the sixteenth century, *ark* was a commonly used word to describe a small chest. The Hebrew word used in Deuteronomy 10:3, *aron*, differs from the word used in Genesis 7 to describe the ark (*teva*) of Noah. The second word means "a chest designed to float," and is also used of the basket into which Moses was placed (Exod. 2:2–5 NKJV). Because the ark of the covenant contained the tablets of stone, it was sometimes called the ark of the testimony (cp.

Exod. 25:22). The tablets were a testimony of God's involvement in the life of his people, and they were also a testimony of their unfaithfulness toward him.

The lid of the ark was known as the *mercy seat* (NIV "atonement cover"). It was decorated by figures of angels known as cherubim and served as the location where sacrificial blood was applied once a year on the Day of Atonement (cp. Lev. 16). The symbolism of the ark prefigures the work of Christ in that God looked down on the broken law through the atoning blood of his Son.

B. The Tribe of Levi (10:8)

The Levites were not all priests. Only the family of Aaron actually served inside the tabernacle (and later the temple). The other portions of the tribe of Levi, however, carried the ark and the other tabernacle furnishings during the wilderness journeys. Later, they engaged in a variety of assignments in the temple, all in connection with its worship procedures and sacrifices.

VII. TEACHING OUTLINE

A. INTRODUCTION

1. Lead Story: Praying Hands
2. Context: Although God promised to forgive Israel for their spiritual waywardness, the inner characteristics that spawned that waywardness were still present among them. They needed repentance and an inner commitment to love God supremely and exclusively.
3. Transition: All believers can increase their commitment to God by reflecting on his faithfulness and by considering the forms such commitment should assume in their experience.

B. COMMENTARY

1. What God Did: The Remembrance of God's Faithfulness (10:1–11)
2. What God Wants: The Results of God's Faithfulness (10:12–22)

C. CONCLUSION: NO SACRIFICE

VIII. ISSUES FOR DISCUSSION

1. Why do you think that holiness and happiness are often regarded as opposites today—or at least as incompatible?
2. Do you think God still administers justice for the fatherless and the widow? How does he do this?

Deuteronomy 10

3. Who are the "aliens" that you come in contact with? How can you "love the alien"?
4. Could God with justification accuse you of being "stiff-necked" in any area of your life? What is the cure for such a spiritual condition?
5. God "separated" the tribe of Levi to minister to him. What kind of separation is necessary in order to serve God faithfully?

Deuteronomy 11

The Choice Is Ours

I. **INTRODUCTION**
Great Is Thy Faithfulness

II. **COMMENTARY**
A verse-by-verse explanation of the chapter.

III. **CONCLUSION**
Missing the Obvious
An overview of the principles and applications from the chapter.

IV. **LIFE APPLICATION**
Storing Real Treasure
Melding the chapter to life.

V. **PRAYER**
Tying the chapter to life with God.

VI. **DEEPER DISCOVERIES**
Historical, geographical, and grammatical enrichment of the commentary.

VII. **TEACHING OUTLINE**
Suggested step-by-step group study of the chapter.

VIII. **ISSUES FOR DISCUSSION**
Zeroing the chapter in on daily life.

Deuteronomy 11

> ### Quote
>
> "All men seek happiness. This is without exception. Whatever different means they employ, they all tend to this end. The cause of some going to war, and of others avoiding it, is the same desire in both, attended with different views. The will never takes the least step but to this object. This is the motive of every action of every man, even of those who hang themselves."
>
> Blaise Pascal

IN A NUTSHELL

In Deuteronomy 11, God offers Israel a choice: either a life of productivity and enjoyment made possible by obedience to him, or a life of difficulty and opposition made necessary by disobedience. The happiness Israel desires can only be theirs by being properly related to him.

The Choice Is Ours

I. INTRODUCTION

Great Is Thy Faithfulness

Christians often sing one of the great hymns of the faith entitled "Great Is Thy Faithfulness":

> Great is thy faithfulness,
> Great is thy faithfulness,
> Morning by morning
> New mercies I see.
> All I have needed
> Thy hand hath provided;
> Great is thy faithfulness,
> Lord, unto me.

You may have sung this hymn without realizing that the writer did not invent those phrases; he was merely quoting Scripture—quoting the prophet Jeremiah, in fact. What is noteworthy about those words is that when Jeremiah wrote them he was not celebrating a great victory of the people of God but reflecting on the greatest defeat in the nation's history. He was looking at the city of Jerusalem as it lay in ruins following the terrible destruction brought on it by the army of Babylon. He wrote, "Because of the Lord's great love we are not consumed, for his compassions never fail. They are new every morning; great is your faithfulness" (Lam. 3:22–23).

The walls were broken down, the gates and the homes were burned, the people had been carted off into servitude, and Jerusalem lay in ruins. The temple of God was destroyed and its furnishings were taken away to Babylon to be used in drinking parties to honor pagan deities. Yet Jeremiah could muse on the faithfulness of God through it all.

It is a faithful God who chastens and disciplines his people when they need it. Man may vacillate, but the God of heaven is always faithful, and his faithfulness doesn't depend on us. We may do our worst, but he remains faithful to his own character. God's faithfulness to Israel was exhibited as much by their removal to Babylon—in fulfillment of his promise to discipline them for waywardness—as by their return seventy years later (also foretold by Jeremiah).

Interestingly, "Great Is Thy Faithfulness" was written not by a pastor or evangelist but by an insurance salesman, Thomas Chisholm. His writing was not provoked by any great crisis in his life, as many hymns are; he simply was overwhelmed one day as he sat meditating on the unfailing kindness of God in his life. He wrote the words to the hymn and sent them to a friend, William Runyan, who set them to music. The church has been singing this great expression of faith ever since.

Of course, it is far better to experience the faithfulness of God in the form of blessing rather than in discipline. That is always the choice that believers face, and especially so with Israel as they stood ready to invade the promised land.

II. COMMENTARY

The Choice Is Ours

MAIN IDEA: *Before addressing the specific stipulations that will come with living inside the land, Moses addresses again the issue of Israel's motivation. He declares the potential blessings and rewards that can be theirs and how their success is tied to their faithfulness to God.*

A Where Obedience Lands: The Objective (11:1–25)

SUPPORTING IDEA: *The land that God is providing his people is highly desirable and better than what they left behind in Egypt.*

11:1. The first twenty-five verses of the chapter alternate between commands to love God and reasons for doing so. Verse 1 could be invoked as a summary of the entire chapter, with its emphasis upon **love** for God and obedience to **his requirements, his decrees, his laws and his commands**.

11:2–4. So Israel would be motivated to obey God, Moses turned in verses 2–7 to the issue of motivation. He urged them to remember as they prepared to invade the land that their own eyes had seen what God could do. **His majesty, his mighty hand, his outstretched arm** became visible to them personally through what God did in humbling **Pharaoh king of Egypt** and **his whole country**. He executed **discipline** upon not only the leaders of Egypt but upon **the Egyptian army** with **its horses and chariots**. He brought the **waters of the Red Sea** against them as they were **pursuing** Israel and **brought lasting ruin** on Israel's enemies as a result. The people whom Moses was addressing did not know this second hand from their **children**, but on the strength of their experience. As a result, they were responsible for paying heed to God's truth and obeying it faithfully.

11:5–7. God operates on the principle that spiritual privilege creates spiritual obligation: "From everyone who has been given much, much will be demanded; and from the one who has been entrusted with much, much more will be asked" (Luke 12:48). Israel was being asked for a great deal, but they were in a position to do what God expected. After all, they did not know him by reputation from accounts given them by their **children**. They **saw** what God did for them in the desert right up until the day they arrived east of the Jordan River. Knowing his power and faithfulness so directly ought to encourage them to live faithfully before him and trust him for their needs.

At the very least, what they saw should keep them far from any form of rebellion. They saw what God did in the case of **Dathan and Abiram** and their companion Korah (who is not mentioned here). Numbers 16 records how these three men, along with 250 others, led a rebellion against Moses and Aaron. They complained that others were as qualified as Moses and Aaron to approach God in the tabernacle, and they demanded an equal participation in the priesthood. Korah was at least a Levite; but Dathan and Abiram were sons of a **Reubenite** man and not even from the priestly tribe.

God dealt severely with this rebellion when **the earth opened its mouth . . . and swallowed them up with their households, their tents and every living thing that belonged to them**. The point of this dramatic act of discipline was to produce a godly fear in the hearts of those whose eyes **saw all these great things**.

11:8. In the pattern of much of this chapter, Moses called the people to **observe . . . the commands** that he was giving them. Failure to do so would put Israel at risk, and they might not have **the strength to go in and take over the land** that they had been promised. God's promises of success include conditions of obedience even while they are being fulfilled. Believers who engage in putting to death the deeds of their bodies (Rom. 8:13) cannot realistically hope to accomplish that objective without his help.

11:9–10. God wanted Israel to **live long in the land**, a land said to be **flowing with milk and honey**. The promised land was **not like the land of Egypt**. Instead of being generally productive, Egypt was fertile only along the banks of the Nile River. The vast bulk of the land was arid and useless.

11:11–12. By contrast, the land that Israel was about to receive was a land of **mountains and valleys** and depended for its water on the **rain from heaven**. Because of its dependence on rain, the promised land was a place closely observed by **the eyes of the LORD**. The rains in the Holy Land fall during a brief period of the year, but the limestone subsoil captures a great deal of the rainfall and holds it in underground reservoirs that can be accessed by drilling.

11:13. The refrain of this summary section again appears, urging Israel to **faithfully obey the commands** that Moses was issuing. Specifically, he called on the nation to **love the LORD** and to **serve him** without reservation. Only in so doing would they find the full blessedness that awaited them.

11:14–15. When Israel obeyed, God promised to **send rain** on the land in the proper **season**. The seasons are specified: **autumn and spring rains**. Rain

Deuteronomy 11:16–17

is seldom seen in Palestine between late March and October. The autumn or early rains permit the ground to be plowed and permit harvests of **grain**. The spring or latter rains permit the harvesting of **new wine and oil**. The two periods of rain together provide grass in the fields so that cattle may be fed. Together, God's provision of rain would permit his people to **eat and be satisfied**.

11:16–17. While God's faithfulness was assured, Israel's was not. In fact, the regularity of the rain and the fertility of the soil might lead his people astray. They might, in fact, be **enticed to turn away and worship other gods**. They could make no greater mistake, for in so doing they would experience **the LORD's anger** against themselves instead of their enemies. Instead of enjoying abundant rainfall, Israel would discover how God would **shut the heavens** so that it would not rain. In turn, the ground would prove unfruitful, and the people would perish. Knowing this in advance through God's repeated warnings, they could prevent this horrible possibility if they would only **be careful**. The suggestion of these words (occurring fifteen times in Deuteronomy) is that more serious blunders occur through neglect than through overt rebellion. People are captured in their sins through inattention, but they are held there through its intrinsic power.

11:18. Being careful meant just that—taking the time and exercising care so that **these words** of God, spoken through Moses, would not be forgotten in the daily routines of life. The best location for them would be in the **hearts and minds** of God's people. Scripture memory programs thus are as old as the Book of Deuteronomy.

11:19–21. These verses are almost an exact repetition of the material in Deuteronomy 6:7–9. God's Word was to be perpetuated through Israel's generations. Parents were to **teach them** in structured ways to their children. They must reinforce such formal instruction by **talking about** God's commandments in informal ways: **when you sit at home and when you walk along the road, when you lie down and when you get up** (see the earlier commentary on 6:7–9). The purpose of this preoccupation with God's truth was to ensure that **the days** of the present generation and the days of their children **may be many in the land**.

11:22–25. Moses closed this large section comprising the general stipulations—the motivational section, if you will—of the covenant (Deut. 5–11) with a summary of all that is contained in these seven chapters. Israel's future success hung upon a critical condition. **If and only if the people would carefully observe** the commands that he was giving them, they would conquer the land. Those commands are summarized under three headings: affection, obedience, and loyalty. They must **love the LORD . . . walk in all his ways and . . . hold fast to him** personally. **Then** they could be sure that the **nations** then occupying the land, although they were **larger and stronger**, would fall before them.

The extent of Israel's success would be determined by the extent of Israel's holy boldness. Every place they would choose to set their foot would eventually be theirs. The territory they had been promised was extensive, running from **the desert** in the south **to Lebanon** in the north, and from **the Euphrates River** in the east to the **western** (what today is called the Mediterranean) **sea**. Although these large areas contained many enemies, **no man would be able to stand against** Israel. Some they would defeat in battle, and others would flee because of God's placing **the terror and fear** of Israel in the hearts of their enemies.

B Where Obedience Leads: The Alternatives (11:26–32)

SUPPORTING IDEA: *Israel's enjoyment of the land is contingent on their behavior. Blessings or curses lie before them; the choice is theirs.*

11:26–28. In this brief section, Moses set forth the options: **a blessing** or **a curse** upon Israel. The former would follow Israel's obedience to God's commands; the latter, their disobedience. **The curse** would be theirs in particular if they turned from the way that God commanded and pursued other gods. Moses cautioned God's people about the dangers of an unbridled curiosity. The practices and ceremonies of pagan deities sometimes contained attractions that would provoke Israel's interest. They were to turn away from such things and hold to Yahweh only.

11:29–30. The choice that lay before Israel was so crucial that God gave orders to formalize the two options once Israel had gained possession of the land. Moses instructed that the entire nation gather to **proclaim** the blessings and the curses on two mountains that stood adjacent to each other: **Mount Gerizim** (for the blessings) and **Mount Ebal** (for the curses). (The instructions given here appear again in Deuteronomy 27 in greater detail.)

These two mountains were **across** (i.e., west of) **the Jordan** and **west of the road**. The road was probably the north-south thoroughfare that linked Jericho with Beth Shan and pointed northward, a road that followed the general course of the Jordan River.

11:31–32. Israel was **about to cross the Jordan to enter and take possession** of the land. Once that had happened, the invitation should go out to all the tribes to gather for a great scene of covenant renewal in keeping with **all the decrees and laws** that Moses was giving Israel. Gathering the tribes would give an opportunity for Israel to rejoice together in the possession of

Deuteronomy 11:31–32

their new homeland and to participate in the solemn ritual of blessings and cursings that would remind them of their covenant obligations.

> **MAIN IDEA REVIEW:** Before addressing the specific stipulations that will come with living inside the land, Moses addresses again the issue of Israel's motivation. He declares the potential blessings and rewards that can be theirs, and how their success is tied to their faithfulness to God.

III. CONCLUSION

Missing the Obvious

Sherlock Holmes and Dr. Watson once went to the mountains on a camping trip. After enjoying a delicious meal, they retired for the night. Around midnight, Holmes awoke and nudged his faithful companion.

"Watson," he said, "look up at the sky and tell me what you see."

Watson, used to Holmes's tests of his observational acumen, observed, "I see millions and millions of stars."

Holmes asked, "What does that tell you?"

Watson pondered for a minute. "Well . . . astronomically, it tells me that there are millions of galaxies and potentially billions of planets. Astrologically, I observe that Saturn is in Leo. Horologically, I deduce that the time is approximately a quarter past three. Theologically, I can see that God is omnipotent and that we are small and insignificant. Meteorologically, I suspect that we will have a beautiful day tomorrow. What does it tell you, Holmes?"

Holmes was silent for a minute, then said, "Watson, someone has stolen our tent."

The world, like Watson, seems to have great difficulty with the obvious. God has built certain consequences into life so we might recognize his authority and power. Numerous scientific studies have documented how people live longer when they live better. Righteousness is good for a person's health.

For example, one magazine offered the findings of a study done at a research center on the University of Michigan campus. The authors of the study concluded that doing regular volunteer work significantly increases life expectancy. Doctors rated it a more important factor than jogging, aerobics, or a healthy diet.

During World War II, it was discovered that people who were suffering from acute anxiety attacks during bombing raids on London improved their condition by setting their own troubles aside and volunteering to help the victims of the German air raids. In helping others, they helped themselves.

Conclusion

An ancient legend recalls the story of a man who was a slave. One day, this downtrodden man met a genie who offered him one wish along with a warning to be careful what he wished for.

The slave decided that he wanted to be the object of servanthood rather than a participant in it. He said, "I wish that I could be waited on hand and foot and have my every longing satisfied." His wish was granted. For three months slaves catered to his every desire.

However, by that time the ex-slave had begun to tire of people jumping each time he snapped his fingers; he had become profoundly bored, and he decided to go looking for the genie in the hopes of having his wish reversed.

Finding the genie, he complained, "Can I have my old life back? I'd rather be in hell than sit around waiting for others to do everything for me."

The genie's response was quick and telling: "Where do you think you've been for the last ninety days?"

PRINCIPLES

- Spiritual strength is connected to faithful obedience to God's commands.
- God supplies the needs of his people according to their needs but does not ordinarily allow stockpiling.
- The worship of false gods is always an outgrowth of spiritual deception.
- Since the success of believers is tied to our knowledge of and obedience to God's Word, the memorizing of portions of the Bible is advisable.

APPLICATIONS

- List two or three areas in which you could do better at obeying God. Use a topical Bible to find passages that address those areas and spend some time reflecting on them.
- Pick one or two of those passages and commit them to memory this week.
- Think of episodes in your life in which you have seen God's unmistakable hand at work. Thank him for those examples of his faithfulness.
- Pray for a believer you know who is facing difficulty morally or theologically. Ask God to help you minister to that person.

IV. LIFE APPLICATION

Storing Real Treasure

Moses urged Israel, "Fix these words of mine in your hearts and minds; tie them as symbols on your hands and bind them on your foreheads" (Deut. 11:18). His words argue for not merely reading the Scriptures, but for memorizing and meditating on them as well.

This emphasis is a consistent theme throughout the Bible. Joshua was told to meditate on God's law, which would produce success in his life: "Do not let this Book of the Law depart from your mouth; meditate on it day and night, so that you may be careful to do everything written in it. Then you will be prosperous and successful" (Josh. 1:8).

David memorized Scripture and recognized it as a key to walking with God: "I have hidden your word in my heart that I might not sin against you" (Ps. 119:11). He knew that memorization was the doorway to constant meditation and all the benefits associated with it: "But [the godly person's] delight is in the law of the LORD, and on his law he meditates day and night" (Ps. 1:2). Fixing God's Word on the heart and mind is both preventative and corrective. Because our values change to conform with Scripture, we become less inclined to engage in foolish and sinful practices. At the same time, God will use Scripture to help us realize it when our actions are not pleasing to him.

V. PRAYER

Father, teach us the joys of loving you and others. Help us to avoid the world's lie that happiness consists of getting our way. Allow us the true fulfillment that you offer—fulfillment that comes from loving others and serving them. In the process, let us bear witness to your reality and goodness. Amen.

VI. DEEPER DISCOVERIES

A. Shut the Heavens (11:17)

God warned Israel that worshiping other gods would cause him to discipline them by means of diminished rainfall (Deut. 11:17). This warning became a reality during the prophetic ministry of Elijah, who came to King Ahab and declared, "As the LORD, the God of Israel, lives, whom I serve, there will be neither dew nor rain in the next few years except at my word" (1 Kgs. 17:1).

Elijah knew that God had promised to withhold the rain if Israel should defect. He could not tell, of course, the exact timing in which such discipline would be inaugurated. That required a prophetic revelation, which he undoubtedly received. In spite of the warning, however, and in spite of the remarkable ministry of the prophet, the danger to Israel became a reality when they perished from the land in 722 B.C. as a result of the Assyrian invasion.

The threat of missing rainfall is given a new use in Zechariah. In describing the age to come and the conditions following the second coming of Christ, the prophet declared: "If any of the peoples of the earth do not go up to Jerusalem to worship the King, the LORD Almighty, they will have no rain" (Zech. 14:17).

B. Gerizim and Ebal (11:29)

These twin mountains of blessing and cursing lay on Palestine's central mountain ridge. Both mountains are about three thousand feet in height, and the area between them forms a natural amphitheater. Joshua would later gather the tribes to fulfill Moses' command to have the blessings and curses read to the nation. The area was rich in Hebrew history.

This area near the little village of Shechem was the first stop Abraham made inside Palestine, and the place where the land first became promised: "Abram traveled through the land as far as the site of the great tree of Moreh at Shechem. At that time the Canaanites were in the land. The LORD appeared to Abram and said, 'To your offspring I will give this land.' So he built an altar there to the LORD, who had appeared to him" (Gen. 12:6–7).

In addition, Jacob lived in the area around the two mountains for a time. The patriarch bought a piece of property adjacent to the town of Shechem and built an altar there (Gen. 33:19–20). He also apparently dug a well, the same one used by Jesus centuries later (John 4:6). Even as they came to the edge of the promised land, the people of Israel were bearing Joseph's bones, dug up in order to be carried back to the land at his own request (Gen. 50:25; cp. Exod. 13:19; Heb. 11:22). They would be buried in the same plot of ground that Jacob had bought near Shechem.

VII. TEACHING OUTLINE

A. INTRODUCTION

1. Lead Story: Great Is Thy Faithfulness
2. Context: Moses places before Israel the choices open to them: for obedience, blessing; for rebellion, discipline.
3. Transition: Believers face the same set of choices. By keeping us conscious of his power to make our lives easy or difficult, God helps us recognize our dependence and his greatness.

Deuteronomy 11

B. COMMENTARY
1. Where Obedience Lands: The Objective (11:1–25)
2. Where Obedience Leads: The Alternatives (11:26–32)

C. CONCLUSION: STORING REAL TREASURE

VIII. ISSUES FOR DISCUSSION

1. What are some of the methods of deception that Satan uses to draw people into spiritual error?
2. Why do you suppose God gives his people strength only at the moment of need rather than allowing them to stockpile it?
3. Have you ever experienced God "shutting off the rain" in your own life? Explain.
4. What are some examples of divine curses that you have seen (or suspected) that resulted from failure to obey God?
5. Have you ever observed what you considered to be a clear case of divine discipline for disobedience in the lives of others? What did you learn from it?

Deuteronomy 12

Only One Way

I. **INTRODUCTION**
Bathed in Mystery

II. **COMMENTARY**
A verse-by-verse explanation of the chapter.

III. **CONCLUSION**
Godly Attachments
An overview of the principles and applications from the chapter.

IV. **LIFE APPLICATION**
No Tools Allowed
Melding the chapter to life.

V. **PRAYER**
Tying the chapter to life with God.

VI. **DEEPER DISCOVERIES**
Historical, geographical, and grammatical enrichment of the commentary.

VII. **TEACHING OUTLINE**
Suggested step-by-step group study of the chapter.

VIII. **ISSUES FOR DISCUSSION**
Zeroing the chapter in on daily life.

Quote

"Worship is the submission of all our nature to God. It is the quickening of conscience by His holiness; the nourishment of mind with His truth; the purifying of imagination by His beauty; the opening of the heart to His love; the surrender of will to His purpose—and all of this gathered up in adoration, the most selfless emotion of which our nature is capable and therefore the chief remedy for that self-centeredness which is our original sin and the source of all actual sin."

William Temple

Deuteronomy 12

IN A NUTSHELL

Deuteronomy 12 declares that Israel will not be free to adapt the old pagan systems to their worship of Yahweh. On the contrary, they must obliterate the local shrines. Once they control the land, God will specify a particular city to serve as the home of their central sanctuary.

Only One Way

I. INTRODUCTION

Bathed in Mystery

One of the central teachings of the Bible is the tri-unity of God, a being who is one in essence yet subsists in three persons. The universe provides no precise parallel to this, although it does contain hints. In their book *Worship: Rediscovering the Missing Jewel,* Ron Allen and Gordon Borror wrote:

> Consider the biblical teaching about the essence of God. He is one God, three persons. Throughout the ages this concept has caused no end of confusion and frustration to theologian and layman alike. Much has been written and said about this eternal truth. But by no available means is it more beautifully expressed than in the music of Bach's trio sonatas for organ. Musicians through the years have marveled at the artistic excellence of these works. They have one melody in the right hand, one melody in the left, and yet another in the pedal line—all sounding at once, each retaining its own identity, yet together forming beautiful harmony. The composer intended this to be an expression, a tonal picture, of the eternal mystery of the Godhead.

While some profess to find such matters disconcerting, it is worth asking whether finite beings have a right to expect God to conform to the limits of their intelligence. If God should be fully understandable and totally predictable, he would not be the infinite God of the Scriptures.

Mortimer Adler came at last to realize this. Adler was one of America's most learned men. The editor of the Great Books series, he advocated the teaching of the classics, opposing the pragmatism of John Dewey that proved such an enormous influence in American education. He thought of himself as a philosopher for the common man, and he championed the idea that truth and values are absolute and unchanging.

Adler was unusual in many ways, not the least of which was his educational accomplishments. He was one of the few people in history to obtain a Ph.D. degree without obtaining a high school diploma or a bachelor's degree. When only fifteen, he dropped out of school to go to work as the secretary of a New York City newspaper. Two years later, while reading Plato for his own pleasure, he determined that he would become a philosopher and enrolled in Columbia University. He finished the four-year program of study in only three years, but he didn't graduate because he would not attend physical education classes or take a required swimming test.

Nonetheless, he obtained a faculty appointment and five years later finished the Ph.D. program (he in time would be awarded ten honorary doctorates). Moving to the University of Chicago, Adler began an extensive writing and lecturing career and made a special investment of effort in popularizing the great books and ideas of Western civilization. He eventually became chairman of the board of editors of the *Encyclopaedia Britannica*.

Although for most of his life he rejected any connection with revealed religion, he eventually became a practicing Christian, claiming that he did so for the very reason that others reject the faith—because only Christianity respected the fact that God at his core was not fully understandable. Adler in his faith recognized that God reserved at the center of Christianity a series of mysteries that he made no effort to explain.

God must be permitted to make the rules when it comes to his own unveiling of himself. As he sought to teach Israel, he must be approached on his own terms.

II. COMMENTARY

Only One Way

MAIN IDEA: *Israel must be careful from the very beginning to worship God properly and on his terms. Those terms include the destruction of the existing pagan system of worship.*

A How False Worship Must End (12:1–4)

SUPPORTING IDEA: *Israel had no more important priority in the settlement of the land than the destruction of the existing worship system.*

12:1. This verse marks a major turning point in Deuteronomy. Chapters 5–11 dealt with general stipulations of the covenant—the motivation for obedience once Israel conquered the land. Beginning here, Moses expounded the specific stipulations of the covenant, building on the motivations of the previous chapters. Verse 1 provides an introduction to the new section, which details **the decrees and laws** Israel **must be careful to follow** once they are **in the land**. These stipulations would apply as long as they were there inside the land God had promised. Moses began by explaining how worship would be carried on once the land was secured.

12:2. Verse 2 gives the general procedure. Before genuine worship could be established by the people of God, the competing pagan systems must be obliterated. The Canaanites typically used **places on the high mountains and**

hills and under every spreading tree to establish their altars. God insisted that Israel destroy these places.

12:3. Verse 3 provides the specific steps that would be used to carry out the general procedure. Moses issued four imperatives, each applying to a different form of pagan ritual. Israel was to **break down** their worship **altars**. The **sacred stones**, which may have been male fertility symbols, were to be smashed (cp. Deut. 7:5; Exod. 23:24; 34:13). The **Asherah poles**, representations of Baal's female consort, Asherah, were to be burned. Other **idols** were to be **cut down** in an effort to **wipe out** the names of the deities from those shrines.

12:4. Finally, Moses gave the rationale for such a process. Israel was not to imitate any pagan system. Just as their God was beyond comparison to any false deity, so must their worship system be. Israel must not worship even the right God in the wrong **way**, the way of the nations they were to drive out of the land.

B Where True Worship Begins (12:5–14)

SUPPORTING IDEA: *Worshiping God's way will require Israel to seek out the place that God would choose. All worship should take place at this central sanctuary.*

12:5–6. Israel had been worshiping at a tabernacle, a portable shrine that could be taken apart, marched some distance, and then reassembled. Once they were in the land, the tabernacle would eventually be replaced by a temple (although this word does not appear in the narrative). The city that would serve as the headquarters of Israel's future worship was not specified by name; it was only called **the place the LORD your God will choose**. It would be inside the land, in the territory of one of the tribes, and would house the building representing God's **dwelling** on earth. It would also be the place where Yahweh would **put his Name**.

To the place of God's choosing Israel was obligated to bring **burnt offerings and sacrifices**. The former term describes an animal offered in its entirety to God; it was a specific subdivision of the larger category of sacrifices. **Tithes** were presentations of one-tenth of the produce of the land or of livestock. These were normally not gifts but mandatory offerings prescribed by law or taxes (cp. Num. 18:21–28; 2 Chr. 31:12; Deut. 14:22–28). The central shrine would also be the place where Israel would bring what they had **vowed to give** to God, as well as their **freewill offerings**. They would also be required by law to bring **the firstborn** of their herds and flocks. In some cases, animals (especially unclean ones) were not offered but were instead redeemed in exchange for cash (cp. Num. 18:15–17).

12:7. At the city God would in time choose—and only **there**, in his **presence**—Israel with its **families** would **eat** and **rejoice** in everything good that had happened. In the worship of God, eating and rejoicing are close partners.

Deuteronomy 12:8–9

In both the Old Testament and the New Testament, the central act of redemption is a sacramental meal. In Hebrew Scripture, the meal is the Passover (Exod. 12); in the New Testament, it is the Lord's Supper. With the exception of the Day of Atonement, Israel's festivals generally included food as part of the event. Many of the sacrifices, in fact, involved killing an animal, a portion of which was offered in fire to God. Another portion was given to the officiating priest, and the rest was given to the worshiper to be enjoyed by him and his family together before the Lord.

More than anything else, however, it was joy that God sought in worship. The believer was to appear before the Lord as one who was satisfied in the wonder and caregiving of his God. The basis of the joy was the fact that the Lord had **blessed** the worshiper and that he was the kind of God who blessed people.

12:8–9. The wilderness travels of Israel by their very nature precluded any stable manner of national life. The nation, however, was approaching **the resting place and the inheritance** that was the land of promise. Since they were soon to arrive "home," their national worship would become more regular. No longer would they be free to improvise about the timing of their worship. When life was stabilized in the land, they would be expected to appear before God at prescribed times and in the one central sanctuary at the place God would choose.

12:10. God viewed Israel corporately as his son: "When Israel was a child, I loved him, and out of Egypt I called my son" (Hos. 11:1). As such, God's son could be expected to receive **an inheritance** that would testify of the Father's love. In earthly fathers, such a bequest would necessitate the death of the father; but with God no such event could be expected. The suitability of using *inheritance* to describe the gift of the land was connected to the idea of a parental largesse. God provided Canaan simply because he wanted to give a gift to his people. He was under no compulsion to do so. He could have made them live as nomads, which they had been before. Instead, he granted them a gift that included not only a place to settle but **rest** from all their **enemies** and a life of **safety**. It is part of God's character to be lavish with his gifts and then call for a response of gratitude rather than to restrain his blessings until humanity takes the initiative.

12:11. Once the land was secure and Israel's enemies were displaced, then God would choose a city that would house **a dwelling for his Name**. The safety referred to in verse 10 would not, in fact, prevail until the time of David: "After the king was settled in his palace and the LORD had given him rest from all his enemies around him, he said to Nathan the prophet, 'Here I am, living in a palace of cedar, while the ark of God remains in a tent'" (2 Sam. 7:1–2).

Even under Saul, his predecessor, the Philistines occupied much of the Holy Land, including its breadbasket, the Jezreel Valley. When Saul died, his head was taken and displayed in the temple of Dagon in Beth Shan on the

Deuteronomy 12:15–16

edge of this region (cp. 1 Chr. 10:8–10). It remained for David to push the Philistines out of the land and secure the borders for Israel. Then he began to consider the possibility of a permanent location for the ark of the covenant.

It was to that city (Jerusalem) that God would in time choose that **burnt offerings and sacrifices . . . tithes and special gifts** should be brought.

12:12. Moses again commanded Israel to **rejoice before the LORD**. This expression appears often in Deuteronomy (cp. 14:26; 16:11,14; 26:11; 27:7) but only once elsewhere (Lev. 23:40). Nonetheless, rejoicing is a central part of worship in Scripture. Such rejoicing was to be universal in Israel. The nation would engage in communal rejoicing at God's appointed intervals. The entire family was expected to participate: **sons and daughters, . . . menservants and maidservants**. In the midst of this celebration, **the Levites**, who had no allotment of property, were not to be forgotten. They were to take part in the festivities even though they were not property owners, living as they did on the food provided by Israel's sacrifices.

12:13–14. God's command to Israel not to sacrifice their burnt offerings anywhere except **the place** that God would **choose** was very clear. Nevertheless, it was persistently disobeyed through the years, giving rise to the frequent remarks later in the Hebrew Scripture about high places. Many of the ancient pagan altars had been built on the tops of hills and mountains, and these were taken over and adapted to the worship of Yahweh down through the centuries. These became widely used in the four centuries between the conquest of the land and the construction of the temple (1 Kgs. 3:2). Even Solomon perpetuated this blunder (1 Kgs. 3:3). Many of Judah's later kings tolerated this practice.

Before David secured the land, of course, local altars were used in genuine worship. Obvious cases include Gideon (Judg. 6:18,26), Manoah (Judg. 13:16), and Elijah (1 Kgs. 18:31). Elijah, as a citizen of the Northern Kingdom (Israel), had to make his case for Yahweh's uniqueness at a location accessible to that kingdom's people.

C How True Worship Takes Place (12:15–28)

SUPPORTING IDEA: *Israel must make a clear-cut distinction between the sacred and the profane, between the consecrated and the ordinary. What is consecrated must be consumed or given only in the place of God's choosing.*

12:15–16. Moses explained that it would not be necessary to offer to God all animals that were slaughtered for their meat. Israelites could enjoy **as much of the meat** as they wanted, assuming that the Lord had blessed their herds and flocks and they could afford it. Eating such meat was permitted those who were **ceremonially unclean** as well as those who were ceremonially **clean**. These categories were not moral ones. Godly people might fit in

Deuteronomy 12:17-19

either category at a given moment, since people could be ceremonially defiled by bodily discharges and diseases that were no fault of their own. Those who were ceremonially unclean were restricted from certain religious celebrations until they had corrected the matter, but such concerns did not apply to the ordinary slaughtering of animals for meat. God only insisted that Israel **not eat the blood** of those animals; they should **pour it out on the ground**.

12:17-19. Although ordinary meat could be eaten in any location, **the tithe** (a one-tenth taxation for the Lord) of agricultural products had to be carried to the future central sanctuary to be offered. **Firstborn** animals had to be dedicated (or redeemed) there as well. Items that were part of a vow or part of freewill offerings or special gifts also must be taken there.

Such consecrated foods must be eaten **in the presence of the LORD** at the place of his choosing. All such items would become avenues of worship and rejoicing **before the LORD** in gratitude for his blessing. Some of these items should be set aside for **the Levites** as well, since they had no farms to sustain them.

12:20-25. It was not God's intent to restrict Israel's diet to vegetable or grain products. Once the land was settled and God had **enlarged** Israel's territory, they could eat all **the meat** they wanted. God merely insisted that they observe his restrictions against eating the **blood** of the animal. Israel's observance of this special restriction would ensure that it would **go well** with them and with their children in years to come.

12:26-28. Consecrated things were a different matter. God put into this category the offerings specified in Leviticus, including items that people had **vowed to give** as well as **burnt offerings**. These must be taken to **the place the LORD will choose**. Even with offerings of prescribed animals, however, the **blood** must not be eaten. Instead, it should be **poured beside the altar**. The prosperity and welfare of present and future generations depended upon careful adherence to these dietary laws.

Ⓓ Why False Worship Must Be Forsaken (12:29-32)

SUPPORTING IDEA: *Although misapplications might take place in the observance of Israel's faith, paganism posed an even greater threat. God's people were to avoid imitating the practices of the peoples they were driving out of the land.*

12:29-30. Curiosity is an enormous challenge to godly living. With Israel, the dangers of curiosity lay in wanting to know more about the Canaanite gods. Moses insisted that Israel not even ask how the peoples of the land went about serving their gods, because if they did they would be tempted to do the same. Their curiosity would lead to their being ensnared by the paganism they were supposed to be displacing.

12:31-32. Specifically, Israel should not imitate the practices of the Canaanites, since they were known to do **all kinds of detestable things** that the Lord hated. A dramatic case in point: they burned their sons and daughters **as sacrifices to their gods**.

Moses concluded this exhortation with a solemn warning about either expanding or detracting from the commandments he had given. Believers have just as much to fear from legalism as from waywardness. The first detracts from the beauty of the message, while the second mars its content.

> **MAIN IDEA REVIEW:** *Israel must be careful from the very beginning to worship God properly and on his terms. Those terms include the destruction of the existing pagan system of worship.*

III. CONCLUSION

Godly Attachments

Charles Bradlaugh, a well-known skeptic, once issued a debate challenge to H. P. Hughes, a British preacher. Hughes, who ran a downtown rescue mission in London, accepted with one condition. He challenged Bradlaugh to show the fruit of the message he advocated. Hughes explained that he planned to bring with him one hundred men and women who would give testimony to what had happened in their personal lives since they had been believers in Jesus Christ. The entire group would be composed of people who had once been drains on society, having been either involved in destructive lifestyles or coming from dysfunctional and/or poverty-stricken homes. He went on to explain to Bradlaugh that his one hundred friends would be willing to submit to cross-examination so that the validity of their testimony could be explored. Hughes challenged Bradlaugh to bring his own group of people, those whose lives had been changed by their lack of faith.

True to his word, at the appointed time Hughes arrived with his one hundred friends. Bradlaugh never showed up, so Hughes used the occasion as a testimony meeting. A number of people in the audience who had come to hear a debate heard of the living reality of the God of the Bible, and many of them were converted.

Worship is accomplished with the life as well as with the words and attitudes of people. Changed and transformed lives testify to the character and supernatural power of the God of heaven. Closeness to him produces changes in character and holiness.

PRINCIPLES

- Attachments to older forms of worship may be comfortable, but they may contain elements of falsehood that make them unacceptable to God.

Deuteronomy 12

- Common sense religion emphasizes the human contributions that are supposed to move the deity. Valid worship always begins with a recognition of what God has already done.
- Religious truth is not false for being narrow any more than mathematical or scientific truth is false for the same reason.
- Rejoicing is the essence of genuine worship. A sad face (apart from remorse for sin or regret concerning the pain of others) is an affront to a gracious and generous God.
- God ought to be given the choice portion of our wealth and not its dregs.

APPLICATIONS

- Set aside some funds to purchase a special gift for a missionary or other Christian servant. (Be sure to find out whether import duties on such a gift are exorbitant before sending it).
- Use a concordance to investigate how the word *rejoice* is used in the Psalms. Make an evaluation of your own worship practices in the light of what you discover.
- Do a frank assessment of the activities of your life that may be crowding out adequate time for worship. Do some housecleaning of your schedule if necessary.
- Consider whether your life is set apart for God's use in significant ways.
- Look at your calendar over the past year and assess how faithful you have been at corporate worship.

IV. LIFE APPLICATION

No Tools Allowed

God in his love did not leave us to figure out his ways by ourselves. He explains his thinking in his Word. One of the more profound teachings of the Bible is the notion that man cannot sit down with his thoughts and come up with a valid approach to God. He will always bungle things.

For example, God warned Israel, "If you make an altar of stones for me, do not build it with dressed stones, for you will defile it if you use a tool on it" (Exod. 20:25). To defile something is to make it ordinary. God insists that any approach crafted by human ingenuity will produce a worship system just like all the pagan systems in the world. In other words, it will be common or profane—just like everyone else's paganism.

By definition, if man contributes anything toward acceptance by God, he loses everything. God expects man to be the recipient, not the originator.

Jesus paid it all, not 99 percent of it. Paul wrote, "For it is by grace you have been saved, through faith—and this not from yourselves, it is the gift of God—not by works, so that no one can boast" (Eph. 2:8–9).

We dare not trim stones to make God an altar, for if we do so we ruin everything. We would spend time bringing people to the altar and saying, "Look at those beautiful stones we trimmed!"

We merely need to accept the work that God has done for us in Christ. The object of his restrictions is to help us see how wonderful he is and to spend the rest of our lives rendering true worship to him.

V. PRAYER

Father, we long to take our eyes off our own flawed efforts to make you reachable and to rest in the perfection of your provision for us. Help us delight in the Savior who made a perfect altar and placed himself upon it for our sakes. Amen.

VI. DEEPER DISCOVERIES

A. Burnt Offerings and Sacrifices (12:6)

Moses told Israel, "Bring your burnt offerings and sacrifices" (Deut. 12:6) to the place God would choose. When these two expressions are used together, the word *sacrifices* often refers to fellowship offerings, consisting of meat that was shared among priest, worshipers, and God: "Sacrifice fellowship offerings there, eating them and rejoicing in the presence of the LORD your God" (Deut. 27:7). *Burnt offerings,* by contrast, were animals offered up entirely in flame to God (Lev. 9:12–14).

B. Special Gifts (12:6)

Among the offerings of worship to God were the *special gifts,* or, as other translations render it, "heave offerings" or "wave offerings." The Hebrew expression means literally "the lifting up of your hand," and it is found only in Deuteronomy, although the first part of the phrase is found elsewhere. The expression may be suggested by the way the offering was presented, since it was held up near the altar by the priest.

C. Consecrated Things (12:26)

Moses instructed God's people, "Take your consecrated things and whatever you have vowed to give, and go to the place the LORD will choose" (Deut. 12:26). The words for *consecrated things* often appear in other translations as "holy things." The Hebrew root may be related to a verb meaning "to cut" or to make a division. Whether the etymology is related or not, Hebrew usage makes clear that the basic notion behind holiness or consecration is *separateness.*

Deuteronomy 12

Whatever is God's is special, segregated from what is shared in common by the rest of the world. The concept applies regardless of the product itself. Clothes, pans, incense, animals, and especially people are made important by their association with God and his command to separate them. The New Testament word *saints* has a direct connection with this Old Testament concept.

VII. TEACHING OUTLINE

A. INTRODUCTION

1. Lead Story: Bathed in Mystery
2. Context: While Israel's practice of worship has been colored by its nomadic condition to this point, God has a new plan for communal worship in the future. When the land is secured, God will select a central place of worship for his people. Anything that belongs to God must be offered there and only there.
3. Transition: True worship takes place according to God's specifications or not at all. Sometimes the first priority in participating in true worship is a destruction of false forms of worship.

B. COMMENTARY

1. How False Worship Must End (12:1–4)
2. Where True Worship Begins (12:5–14)
3. How True Worship Takes Place (12:15–28)
4. Why False Worship Must Be Forsaken (12:29–32)

C. CONCLUSION: NO TOOLS ALLOWED

VIII. ISSUES FOR DISCUSSION

1. Is walking in the woods a valid substitute for corporate worship?
2. In what ways do people in Western countries today "do what is right in their own eyes"?
3. What are the personal costs of genuine worship?
4. Does God "place his name" in a particular place today? Why or why not?
5. Why did God ask Israel for the firstborn of their flocks and herds?

Deuteronomy 13

Confronting Error

I. **INTRODUCTION**
Subliminal Neckties

II. **COMMENTARY**
A verse-by-verse explanation of the chapter.

III. **CONCLUSION**
Tolerance and the Love of Truth
An overview of the principles and applications from the chapter.

IV. **LIFE APPLICATION**
Thomas Jefferson's Bible
Melding the chapter to life.

V. **PRAYER**
Tying the chapter to life with God.

VI. **DEEPER DISCOVERIES**
Historical, geographical, and grammatical enrichment of the commentary.

VII. **TEACHING OUTLINE**
Suggested step-by-step group study of the chapter.

VIII. **ISSUES FOR DISCUSSION**
Zeroing the chapter in on daily life.

Deuteronomy 13

Quote

"Man is nothing but a subject full of natural error that cannot be eradicated except through grace. Nothing shows him the truth; everything deceives him. The two principles of truth, reason and senses, are not only both not genuine, but are engaged in mutual deception. The senses deceive reason through false appearances, and, just as they trick the soul, they are tricked by it in their turn: it takes its revenge. The senses are disturbed by passions, which produce false impressions. They both compete in lies and deception."

Blaise Pascal

In a Nutshell

Theological error is the most pernicious of errors; it strikes at man's center and separates him from his Creator and Redeemer. God insisted not only that Israelites should judge their own hearts and cast aside falsehood about him but that they should also confront it wherever it emerged.

Confronting Error

I. INTRODUCTION

Subliminal Neckties

Some years ago, Christians scattered across the United States received flyers advertising subliminal neckties. They appeared to be moderately stylish paisley ties, with nothing remarkable about them to the casual glance. The ad copy, however, informed the targeted buyer that "hidden in the fabric, almost totally undetectable to the human eye, are the words 'Jesus Saves.' The ties are made from anointed cloth and can be yours for a tax deductible love gift of $30. You could also buy seven for a tax-deductible gift of $200 to help us feed the hungry."

Readers were not told the precise nature of the fabric's anointing, nor who the hungry were whom the advertiser had in mind to feed. The sales copy did, however, give the ideological wellspring of this remarkable new evangelistic tool: "For years Russian and Communist scientists have experimented with subliminal advertising designed to influence unsuspecting consumers to their ideology and propaganda. Now, the Lord has revealed to his people how to use it for his glory."

A magnified picture of one of the ties revealed that indeed the words "Jesus Saves, Jesus Saves, Jesus Saves, Jesus Saves," were repeatedly interspersed throughout the fabric. "When worn," the leaflet promised, "the words 'Jesus Saves' are actually being planted in the subconscious minds of everyone who sees it." What glory God would obtain from this subconscious change was not specified.

Because of the subliminal message, wearers of these remarkable ties could do their witnessing without ever having to say a word to anybody. At the time it struck me as a bizarre approach to evangelism, but in retrospect I see that it was a harbinger of the arm's-length sort of personal ministry that has become popular in many circles. Subliminal ties play to the common human dislike of having to differentiate between truth and falsehood. We find that necessity as disturbing as Israel did.

Ideas do, however, have consequences. God's people had to learn from the very inception of their national life the dangers inherent in false ideas. While laws matter a great deal, ideas have consequences that reach much further, for they are carried around inside one's mind. Falsehood on any level is lethal.

Deuteronomy 13:1–2

II. COMMENTARY

Confronting Error

> **MAIN IDEA:** *False teaching—anything that would weaken the believer's ties to his Lord—must be confronted wherever it appears, even if that confrontation requires painful correction. The life of the nation is at stake.*

A Confronting Those with Supernatural Credentials (13:1–5)

> **SUPPORTING IDEA:** *Israel is warned not to yield her ties to Yahweh even in the face of signs or wonders. The ultimate test of a prophet is his teaching.*

13:1–2. Prophets were people who spoke for God, and they deserved the most careful attention, provided their credentials were in order. This paragraph (vv. 1–5) provides the acid test of a **prophet** in the Israelite economy. Although supernaturally given revelations gave credibility, the core qualification of a prophet was fidelity to Yahweh. If this was lacking, as with the prophet or one who foretold **by dreams** in verses 1–2, the credibility of the prophet was ruled out.

It is noteworthy that the person in question would be able to provide **a miraculous sign or wonder**. While miracles do validate legitimate prophets (cp. 18:15–18; Heb. 2:1–4), they could never do so for someone who said, **Let us follow other gods**.

13:3–4. Israel's protection lay in two sets of actions. First, they **must not listen** to the words of the discredited prophet. Instead, they were to see in those very words how the Lord was **testing** them to reveal the depth of their **love** for him. God did such testing not because his knowledge was insufficient but because theirs was. While many believers profess the deepest commitment to God, when they face tests they discover their love for God to be less than they thought. Loving God supremely is not a convenience; it is essential for survival in a dark world. Those who fly his banner must **follow** him, **revere** him, **keep his commands**, and **obey him**.

13:5. The other half of Israel's protection from error was preventive. Since the **prophet or dreamer** had gone on record as advocating **rebellion**, he must be **put to death**. Capital punishment was never to be invoked thoughtlessly or without investigation, but in such a case, when witnesses were plentiful, no mercy was to be extended. The false prophet had committed the most dangerous crime possible, one that had repercussions for the moment as well as the future. Further, he had insulted the one who **brought** Israel out of Egypt and **redeemed** her from the land of slavery. Only through execution could the nation **purge the evil** of such an act.

B Confronting Those with Family Ties (13:6–11)

SUPPORTING IDEA: *Ties to Yahweh transcend even family loyalty. Error must be challenged wherever it appears.*

13:6–7. Although the execution of a prophet might be difficult, many people would find the process easier than confronting members of one's own family. However, God insisted that even that horrible duty must be carried out when family members were guilty of spiritual sedition. The language of verse 6 emphasizes the possible closeness of family ties. The danger might come in the form of **your very own brother**, or a **son or daughter**, or even **the wife you love**. It might be outside the physical family in the form of one's **closest friend**. It could be all the more insidious for being something done **secretly**, an enticement that would be unknown to those outside one's intimate circle. Failure to expose such a person, however, would open the gates to further infiltration. Like a cancer eating away quietly from within, the life of the nation would be threatened.

13:8–10. The close friend or family member guilty of rebellion against the Lord must not be extended **pity**. The one who heard the appeal to abandon Yahweh must be **first** in putting the guilty party **to death**. It is unlikely that this could be done, however, without corroboration: "One witness is not enough to convict a man accused of any crime or offense he may have committed. A matter must be established by the testimony of two or three witnesses" (Deut. 19:15). The prescribed punishment in Israel was death by stoning, perhaps because it emphasized the action of the community as over against private vengeance. What a single person could not do, the community could.

13:11. Many people today declare that the execution of capital offenders carries no preventative weight, but the Scriptures insist otherwise. All Israel would **hear and be afraid** when the news of such executions passed through the land. The benefits to the community would be substantial: **no one among you will do such an evil thing again**. The mere existence of a death penalty in a code of legislation was, of course, valueless. Only the carrying out of the death penalty would produce the desired results. Failure or even delay of executions would cause severe societal problems (see Eccl. 8:11).

C Confronting Those Within the Community of Faith (13:12–18)

SUPPORTING IDEA: *If wholesale defection from the Lord should occur in a community, the people who are guilty must be executed and their community destroyed.*

13:12–13. The third realm of ideological confrontation Moses described was more remote. Prophets were public by their very nature. Family members and close friends might speak in secret, but at least their intent was clear to those who heard them. However, Moses explained, at some point an Israelite might **hear it said** that a community nearby had fallen under the influence of false teachers. Wicked men might lead the people of their whole town astray, invoking the formula, **Let us go and worship other gods**. In other words, the report would be just that—something heard secondhand.

13:14–15. Since the penalties for rebellion were absolute, any such report could not be taken at face value. The hearers **must enquire, probe and investigate it thoroughly**. Only when they were sure that the report was **true** and it had **been proved** to be so could the people of neighboring towns proceed.

Such a **detestable thing** was to be dealt with radically. **All who live** in the town would be **put to the sword**. Both the **people** and the **livestock** should be destroyed. The sentence is pronounced upon the entire community for one of two reasons. Either they had subscribed to the error and become idolaters themselves, or they had failed to report the existence of error among them. To tolerate spiritual rebellion or to subscribe to it placed offenders under the sentence of death. The livestock of the city were included in the destruction, perhaps to forestall the false accusations that might be made if people should come to covet the animals of others.

13:16–18. To prevent the spread of such false teaching, the offending town would become an object lesson. None of its goods would accrue to anyone. Moses ordered those responsible to **gather all the plunder** of the community into the square and burn it **as a whole burnt offering to the LORD**. The property was **condemned** and could never become the goods of observers. Only by turning the town into **a ruin forever** could the Lord be turned away **from his fierce anger**, an anger justified by Israel's abandonment of him.

As heinous as the crime was, God would **show . . . mercy** and **have compassion** on the survivors, and even **increase** their numbers if people would confront error in this distasteful but responsible way, in recognition that they were doing what was **right** in God's eyes.

MAIN IDEA REVIEW: *False teaching—anything that would weaken the believer's ties to his Lord—must be confronted wherever it appears, even if that confrontation requires painful correction. The life of the nation is at stake.*

III. CONCLUSION

Tolerance and the Love of Truth

The dictionary defines *tolerance* as "the capacity for or the practice of recognizing and respecting the beliefs or practices of others." Tolerance in this traditional sense is merely an outgrowth of Christian love, part of practicing the Golden Rule. We like to have our own views and practices respected. The

Lord Jesus insisted that the best way to encourage this is to grant it to other people.

But as is so often the case, the dictionary is running behind the culture. Today we are hearing a new definition of *tolerance* in the modern world. To respect people as people is not enough. To grant them the right to their practices is inadequate. Today, we must accept their ideas as equally valid with our own. We are constantly asked to jettison a love for the truth for the sake of harmony.

In the Western world, tolerance has now become the highest of all virtues. No one should be made uncomfortable by raising questions about the validity of their beliefs. Still less acceptable are people who have strong spiritual convictions. Christian evangelism is now often viewed as a form of hate speech.

Many Christians today subscribe to this perspective, not realizing that this modern brand of tolerance brings with it a diminished concern for lost people. We now can comfort ourselves when we are indifferent to people without Christ by explaining that we dare not cause them discomfort. As our biblical text shows, however, spiritual truth is literally a matter of life and death. Christians must not fail to show loving spiritual concern for others by justifying such neglect in the name of good manners. Our witness must always be winsome, but it must be a winsome *witness*.

PRINCIPLES

- Truth can be attested by the supernatural, but so can falsehood.
- A concern for doctrinal purity should always be based on the love of the Lord, not a desire to express spiritual pride.
- Some believers tend to forget God's persistent faithfulness in the face of the spectacular and showy.
- There is a kind of misguided pity that deals gently with false teachers at the expense of their victims.
- Error is most painful when it is found inside the family.

APPLICATIONS

- Make a list of several occasions in your life when your love for God has been tested by the popularity of a false point of view.
- Pray for the doctrinal purification of the church in the Western world and for the guarding of your own home church.
- If you have a faithful pastor who teaches the truth, thank God and that pastor for the blessing of sound teaching.
- Write a note or letter of appreciation to someone who has been instrumental in your spiritual development.

Deuteronomy 13

IV. LIFE APPLICATION

Thomas Jefferson's Bible

As one of the nation's founding fathers and the author of the Declaration of Independence, Thomas Jefferson left many positive contributions to the United States, including model legislation preserving religious liberties that he wrote for the state of Virginia.

However, in his personal life Jefferson was deeply influenced by European rationalism, and this set of errors colored the way he viewed God's truth. One of Jefferson's sadder bequests to history was his personal Bible. He composed it by going through the New Testament and editing out any statement that seemed to suggest that Jesus was more than an ordinary man. His assembled clippings from the Gospels lie in a notebook in a Washington museum. They bear the title, "The Life and Morals of Jesus of Nazareth."

In his notes, Jefferson explained that he wanted to separate "the moral teachings of Jesus from the speculations of crazy theologians . . . abstracting what is really his from the rubbish in which it is buried . . . omitting every verse or paragraph that was ambiguous or controversial." His mutilated "Bible" closes with Matthew 27:60: "And he rolled a great stone to the door of the sepulchre, and departed" (KJV).

It seems to have escaped the great statesman's notice that the very book from which he extracted his distilled preferences never would have come into existence if Jesus had not risen from that tomb. Destructive error can be introduced even by the mighty and must be exposed regardless of its source.

V. PRAYER

Father, we ask that you give us a passion for the truth and not merely a hatred of falsehood. Keep us concerned for the spiritual health of people but open to your own rebukes from your mighty Word. Amen.

VI. DEEPER DISCOVERIES

A. Prophet (13:1)

The derivation of the Hebrew word for *prophet* is uncertain. Many older lexicographers connected it with a Semitic root meaning "to bubble up, boil forth." However, many of these scholars seemed to have a theological axe to grind, using this supposed derivation to suggest that prophecy was done by a person in a state of ecstasy (i.e., one who had lost control of his rational faculties).

The expositor is on safer ground to draw the meaning of the word from its usage rather than its origins. In this connection several key texts are determinative. One is God's commission to Moses on his reluctant entry into the prophetic office. When Moses complained that he lacked the skill to speak for God, he received a divine rebuke and was told that he could use his brother Aaron as his spokesman: "You shall speak to him and put words in his mouth; I will help both of you speak and will teach you what to do. He will speak to the people for you, and it will be as if he were your mouth and as if you were God to him" (Exod. 4:15–16).

A prophet thus spoke for God and as such was to be feared because of the power behind his speech, as the following text implies: "If anyone does not listen to my words that the prophet speaks in my name, I myself will call him to account" (Deut. 18:19). How a prophet received his divine revelation is described in Numbers 12:6–8: "When a prophet of the LORD is among you, I reveal myself to him in visions, I speak to him in dreams. But this is not true of my servant Moses. . . . With him I speak face to face, clearly and not in riddles; he sees the form of the LORD. Why then were you not afraid to speak against my servant Moses?"

Although predictions formed only part of the prophet's ministry, they were critical in establishing him as one who deserved a hearing. The bulk of his speech might contain exhortations to godly conduct, but his predictive powers had first to provide the platform from which he spoke, as they did with Samuel: "The LORD was with Samuel as he grew up, and he let none of his words fall to the ground. And all Israel from Dan to Beersheba recognized that Samuel was attested as a prophet of the LORD" (1 Sam. 3:19–20).

B. Detestable Thing (13:14)

Moses described false teaching as *detestable*: "If it is true and it has been proved that this detestable thing has been done among you" (Deut. 13:14). The older translations used the word *abomination* to describe such counsel.

Moses lumped spiritual sedition into the same repulsive category as sexual irregularities (cp. Lev. 18:22), child sacrifice to pagan gods (Deut. 12:31; 2 Kgs. 16:3), the abuse of power (Prov. 16:12), perversions of justice (Prov. 17:15), and practices like necromancy and wizardry (Deut. 18:10–12). Clearly, the modern view of false teaching as simply the expression of alternate opinions must be challenged.

VII. TEACHING OUTLINE

A. INTRODUCTION

1. Lead Story: Subliminal Neckties

Deuteronomy 13

2. Context: Israel's imminent possession of the promised land will expose them to terrible danger in the form of theological error. This must be eliminated with the same courage and persistence required to possess the land.
3. Transition: Falsehood about God strikes at core values in human experience. The modern exaltation of a false kind of tolerance at the expense of truth is dangerous.

B. COMMENTARY
1. Confronting Those with Supernatural Credentials (13:1–5)
2. Confronting Those with Family Ties (13:6–11)
3. Confronting Those Within the Community of Faith (13:12–18)

C. CONCLUSION: THOMAS JEFFERSON'S BIBLE

VIII. ISSUES FOR DISCUSSION

1. What is the difference between testing and temptation?
2. How can compassion sometimes produce a tolerance for wickedness and false doctrine?
3. What kind of investigation should be done upon the report of false teaching?
4. Why do you think the accuser had to be first in line at the execution of false teachers?
5. Why do you think all the people involved had to cast a stone at such an execution?

Deuteronomy 14

Distinctive Lord, Distinctive Life

I. **INTRODUCTION**
Who Can He Tell?

II. **COMMENTARY**
A verse-by-verse explanation of the chapter.

III. **CONCLUSION**
Why Poison Ivy?
An overview of the principles and applications from the chapter.

IV. **LIFE APPLICATION**
The House We Build
Melding the chapter to life.

V. **PRAYER**
Tying the chapter to life with God.

VI. **DEEPER DISCOVERIES**
Historical, geographical, and grammatical enrichment of the commentary.

VII. **TEACHING OUTLINE**
Suggested step-by-step group study of the chapter.

VIII. **ISSUES FOR DISCUSSION**
Zeroing the chapter in on daily life.

Deuteronomy 14

> Quote
>
> "God loves us as we are, but he loves us too much to leave us that way."
>
> Anonymous

Deuteronomy 14

IN A NUTSHELL

God decreed that the people of Israel should be distinctive in their behavior, their diet, and their worship practices. In everything they were to remember their special standing before him and rejoice in his goodness.

Distinctive Lord, Distinctive Life

I. INTRODUCTION

Whom Can He Tell?

A minister was quite accomplished on the golf links but seldom could find time for the game in his busy schedule. It had been many months since he had played, so one day he sat down with his desk calendar and determined that he was going to find a day when he could play a round of golf.

Unfortunately, the one day he decided he could work in some recreation time fell on a Sunday. Since he had made quite a few negative comments about golfers who abandoned church for the links, he decided he would have to go out of town for his round of golf. So he arranged for a substitute preacher and traveled some distance away to a public course, hoping that no one he knew would be there.

As he approached the first hole, he looked around nervously and was glad to discover that no acquaintances were in sight. He placed his ball on the tee of the 195-yard, par-three hole. Observing the pin placement, he stepped up to the ball.

As he took a few practice swings, an angel looked down from heaven, greatly disturbed as he noted this minister skipping church to play golf on Sunday. Quickly informing the Almighty, the angel was given instructions about what to do.

Just as the minister teed off, the angel arranged for a gust of wind that picked up the ball and dropped it directly into the cup. When the angel asked about the purpose of God's method of discipline, he was told: "Think about it. . . . Who can he tell?"

God designed his world so that people who knew him would always be in position to tell others who didn't. If the lips of a Christian are silent, he still bears testimony to his God by the life that he lives. Unfortunately, sometimes his testimony is impeded by inconsistency or hypocrisy. A distinctive lifestyle is one that is the same in private as it is in public.

II. COMMENTARY

Distinctive Lord, Distinctive Life

> **MAIN IDEA:** *If Israel is to please the Lord fully, they will live lives that are as distinctive among the nations as their Lord is different from pagan deities.*

A Distinctive Deeds (14:1–2)

SUPPORTING IDEA: *God's people must not display a paganistic loss of hope in their behavior even when bereaved.*

14:1. Since Israel had been chosen by God both to be blessed and to serve as a channel of blessings (cp. Gen. 12:1–3) to the world, they were to be thought of as **children of the LORD**. Their behavior should be distinctive and not merely a continuation of the common practices of the pagan nations of the region. Everything they did was to reflect glory on their God, just as Jesus later instructed his disciples: "In the same way, let your light shine before men, that they may see your good deeds and praise your Father in heaven" (Matt. 5:16).

One example of reflecting God's light to the nations would be Israel's actions when a death occurred. Although the nations might **cut** themselves or **shave the front** of their heads when they suffered the loss of a loved one, Israel was not to behave this way. They were not to imitate the practices of the pagans around them. Yahweh had the power to overcome even death; his people were to reflect his great power in their reactions to death itself.

14:2. The people of Israel were not to imitate any pagan custom. Distinctiveness was the central feature of their faith and lifestyle: **you are a people holy to the LORD your God**. This distinctiveness was based on God's choice in making Israel separate from **all the peoples**, a choice that made them **his treasured possession**.

There has always been a tendency among the people of God to want to be like the rest of the world. We draw comfort from the fact that we are like others in important ways. Although there is a core of common humanity shared by believer and unbeliever alike, when it comes to the central tenets of our faith, we are not to be concerned with being accepted by others but with pleasing the Lord. Unfortunately, Israel found this basic principle hard to observe: "They said to [Samuel], 'You are old, and your sons do not walk in your ways; now appoint a king to lead us, such as all the other nations have'" (1 Sam. 8:5).

B Distinctive Diet (14:3–21)

SUPPORTING IDEA: *Israel's meat diet is to be restricted to those foods that are ceremonially clean as defined by Yahweh.*

14:3. The people of Israel were to be different not only in their expressions of mourning, but in the very food they ate. Moses summarized the dietary restrictions that followed as critical so that Israel might not eat **any detestable thing**. The Hebrew word (see "Deeper Discoveries," ch. 13) signifies something that is repulsive in God's sight (or even man's). God wanted to save Israel from eating what was unsafe and thus making itself subject to certain food-related illnesses.

The line between clean and unclean was based solely on God's arbitrary choice—made in the same way as his choice of Israel was made. In the New Testament, God *declared* all foods clean; he did not *make* all foods clean: "[Deceivers] forbid people to marry and order them to abstain from certain foods, which God created to be received with thanksgiving by those who believe and who know the truth. For everything God created is good, and nothing is to be rejected if it is received with thanksgiving, because it is consecrated by the word of God and prayer" (1 Tim. 4:3–5).

14:4–5. Israel had a broad choice of animals that they might consume for food. Among them were domesticated animals that they might raise for this purpose: **the ox, the sheep**, and **the goat**. These were all permitted in Israelite diets.

Many wild animals were also permitted. These could be hunted and killed for their meat. The animals mentioned in verses 4–5 were all split-hoofed ruminants (cud chewing), a characteristic that is made explicit in verse 6.

14:6. Moses provided the general principle that Israelites were to use in deciding which animals were permitted for food. Any animal characterized by **a split hoof divided in two** and rumination fell into the permitted category. Like the clean/unclean distinction generally, this combination of factors appears to have been arbitrary.

14:7–8. Both requirements were important. Some animals met one characteristic but not the other. The **camel, rabbit,** and **coney** serve as examples. The last animal is also called the Syrian rock hyrax, a small animal that lives in loose rock formations and seldom ventures far from its home. It is still seen in parts of northern Galilee and sometimes is mistaken for a rabbit. Although all three animals were ruminants, they did not have a split hoof and so were ceremonially unclean.

The pig has **a split hoof** but **does not chew the cud**, so it was also forbidden as food. Moses added that Israelites must neither **eat** the meat of unclean animals nor **touch** the **carcasses** of those that had died or had been slaughtered.

14:9–10. Moses described the criteria for determining whether an aquatic creature might be eaten. Here he only mentioned the general principle (both positively and negatively). Fish that had **fins and scales** could be eaten for food, thus eliminating sharks, shellfish, and eels.

14:11. A third category of animal life is now considered. Moses gave the general principle first: **you may eat any clean bird**. No differentiating principle is enunciated here, but the prohibited individual varieties are specified.

14:12–18. Twenty-one varieties of birds are placed on the unclean list, some of which are difficult to identify with confidence. **The vulture, the black vulture, the red kite, the black kite, the horned owl, the screech owl,** the white owl, and **the desert owl** are birds whose exact modern equivalent is uncertain. The common denominator of the prohibited birds seems to be that they were carnivores and that most of them consumed dead animals.

The hoopoe is a bird that is primarily an insect-eater. It has a long curved bill and a notable crest that it displays when stationary. Its black-and-white wing plumage and its peculiar walk make it easy to identify even from a distance.

14:19–20. These verses describe a fourth category of animals: **flying insects that swarm**. These were decreed to be unclean, in contrast to the other **winged** creatures that were clean. The discussion does not provide much information for the person who was concerned to observe these details, but Moses had already specified the nature of the forbidden insects earlier in Leviticus. In 11:20–23, we see the details: "All flying insects that walk on all fours are to be detestable to you. There are, however, some winged creatures that walk on all fours that you may eat: those that have jointed legs for hopping on the ground. Of these you may eat any kind of locust, katydid, cricket or grasshopper. But all other winged creatures that have four legs you are to detest."

14:21. Two other restrictions remained to be introduced. First, carrion was ruled out across the board. Although what was **already dead** could be given to a resident **alien**, or it could even be sold to a non-Jew, Israelites were not to eat carrion since the manner of the animal's death could not be assured. Among other things, the lifeblood of the animal dying on its own was not poured out according to divine instructions (cp. 12:16,24). Avoidance of such commonly consumed foods would allow Israel to be a distinctive **people holy to the Lord**.

The other restriction is more curious: **Do not cook a young goat in its mother's milk**. The reason for this prohibition, which is unclear, has created a considerable body of literature. The most reasonable conjecture suggests that such a practice was a pagan ritual of the Canaanites. Support for this idea is found in the observation that the restriction appears in two other places, both of which are associated with religious festivals (Exod. 23:19; 34:26). God insisted that practices associated with paganism form no part of Israel's religious life.

Ⓒ Distinctive Devotion (14:22–29)

SUPPORTING IDEA: *The worship practices of the people of God are to be marked by devotion to him and compassion for the needy.*

14:22–23. Israelites were obliged to **set aside a tenth** of the produce of their fields **each year**. This portion of their income was to be used to pay the cost of travel to the central sanctuary each year and to provide for communal worship meals. For those who lived within a reasonable distance of the central worship center, they were to consume **the tithe** of their grain, new wine, and oil themselves. For meat, they were to consume **the firstborn** of their herds and flocks in the presence of the Lord. Worship and celebration, devotion and joy were routinely linked in the Israelite economy. Reveling in the goodness of God who had provided such things was part of learning **to revere the** LORD. (For more on the tithe, see "Deeper Discoveries.")

14:24–26. For people who lived at places **too distant** from the central sanctuary, an alternate plan was given. If the tithe was so abundant that transporting it would be difficult, Israelites were permitted to **exchange** the tithe of their increase **for silver**. This silver could be more easily transported as Israelites set out to **go to the place** the Lord would choose.

Once at the worship center, the coins of the tithe could be used to provide for whatever the worshiper desired: **cattle, sheep, wine or other fermented drink, or anything** (within the dietary restrictions) that they wished. Israelite families were to eat there **in the presence of the** LORD (cp. v. 23). They were to **rejoice** in his sufficiency for their needs.

14:27–29. In all the excitement that would be associated with the festivals, Israelites might easily **neglect the Levites** who were scattered throughout their towns. Since they owned no allotment or inheritance of land, the Levites were unable to farm and provide for their own needs. As a result, Israelites every three years were to set aside a special tithe in each town to provide for the Levites and their financial needs. Neither they, nor the resident **aliens, the fatherless and the widows** were to be omitted from the worship celebrations. By paying attention to this provision of the covenant, the people of God would be investing in their own future: **so that the** LORD **your God may bless you in all the work of your hands.**

> **MAIN IDEA REVIEW:** If Israel is to please the Lord fully, they will live lives that are as distinctive among the nations as their Lord is different from pagan deities.

III. CONCLUSION

Why Poison Ivy?

During a Christian summer camp for children, a counselor raised the issue of God's purposes in the world. He asked the children why they thought God created certain features in the world: trees, rocks, rivers, animals, and other parts of the created order. The discussion grew quieter when one of the students asked, "If God has a purpose for everything, why did he create poison ivy?"

The counselor paused for a moment, scratching his brain for a suitable answer. He was rescued by another camper, who opined, "The reason God

Deuteronomy 14

made poison ivy is because God wanted us to know there are certain things we should keep our cotton-pickin' hands off of!"

Holiness is essentially a positive concept. God separates people who know him by faith from humanity at large so that as his children they can bear witness to him and enlarge the family circle. Part of that separation, however, requires a recognition and submission to what God has placed off limits. What we do as well as what we don't do mark us out from the general population.

PRINCIPLES

- God chose Israel not because they were superior but because of what he could do through them for others.
- The fear of God does not come naturally to human beings; it must be learned through Scripture, worship, and the hard knocks of experience.
- God not only allowed for joyful worship but commanded it.
- Compassion is easily forsaken in the midst of prosperity, even when this prosperity is God given.
- God is glorified when his people find satisfaction in him and in his provisions for them.

APPLICATIONS

- Spend some time thinking about what you may be doing that originates not from the Scriptures but from the influence of the world.
- Do a frank evaluation of your financial ministry, both that which goes to your home church and the funds you give elsewhere. Make changes as needed.
- Take some time off work to spend alone or with your spouse on a spiritual retreat with God.
- Consider the people in your community who may be neglected in the worship of God, and consider creative ways of helping them participate.

IV. LIFE APPLICATION

The House We Build

You may have heard the story of the rich man who had been so blessed that he wanted to do something kind for others. As he passed through his community, he noticed the decrepit house of a local carpenter. The wealthy man went to see the poor craftsman and offered him a contract. He said, "I want you to build a new house here in the neighborhood. Use only the best materials. Hire the best craftsmen. Spare no expense." The rich man explained the he was going on a long vacation and he hoped the house would be completed by the time of his return.

The carpenter, however, was poor largely because he was dishonest. He saw his new contract as an opportunity to cheat his benefactor. So he cut corners when he bought materials and negotiated kickbacks from people who sent less-skilled workmen to do the job. Finally the house was finished, and the rich man returned to inspect it. After looking it over, he handed the carpenter the keys he had just received.

"Here are your keys. I had you build this house for yourself. You and your family are to have it as my gift."

In the years that followed the carpenter never ceased to regret the way in which he had cheated himself. "Had I only known," he would say to himself, "that I was building this house for myself!"

All of us live in the moral house we build for ourselves. The cheating we do when we think no one is looking affects us far more than it affects others. True wisdom comes when we recognize that all we do affects our inner person.

V. PRAYER

Father, we ask that we be always conscious that our moral and spiritual choices affect others sometimes and ourselves always. Make us people who appreciate the beauty of holiness and practice it as well. Amen.

VI. DEEPER DISCOVERIES

A. The Tithe of Your Grain (14:23)

Moses instructed Israel, "Eat the tithe of your grain, new wine and oil, and the firstborn of your herds and flocks in the presence of the LORD" (Deut. 14:23). A tithe was one-tenth of any item, but the number and purpose of Israel's tithes is a matter of some debate. It seems clear that the tithe mentioned in Deuteronomy 14:22 was intended to finance the worshiper's trips to the central sanctuary. However, God indicated earlier that Israel's tithes were to be contributed directly to the Levites (Num. 18:21–32). For that reason, we may be correct in thinking there were two tithes. The first was 10 percent of each family's produce and was given to support the Levites in their function as Israel's worship specialists. The second (a tenth of the remaining 90 percent) was saved for trips to the central worship center. Since these took place three times a year (at Passover, Pentecost, and Tabernacles), the expense was considerable. God wanted no person in Israel to be unable to afford the expense of worship because of inadequate funds.

Deuteronomy 14

Tithes were not considered voluntary contributions. The Israelite who did not provide his tithe had disobeyed God. Tithes were taxation to support the theocratic state and to tie the worshiper's heart to God. Israel's worship did include giving in the form of freewill offerings which were contributed in addition to the mandatory tithes: "When anyone brings from the herd or flock a fellowship offering to the LORD to fulfill a special vow or as a freewill offering, it must be without defect or blemish to be acceptable" (Lev. 22:21; cp. Exod. 35:29; Num. 15:3; Ezra 3:5).

The tithe mentioned in Deuteronomy 14:27–29 appears to be a third tithe, collected from the produce every third year and used not for the worship apparatus but for the Levites. If the above analysis is true, the annual taxation rate of the Israelite averaged around 22 percent of their farm production.

VII. TEACHING OUTLINE

A. INTRODUCTION
1. Lead Story: Whom Can He Tell?
2. Context: In a world of paganism, God calls on Israel to be different, and to recognize that in their distinctiveness lay the key to influencing a pagan world.
3. Transition: Part of being better is being different. Just as Israel was commanded by God to be holy, so are we. We must be identifiable to our generation if we hope to influence it for good.

B. COMMENTARY
1. Distinctive Deeds (14:1–2)
2. Distinctive Diet (14:3–21)
3. Distinctive Devotion (14:22–29)

C. CONCLUSION: THE HOUSE WE BUILD

VIII. ISSUES FOR DISCUSSION

1. What characteristics mark a genuinely holy person today?
2. What did it mean to eat before the Lord? How did such eating differ from a normal meal?
3. What steps would you suggest that a person take to learn to fear the Lord?
4. Why were the annual tithes a regular test of faith and obedience?
5. What does it mean to be a special treasure to the Lord above other people?

Deuteronomy 15

Developing a Generous Heart

I. **INTRODUCTION**
A Frozen Attitude

II. **COMMENTARY**
A verse-by-verse explanation of the chapter.

III. **CONCLUSION**
Reflecting God's Liberality
An overview of the principles and applications from the chapter.

IV. **LIFE APPLICATION**
The Angel of Fredericksburg
Melding the chapter to life.

V. **PRAYER**
Tying the chapter to life with God.

VI. **DEEPER DISCOVERIES**
Historical, geographical, and grammatical enrichment of the commentary.

VII. **TEACHING OUTLINE**
Suggested step-by-step group study of the chapter.

VIII. **ISSUES FOR DISCUSSION**
Zeroing the chapter in on daily life.

Deuteronomy 15

Quote

"In glory God is incomprehensible, in greatness unfathomable, in height inconceivable, in power incomparable, in wisdom unrivaled, in goodness inimitable, in kindness unutterable."

Theophilus of Antioch

IN A NUTSHELL

Deuteronomy 15 teaches that God is openhanded and generous toward his people. He also desires them to be generous in return and to reflect his holy character.

Developing a Generous Heart

I. INTRODUCTION

A Frozen Attitude

A creative minister in a growing church stood in the pulpit one Sunday morning and announced: "I have some good news and some bad news. The good news is that we have ample funds to pay for our new building program. The bad news is that it's still out there in your pockets."

While many funny stories have been told about pastors trying to wheedle more money out of their congregations, it is regrettable that such efforts are necessary. Christians are supposed to be generous, since they serve a God of incredible liberality.

Clovis Chappell, the noted authority on preaching, tells in one of his books about the excavation of Pompeii some years ago. The city was destroyed by the eruption of nearby Mount Vesuvius. The huge quantity of falling ash literally fixed people in mid-motion for centuries. Chappell noted that one woman's feet were turned toward the city gate, but her face had turned back toward something behind her. Excavators discovered that at the moment of her death she was reaching for a bag of pearls. Although her life was at risk, she thought so much of her pearls that she could not bear to live without them. She was literally frozen in an attitude of greed.

So are many Christians. We often manage to provide for the essentials of ministry, but often without showing a liberal spirit. God wants his people to rejoice in his generosity and let it be the basis for our own. He longs to produce generous hearts that reflect his faithfulness.

Deuteronomy 15:1

II. COMMENTARY

Developing a Generous Heart

MAIN IDEA: *Since God has demonstrated his own generosity toward Israel, they are to imitate that generosity toward one another and in worship.*

A Generosity Toward the Poor (15:1–11)

SUPPORTING IDEA: *The wealthy in Israel must cancel debts to their countrymen every seven years. They are not to insist on repayment of loans but to suffer financial losses gladly in the interests of others.*

15:1. God instructed Israel to issue a general cancellation of personal debt **at the end of every seven years**. The debts in question would range from minor to substantial and required the people of Israel to decide whether money was their primary standard of value in life. Only those who recognized that financial success was secondary to other kinds of success would be likely to participate in such a cancellation. Whether this ever happened on a large scale in Israel is open to question.

There is some uncertainty about whether the debt cancellation was permanent or simply was to be deferred during the sabbatical year when crops were not grown (cp. Lev. 25:1–7; Exod. 23:10–11). Verse 9, however, strongly suggests that the temptation would be strong to withhold a loan to the needy just before the sabbatical year, a prohibition that has more bite if the debt cancellation was to be a permanent one.

15:2. The mechanics of the periodic cancellation were simple. Each person would **not require payment from his fellow Israelite or brother**. He would do so on the basis of God's Word, recognizing that in the seventh year it was **the LORD's time for canceling debts**. Each member of the covenant community was to extend freedom from obligation to those who were in debt. In other words, the painful character of the process would be ameliorated by the fact that it was shared by all. Most of all, however, it was to be recognized that the entire process reflected the openhanded generosity of the God of heaven, who had given Israel a national life and had freed the people from slavery in Egypt. The clock was to be a regular one: "At the end of every seven years, in the year for canceling debts, during the Feast of Tabernacles" (Deut 31:10).

15:3. Israel's distinctiveness would be evident to nations surrounding them if they obeyed the sabbatical cancellation provisions. None of Israel's neighbors were subject to any such statute, and Israel's obedience to it would testify to their convictions about the adequacy of Yahweh. The love of God would thus be reflected inside the covenant people, although they were permitted to continue to collect debts owed by **a foreigner**.

15:4–5. Regular cancellations of debt would go a long way toward insuring that there would **be no poor** among the tribes of Israel. The lost income to the wealthy would be replenished by the generosity of Israel's benefactor, Yahweh. The disappearance of debt would ensure that individual family farms would remain in those families and that poverty in Israel would be virtually unknown. Everything depended on the individual Israelite's convictions. Would he be content to trust in God to **richly bless** him as he obeyed his commands? Only if Israel proceeded to **fully obey** would they experience a land that was poverty-free.

15:6. In order to encourage the people to take God seriously, Moses noted that the Lord would **bless** them as he had promised. Their prosperity would be extraordinary. They would **lend to many nations but . . . borrow from none**. They would never know the heel of a foreign oppressor if they followed the Lord. These lofty possibilities were realized only briefly. The nation that was to have been a blessing to others by their disobedience forfeited this privilege and repeatedly had to be rescued from oblivion.

15:7–8. Although faithfulness to the covenant would have made Israel free from poverty, God allowed for the possibility that some people in the land would be impoverished. If this should happen **in any of the towns of the land**, people were not to pass moral judgment on the causes of such poverty. They were not to avoid contributing to the financial betterment of a **poor brother**. Rather, they were to **be openhanded and freely lend him** whatever he needed.

15:9–11. Since debts were to be cancelled every seven years, some people would likely be tempted to avoid loaning money in the sixth year, and by their tightfistedness they would be expressing **ill will** toward the needy brother. If this should happen, the poverty-stricken brother might **appeal to the Lord** against those who were stingy and cause them to be found **guilty of sin** against the Lord. God is generous, and so should Israel **give generously**. Stinginess is unbecoming a person who professes to know the one who owns all the resources of heaven (cp. Ps. 50:10). **A grudging heart** should not be found in a people so blessed as Israel had been, especially since God was promising still further blessings for obedience: **Because of this the Lord your God will bless you in all your work and in everything you put your hand to**.

Since poverty is sometimes connected with uncontrollable events, and since unredeemed humanity is selfish by nature, Moses noted that there would **always be poor people in the land** (cp. Mark 14:7). Because anyone might be affected, Israel was always to be **openhanded** toward their kinsmen specifically and **toward the poor and needy** generally.

B Generosity Toward the Desperately Poor (15:12–18)

SUPPORTING IDEA: *Israel must proclaim liberty to those who have sold themselves as slaves and allow them to reclaim their property. Those who are slaves must be treated with kindness.*

15:12–13. God warned the people of Israel that they were never to sell the property that had come into their family by God's generosity: "The land must not be sold permanently, because the land is mine and you are but aliens and my tenants" (Lev. 25:23; cp. 1 Kgs. 21:3). Still, Israel's citizens themselves were assets that could be used to satisfy a debt. A **fellow Hebrew** might decide to sell himself to someone more prosperous in exchange for funds or goods to solve an immediate financial crunch.

If this should happen, the self-imposed slavery could only continue, like other debts, for **six years. In the seventh year**, the desperately poor man would be able to return to his own land and resume his life. His benefactor would be required at that time to **release him**. However, the problems that had caused him to sell himself in the first place still might be there, and without some kind of stake he might soon be forced to endure such an experience again. To forestall that, the employer/lord was expected not to send the poor man away **empty-handed**.

15:14–15. On the contrary, the newly liberated Hebrew was to be supplied **liberally** from the owner's **flock, threshing floor**, and **winepress**. The standard by which these gifts were extended should be **as the LORD your God has blessed you**. Generosity, if not lavishness, was to be the order of the day. The memories of days in Egypt were to inform and strengthen the entire process: **Remember that you were slaves in Egypt**. The contrast between their present prosperity and their former misery ought to impel the Israelites toward love and generosity.

15:16–17. Nor was this generosity to begin at the time the slavery ended. It was, in fact, to characterize the entire experience. The treatment of the impoverished brother might make him want to live with his master permanently. Love and liberality combined might encourage him to come to the master and say, **I do not want to leave you**. Such a proposal would certainly be made only after the most cautious deliberation. It would have to grow from the realization that the master had demonstrated faithful love during the time of the slave's servitude, and that the slave's condition at the end of the six years was superior to life on his own.

When a slave decided that he wanted to stay permanently with such a beneficent master, he was to be marked for life. The master was to **take an awl and push it through his ear lobe** to signify the lifelong commitment. Thus the slave would bear in his own body a visible testimony to the goodness and generosity of his master.

15:18. Voluntary slavery, however, would rarely be chosen as a lifestyle. For most Israelites, the choice to be generous would still rest with the person lending money to his less fortunate Hebrew brother. To help bring matters into perspective, Moses insisted that owners **not consider it a hardship** to set their servant free. After all, they were receiving better **service** than they could ever expect from **a hired hand**. They were to recognize that in liberating a slave in the seventh year, they were behaving in a fashion that would encourage the Lord to bless them **in everything**.

Generosity Toward the Lord (15:19–23)

SUPPORTING IDEA: *The Israelite worshiper must set apart the first and the best for the Lord.*

15:19–20. Since God had saved all the firstborn of Israel, he expected the nation to offer him **every firstborn male** of their herds and flocks. Since this could only be done at the central sanctuary, such animals would first have to be **set apart** for the Lord. This separation would be realized in not allowing the firstborn oxen to work and in not shearing the firstborn sheep of each ewe. Such behavior would mark Israel out as distinctive and provoke questions on the part of neighbors and resident aliens about the rationale for such decisions. The segregated animals would be taken to the central worship center and be slaughtered by a priest and shared in the presence of the Lord. In this way, Israelites would be offering God the first and best of what they owned.

15:21–23. God would accept only the best from Israel. Any animal that had a **defect**, or was **lame or blind**, was not to be sacrificed to God. The worship system was built on the recognition that God was the source of Israel's breath and national life. This primacy should be recognized through costly sacrifices. God knew that humanity's affections tend always to follow their actions: "Store up for yourselves treasures in heaven, where moth and rust do not destroy, and where thieves do not break in and steal. For where your treasure is, there your heart will be also" (Matt. 6:20–21).

A flawed animal could not be offered to God, but it could be eaten at home, and Moses made that possibility explicit: **You are to eat it in your own towns. Both the ceremonially unclean and the clean may eat it.** At the same time, even this nonreligious feast was required to observe the regulations concerning the blood of the animal: **pour it out on the ground like water**.

MAIN IDEA REVIEW: *Since God has demonstrated his own generosity toward Israel, they are to imitate that generosity toward one another and in worship.*

III. CONCLUSION

Reflecting God's Liberality

Henry Crowell was only nine years old when his father died of tuberculosis. When he was seventeen, Crowell discovered he had the same disease. To all appearances, he was dying.

That may have moved Crowell to attend an evangelistic meeting in Cleveland, Ohio, where the featured speaker was a man by the name of Dwight L. Moody. Moody told the crowd that the world had yet to see what could be done through a person whose life was fully consecrated to Jesus Christ.

As Crowell reflected on this statement, he decided that he wanted to be that person. But how could God use him? He had no idea. He was convinced that he could never preach. He did believe, however, that he could be a businessman useful in the service of the king. He didn't know how long he would live, but he told God that in the time he had left he would support people like Dwight Moody who could proclaim the gospel. He also asked for healing as he consecrated the remainder of his life to God.

Crowell applied himself and invested his funds intelligently as the days passed. His health began to improve, and that encouraged him to buy a mill. It had been owned by Quakers and was designed to produce cereal products. The Quaker Oats Company had begun.

As Crowell's health continued to improve, he also enjoyed a great deal of business success. God prospered the business, and Henry Crowell put the funds that came in to work, giving 70 percent of his income to Christian causes. He was especially glad to be able to assist Moody Bible Institute in the midst of a dark financial time. He also helped begin the ministries of Moody Press, *Moody* magazine, and Moody's radio ministries. The man who thought he was headed for an early grave instead left his mark on the Christian church through his liberal giving and the wisdom he used in applying God's resources.

PRINCIPLES

- God demonstrates generosity, then asks it from his people.
- Giving works best when the Lord's portion is removed first and believers learn to live within the remainder.
- The generous giver, demonstrating the nature of God by his behavior, can never outgive God.
- God expects believers to improve their attitude in giving as well as their giving itself.

- Since all wealth ultimately comes from God, his people ought to acknowledge his primacy by offering him the best of their wealth, time, and abilities.

APPLICATIONS

- Set aside a portion of your income this month for a person in need and ask God for wisdom in distributing this income.
- Get involved as a volunteer in a local ministry that addresses the needs of the poor.
- Do an assessment of the level of your personal giving to the Lord.
- Do a similar assessment of your time and abilities. Make changes as needed.

IV. LIFE APPLICATION

The Angel of Fredericksburg

December 13, 1862, was one of the bloodiest days of the Civil War. Wave after wave of Union troops were injured or killed as they assaulted the virtually impregnable Confederate town of Fredericksburg, Virginia. So many men cried for help and for water that a continuous moan seemed to move across the field.

Secure behind strong breastworks, Sergeant Richard Kirkland of the Second South Carolina Regiment listened with increasing sympathy. Kirkland was a new Christian, having received Jesus Christ as his Savior as the result of evangelistic efforts among the Confederate troops. He approached his commanding officer and said, "All day I have heard those poor people crying for water, and I can stand it no longer. I come to ask permission to go and give them water."

When permission was granted, Kirkland took all the canteens he could carry, slowly crawled over the barrier, and began to move among the pitiful men. The Union troops quickly saw what he was doing and held their fire. For several hours he ministered, doing what he could to ease the agony of the suffering, and as a result became known to military historians as the "angel of Fredericksburg."

Kindness and generosity do not usually require heroism. They must, however, issue from hearts that have been changed and are tuned to the frequency of human suffering wherever it exists. Jesus Christ is exalted when Christians supply the essentials of those in need.

Deuteronomy 15

V. PRAYER

Father, help us to see how what we do always testifies to what we believe about you. Keep us from being indifferent to the pains and misfortunes of others, and help us to live in a way that adorns our convictions. Amen.

VI. DEEPER DISCOVERIES

A. Hebrew (15:12)

The term *Hebrew* is often thought of as being a synonym for *Israelite*. Some texts, however, suggest that the terms were not precisely the same. For example, 1 Samuel 14:21 states, "Those Hebrews who had previously been with the Philistines and had gone up with them to their camp went over to the Israelites who were with Saul and Jonathan." The suggestion has been made that the word in this verse refers to a group known to history as the *Hapiru*, who may have earned their living as mercenaries.

It is noteworthy that in Hebrew Scripture Israelites rarely refer to themselves as Hebrews. The exception is Jonah, who described himself to the crew of his ship as a Hebrew. The term sometimes is used by non-Jews to describe the descendants of Jacob, often in a derogatory way: "[Potiphar's wife] called her household servants. 'Look,' she said to them, 'this Hebrew has been brought to us to make sport of us! . . . That Hebrew slave you brought us came to me to make sport of me'" (Gen. 39:14,17). The term may have been applied in Abraham's time to migrating tribesmen in general, a description that certainly would have included Abraham.

B. Redemption (15:15)

Moses instructed Israel, "Remember that you were slaves in Egypt and the LORD your God redeemed you" (Deut. 15:15). The theme of redemption appears often in Scripture, and sometimes as a summary of the work that God does in the life of Christian converts. The Old Testament speaks of a "kinsman-redeemer" who was expected to avenge or pay back a wrong done to a near relative or to buy back property that had been sold out of the family (a key feature of the Book of Ruth).

Redeem at its root is a financial word. It means "to pay the price required to possess what was once owned and later lost." It provides a rich picture of the work of God, who owned man fully, then lost him through his rebellion, and in love determined to buy him back. The term held a special significance for Israelites in connection with the exodus. Since God spared the firstborn of Israel on the night of the first Passover, he placed a claim on all subsequent generations of their firstborn. They were to be dedicated to God's service, and they could be bought back from God or redeemed by the payment of the appropriate redemption price (cp. Num. 3:46–51).

VII. TEACHING OUTLINE

A. INTRODUCTION
1. Lead Story: A Frozen Attitude
2. Context: Moses instructs Israel to take responsibility for the poor within their nation. They are to avoid turning away from the less fortunate and to practice a gracious generosity.
3. Transition: Openhanded generosity, so evident in the character of God, is also to characterize his people. We are never more like him than when we exercise compassion toward others.

B. COMMENTARY
1. Generosity Toward the Poor (15:1–11)
2. Generosity Toward the Desperately Poor (15:12–18)
3. Generosity Toward the Lord (15:19–23)

C. CONCLUSION: THE ANGEL OF FREDERICKSBURG

VIII. ISSUES FOR DISCUSSION

1. What effect might a general cancellation of debts have in modern society?
2. What effect might such policies of compassion and openhandedness have had on Israel's neighbors?
3. Why do you think God commanded Israel not to be grieved over the loss of a loan repayment?
4. Should Christians base their giving on the needs of others or on their own ability to give?

Deuteronomy 16

Seeking the Center

- I. **INTRODUCTION**
  The Red Couch

- II. **COMMENTARY**
  A verse-by-verse explanation of the chapter.

- III. **CONCLUSION**
  My Grace Is Sufficient
  An overview of the principles and applications from the chapter.

- IV. **LIFE APPLICATION**
  The Joy Set Before Him
  Melding the chapter to life.

- V. **PRAYER**
  Tying the chapter to life with God.

- VI. **DEEPER DISCOVERIES**
  Historical, geographical, and grammatical enrichment of the commentary.

- VII. **TEACHING OUTLINE**
  Suggested step-by-step group study of the chapter.

- VIII. **ISSUES FOR DISCUSSION**
  Zeroing the chapter in on daily life.

Deuteronomy 16

Quote

"All human beings pass away. Do not let your happiness depend on something you may lose. If love is to be a blessing, not a misery, it must be for the only beloved who will never pass away."

C. S. Lewis

IN A NUTSHELL

In Deuteronomy 16, Moses instructs God's people to make the Lord the center of their celebrations, the focus of their public life, and the sole possessor of their hearts.

Seeking the Center

I. INTRODUCTION

The Red Couch

In his book *The Parable of Ten Preachers*, Thomas Troeger describes a fictional but plausible pastor by the name of Jason Kirk. Kirk came to Clyde's Corner Church at the beginning of the twentieth century and found himself in the midst of a strange and destructive dispute.

It seems that the founder of Clyde's Corner Church, the late Cedric Clyde, was a highly successful farmer near Clyde's Corner. Wanting to show his gratitude to God, he assumed the full financial burden of building the local church. Shortly before his death, Cedric also donated a number of pieces of furniture, including one item that was designated for the church platform: "a giant red horsehair couch whose rich color Cedric fancied would brighten the front of the church." The couch was imposing both for its color and for its curved arms and mahogany legs carved into the shape of lion's claws.

When Kirk came to Clyde's Corner Church, he did not realize that the church had split into two factions over that couch. The Clyde family (including several descendants of the aforementioned church benefactor) adored the red couch and loved its presence on the church platform. The newer members of the church thought it unattractive and ill suited for such a prominent position in the church auditorium. The new families were generally affluent and accustomed to seeing fine furnishings in their homes. They regarded the couch (which they called "the Victorian Leviathan") an affront to good taste. The Clyde family, which had come down in the world since their great ancestor had passed on, liked to point out that had it not been for their family, there would be no Clyde's Corner Church.

Pastor Kirk found that every utterance he made from the pulpit was carefully interpreted by each faction in the light of the pressing question, "Is Pastor Kirk for or against the red couch remaining in its present location?"

In Troeger's parable, Pastor Kirk is able to concoct an ingenious compromise to mollify both sides, a compromise that included placing a cross in the most prominent position on the church platform. Once he was able to convince both factions that the Lord Jesus Christ deserved first billing in Clyde's Corner Church, the squabble was brought down to size (Troeger, pp. 20–22).

Someone has said that the continuing challenge of the church is keeping the main thing the main thing. God will never settle for second place in the lives of his people. As long as our eyes are centered on secondary things, we will miss the full measure of his blessing.

Deuteronomy 16:1

II. COMMENTARY

Seeking the Center

MAIN IDEA: *Yahweh is to be the centerpiece of Israel's national life. The people are to enjoy him fully at his appointed festivals, pursue the justice that reflects his character, and worship him exclusively.*

A The Joy of Israel's Celebrations (16:1–17)

SUPPORTING IDEA: *God's festivals were to be times of great rejoicing and celebrating in his sufficiency and generosity.*

16:1. God expected Israel to rejoice in his faithfulness and provision for their national life. That corporate life had begun **in the month of Abib** (mid-March to mid-April on modern solar calendars) forty years before, when God brought the nation **out of Egypt by night**. (The month *Abib* is elsewhere sometimes called *Nisan*.) They were therefore to **celebrate the Passover** and commemorate their national origins, recognizing that the Lord their God had done a mighty work in bringing them into existence as a people.

16:2. The year was to begin with a remembrance of the events of the first **Passover** to the Lord. Instead of a homebound celebration as the original had been, future Passovers were to be enjoyed **at the place** the Lord would **choose as a dwelling for his Name** (cp. Exod. 12:1–14). For the Passover meal itself, God had specified that the animal to be eaten had to be a lamb (Exod. 12:3), but since the Passover was just the beginning of a much larger weeklong celebration called the Feast of Unleavened Bread, God directed that the animal to be sacrificed for the feast proper could be either from the **flock** (i.e., a sheep or goat) **or herd** (i.e., a steer or calf). For examples of both being offered in connection with the feast, see 2 Chronicles 30:24; 35:6–9.

16:3–4. When Israel left Egypt, they were in a hurry and could not wait for their bread to rise. As a result, the Passover bread was not to be **made with yeast**. Unleavened bread alone could be eaten at the festival, the flat cakes serving as a reminder of **the bread of affliction** that Israel had eaten in Egypt. The **departure from Egypt** itself was a great victory that God had gained over the resistance of a stubborn Pharaoh. God insisted that Israel remember that special time as long as they lived.

Since leavening suggested a condition of business as usual, yeast was to be removed from the dwellings of Israel for the entire **seven days** of the feast. For similar reasons, the meat Israel would sacrifice on the evening of the first day of the Feast of Unleavened Bread (i.e., the Passover meal itself) was to be eaten completely. None was to remain until morning, since cleanup of the remains would have delayed Israel's departure from Egypt. The exodus legislation suggests the tone of the first Passover: "This is how you are to eat it: with your cloak tucked into your belt, your sandals on your feet and your staff in your hand. Eat it in haste" (Exod. 12:11).

16:5–6. Moses again connected the Passover celebration with the central sanctuary (cp. Deut. 12:1–5,11,13). There and only there could the festival be celebrated. The Passover was **not** to be sacrificed **in any town** other than the one he would **choose**. The festival must begin **in the evening, when the sun goes down**, on the anniversary of the departure of Israel. In Exodus 12:10,29–31, the text suggests that Israel stayed awake through the night as a recognition of how Yahweh had kept watch over them in the crisis. In time, Jesus was to transform elements of the Passover into the Lord's Supper, a recognition of the redemption that he would bring about through his death (cp. Luke 22:1,7,13,15–20).

16:7–8. The sacrificial animal at Passover was to be eaten roasted and only at the city of the central sanctuary. Once the meal was over, people were directed to **return** to their tents.

Some have seen in this last word an indication of a nomadic setting, but this need not be the case. Records show that the population of Jerusalem would mushroom to ten times its normal size for the Passover, and the local dwellings simply could not accommodate such an enormous increase. The overflow would camp in tents—either those that they brought or that they rented from local merchants. At any rate, **to your tents** remained an idiom for "to your homes" for many generations to come (cp. 2 Kgs. 8:21; 13:5; 14:12 NASB).

For the **six days** following the evening of Passover, Israel was to **eat unleavened bread**. On the **seventh day** people would gather in **an assembly** to worship the Lord, and then be dismissed to their homes.

16:9–10. Passover/Unleavened Bread marked the first religious festival of Israel's year. The second was **the Feast of Weeks**, or, as it became more commonly called later, the Feast of Pentecost. It began exactly **seven weeks from the time** corn began to be harvested. It, too, was a celebration; not of deliverance, but of blessing. Worshipers were to bring **a freewill offering** that was **in proportion to the blessings** of the harvest.

16:11–12. The Feast of Weeks, like the other festivals (except the Day of Atonement, which involved mourning for sin), was above all a time to **rejoice before the LORD**. God intended that the corporate life of the nation and the individual life of the believer be driven by joy. Only as Israel rejoiced in God could they show the world his sufficiency and greatness. In fact, God insisted that Israel's rejoicing be all-inclusive. **Sons, daughters, menservants, maidservants, the Levites**, and **aliens** were all to participate in the celebration that recognized God's blessing upon them all. As they rejoiced, the people of God were also to **remember** that they had been **slaves in Egypt**. Those memories would serve to reinforce their joy as they contemplated the contrast between what they were and what they had been.

In the same spirit, Christians are to rejoice continuously as we consider the changes that God brings into our lives. The joyful life is a winsome life and a solid recommendation of the faith we represent.

16:13–15. Israel's third annual major festival was the **Feast of Tabernacles** ("Booths"). It was celebrated for **seven days** after the people had

Deuteronomy 16:16–17

harvested grain and grapes. According to Leviticus, this feast was to take place in the fall: "On the fifteenth day of the seventh month the Lord's Feast of Tabernacles begins, and it lasts for seven days" (Lev. 23:34). The seventh month was Tishri (mid-September to mid-October), marking the end of the wheat-growing season as Weeks had signified its beginning.

The name *Tabernacles,* however, derives not from agricultural associations but from God's insistence that Israel remember its wilderness wanderings: "Live in booths for seven days: All native-born Israelites are to live in booths so your descendants will know that I had the Israelites live in booths when I brought them out of Egypt. I am the LORD your God" (Lev. 23:42–43).

Again, the dominant motif of Tabernacles was to be universal joy over what God had done in providing for Israel's needs. They were to celebrate for seven days at the place of the central shrine. Every part of every Israelite household was to **be joyful** at the feast in recognition of the goodness of God.

16:16–17. These verses summarize the festival year. **Three times** each year the **men** of Israel were required **to appear before the** LORD, and verses 11 and 14 strongly suggest that the females of each household were expected to attend all or part of these events as well. On each occasion, **the Feast of Unleavened Bread, the Feast of Weeks and the Feast of Tabernacles**, Israelites were to come to the place God would choose; and **no man should appear before the** LORD **empty-handed.** Sacrifice is the essence of worship, so each person was to bring a gift **in proportion to the way** God had blessed.

B The Justice of Israel's Communities (16:18–22)

SUPPORTING IDEA: *Worshiping Yahweh involves not only regular periods of rejoicing, but a careful pursuit of the justice that is characteristic of Yahweh himself.*

16:18. While the periodic worship of the festivals called Israel to the central sanctuary, the regular life of the nation could honor God best by a consistent display of justice in every town that the Lord was giving them. Moses instructed the people to **appoint judges and officials** in each tribe. These leaders would be expected to **judge the people fairly.**

16:19–20. The principles upon which Israelite justice would be based are given. Judges were prohibited from showing partiality in the administration of justice. They were warned against accepting **a bribe**, since a bribe **blinds the eyes of the wise.** Judges were to operate on the principle of following **justice and justice alone.** If they did so, the judges and the people who came to them for justice would **live and possess the land.**

16:21–22. The standard of justice in the promised land was always to be the character of Yahweh himself, upon whom everything depended. The judges of Israel were not to tolerate spiritual defection in any form. As an example, Moses excluded the setting up of **any wooden Asherah pole** beside the central **altar** of Israel. The proximity of such a pole would invest it with the authority of divine associations and was therefore prohibited, as was a **sacred stone** or pillar. These items were associated with the worship of Canaanite false gods and represented objects that the Lord hated.

> **MAIN IDEA REVIEW:** Yahweh is to be the centerpiece of Israel's national life. The people are to enjoy him fully at his appointed festivals, pursue the justice that reflects his character, and worship him exclusively.

III. CONCLUSION

My Grace Is Sufficient

Charles Spurgeon was in his day the best-known preacher in the English-speaking world, and he was a man who was prone to fits of depression. On one occasion while riding home after a long day at work, his spirits were low. Remembering a text he had read earlier in the day, he began to meditate upon it: "My grace is sufficient for thee: for my strength is made perfect in weakness" (2 Cor. 12:9 KJV).

He considered his own smallness compared to God's greatness and compared it to a small fish that feared lest he drink the river dry. God might say to such a fish, "Drink up, little fish, my stream is sufficient for you."

Then he thought of a mountain climber who was concerned that he might consume all the air in the atmosphere and was instead assured, "Breathe away, young man, and fill your lungs; my atmosphere is sufficient for you."

His meditation had the desired result. He said, "I experienced the joy that Abraham felt when he rejoiced in God's provision." God's well never runs dry. His resources are limitless, so we need never fear drinking deeply of his goodness. It is given to us for our joy.

PRINCIPLES

- God delights to see his people rejoice in what he has provided.
- A good memory is one of the most precious assets of spiritual living.
- Recalling what our lives were like before Jesus Christ entered them will help keep our daily problems in perspective.
- Prosperity is often the enemy of spiritual development.

APPLICATIONS

- Make a list of contrasts between life before and after conversion. Let your list guide your devotions this week.

- Give an honest answer to the question, "Do I serve the Lord joyfully or reluctantly?"
- If you are unhappy with your answer to the previous question, spend some time doing a concordance study of the word *rejoice* in Scripture (particularly in the Psalms).
- Give God a freewill financial gift of appreciation for some recent blessing.

IV. LIFE APPLICATION

The Joy Set Before Him

The righteous life is a joyous life. What took Jesus to the cross was the possibilities that lay on the other side of the cross, as the author of Hebrews explains: "Let us fix our eyes on Jesus, the author and perfecter of our faith, who for the joy set before him endured the cross, scorning its shame, and sat down at the right hand of the throne of God" (Heb. 12:2).

Jesus knew that carrying out his mission of being an atonement for sin would yield him the joy of having completed the job and knowing the Father's approval on his life. Now he awaits the time when he will be granted the nations as his inheritance (cp. Ps. 2:7–9).

Deuteronomy 16, Hebrews 12, and other texts explode the myth that Christianity is altruistic—a dangerous heresy. Did Jesus Christ lay down his life for you and me? He certainly did. Did he go to the cross *only* for you and me? No; he also did it for himself. It was in *his* interests to go to the cross, because now he enjoys the prospect of a worthy rule over and with his people.

That same motivation should be ours, too. Jesus once told a parable about servants who were given money to use in commerce while the investor was away. When the one who supplied the money returned, he called his servants to him for an accounting. When one explained how he had doubled the master's earnings, the lord said to him, "Well done, good and faithful servant; you have been faithful over a few things, I will make you ruler over many things. Enter into the joy of your lord" (Matt. 25:23 NKJV). Contemplating the joy that will be ours when we hear the Lord Jesus commending our labors is something that ought to make us stronger believers.

Among other things, letting joy drive us will keep us from the ugly business of wearing a martyr complex. Few things are as unattractive as the person who engages in Christian service reluctantly, calling attention to the price he is paying to serve God.

We are supposed to do what we do in obedience to God and from love for people because it is a delight to serve God and a thrill to know that his commendation lies ahead. Christian living should be a joy-driven experience.

V. PRAYER

Father, allow our hearts to be captured by your joy. Keep us from focusing on obstacles and difficulties that obscure our vision of you. Amen.

VI. DEEPER DISCOVERIES

A. The Calendars of Israel (16:1)

In Old Testament times, Israel's sacred year began officially in the spring with a month that was variously called *Abib* (six times) or *Nisan* (twice). At the institution of the Passover, God told Israel, "This month is to be for you the first month, the first month of your year" (Exod. 12:2). Apparently the year had previously begun in the fall with the month *Tishri* (September-October) at the time of the early rains, and in some instances the civic year seems to have continued on a Tishri-Tishri basis: "Celebrate the Feast of Weeks with the firstfruits of the wheat harvest, and the Feast of Ingathering at the turn of the year" (Exod. 34:22). The ancient months with their modern equivalents appear below:

Abib/Nisan	March-April
Iyyar	April-May
Sivan	May-June
Tammuz	June-July
Ab	July-August
Elul	August-September
Tishri	September-October
Heshvan	October-November
Kislev	November-December
Tebeth	December-January
Shebat	January-February
Adar	February-March

Because the Hebrew year was based on a lunar cycle (twelve months, alternately of thirty or twenty-nine days), about every three years a thirteenth intercalary month was added, called "second Adar."

B. Leaven (16:3)

Moses explained to Israel that for one week a year leavening agents should not be present in the Jewish home: "Do not eat [the Passover] with bread made with yeast, but for seven days eat unleavened bread, the bread of affliction, because you left Egypt in haste—so that all the days of your life you may remember the time of your departure from Egypt" (Deut. 16:3). Leavened bread was part of the basic diet of Israel from ancient times: "They are all adulterers, burning like an oven whose fire the baker need not stir from the kneading of the dough till it rises" (Hos. 7:4).

Deuteronomy 16

Because of some New Testament references to leaven, it is often taught that unleavened bread was eaten at Passover because leaven's penetrating quality made it a natural symbol of evil. For example, Paul wrote: "Therefore let us keep the Festival, not with the old yeast, the yeast of malice and wickedness, but with bread without yeast, the bread of sincerity and truth" (1 Cor. 5:8). However, in the original Passover, leaven was excluded not because it connoted evil, but because Israel left Egypt in haste, without time for bread to rise (cp. Exod. 12:11,33; Deut. 16:3).

While leaven was prohibited in the blood offerings made by fire (cp. Lev. 2:11; 6:17; 7:12), God accepted leaven made in peace or fellowship offerings and in firstfruit offerings (Lev. 7:13; 23:17). Although Scripture is silent about the presence or absence of leaven in the shewbread of Israel, the ancient Jewish historian Josephus reports that the shewbread was in fact unleavened.

VII. TEACHING OUTLINE

A. INTRODUCTION
1. Lead Story: The Red Couch
2. Context: The people of Israel would find themselves drifting away from the Lord unless they set aside regular periods to refresh themselves in God's goodness. He was to be their joy and the moral standard of their communities.
3. Transition: God desires that his people rejoice frequently and enthusiastically in his goodness. He gains great glory when we find ourselves satisfied in his grace.

B. COMMENTARY
1. The Joy of Israel's Celebrations (16:1–17)
2. The Justice of Israel's Communities (16:18–22)

C. CONCLUSION: THE JOY SET BEFORE HIM

VIII. ISSUES FOR DISCUSSION

1. Why is it important to memorialize significant events in one's spiritual life?
2. Why do you think God insisted on one central place for the celebration of Israel's major festivals?
3. Can you think of some reasons why Jesus used the Passover as the basis for the Lord's Supper?
4. Why was God so insistent that worshipers not appear before him empty-handed?

Deuteronomy 17

The Great Society

I. INTRODUCTION
The Gift of the Fortunate

II. COMMENTARY
A verse-by-verse explanation of the chapter.

III. CONCLUSION
Faithful to His Commitments

An overview of the principles and applications from the chapter.

IV. LIFE APPLICATION
Ernest's Gun

Melding the chapter to life.

V. PRAYER
Tying the chapter to life with God.

VI. DEEPER DISCOVERIES
Historical, geographical, and grammatical enrichment of the commentary.

VII. TEACHING OUTLINE
Suggested step-by-step group study of the chapter.

VIII. ISSUES FOR DISCUSSION
Zeroing the chapter in on daily life.

Deuteronomy 17

> ### Quote
>
> "Christianity, rightly understood, is utterly unlike religion that man invents. It is so completely contrary to the way man does things that it must have come from God. Take Christmas, for example; only God could have thought of that. When man invents a super being, he comes up with a Superman, or a Captain Marvel. God gives the world a baby."
>
> Richard Halverson

IN A NUTSHELL

In Deuteronomy 17, God calls on his people to revere him and to translate this reverence into the establishment of a just society marked by respect for others.

The Great Society

I. INTRODUCTION

The Gift of the Fortunate

In one of his books, Roy Laurin tells about a Christian businessman who was traveling in Korea. As he and the missionary who was his guide and interpreter moved along, they observed an unusual scene. In a field by the side of the road was a young man pulling a primitive plow while an old man was holding the handles. The businessman was amused and took a snapshot of the pair.

"That is curious!" he said. "I suppose these people are very poor."

"Yes," the guide noted. "Those two men happen to be Christians. When their church was being built, they were eager to give something toward it; but they had no money. So they decided to sell their one and only ox and give the proceeds to the church. This spring they are pulling the plow themselves."

The businessman was silent for a while. Then he said, "That must have been a real sacrifice."

"They did not call it that," said the missionary. "They thought it was fortunate that they had an ox to sell."

There are gifts to God that are valuable for the good they can do, and there are gifts to God that are priceless for the statement they make about the heart of the giver. The Korean farmers' gift fell into the second category.

God calls on his people to delight in him so much that they make consistent statements in their worship of the way they esteem him. Only a person who has an eternal perspective on things can live joyfully in the present.

II. COMMENTARY

The Great Society

MAIN IDEA: *Israel was to be a nation that fostered respect for all its citizens, a respect built on reverence for God and obedience to his Word.*

A The Precedence of Respect for Yahweh (17:1)

SUPPORTING IDEA: *God's people were to build respect into their society by first reverencing Yahweh in their worship.*

17:1. One thing that made Israel distinctive was its policy of respect for all its citizens. Human life was important, in God's frame of reference, because it was his invention and it was made in his image. Respect could

Deuteronomy 17:2–6

never rise any higher in Israel than the individual worshiper's reverence for his God. Yahweh insisted that Israelites **not sacrifice to the LORD** an animal that had **any defect or flaw in it**. The Lord was to be given the best as an expression of the worshiper's heart. He could not hold Yahweh close to his heart and at the same time offer a flawed sacrifice, something that would be detestable to God. Human affections always follow the soul's investment. Loving motions create loving emotions.

🅱 The Principle of Respect for Justice (17:2–13)

> **SUPPORTING IDEA:** *Israel was required to deal respectfully with those accused of crimes, to submit to those responsible for rendering justice, and to revere the law itself.*

17:2–6. The person in Israel who was **found doing evil** in the eyes of the Lord was subject to severe penalties, but they were to be given due process of divine law and the benefit of a doubt. Even if they had **worshiped other gods**, the matter would have to be handled carefully. Community leaders were to **investigate** everything **thoroughly** and determine whether it was true that such **a detestable thing** had taken place. Only if the offense had actually occurred would the people of the community proceed. They were to take the offender and **stone that person to death**. The sentence would be carried out at the **city gate**, the area of heaviest traffic and the seat of local law courts, so the community could see for itself the gravity of disobedience of Yahweh. Both **a man** and a **woman** were subject to the death penalty in Israel.

Under no circumstances, however, could a person **be put to death on the testimony of only one witness**. An individual's testimony could be false, but it would be far less likely that **two or three witnesses** would conspire to pervert justice. Because of this prohibition, there were undoubtedly apostates and murderers in Israel who escaped the justice of community law; but the safeguard was necessary to respect the interests of people who were falsely accused.

17:7. In Israel, the law was never to be a vehicle of private vengeance. **All the people** had a stake in justice, but the accuser was required to bear responsibility for his testimony and to **be the first in putting** the offender **to death**. No doubt this precept must have given many witnesses pause before bringing a report to the community authorities. This statement lies behind Jesus' caution, "If any one of you is without sin, let him be the first to throw a stone at her" (John 8:7).

17:8–13. Matters of justice are seldom simple, and Moses recognized that **cases** might **come before** Israel's **courts** that would prove **too difficult** for settlement at the local level. Israelite justice therefore had to contain an appeals process. The matter would be taken **to the place the LORD** would **choose**—presumably the same place as the central sanctuary, although the language is less specific—and submitted to higher authority. **The priests** were to be consulted, as well as **the judge** who was **in office at that time**. They were to render a **verdict**.

Since there were two sides to every matter of justice (and particularly so in appeals cases), it would be tempting to reject the decision of the appellate judge. Israel was solemnly warned not to do so. People **must act** according to the judicial decisions they receive and not take the law into their own hands or show **contempt** of the **judge** or **priest**. To show such disrespect to God's duly constituted system of justice was to call down grave consequences. Rebels must be **put to death**.

C The Practice of Respect for the People (17:14-20)

SUPPORTING IDEA: Although Israel would in time ask for a king and reject Yahweh's rule in the process, they were cautioned to appoint a ruler who would humble himself before God and respect his people.

17:14. Three centuries later perilous times would cause Israel to reject God's personal rule over their land and to call instead for **a king**. This happened during the latter years of Samuel, who was a wonder as a judge and prophet but less successful as a parent. When his sons, who were appointed judges by Samuel, proved to be disappointing leaders, the people complained (cp. 1 Sam. 8:1-5). In calling for a king to rule over them **like all the nations** around them, Israel jettisoned the distinctive position that God wanted them to enjoy. Still, God's concern at this time was to make sure that the king, who might pose a terrible threat to justice himself through an autocratic rule, should be the right kind of person.

17:15-17. Moses gave Israel a series of four external safeguards to minimize the potential for authoritarian abuse by a king. If he should violate any of these provisions, his disobedience would be a matter of public scrutiny. First among God's warnings was his insistence that only an Israelite rule in Israel. The king must be **from among** the native Jewish population and could not be **a foreigner**.

A second external safeguard lay in the provision that the king refrain from collecting **great numbers of horses** that would enlarge his army's power and inflate his ego. In addition to these obvious pitfalls, amassing large numbers of horses would tempt the people to **return to Egypt**, where the best animals were to be found.

A third warning concerned the accumulation of **wives** who could lead him **astray** toward pagan worship. Solomon himself, the wisest of Israel's kings, blundered in this regard: "King Solomon, however, loved many foreign women . . . They were from nations about which the LORD had told the Israelites, 'You must not intermarry with them, because they will surely turn your

Deuteronomy 17:18-20

hearts after their gods'" (1 Kgs. 11:1–2). Solomon also disregarded the fourth warning not to **accumulate large amounts of silver and gold**. God wanted the leader of his people to trust in him, not in material goods. This principle was violated by David much later when he called for a census of Israel: "Satan rose up against Israel and incited David to take a census of Israel" (1 Chr. 21:1). By trusting in the size of his battalions, David was turning away from faith in Yahweh.

17:18–20. God desired the king's (and Israel's) security to be connected not with the accumulation of armies or financial reserves but with a strong inner loyalty to Yahweh. To emphasize this point, Moses instructed that each new king, in the aftermath of his coronation, should **write for himself on a scroll** a copy of God's law. By having the words personally written, God ensured that a measure of interaction with the text would take place.

The king was not only to copy the text, he was to **read it all the days of his life**. In so doing, he would learn to **revere the LORD**. In God's view, the primary qualifications for kingship were moral and spiritual rather than diplomatic skills or military prowess.

By making himself subject to God's law and decrees, the king would make it clear that he did **not consider himself better than his brothers** and as a result would not **turn from the law**. Although God tolerated rather than prescribed a monarchy in Israel, he would not have caused further harm to his people by having tyrants rule over them. In fact, obedience would tend toward protracting royal rule in Israel: **Then he and his descendants will reign a long time over his kingdom**.

> **MAIN IDEA REVIEW:** Israel was to be a nation that fostered respect for all its citizens, a respect built on reverence for God and obedience to his Word.

III. CONCLUSION

Faithful to His Commitments

Stuart Briscoe, former pastor of Elmbrook Church in Brookfield, Wisconsin, tells about an episode that took place when he was still in the banking business in England. He was called on one day to confront a coworker who was discovered to have embezzled an enormous sum of money from the bank. The embezzler's explanation? He was leading a double life that was too expensive. He had two wives, two families, and two homes.

When he was presented with the evidence of his theft, he "apologized" by saying, "I am very sorry for what I have done; now I need to know whether I should fulfill my preaching commitments on Sunday in our local church." The contradiction between his moral standards and those of the God whom he professed to serve was obvious to others but not to himself. Briscoe notes that he spent a great deal of time in the following months attempting to repair some of the damage done by that embezzler's absurd "testimony."

Christians have the potential to cause either great harm or great good to the cause of the Lord by their moral lives. Just as Israel was expected to make a statement about the moral principles of Yahweh by the way they operated their communities, so Christian believers declare the character of Jesus Christ—either truly or falsely—by their actions in the world.

PRINCIPLES

- A worshiper's gift makes a statement about the worshiper and his God.
- In God's pattern of justice, he takes the risk of the guilty going free but not of the innocent being punished.
- Man's sinful nature causes him to deny his guilt as well as pervert the judicial system that seeks to discover the truth.
- God is not naïve in the giving of his laws; he anticipates our disobedience even as he commands our obedience.
- There is no substitute for a firsthand encounter with the Word of God.

APPLICATIONS

- Assess your pattern of giving to determine whether any gifts have "flaws."
- Recognize the common tendency for people of faith to want to be like the rest of the world.
- Understand the connection between worship and financial giving.
- Judge any inclinations in your heart to prefer accumulated resources over trust in God.
- Begin to read the Scriptures on a daily basis.

IV. LIFE APPLICATION

Ernest's Gun

Ernest Hemingway was the envy of his generation. He was a celebrated author and a hard-drinking ladies' man who had been everywhere and done everything. Hemingway first began to be noticed as a reporter for the *Kansas City Star*. He served as an ambulance driver in World War I, spent summers in Europe, and became a noted participant in the Spanish Civil War.

Deuteronomy 17

He knew everyone of importance—movie actresses, the famous bullfighter Manolete, F. Scott Fitzgerald—the list was long and important. He was a big-game hunter, soldier of fortune, and prize-winning novelist. He knew how to live.

But Hemingway didn't know what he was living for. Without a core to his life, the experiences began to lose their flavor. His drinking began to take its toll on his body, and the emptiness within finally became too much. One beautiful Sunday morning he went downstairs in his Key West home and opened the gun closet. He took out a favorite shotgun, dropped in two shells, and placed the gun butt on the floor. Turning the gun toward himself, he placed the twin barrels just above his eyebrows, and pulled both triggers.

Hemingway could have sympathized with fellow novelist Jack Higgins, who was asked what he would like to have known when he was younger. He replied, "I wish I had known that when you get to the top, there's nothing there."

The world's beautiful people suffer from the sorrows that arise from disillusionment. Unless they have a vital connection with God, they are likely to regard the problem as being caused by the emptiness of the world rather than the emptiness of their own hearts. Only God can fill the vacuum and give meaning to human experience.

V. PRAYER

Father, teach us lasting and eternal values so we might know you deeply. Save us from the disappointments that come when we turn our eyes toward the trinkets of our world and away from you, its only genuine treasure. Amen.

VI. DEEPER DISCOVERIES

A. Purging the Wicked (17:7,12)

Twice in this chapter Moses urged upon Israel the importance of separating itself from people who had brought guilt upon the land. In verse 7, he warns, "You must purge the evil from among you." Again, in verse 12: "You must purge the evil from Israel." These words, or slight variations on them, also appear six times elsewhere in Deuteronomy.

The apostle Paul used this language when describing the treatment of a sinning Christian in Corinth. A believer had begun an incestuous relationship with his stepmother (cp. 1 Cor. 5:1), and the church in Corinth had done nothing about it. Paul directed that unless the offender repented, he should be banned from the life of the church and even from table fellowship with believers (1 Cor. 5:7,9–13). If they refused to carry out such measures, the apostle himself would deliver the sinning brother over to the devil for destruction (1 Cor. 5:5).

Although Christians are not to inflict capital punishment on one another, they are to withhold fellowship with a view to provoking repentance. God acknowledges that one believer who displays scandalous behavior can stain the testimony of the entire believing community.

B. Horses (17:16)

Moses warned Israel's kings to trust in God rather than in the might of their armies: "The king, moreover, must not acquire great numbers of horses for himself or make the people return to Egypt to get more of them, for the LORD has told you, 'You are not to go back that way again'" (Deut. 17:16). Horses were often associated with royalty and excessive pageantry, but they were especially important in the ancient world for pulling chariots. God's warning about returning to Egypt to acquire such animals might only imply the sending of trading deputations, but it might also infer that some Israelites themselves would be traded to the Egyptians for horses. Solomon once exchanged several towns (apparently in the form of tax revenues) to Hiram for lumber (see 1 Kgs. 9:11–14).

The most serious violation of these warnings took place during the reign of Solomon:

> Solomon accumulated chariots and horses; he had fourteen hundred chariots and twelve thousand horses, which he kept in the chariot cities and also with him in Jerusalem. . . . Solomon's horses were imported from Egypt and from Kue—the royal merchants purchased them from Kue. They imported a chariot from Egypt for six hundred shekels of silver, and a horse for a hundred and fifty (1 Kgs. 10:26,28–29).

VII. TEACHING OUTLINE

A. INTRODUCTION
1. Lead Story: The Gift of the Fortunate
2. Context: A great society begins with reverence, but it does not end there. Respect for God should issue in respect for justice for everyone.
3. Transition: God insists that his people recognize the connection between the way they behave in their communities and the way they proclaim his message.

B. COMMENTARY
1. The Precedence of Respect for Yahweh (17:1)

Deuteronomy 17

2. The Principle of Respect for Justice (17:2–13)
3. The Practice of Respect for the People (17:14–20)

C. CONCLUSION: ERNEST'S GUN

VIII. ISSUES FOR DISCUSSION

1. How does God balance the rights of the accused and the rights of the victim?
2. How can the church promote a more just society? Does such a society hold any benefits for the propagation of the gospel?
3. What are the dangers to society when a ruler exalts himself as superior to his countrymen?

Deuteronomy 18

A Prophet like Moses

- **I. INTRODUCTION**
  Can You Keep a Secret?

- **II. COMMENTARY**
  A verse-by-verse explanation of the chapter.

- **III. CONCLUSION**
  The Exalted Stove

  An overview of the principles and applications from the chapter.

- **IV. LIFE APPLICATION**
  The Lady Be Good

  Melding the chapter to life.

- **V. PRAYER**
  Tying the chapter to life with God.

- **VI. DEEPER DISCOVERIES**
  Historical, geographical, and grammatical enrichment of the commentary.

- **VII. TEACHING OUTLINE**
  Suggested step-by-step group study of the chapter.

- **VIII. ISSUES FOR DISCUSSION**
  Zeroing the chapter in on daily life.

Deuteronomy 18

Quote

"If someone considers the prophetic writings with all the diligence and reverence they are worth, while he reads and examines with great care, it is certain that in that very act he will be struck in his mind and senses by some more divine breath and will recognize that the books he reads have not been produced in a human way, but are words of God."

Origen of Alexandria

IN A NUTSHELL

Deuteronomy 18 explains how Israel, soon to be without Moses, will not lack for divinely ordained leadership. The priests and Levites will attend to regular matters of worship, and God will raise up prophets to reveal his will.

A Prophet like Moses

I. INTRODUCTION

Can You Keep a Secret?

The Duke of Wellington is best known as the British general who defeated Napoleon at Waterloo in 1815, altering the course of European history. During Wellington's earlier service in India, he was placed in charge of negotiations when authority over various parts of India was being divided among the maharajahs. The emissary of one of these Indian rulers, anxious to know what territories would be ceded to his master, tried to obtain advance information about the division. When nothing worked, he offered Wellington a large sum of money to disclose the information to him.

Wellington motioned for him to come near. "Can you keep a secret?" asked Wellington.

"Yes, indeed," the man replied.

"So can I," replied Wellington.

God has decreed many plans for this age that remain undisclosed. As Moses explained to Israel, "The secret things belong to the LORD our God, but the things revealed belong to us and to our children forever, that we may follow all the words of this law" (Deut. 29:29). The "things revealed" to humankind have been revealed through the ministry of the prophets.

God in his grace has through the ministry of the prophets of the Old and New Testaments laid out the outline of his plan of the ages. In it we see at the end Jesus Christ glorified and triumphant, reigning with his followers throughout eternity. Because of the prophets, the ancients knew the lineage, birthplace, and character of the coming Messiah, and the New Testament prophets became part of the foundation of the church (Eph. 2:20).

God in revealing his plans has decreed that they should not be a secret but instead should be proclaimed throughout the world, that all people might come to know his plans to exalt Jesus Christ. Because of God's love expressed through the prophets, the plan of the ages is available for all.

Deuteronomy 18:1-2

II. COMMENTARY

A Prophet like Moses

MAIN IDEA: *Although Moses will soon pass off the scene, God will continue to provide for his people's spiritual needs through Levites and prophets.*

A Providing for Leadership: Defending the Levites (18:1-8)

SUPPORTING IDEA: *Israel must provide for those who exercise leadership in worship among the Levites.*

18:1-2. Because of their zeal for God at the time of the golden calf incident (Deut. 10:8), the **Levites** were set apart for service in connection with the tabernacle and its worship. Out of this tribe, the family of Aaron was designated to serve as **priests**. However, **the whole tribe**—priests and those who engaged in setting up and dismantling the worship system—was prohibited from owning property in the promised land. God instructed that they should **live on the offerings made to the LORD by fire**, which would serve as their **inheritance**. Those offerings included the meal or grain offering, the sin offering, and the guilt offering (Num. 18:9). The Lord himself would serve as **their inheritance** and give them blessings that more than compensated for the Levites' loss of material wealth.

18:3-5. Israel was commanded not to neglect the Levites, since their work was so important and since the ordinary methods of income production were closed off to them. In these verses Moses specified the nature of the offerings he mentioned in verse 1. When a bull or sheep was offered to God, the priests were to receive designated portions of the animal. Specifically, they were to be given **the shoulder, the jowls and the inner parts**. When the worshipers brought other items, the priests were to receive **the firstfruits** of the country's **grain, new wine and oil, and the first wool** when the sheep were sheared. The gifts of Israel were to be given in recognition of the Levites' **chosen** role among the tribes: **to stand and minister in the LORD's name**.

The Levites were in relation to Israel what Israel was in relation to the rest of the nations. Levites were chosen for a special spiritual role, and they were dependent on the other tribes for survival, just as the nation was dependent on God.

18:6-8. Moses recognized that Levi's designated role might prompt some in the tribe to move from **one** of the **towns** where they were **living** and take up residence (at least temporarily) at **the place the LORD will choose**. This move would be fueled by the **earnestness** a Levite would feel about his responsibility to **minister in the name of the LORD**. Moses insisted that anyone who did so should not be penalized because he had left a more secure situation. The one whose zeal prompted him to move was **to share equally** in the **benefits** of those serving in the temple of the future.

B Protecting the Leadership: Detestable Practices (18:9-14)

SUPPORTING IDEA: *Israel must beware of substituting pagan religious practices for those revealed by God.*

18:9. For forty years, Moses had served God faithfully in the leadership of his people (cp. Num. 12:7), but as a mortal man he would soon pass off the scene. Once Israel was settled in their land, the time would come when they would want to know the mind of God as it applied to them, and Moses would not be available. When that happened, they were not **to imitate the detestable ways of the nations** they were dispossessing. All the Canaanite nations had invented or copied methods of knowing the future; these methods must be shunned by Israel.

18:10-11. The general principle is translated into specific prohibitions. Israel was not to imitate the practice of child sacrifice in an effort to appease a pagan deity and influence the course of the future. They were not to practice **divination**, the consulting of objects or people (living or dead) to discover what would happen in the future (see "Deeper Discoveries").

Israel was also prohibited from engaging in **sorcery**, the art of the occult. Sorcerers were, according to the literal meaning of the Hebrew text, "those who cause to appear." Their apparitions could seduce Israel into abandoning the worship of Yahweh. The Old Testament recognizes the reality of the spirit world and does not prohibit Israel from dabbling in it because of its ineffectiveness but because of its association with pagan deities.

Nor could the people of God tolerate the presence among them of one who interpreted **omens**, predicting the future on the basis of how objects fell out of a cup (cp. Gen. 44:5), for example.

Witchcraft was also excluded as a method of discovering future events. The category includes those who performed what were (or appeared to be) supernaturally caused signs. Often these were designed to expel evil (Isa. 47:9,12).

The person who **casts spells** was thought to be able to use curses to control the destiny of others. The **medium** was one who practiced necromancy (as did the **spiritist**), attempting to contact **the dead** to obtain special information. Sometimes special vocal sounds were used to invoke these spirits (Isa. 8:19; cp. Lev. 20:6,27; 1 Sam. 28:3,9; 2 Kgs. 21:6).

18:12-14. Such **detestable practices** as those Moses cataloged had led God to **drive out those nations** who were in the land. Israel would risk a

Deuteronomy 18:15

similar expulsion if they should take part in such exercises. Nor could such black arts be pursued as a sideline by only a few people in Israel. **Anyone** who engaged in these practices was **detestable to the LORD**. Israel was to be upright or **blameless** and to abhor such practices.

C Pruning the Leadership: Detecting Prophets (18:15–22)

SUPPORTING IDEA: *God will reveal himself through genuine prophets, to whose word Israel must pay the closest attention.*

18:15. God did not, however, close off a knowledge of the future from his people. But instead of using the magical practices common to the nations, they were to listen to the **prophet** whom God would **raise up** for them in the future. He would be like Moses in the sense that he would reveal God's truth to them with fidelity and accuracy. When the prophet spoke, God would be speaking; consequently, Israel **must listen** to his words.

18:16–18. The provision of the Word of God by means of a prophet lay in the request of the nation when they were still **at Horeb on the day of the assembly**. They had asked Moses to act as their intermediary. The people were frightened by **the voice of the LORD** and alarmed by the **great fire** on the mountain. Concerned that they might die, the people requested that Moses receive the **words** of God on their behalf. God regarded their request as a good and reasonable one, and granted it. In the same spirit, he would again do so in the future, raising **up for them a prophet** like Moses. The task of the prophet appears in a succinct form in verse 18: **I will put my words in his mouth, and he will tell them everything I command him.**

18:19. Because the prophet was God's mouthpiece, his **words** held divine authority. To reject the words that the prophet spoke was to reject God, and he would not permit such rebellion to go unchallenged: **I myself will call him to account**. On some occasions, the prophet might be able to execute divine judgment himself, as Paul did with Elymas the sorcerer (see Acts 13:9–11).

18:20. The office of prophet carried a great potential for abuse, since prophets would say some things that could not be tested immediately. To prevent such abuse, God declared that **a prophet** who presumed to speak what God had **not commanded** would be subject to the **death** penalty. This text should be compared carefully with the description of a false prophet in Deuteronomy 13:1–11. The two passages together describe two categories of false prophets: those who prophesied in the interests of another God and those who spoke falsely in Yahweh's name.

18:21–22. Because of the dangers inherent in prophetic ministry, the people would naturally want to know, **How can we know when a message has not been spoken by the LORD?**

The answer to this question was simple and straightforward: The prophet who proclaimed something that did **not take place or come true** was a false prophet, setting forth **a message the LORD has not spoken**. It can be seen clearly from this text that prediction was the essence of prophetic ministry. Although not everything that a prophet spoke was a prediction, he had to earn his credibility by means of his predictive utterances. Once he had gained the confidence of the public by means of prophetic accuracy, his ministry in other areas would be enhanced. Thus the writer of 1 Samuel 3:19–20 notes, "The LORD was with Samuel as he grew up, and he let none of his words fall to the ground. And all Israel from Dan to Beersheba recognized that Samuel was attested as a prophet of the LORD."

The prophet held a place of high honor in Israel. Moses' remark that Israel should **not be afraid** of false prophets carries with it the necessary implication that they should extend a healthy respect to those who were true prophets.

> **MAIN IDEA REVIEW:** Although Moses will soon pass off the scene, God will continue to provide for his people's spiritual needs through Levites and prophets.

III. CONCLUSION

The Exalted Stove

In *Laughing Out Loud and Other Religious Experiences*, author Tom Mullen tells about an engineer, a psychologist, and a theologian who were on an extended hunting trip in northern Canada. The weather turned stormy, so they sought shelter at an empty cabin.

As they went into the cabin, they saw something striking: a cast-iron potbellied stove suspended in midair by wires attached to the ceiling beams. The trio could not keep themselves from speculating on the reason for the stove's elevation. They each began to express the meaning of such a phenomenon. The psychologist opined, "It is obvious that this lonely trapper, isolated from humanity, has elevated his stove so he can curl up under it and vicariously experience a return to his mother's womb."

The engineer disagreed, saying, "The man is practicing the laws of thermodynamics. By elevating his stove, he has discovered a way to distribute heat more evenly throughout the cabin."

The theologian offered a more profound explanation: "I'm sure that hanging his stove from the ceiling has a religious meaning. Fire lifted up has been a religious symbol for centuries."

The three continued their debate for some time without resolving the issue. Finally, when the trapper returned, they asked him why he had hung his potbellied stove by wires from the ceiling.

Deuteronomy 18

"I had plenty of wire but not much stovepipe," he replied.

Speculation can carry even the wisest of men only so far. The meaning of life, like the purpose of an exalted stove, can be known only when it is declared openly by the one who designed it. Thanks be to God for the glorious gift of his intent for the world, revealed to humanity through the prophetic Scriptures!

PRINCIPLES

- Those who serve God in vocational ministry must learn to trust him for their daily needs before they can encourage others to do so.
- Intimacy with God is to be preferred above material wealth.
- Giving to God should come from the firstfruits of a person's labor rather than from what is left after the bills are paid.
- When believers neglect the revealed Word of God, they are likely to turn to silly and unprofitable methods of insight.

APPLICATIONS

- Don't allow your curiosity about occult or New Age religion to lead you away from God's truth.
- Understand the relationship between a prophet's ministry of foretelling the future and his exhortation of the people of God.
- Work to be able to explain the gospel of Christ by using the Scriptures.

IV. LIFE APPLICATION

The Lady Be Good

The crew of a B-24 Liberator known as *Lady Be Good* finished its mission over Europe on one occasion late in the war and headed for its assigned landing field in North Africa. As the day waned and darkness fell, they were required to find their base by using their radar and their instruments. Because they had flown the route before, they knew the approximate amount of time they would be airborne.

However, they were unaware of the fact that they were being pushed along by a strong tailwind. When their instruments indicated they were over their landing field far earlier than they expected, they refused to believe it. They continued to fly into the night while they looked for the familiar lights of their destination. Eventually their fuel supply ran out, and they crashed in the desert.

The bomber was found weeks later. All the crew members were dead because they preferred to trust their instincts rather than the instruments that would have brought them home safely.

God in his kindness has given his Word to the world as a certain guide. Life is too complicated to be lived on the basis of instincts. It is far better to trust the Creator's revelation of himself than to do what "seems right."

V. PRAYER

Father, thank you for the richness, beauty, and truth of your Word. Grant that we may seek you through its words, trust you in its promises, and rejoice in you because of its revelation. Help us to believe it and to share it with others. Amen.

VI. DEEPER DISCOVERIES

A. Sacrifices His Son or Daughter in the Fire (18:10)

The Hebrew text of this verse says literally, "Makes his son or daughter pass through the fire." In some cases in the Hebrew Scriptures, the destination is made explicit: "Do not give any of your children to be sacrificed to Molech, for you must not profane the name of your God" (Lev. 18:21; cp. 2 Kgs. 23:10; Jer. 32:35). Molech was the name of an Ammonite deity that demanded child sacrifice. Although the expression "pass through the fire" is sometimes asserted to be a ritual that did not involve the death of the child, this is highly unlikely. Second Kings 16:3 describes how King Ahaz of Judah violated this precept: "He walked in the ways of the kings of Israel and even sacrificed his son in the fire, following the detestable ways of the nations the LORD had driven out before the Israelites." It is unlikely that this is a reference to anything other than the practice of child sacrifice referred to in Deuteronomy 18:10.

The practice of child sacrifice is also well attested among the Canaanites both from literary remains and from artifacts. King Josiah, as part of his reforms in Judah, "desecrated Topheth, which was in the Valley of Ben Hinnom, so no one could use it to sacrifice his son or daughter in the fire to Molech" (2 Kgs. 23:10).

B. Divination (18:10)

Divination was the practice of determining the future by means of occult practices. These included oneiromancy (the interpretation of dreams), astrology, necromancy, augury (the analysis of the movements of birds and animals), pyromancy (the observation of patterns in fire), and especially haruspicy, the study of the entrails—especially the liver—of specified animals. Some of these

Deuteronomy 18

methods are described in Ezekiel 21:21: "For the king of Babylon will stop at the fork in the road, at the junction of the two roads, to seek an omen: He will cast lots with arrows, he will consult his idols, he will examine the liver."

Joseph, unrecognized by his brothers, said to them, "What is this you have done? Don't you know that a man like me can find things out by divination?" (Gen 44:15). Benjamin had been arrested for having a divining cup in his grain sack, and Joseph was playing his role of pagan Egyptian viceroy to the hilt, so it is probable that his statement should not be taken as a description of what he actually did. However, it certainly can be regarded as typical of what Egyptian officials were expected to do at that time.

All forms of divination and magic are off limits for God's people.

VII. TEACHING OUTLINE

A. INTRODUCTION

1. Lead Story: Can You Keep a Secret?
2. Context: Moses continues to outline God's plan for spiritual and societal leadership in Israel by declaring his plan for supporting the Levites and for revealing his will through the prophets.
3. Transition: God intends for his people to know his mind through his Word instead of through the varied methods that are used by the world.

B. COMMENTARY

1. Providing for Leadership: Defending the Levites (18:1–8)
2. Protecting the Leadership: Detestable Practices (18:9–14)
3. Pruning the Leadership: Detecting Prophets (18:15–22)

C. CONCLUSION: THE *LADY BE GOOD*

VIII. ISSUES FOR DISCUSSION

1. Why do you think that people in ministry in both the Old Testament and the New Testament expected to receive contributions toward their livelihood from people to whom they ministered?
2. What is the relationship between blamelessness and sinlessness? What is the difference between them?
3. Can you think of some similarities between Moses and the Lord Jesus Christ?
4. What do you think might have been the qualities in God's voice that frightened Israel?

Deuteronomy 19

God Our Refuge

- I. **INTRODUCTION**
  A Mighty Fortress

- II. **COMMENTARY**
  A verse-by-verse explanation of the chapter.

- III. **CONCLUSION**
  Rinkart's Refuge
  An overview of the principles and applications from the chapter.

- IV. **LIFE APPLICATION**
  A Light in the Darkness
  Melding the chapter to life.

- V. **PRAYER**
  Tying the chapter to life with God.

- VI. **DEEPER DISCOVERIES**
  Historical, geographical, and grammatical enrichment of the commentary.

- VII. **TEACHING OUTLINE**
  Suggested step-by-step group study of the chapter.

- VIII. **ISSUES FOR DISCUSSION**
  Zeroing the chapter in on daily life.

Deuteronomy 19

> **Quote**
>
> "There is no merit where there is no trial; and till experience stamps the mark of strength, cowards may pass for heroes, and falsehood for faith."
>
> Aaron Hill

IN A NUTSHELL

In pursuit of a just society, God in Deuteronomy 19 establishes protections for those who are falsely accused, for society itself, and for its legal institutions.

God Our Refuge

I. INTRODUCTION

A Mighty Fortress

On October 31, 1517, an Augustinian monk named Martin Luther posted a list of items on the door of the cathedral in Wittenberg, Germany. Known to history as *The Ninety-Five Theses,* Luther's document created a firestorm of controversy. He challenged the validity of practices that had dominated church life for centuries. Its rapid dissemination, along with other writings from Luther, fostered what has come to be called the Protestant Reformation.

For several years, Luther was the most wanted man in Europe. Although the masses admired him, he was excommunicated by the pope and called to the city of Worms to defend the contents of his books and pamphlets. Proclaiming that his conscience was captive to the Word of God, Luther refused to recant the theological contents of his writings.

As a result, the authorities sought to arrest him; a friend, however, came to his aid and had him "kidnapped" for his own protection. For months Luther was hidden away at the Wartburg Castle where he continued to write new treatises and to translate the New Testament into German (virtually creating the modern German language). The castle became his refuge from his enemies for many months while his enemies sought him in vain.

Some years later, Luther penned the words of a hymn based on Psalm 46, words that became the anthem of the Protestant Reformation. The hymn's lyrics celebrate the great truth that God himself becomes the refuge of the one who puts his trust in Jesus:

> A mighty fortress is our God,
> A bulwark never failing.
> Our shelter he amid the flood
> Of moral ills prevailing.
> But still our ancient foe
> Doth seek to work us woe.
> His craft and pow'r are great
> And armed with cruel hate
> On earth is not his equal.

II. COMMENTARY

God Our Refuge

MAIN IDEA: *God establishes his system of justice for Israel by insisting on safeguards for the protection of the defenseless and weak and of the process of justice itself.*

A Protecting the Accused (19:1–10)

SUPPORTING IDEA: *By establishing regional cities of refuge, Israel must protect persons who are falsely accused of crimes from suffering unjust retribution.*

19:1–2. Moses began this section, as he did many others, by the familiar refrain **when the LORD your God has destroyed the nations whose land he is giving you**. Principles of civil justice could be partially implemented while Israel was still nomadic, but an entirely new situation would prevail when Israel had **driven . . . out** the Canaanites and **settled** in **their towns**. Yahweh's statutes for the establishment of criminal justice would require that Israel set aside **three cities centrally located in the land**. These cities would be centrally located on a regional basis: one in the north, one in the south, and one in the center of the promised land.

19:3. To ensure that they could serve their purposes as cities of refuge, these three cities should have easy access to roads; and if no such roads existed, the issue was sufficiently important that the nation should **build roads** to them. Then the land should be divided into **three** districts of jurisdiction with one city in each part, giving ease of access **so that anyone who kills a man may flee there**.

19:4–7. The purpose of the cities of refuge was to provide a haven for people who were falsely accused of murder. So that Israel might understand that all homicide does not fall into that category, Moses carefully differentiated in verses 4–13 between murder with **malice aforethought** and what Western law now calls manslaughter.

The cities of refuge would serve as places for the person who killed his neighbor **unintentionally**. Verse 5 provides a concrete example: two persons working in the forest. One **swings his ax to fell a tree** and the **head** of the ax **flies** off and kills the other. Although such an event would be clearly regarded as accidental if witnessed, the perpetrator might, in the absence of eyewitnesses, suffer death from **the avenger of blood** when the episode was revealed.

The "avenger of blood" refers to a near kinsman who had the legal responsibility to right wrongs perpetrated on his family (see "Deeper Discoveries"). There was no police force in Israel, and the avenger of blood served as a rough approximation of one at this time. Since the avenger might conclude in the heat of the moment that his relative had been murdered, the person who did the accidental killing was allowed to **flee** to one of the cities of refuge to **save his life**. This provision is spelled out in much greater detail in Numbers 35:9–28, which includes the additional provision that the elders of the city of refuge must hold a hearing to determine the legitimacy of a person's claim that the death in question was accidental. If his claim was upheld, he was permitted to stay in the city of refuge until the death of the high priest. He wandered outside its walls, however, at his own risk.

19:8–10. Israel had already set aside three cities of refuge in the territory east of the Jordan River: Golan in the northern area in the tribe of Gad, Ramoth in the central region assigned to Manasseh, and Bezer in the south where Reuben dwelled. At the time of Joshua when the conquest was largely finished, the people set aside three other cities: Kedesh, Shechem, and Kiriath Arba or Hebron (see Josh. 20:7). Verse 8 allows for the possibility that Israel might expand still further to the full measure of the territory described to the **forefathers**. If God should enlarge their **territory**, they were to set aside **three more cities**, making nine in all. There is no record that this provision was ever invoked, since Israel's conquest of the land never extended to the full boundaries promised to the patriarchs.

B Protecting Human Life (19:11–13)

SUPPORTING IDEA: *Although those who are falsely accused must be protected, those who commit murder with malice must be forced to pay the price for their actions.*

19:11. While manslaughter involved an accidental death, murder was planned: **if a man hates his neighbor and lies in wait for him, assaults and kills him**. Yahweh's plan for criminal justice was based on the recognition that bearing grudges and nursing resentments were bound to foster hatreds leading to violence: "Do not seek revenge or bear a grudge against one of your people, but love your neighbor as yourself. I am the LORD" (Lev. 19:18). A murderer, like one who committed manslaughter, might flee **to one of these cities** of refuge and attempt to invoke the protections it afforded.

19:12–13. Such protections were to be denied once it had been established that the person had committed murder. The **elders of his town** were to **send for him, bring him back from the city** of refuge, and **hand him over to the avenger of blood**, who would then serve as the officially ordained executor of the community's justice.

Since the process was troublesome and distasteful, those involved would be tempted to neglect their duty in such matters. However, more was at stake in each case than one person's guilt or innocence. Although the community might forget, God did not overlook the guilt placed on the community by its failure to act justly. Officials were to show **no pity** and in so doing **purge** from the land the **guilt of shedding innocent blood**. To neglect to do so might cause them to forfeit God's blessing on his people: **so that it may go well with you**.

C Protecting the Process of Justice (19:14–21)

SUPPORTING IDEA: *The process of justice must not be compromised. Israel must respect principles of equitable investigation and punish those who would impede them.*

19:14. The placement of this verse, which seems at first blush not to fit the context, is in keeping with the theme of the section, which is the ensuring of a valid process of justice. The **boundary stone** was a mute but eloquent witness to the property rights of individuals. To **move** it was to set aside the testimony of previous generations about the exact location of each family's **inheritance** in the promised land.

19:15. Although it was important to find and prosecute lawbreakers in Israel, this process was less important than avoiding the prosecution of innocent people. Therefore, every **matter** involving a crime **must be established by the testimony of two or three witnesses**. Better to allow criminals to escape than to prosecute the innocent.

19:16–20. One of the greatest threats to the judicial process was the **malicious witness** who accused someone falsely. From time to time it would be clear in a court action that someone was lying. In such a situation, the two men involved in the dispute were to **stand in the presence of the LORD before the priests and the judges** charged in the case. If a **thorough investigation** revealed that the accusing witness proved **to be a liar**, then the penalties that he sought to have imposed on the accused would be levied upon him. This does not necessarily imply the death penalty but merely that the court should **do to him as he intended to do to his brother**. In so doing, the officials would keep the judicial process free from **evil** and from a loss of confidence among the population. Their action would also make a potential witness think twice before making false assertions, since the carrying out of the penalty would cause **the rest of the people** to hear and be afraid, and **never again** engage in such accusations.

19:21. Although compassion on an individual level is a virtue, **pity** extended by the community toward proven lawbreakers would prove to be destructive to communal existence. The principle of Israelite justice was not built on individual vengeance but upon community concern to honor divine justice and create a just society. The commonness of statements like verse 21 suggests that Yahweh recognized the reluctance of people to carry out needed actions in the interests of the community (cp. 7:16; 13:9; Isa. 13:18; Ezek.

7:14; 20:17). The principle to be used was *lex talionis:* **life for life, eye for eye**. The lawbreaker would suffer equally with his victim. It does appear that in some cases fines could serve as compensation for victims (see Exod. 21:22).

> **MAIN IDEA REVIEW:** God establishes his system of justice for Israel by insisting on safeguards for the protection of the defenseless and weak and of the process of justice itself.

III. CONCLUSION

Rinkart's Refuge

Martin Rinkart was the son of a German coppersmith who grew up to be a pastor and church musician. Although his family was poor, Rinkart managed to work his way through the University of Leipzig and to become ordained as a Lutheran pastor. He was eventually called to the church in his hometown of Eilenberg, Saxony, at a strategic time. The Thirty Years War was in full swing, and Protestant and Catholic armies were laying waste to the land.

In addition to the perils of a terrible war, Germany was subject to famines and outbreaks of devastating diseases. Because Eilenberg was a walled city, it attracted many refugees, making it particularly vulnerable to various epidemics.

In 1637, a virulent outbreak of disease hit Eilenberg. At its crest, Martin Rinkart was the only minister able to function in the city. He often conducted forty to fifty funerals in the course of a single day. Nevertheless, he did not neglect his regular pastoral and musical work during the years of peril, composing seven different dramas about the Reformation and writing sixty-six hymns.

One of those is the hymn for which he is best known, "Now Thank We All Our God." In this hymn, Rinkart celebrates the sufficiency of God to make his people equal to the darkest hours. Millions who have sung it have never made the connection of its glorious words with the setting in which they were composed. Its words testify to the faithfulness of God in the midst of great peril:

> Now thank we all our God
> With hearts and hands and voices,
> Who wondrous things hath done,
> In whom his world rejoices;
> Who from our mothers' arms
> Hath blessed us on our way
> With countless gifts of love,
> And still is ours today.

Deuteronomy 19

PRINCIPLES

- God realizes his people need protection from the pains and heartaches of the world.
- The agonies of those who are falsely accused are of great concern to the living God, and he acts as their defender.
- The task of evangelism often involves preparing an open road so offenders can find their refuge in Christ.
- Compassion for victims is sometimes forgotten in a misapplied concern for their oppressors and murderers.

APPLICATIONS

- Develop the spiritual eyesight that helps you appreciate God's intent to shape your life through adversity.
- Learn the words of several good hymns that celebrate God's role as a refuge to his people.
- Memorize a psalm (or portion of a psalm) that points believers in the direction of God's adequacy during trials.
- Instead of accepting critical rumors at face value, develop a cautious attitude that waits until all the facts are known.

IV. LIFE APPLICATION

A Light in the Darkness

Vice President George Bush represented the American government at the funeral of the late Soviet Premier Leonid Brezhnev. The funeral was impressive but solemn and utterly without hope. The godless government of the U.S.S.R. permitted neither prayers, nor the mention of the name of God, nor any reading of Scripture or singing of hymns.

Upon his return, Bush told of an action by Brezhnev's widow at the time her husband's casket was being closed. Just before the lid came down, she reached over her husband's body and made the sign of the cross on his chest.

Vice President Bush remarked that it was a courageous act to perform in the heart of an atheistic empire. It also testified loudly that all the efforts of a godless regime had been unable to quench the power of faith—not even in the household of the man who epitomized a godless ideology while he lived. Even in the greatest darkness, it is possible to live in acknowledgement that a light does exist.

Christians who live under oppressive governments have had to learn by experience the sufficiency of God during their deepest distress. By calling upon him to comfort them in the midst of darkness, they have shown to the world the living reality of the God who is there. By trusting in Jesus Christ, the believer finds the only sure place of safety in the universe. None of those who believe in him will ever be disappointed.

V. PRAYER

Lord, thank you that in a world that seems more stable than it is you are still our refuge and strength. When you attempt to teach us of your reality by permitting adversity to enter our lives, help us not to chafe or complain, but to run to you for safety. Amen.

VI. DEEPER DISCOVERIES

A. The Avenger of Blood (19:6)

The Hebrew term for *avenger* is *go'el*, a word that means "redeemer." A redeemer was one who paid a price to return a person to his previous condition. If a person had become a slave to pay off debts, the redeemer bought the enslaved person out of slavery and returned him to freedom.

In the context of verse 6, and attached to the word *blood*, the redeemer became an avenger, attempting to right a wrong that had been committed. As such, the avenger of blood was acting in a civil rather than a private capacity. He was not seeking personal vengeance, which was prohibited under divine law (Rom. 12:19; cp. Lev. 19:18; Deut. 32:25). The avenger of blood was God's mediator of justice in Israelite society, and he was appointed in certain cases to execute capital offenders (cp. Deut. 19:12).

However, vengeance is never to be sought on a personal level; it is God's function, normally mediated through civil government. Paul instructed the Roman Christians, who were under the heel of an oppressive government, that even an evil regime like Nero's had a place in the divine scheme of justice: "[Government] is God's servant to do you good. But if you do wrong, be afraid, for he does not bear the sword for nothing. He is God's servant, an agent of wrath to bring punishment on the wrongdoer" (Rom. 13:4; cp. Num. 35:16–21).

B. An Eye for an Eye (19:21)

The Lord Jesus in the Sermon on the Mount declared, "You have heard that it was said, 'Eye for eye, and tooth for tooth.' But I tell you, Do not resist an evil person. If someone strikes you on the right cheek, turn to him the other also" (Matt. 5:38–39). Some have drawn from this the mistaken notion that Jesus was dismissing Deuteronomy 19:21 as an example of inferior morality. Nothing could be further from the truth. Jesus prefaced his remark by saying, "Do not think that I have come to abolish the Law or the Prophets; I have not come to abolish them but to fulfill them. I tell you the truth, until heaven and earth disappear, not the smallest letter, not the least stroke of a pen, will by any means disappear from the Law until everything is accomplished" (Matt. 5:17–18).

His intent was to correct the common misuse of Deuteronomy 19:21 to authorize personal retribution. The passage was never intended to be used in such a manner. He substituted for the common misinterpretation the correct one, emphasizing gentleness when wronged. Societal justice is a state rather than an individual function.

VII. TEACHING OUTLINE

A. INTRODUCTION

1. Lead Story: A Mighty Fortress
2. Context: Moses provides in Deuteronomy 19 God's methods of safeguarding a civil society and its institutions. Israel is to protect those who are falsely accused without inviting anarchy and to protect the process of justice itself.
3. Transition: God wants his people to recognize that in him they may find refuge and security.

B. COMMENTARY

1. Protecting the Accused (19:1–10)
2. Protecting Human Life (19:11–13)
3. Protecting the Process of Justice (19:14–21)

C. CONCLUSION: A LIGHT IN THE DARKNESS

VIII. ISSUES FOR DISCUSSION

1. How have you found Jesus Christ to be a refuge in your life?
2. Can you think of ways society has suffered through exercising pity toward the guilty?
3. What are the dangers of holding grudges?
4. How can Christians serve as a channel to bring hurting people to Jesus Christ as their refuge?

Deuteronomy 20

The Qualities of a Christian Warrior

I. **INTRODUCTION**
No Prisoners

II. **COMMENTARY**
A verse-by-verse explanation of the chapter.

III. **CONCLUSION**
The Perils of Superman
An overview of the principles and applications from the chapter.

IV. **LIFE APPLICATION**
Nothing to Play With
Melding the chapter to life.

V. **PRAYER**
Tying the chapter to life with God.

VI. **DEEPER DISCOVERIES**
Historical, geographical, and grammatical enrichment of the commentary.

VII. **TEACHING OUTLINE**
Suggested step-by-step group study of the chapter.

VIII. **ISSUES FOR DISCUSSION**
Zeroing the chapter in on daily life.

Deuteronomy 20

> ## Quote
>
> "The meaning of earthly existence lies, not as we have grown used to thinking, in prospering, but in the development of the soul."
>
> Aleksandr Solzhenitsyn

Deuteronomy 20

IN A NUTSHELL

Courage, conviction, and self-control are necessary attributes of those who would engage in divinely ordained warfare.

The Qualities of a Christian Warrior

I. INTRODUCTION

No Prisoners

The New Testament is filled with the language of violence. Paul wrote, "If you are living according to the flesh, you must die; but if by the Spirit you are putting to death the deeds of the body, you will live" (Rom. 8:13 NASB). The apostles spoke often of internal warfare, and that warfare is no less real for being cast in the shape of a metaphor. Most of us will confess that we ourselves are to blame for most of the troubles we experience.

Shakespeare has King Richard III soliloquize,

My conscience hath a thousand several tongues,
And every tongue brings in a several tale,
And every tale condemns me for a villain.

Our internal "tongues" confirm what we know: an internal war rages within us. We find righteousness unfamiliar and challenging. Sin comes easily to us. After we are converted, our inner warfare is all the more evident. Now our consciences are sensitized by the Holy Spirit to be more tender about sin. Scripture challenges us toward godliness and the offering of our lives daily to the Savior. Although we want to do right, the "deeds of the body" that Paul described still lie within us, waiting for an opportune moment to do our souls harm.

Christian living, as Romans 8:13 declares, is a continual battle that involves doing violence to those inner sinful impulses that Paul calls "the flesh." Like Israel of old, we have a territory to conquer, a country to which God assigned us and one that is occupied by forces that have our destruction in mind. As Moses warned Israel, we are to go into our spiritual battles with one thought in mind: take no prisoners.

II. COMMENTARY

The Qualities of a Christian Warrior

> **MAIN IDEA:** *In a fallen world, conflict is sometimes necessary. To engage in any spiritual struggle successfully, God's warrior needs to display courage, conviction, and self-control.*

Deuteronomy 20:1

A Courage (20:1–4)

SUPPORTING IDEA: *Spiritual challenges become manageable when we are reminded that God is present and active in the struggle.*

20:1. Israel's policies of warfare, like everything else in its corporate life, were to be guided by the principle of glorifying Yahweh. The nation's soldiers were not to be intimidated by their enemies' legions or arsenals. If Israel's **enemies** had **horses and chariots** and **greater** numbers than theirs, they were first to do battle with their own fears and recognize that the Lord would be with them in battle.

20:2–4. Not only would Yahweh be present on the battle line; he would be engaged in the fight itself: **the LORD your God will fight for you against your enemies**. The **priest** (presumably the high priest of Israel) would have the responsibility of addressing **the army** before the battle to reinforce this truth.

B Conviction (20:5–9)

SUPPORTING IDEA: *God does not require superior numbers to achieve his spiritual goals; he can win with smaller armies and lesser abilities if his people put their trust in him.*

20:5–7. Instead of seeking to expand the size of the nation's regiments, Israel was to seek out those whose enthusiasm for the conflict was less than it should have been and to dismiss them. The officers were to take responsibility for giving the halfhearted warriors an early exit from the fighting.

Men could be dismissed for a distraction as small as the completion of a **new house**. **Dedicated it** is a possible rendering of the Hebrew words in verse 5, but a better translation would be "begun to live in it." Three times in these verses it is said about the distracted soldier, **Let him go home**. God does not have to use more soldiers in order to win battles (see 1 Sam. 14:6). A recently planted **vineyard** or a recent engagement were also reasons to be sent home. Such prescriptions betray a philosophy of warfare that was different from that among the nations around Israel. Israel's profession of confidence in Yahweh was not to be merely lip service. They were to act upon their conviction that God could do great things with only a few who were thoroughly dedicated to him.

20:8–9. **To go home**, a soldier needed only to declare the fact that he was **afraid or fainthearted** and he could leave the battlefield. Fear has a way of permeating the ranks, and the officers were to make an effort to eliminate such people from the battle line. **The officers**, only after the fearful had left the scene, were to **appoint commanders**.

Deuteronomy 20:19–20

[C] Control (20:10–20)

SUPPORTING IDEA: *God's people are to wage war within self-imposed restraints toward enemies and toward nature itself.*

20:10–11. It seems clear from verse 15 that this paragraph is not designed to apply in the coming battle against the Canaanites. Moses explained there that the provisions of verses 10–14 were to apply to "cities . . . at a distance" from Israel and did not belong to the occupants of Canaan.

Since Israel was not to pursue aggressive war on other nations, under what circumstances could these words apply? The likelihood is that from time to time Israel would be subject to foreign aggressors. Israel was not prohibited from making reprisals against such raids. God's people had the freedom to protect her boundaries.

In that case, Israel was to issue a measured response and not simply seek the indiscriminate slaughter of their opponents. When they surrounded a city **to attack** it, they should first, before shedding blood, offer the town the option of **peace**. The primary condition of the offer was that the people would be **subject to forced labor**. If the plunderers were willing to work for Israel, at least they could survive.

20:12–15. If Israel's enemy should be unwilling **to make peace** under those terms, and instead engaged the Israelite army **in battle**, the city should be surrounded and put under **siege** until its surrender. Even then, only **the men** in the city were to be executed. The **women, the children, the livestock**, as well as the material wealth of the town, were to become spoils of war.

20:16–18. Before any of the aforementioned conditions could apply, however, Israel would have to secure its homeland. In the cities of the Canaanite nations, a different attitude would prevail. Even if the Canaanites, after their defeat, posed no military threat, they would constitute a lethal spiritual danger. There, Israel was instructed, **Do not leave alive anything that breathes**. This instruction would apply to those who remained after most of the people had fled (see the exposition of ch. 7).

God repeated the instructions to **completely destroy** the resident nations frequently in Deuteronomy because he knew that Israel would be reluctant to carry out such a distasteful assignment, and his concern was well founded, as Judges 2:1–4 confirms. (To the six nations mentioned in v. 17, Deut. 7:1 adds a seventh, the Girgashites.)

The neglect of his horrendous but necessary task proved fatal to Israel's life in succeeding generations. The violation of God's command led directly to the Babylonian captivity eight centuries later, because Israel did learn **to follow all the detestable things** the Canaanites did **in worshiping their gods**.

20:19–20. Even in the business of warfare, Israel was to live as a people who exhibited self-control. They were not to be destructive for destruction's

Deuteronomy 20:19–20

sake nor give vent to rage when difficulties emerged. When Israel laid **siege to a city for a long time**, their boredom and frustration might lead them to forget that there would be a life after the war was ended. Israel was to exercise a restrained approach toward the ecology of the Holy Land by refusing to **destroy its trees** in order to build siege works. God reminded the Israelite army that those trees could sustain future generations and that their removal might hasten the battle but spoil the peace that followed.

The plaintive question that ends verse 19, **Are the trees of the field people, that you should besiege them?** places the sinfulness of man against the backdrop of the rest of God's creation. Only man, the pinnacle of God's creation, is capable of so egregious an action as to destroy what God gave him to sustain his life. Israel might easily win external battles while losing inner struggles if they ignored God's design.

> **MAIN IDEA REVIEW:** *In a fallen world, conflict is sometimes necessary. To engage in any spiritual struggle successfully, God's warrior needs to display courage, conviction, and self-control.*

III. CONCLUSION

The Perils of Superman

In the years when Muhammad Ali dominated the world of heavyweight boxing, he was more famous for his braggadocio than for his hitting ability. On one occasion he boarded an airplane to travel to his next fight. A few minutes before the flight was scheduled to leave, the stewardess reminded him to fasten his seat belt.

Ali replied indignantly, "Superman don't need no seat belt."

The stewardess proved equal to the occasion, answering, "Superman don't need no airplane, either."

Christians are not supermen and shouldn't claim to be. We do not have the resources in ourselves to wage warfare against the natural man (cp. Eph. 4:22). However, when we put our trust in Christ, the Holy Spirit comes to reside within. He is the only weapon we need to do battle against sin (Rom. 8:13). Just as Israel was told to claim the promised land by putting the soles of their feet upon it, so Christians are to lay claim to their inner lives for Jesus Christ. The battle may be long and challenging, but with God's help success is assured.

PRINCIPLES

- The faithfulness of God in the past fortifies believers for future challenges.

- Courage is the most fundamental of all virtues.
- Discouragement is contagious and is easily transmitted to others.
- Exposure to false doctrine places a person at risk not just for theological errors but for moral failure.

APPLICATIONS

- Identify the aspects of your life that are not yet under God's control and go to war with them.
- Know your spiritual weapons and use them to do battle with sin in your life.
- Ask people who are spiritually mature about the most valuable lessons they have learned in their spiritual lives.
- Ask God for help in some area of your life that needs conquering.

IV. LIFE APPLICATION

Nothing to Play With

In 1977, French aristocrat Baron Richard D'Arcy was killed by his two-year-old pet lion. He had raised it from birth, and it had behaved well in his household. On the evening of his death, however, he attempted to force it into the bathroom where it usually spent the night. The animal turned on him and clawed him to death.

Sin in the Christian life can behave the same way. Believers do well not to keep sins as pets, for they are untamed by definition. Sooner or later they will turn and do terrible damage to the one who accommodates them. The only safe way to deal with sin is to put it to death when it is found. Tolerating it to any degree will lead to pain and regret.

V. PRAYER

Father, grant us the determination to put our sins to death for your sake as well as our own. Keep us from developing a peaceful coexistence with the habits and practices that could destroy us. Amen.

VI. DEEPER DISCOVERIES

A. Forced Labor (20:11)

Israel was permitted to keep laborers from distant cities they conquered but not from among the Canaanites: "If they accept [your offer of peace] and open their gates, all the people in it shall be subject to forced labor and shall

Deuteronomy 20

work for you" (Deut. 20:11). Israel was specifically forbidden to permit the seven nations of Canaan from remaining in the land as forced laborers (20:16–18). Nonetheless, when the inhabitants of the land fought stubbornly, that is precisely what Israel did (see Josh. 17:13). The practice was still continuing as late as Solomon's time (see 1 Kgs. 9:20–21).

B. Nations (20:15)

Although the term *nation* refers today to collections of various ethnic groupings united under a political commonality, at the time of the Bible *nation* referred not to a political but an ethnocultural entity. A *nation* might contain only a few thousand people (the Jebusites are an example) who were united by kinship, language, and customs. When the Lord Jesus commanded his followers to disciple the nations (Matt. 28:19–20), he referred not to the few hundred modern political states but to the thousands of ethnic groupings scattered around the globe.

VII. TEACHING OUTLINE

A. INTRODUCTION

1. Lead Story: No Prisoners
2. Context: Although Israel was to be a peace-loving nation, they did have permission to drive others out of the land that God had promised to them. But even their warfare had to be regulated by God's commands.
3. Transition: God calls Christians to engage in inner warfare within the confines of his commandments.

B. COMMENTARY

1. Courage (20:1–4)
2. Conviction (20:5–9)
3. Control (20:10–20)

C. CONCLUSION: NOTHING TO PLAY WITH

VIII. ISSUES FOR DISCUSSION

1. What are some of the battles you are fighting at this point in your life?
2. What are the differences between physical warfare and spiritual warfare?
3. What part does courage play in the inner warfare of the Christian believer?
4. Why do you think so few people are concerned about a lack of personal self-control today?

Deuteronomy 21

Matters of Life and Death

I. **INTRODUCTION**
Granny Dumping

II. **COMMENTARY**
A verse-by-verse explanation of the chapter.

III. **CONCLUSION**
Accidental Baptists
An overview of the principles and applications from the chapter.

IV. **LIFE APPLICATION**
Lincoln's Miracle
Melding the chapter to life.

V. **PRAYER**
Tying the chapter to life with God.

VI. **DEEPER DISCOVERIES**
Historical, geographical, and grammatical enrichment of the commentary.

VII. **TEACHING OUTLINE**
Suggested step-by-step group study of the chapter.

VIII. **ISSUES FOR DISCUSSION**
Zeroing the chapter in on daily life.

Deuteronomy 21

> **Quote**
>
> "Never yet did there exist a full faith in the divine word which did not expand the intellect while it purified the heart; which did not multiply the aims and objects of the understanding, while it fixed and simplified those of the desires and passions."
>
> Samuel Taylor Coleridge

IN A NUTSHELL

In Deuteronomy 21, Moses calls on Israel to respect human life even in its weakest and most degraded forms, and to balance the rights of the individual with the life of the community before God.

Matters of Life and Death

I. INTRODUCTION

Granny Dumping

In all the wars in which Americans have participated, about 1.1 million of our citizens have been killed. Since the *Roe v. Wade* ruling in 1973, more than twenty-eight times that number have been exterminated through abortion. According to the Alan Guttmacher Institute (the research arm of Planned Parenthood), over 95 percent of the abortions in America take place for reasons of convenience—not because of incest, rape, or the threatened health of the mother.

In recent years, a matching phenomenon for the end of life (albeit in smaller numbers) has appeared on the American scene. Harshly dubbed "Granny-dumping," it describes the practice of abandoning elderly people in places where they are most likely to receive the notice of community authorities. Often these elderly victims are left at the doors of hospitals or clinics by their relatives, who leave the hospital staff to extend care to the person left behind. The standard approach is to leave the victim with no identification so he cannot be traced to his kin and thus will become a ward of the state.

Several years ago, an eighty-two-year-old man was left by his daughter at an Idaho racetrack. When his story made the newspapers, there was a brief outcry because of what was thought to be an unusual practice. However, one past president of the American College of Emergency Physicians estimates that about two hundred thousand elderly people are abandoned at hospitals annually. Americans are exhibiting an increasing disregard for life at its end as well as its beginning.

II. COMMENTARY

Matters of Life and Death

> **MAIN IDEA:** *Israel is to maintain respect for life in every form and recognize that it always issues from God. The victors and the strong must respect the rights of the vanquished and the weak, and each must recognize God's interest in the other.*

Deuteronomy 21:1-2

▲ The Death of an Unknown Individual (21:1-9)

SUPPORTING IDEA: *Although the victim of a crime may be unknown to the community, he is neither unknown nor forgotten before God. The community must declare its disapproval and its separation from such crimes.*

21:1-2. Israel was not to regard a murdered person as merely an unsolved crime. If someone should be **found slain** in the land that God was giving them and if the crime should be unsolved, the fact remained that murder had been committed in the land that God regarded as holy. Although the perpetrator might not be known, the **elders** and the **judges** of the nearest community had a responsibility to atone for the deed.

21:3-5. The town leaders of the community nearest the body were to procure a **heifer** that had **never been worked** or **worn a yoke**. The ritual of cleansing was to be performed **in a valley** that had **not been plowed or planted**. These two features suggest that both the place and the animal were undefiled.

The animal was to be killed in a rite of atonement for the community. Two proposals are commonly forwarded for the rationale behind this ritual. One suggests that the rite substituted the death of the heifer for the death of the murderer. By killing the animal, the community displayed their recognition of the need to cleanse the land of such offenders.

The other option is to regard the rite as symbolic of the cleansing of community guilt. Just as the blood of the animal was washed away by the **flowing stream**, the bloodguilt of the community was cleansed by the rite. In favor of the second suggestion is the location prescribed and the ritual of hand-washing by the elders (cp. v. 6). In this respect the rite of atonement resembles other prescribed rituals for the elimination of guilt (cp. the released bird in Lev. 14:1-7 and the scapegoat on the Day of Atonement in Lev. 16:20-22). Although the community leaders were responsible to take the initiative in this communal cleansing, **the priests, the sons of Levi**, were also to have a part.

21:6-9. Although the ritual for communal atonement contained aspects of worship, it was not properly a sacrifice. It was not offered at the central sanctuary (cp. Deut. 12:5-7), or on an altar of any kind, but in a valley adjacent to the responsible community. No reference is made to the pouring out of the blood in a ritualized way, but rather **the elders of the town** were to **wash their hands over the heifer** and declare their innocence before Yahweh.

The elders (perhaps through or in partnership with the Levites) were to accompany this declaration with a prayer: **Accept this atonement for your people Israel**. Although not a sacrifice in the strictest sense, the ritual would have the effect of a sacrifice since **the bloodshed** would **be atoned for**.

The strangeness of this rite should not blind our eyes to the values that lie behind it. God was concerned for even one unknown and unclaimed life in Israel. Any wrongful death produced a moral stain on the whole nation. The guilt of innocent blood was not to be dismissed but purged by prescribed ritual.

B The Life of the Prisoner of War (21:10–14)

> **SUPPORTING IDEA:** *Israel in victory must show respect for the life and feelings of the vanquished. The weak are not to be crushed at the whims of the strong.*

21:10–11. Moses presented a scenario that Israel would face in its defensive wars. It might be that when Israel went **to war against** her **enemies** that **captives**, prisoners of war, would be taken in keeping with Deuteronomy 20:11. The possibility could not apply to the imminent invasion of Canaan, since no survivors were to be permitted to live from among the Canaanites (cp. 20:16–17).

Among the possible captives, an Israelite soldier might notice **a beautiful woman**. If the soldier was attracted to her, he was permitted to **take her** for a **wife** subject to certain qualifications. God's laws dealt with life in the real world. Although we might wish for a world without war, crime, and prisoners of war, the Hebrew Scriptures deal with the realities rather than the utopian vision. This law for the treatment of female prisoners of war benefited the vanquished and placed restrictions upon the victors.

21:12–13. To begin with, the woman was not to be treated as a piece of property but as a human being with emotions. She was not to be raped and discarded or made a slave. Since her parents were no longer to be a part of her life, she was initially allowed a month of mourning to help her face life under her new conditions. She was to be brought into the Israelite's **home** and have **her head** shaved and **her nails** trimmed as a symbol of her sorrow and her new beginning.

In the same vein, she was to **put aside the clothes she was wearing when captured** and to be dressed in fresh garments that were suggestive of the new life she had begun. Only after her mourning was completed could the marriage be consummated. The new bridegroom was required to restrain himself for a **full month**.

21:14. At the same time, the difficulties of such an intercultural marriage were significant. In a short time it would be apparent whether these could be overcome. If the Israelite was **not pleased with** his new bride, he was to set her free. He was not to **sell her** or otherwise profit from his possession of her, but he was to allow her to go wherever she wished. Strength was not to take advantage of weakness but to respect her as a person made in the image of God.

C The Life of the Firstborn Son (21:15–17)

> **SUPPORTING IDEA:** *Sons are not to be punished for the wrongs of their mothers, whether perceived or real. Israelites must respect the lives and status of their children.*

21:15. Polygamy was permitted in Israel, but it was neither encouraged nor often practiced. Practical and economic problems connected with it guaranteed that only the wealthy and powerful could afford to engage in marriage

Deuteronomy 21:16-17

to more than one wife. Even so, it was fraught with difficulty, as the Scriptures abundantly testify (cp. the troubles described in the narratives concerning Abraham in Genesis and Hannah in 1 Samuel 1).

Moses proposed the possibility that a man with two wives might love **one but not the other**. If his firstborn son came from the unloved wife, he was not to despise the rights of the **firstborn** because of the identity of his mother. The child should be treated according to his proper status and not disregarded because of his mother.

21:16–17. The Hebrew father was to **acknowledge the son of his unloved wife as the firstborn**. This meant that he was to receive a **double share** of the father's wealth. The father must not treat the son of the unloved wife prejudicially but preserve for him **the right of the firstborn**. This legislation does not deny the special circumstances surrounding the experience of Jacob and Esau or Isaac and Ishmael where God specifically set aside the normal prerogatives of the firstborn. Apart from some such intervention, however, the rights of the firstborn were not to be transferred.

D The Death of the Rebellious Son (21:18–21)

SUPPORTING IDEA: *Sons must respect the position and status of their parents. Those who do not will be subject to the discipline of the community.*

21:18. Moses balanced the principle of the previous section. If sons should not suffer because of the whims of their fathers, then neither should fathers (and mothers) suffer because of the misbehavior of their children.

The **stubborn and rebellious son** in question was not a toddler who had proven naughty but a young adult who had accumulated a long track record of disobedience and willfulness. His life had been characterized by a refusal to **listen** to his parents when they disciplined him. He was now in a position to inherit their wealth and extend his unruly behavior into the community at large.

21:19–20. All attempts at curbing his waywardness having failed, **his father and mother** were directed to **bring him to the elders** to have the case adjudicated. Parental rights in Israel did not include the right of life and death over their children. They had to present their case to civil authority to ensure that they were not at fault in their analysis of the incorrigibility of their son. The trial was to take place in the standard location, **at the gate** of the town. **This son of ours . . . is a profligate and a drunkard** was not a listing of specific capital offenses but evidence to support their contention that the young man was hopeless in his unwillingness to conform to sound wisdom.

21:21. If the parental complaint was sustained by civil authority, the execution of the young man was to be undertaken as a community obligation. All the men of the community were to **stone him to death**. The community would benefit not only by the removal of the young man but by the fact that his death would become known to **all Israel** and would cause others who might follow in his steps to **be afraid**.

E The Death of the Capital Offender (21:22–23)

SUPPORTING IDEA: *The land of promise is desecrated by a lack of respect for human life.*

21:22. While this chapter begins with reference to a murder victim, it ends with the description of a person **put to death** because of a **capital offense**. Even such an offender is not to be treated in death as human garbage. The body of such a man might in certain cases be **hung on a tree** as a display of justice and to serve as a deterrent to lawlessness (cp. Num. 25:4; Josh. 8:29; 10:26–27; 2 Sam. 21:5–9). Stoning, not hanging, was the means of execution in Israel.

21:23. Those purposes must give way before the importance of respect for the humanness of the offender. Israelite communities **must not leave his body on the tree overnight**. He was to be buried before sundown, since **anyone who is hung on a tree is under God's curse**. The cursing is the cause rather than the effect of the hanging.

Paul quoted this verse in connection with the crucifixion of Christ: "Christ redeemed us from the curse of the law by becoming a curse for us, for it is written: 'Cursed is everyone who is hung on a tree'" (Gal. 3:13). By proper burial of even such a person, Israel would not **desecrate the land** God was giving them **as an inheritance**.

MAIN IDEA REVIEW: *Israel is to maintain respect for life in every form and recognize that it always issues from God. The victors and the strong must respect the rights of the vanquished and the weak, and each must recognize God's interest in the others.*

III. CONCLUSION

Accidental Baptists

In 1992, Southern Baptist missionary Rob Moor was traveling in Tanzania with a local pastor by the name of Sostenes Karoli. About sixty miles from their homes in Bukoba, the two were involved in a head-on collision with another car carrying five passengers. Neither Rob nor Sostenes was injured, but all five passengers in the other vehicle were hurt, one quite seriously. The most severely injured passenger was rushed to a hospital where he was taken directly into the emergency room.

Back at the scene, Rob and Sostenes led in prayer for all the accident victims. The spectators who gathered at the location of the wreck were fascinated by the impromptu prayer meeting, so the two Christians took the opportunity to distribute tracts and share their faith.

Rob was eventually able to catch a ride into Bukoba. Sostenes waited for two days for a truck to take him and his wrecked vehicle back home. During the delay, he was joined by some Baptist laymen and another local pastor who had heard of his mishap. Together they were able to lead fourteen people to a knowledge of Jesus Christ. The new converts came together, and some two weeks after the accident began a new church with the title *Kanisa la Ajali*—which in Swahili means "Accident Baptist Church."

In the providence of God, there are no accidents. When God's people display his character and express his love and respect for people, he uses it for his glory. What we see as "accidents of providence" are actually expressions of his government of human affairs.

PRINCIPLES

- Love is one factor—but not the only one—that God uses to promote the permanence of the marriage bond.
- People are not free to violate law or convention to satisfy their wants and cravings.
- Even guilty people deserve to be treated as those made in the image of God.

APPLICATIONS

- Identify any injury (physical or otherwise) you may have caused to another, and take steps to set things right.
- Know the arguments for the personhood of the unborn child.
- Assess your life for evidence of stubbornness and rebellion.
- Keep your life free from the defilements of the world.

IV. LIFE APPLICATION

Lincoln's Miracle

Abraham Lincoln lost his mother at a young age, suffered from a lack of formal education, and faced long odds at each step of his life. He lost most of the elections in which he was a candidate. He even failed at running a country store near his home in Illinois.

When Lincoln and his partner in the store were contemplating closing their doors, Abe reflected, "You know, I wouldn't mind so much if I could just do what I want to do. I want to study law. I wouldn't mind so much if we could sell everything we've got and pay all our bills and have just enough left over to buy one book—*Blackstone's Commentary on English Law;* but I guess I can't."

As they were talking, a wagon approached. The driver pulled up close to the store porch, looked at Lincoln and said, "I'm trying to move my family out west, and I'm out of money. I've got a good barrel here that I could sell for fifty cents."

Lincoln looked at the haggard-looking man and his too-thin wife. He thought for a few seconds, then reached into his pocket and pulled out the last fifty cents he had. Handing it to the traveler, he said, "I reckon I could use a good barrel."

All day the barrel sat on the porch of that store. Lincoln's soon to be ex-partner kidded him about his too-compassionate nature. As the day drew to a close, Lincoln walked over and peered into the barrel. He saw something in the bottom of it that he hadn't noticed before. He reached down and pulled out a book and stood astonished. It was a copy of *Blackstone's Commentary on English Law*. Lincoln later wrote, "I stood there holding the book and looking up toward the heavens. There came a deep impression on me that God had something for me to do and he was showing me now that I had to get ready for it. Why this miracle otherwise?"

In God's plan, law books in barrels, unexpected pregnancies, and handicapped children are no more accidental than the opening of the Red Sea. His ways may be mysterious and disturbing to us, but that says more about us than about him: "He is the Rock, his works are perfect, and all his ways are just. A faithful God who does no wrong, upright and just is he" (Deut. 32:4).

V. PRAYER

Father, give us the insight to appreciate your goodness even when we don't know your intent. Help us to have the humility to admit that there are aspects to your plan we don't understand and to trust your character when we don't know what you're doing. Amen.

VI. DEEPER DISCOVERIES

A. Firstborn (21:16)

Israelites were warned not to tamper with reality when it came to writing their wills: "It shall be, on the day he bequeaths his possessions to his sons, that he must not bestow firstborn status on the son of the loved wife in preference to the son of the unloved, the true firstborn" (Deut. 21:16 NKJV). *Firstborn*, as this verse makes clear, is a term that refers to legal status as well as chronological precedence. The firstborn of the family received a double portion of his father's estate and was regarded as senior among surviving sons.

Cults often teach that applying the term *firstborn* to Jesus proves that he was a created being and thus is not God. Nothing could be more misguided. Jesus' *firstborn* status relates him to us, not to creation: "For those God

Deuteronomy 21

foreknew he also predestined to be conformed to the likeness of his Son, that he might be the firstborn among many brothers" (Rom. 8:29). As the senior member of God's human family, Jesus is deserving not simply of respect, but of worship: "When He again brings the firstborn into the world, [God] says: 'Let all the angels of God worship Him'" (Heb. 1:6 NKJV).

B. Stubborn and Rebellious (21:18)

It is no accident that the expression used in verse 18 to describe a wayward son is elsewhere used of Israel, God's own wayward son. In Jeremiah 5:23, God describes the imminent destruction of Judah with the plaintive words, "But these people have stubborn and rebellious hearts; they have turned aside and gone away." Identical language is used to describe the generation of the exodus: "They would not be like their forefathers—a stubborn and rebellious generation, whose hearts were not loyal to God, whose spirits were not faithful to him" (Ps. 78:8). The Israelite parent whose child ignored all his instruction could know in a small measure the sorrow that Israel caused Yahweh.

VII. TEACHING OUTLINE

A. INTRODUCTION
1. Lead Story: Granny Dumping
2. Context: God charges Israel to observe his commands about life and death.
3. Transition: God expects believers to recognize his hand in human affairs and to respect all human life, even when extending such respect may be painful or troublesome.

B. COMMENTARY
1. The Death of an Unknown Individual (21:1–9)
2. The Life of the Prisoner of War (21:10–14)
3. The Life of the Firstborn Son (21:15–17)
4. The Death of the Rebellious Son (21:18–21)
5. The Death of the Capital Offender (21:22–23)

C. CONCLUSION: LINCOLN'S MIRACLE

VIII. ISSUES FOR DISCUSSION

1. How can you distance yourself from the moral blunders of other people?
2. Why do you think stubbornness is viewed by God as such a serious matter?
3. Can a community secure corporate atonement today? Why or why not?
4. Can war be totally avoided in the world we live in? Why or why not?

Deuteronomy 22

Preserve and Protect

I. **INTRODUCTION**
The Apology of Aristides

II. **COMMENTARY**
A verse-by-verse explanation of the chapter.

III. **CONCLUSION**
Fractured Scriptures

An overview of the principles and applications from the chapter.

IV. **LIFE APPLICATION**
Misplaced Confidence

Melding the chapter to life.

V. **PRAYER**
Tying the chapter to life with God.

VI. **DEEPER DISCOVERIES**
Historical, geographical, and grammatical enrichment of the commentary.

VII. **TEACHING OUTLINE**
Suggested step-by-step group study of the chapter.

VIII. **ISSUES FOR DISCUSSION**
Zeroing the chapter in on daily life.

Deuteronomy 22

> **Quote**
>
> *"Simplicity reaches out after God; purity discovers and enjoys him."*
>
> Thomas à Kempis

IN A NUTSHELL

Deuteronomy 22 insists that Israel's people should take steps to protect life and to promote purity at all levels of national experience.

Preserve and Protect

I. INTRODUCTION

The Apology of Aristides

Aristides was a second-century Greek philosopher who, in his late fifties, became a Christian believer after he was already famous throughout the Roman Empire. He became disturbed when he saw what was happening to Christians under the government of the emperor Hadrian. Believers were being harassed, persecuted, and killed for their faith because they would not subscribe to the official Roman state religion. Aristides wrote the emperor and appealed to him to end his regime's persecution of Christians. Here is part of what he wrote in what has become known as the *Apology of Aristides* (*Apology* in this context means "a reasoned legal defense"):

> Christians abstain from all impurity in the hope of a recompense that is to come in another world. As for their servants or handmaids or children, they persuade them to become Christians by the love that they have for them. And when they have become so, they call them without distinction, "Brothers." They do not worship strange gods and they walk in all kindness and humility and falsehood is not found among them. And they love one another. When they see a stranger, they bring him to their homes and rejoice over him as over a true brother. But they do not call brothers those who are after the flesh but those who are in the spirit and in God. And if there is among them a man who is poor and needy, and if they have not an abundance of necessities, they fast two or three days that they may supply the needy with necessary food. They observe scrupulously the commandment of their Messiah. They live honestly and soberly as the Lord their God commanded them. They praise and laud him and over their food they render him thanks. And if any righteous person of their number passes away from this world, they rejoice and give thanks to God, and they follow his body as though he were moving from one place to another. And when a child is born to them, they praise God and again, if it chances to die in its infancy, they praise God mightily as for one that has passed through the world without sins. Such is the law of the Christians, and such is their conduct.

That such a statement could be written to a public figure without fear of contradiction explains, perhaps more than anything else, the rapid spread of Christianity through the early Roman Empire. The second-century Christians behaved as advertised; they produced real benefits to the society in which they lived. And it started, as Aristides noted, with their passion for purity. Those early believers rarely permitted their testimony to be adulterated by attachments to the values of the world or the precepts of Roman religion. The stakes were too high . . . as they still are.

The power of the testimony of Christians rises in direct proportion to their unwillingness to mix truth with error and to trim their sails to the prevailing winds of the culture. Purity brings no one to Christ, but it does give credibility to those who proclaim him.

II. COMMENTARY

Preserve and Protect

MAIN IDEA: *God's people must love one another in responsible ways, showing respect for life and property and for the purity that makes believers distinct from their neighbors.*

A Promote the Preservation of Life (22:1–8)

SUPPORTING IDEA: *Israelites must take responsibility for one another by acts that preserve the lives and property of their neighbors.*

22:1–2. Moses adorned the command "you shall love your neighbor as yourself" (Lev. 19:18 NKJV) with the clothing of specific examples in these opening verses of the chapter. The opposite of love is not hatred but indifference. The Israelite who saw a **brother's ox or sheep straying** was not to **ignore it**. He was to go to the trouble to **take it back to him**. The fact that the brother did not live nearby was irrelevant; he lived somewhere. If he could not be located, the Israelite was to take the animal home where it could be fed and kept until the owner came **looking for it**. By these words, Moses invested love for one's neighbor with a healthy dose of reality. The Israelite who names the name of Yahweh must exhibit Yahweh's attribute of personal concern.

22:3–4. In these verses, the principle is expanded to cover any personal property of another. It mattered little whether the possession was a **brother's donkey or his cloak**, or for that matter **anything** that he might lose. The person who loves is never indifferent to what might bring pain or loss to another.

Nor was he to be unconcerned with regard to the need for unusual personal exertions. The donkey or ox of a brother need not be lost; it might just be struggling with its load. If it had **fallen on the road**, then the caring person would help the brother **get it to its feet**. It should be remembered that these animals were not pets. The beast of burden enabled the farmer to grow his goods and take them to market. If an ox or donkey was missing or injured, the owner's livelihood was in jeopardy.

22:5–7. Verse 5 might appear to be out of place in a discussion of the preservation of life, but that is not the case. Moses insisted that Israel not blur distinctions that go to the continuance of life itself. **A woman must not wear men's clothing, nor a man wear women's clothing.** The prohibitions against cross-dressing are not pointed at masquerade parties but at a larger issue—the loss of male and female roles in a healthy society. Israelites were to respect God's design and not call their assigned sexuality into question by wearing inappropriate clothing. Moses knew that behavior provokes values just as values promote behavior. The Lord **detests** such behavior because it places a fog around distinctions that he constructed. God is against anything that blurs the lines between the sexes.

In the same way, Israel must recognize that even in the animal world the continuation of life depends on respect for motherhood. Even in such a mundane matter as a **bird's nest beside the road**, the life of **the mother** must be preserved to continue life into the next generation. Israel's future prosperity and even their longevity depended on their respect for life.

22:8. If the previous two examples were somewhat subtle, Moses' third illustration of love for one's neighbor is quite direct. Israelites were to build into the cost of any new house they constructed the expense of a **parapet** wall around the **roof**. Israelites were to take into account the possibility that a neighbor may stray near the edge and suffer an accidental injury or death. Since a parapet could preserve life, they were to build it onto their homes so they **may not bring the guilt of bloodshed** on their homes.

B Protect the Purity of Life (22:9–30)

SUPPORTING IDEA: *The people of God should take positive steps to display a concern for purity in private actions as well as public institutions.*

22:9–12. The apostle Paul, at a crucial point in the argument of 1 Corinthians, used an obscure law about muzzling a working ox (Deut. 25:4) to establish the validity of remuneration for ministers. In his discussion (1 Cor. 9:1–10), while not denying the validity of the muzzling law for its own sake, he was clear in stating that the overriding principle was still more important than the original law (1 Cor. 9:9–10).

The laws given in verses 9–12 fit into the same category. Moses warned Israel against the principle of adulteration. Wearing **clothes of wool and linen woven together** would not destroy a person morally; nor would mixing **two kinds of seed** in a vineyard. However, mixing the truths of Scripture with the viewpoints of pagan culture will always prove deadly. Israel was not to yoke herself into the same theological **plow** with the surrounding cultures and become defiled. Instead, the nation was to take pains to wear the symbols of her distinctiveness.

The **tassels** worn on the **corners** of the Israelite's **cloak** served a critical purpose: "Throughout the generations to come you are to make tassels on the corners of your garments, with a blue cord on each tassel . . . and so you will remember all the commands of the LORD, that you may obey them and not prostitute yourselves by going after the lusts of your own hearts and eyes" (Num. 15:38–39).

22:13–15. Moses turned from the metaphors of godly life to the place where it receives its most severe test: the home. Contrary to the pagan cultures around them, Israelites were to live with a sense of their accountability to Yahweh in their dealings with mates and children. An Israelite man was not to slander the reputation of his new wife by attempting to cloak his distaste for her by accusing her of a moral offense. If he should give her **a bad name** by asserting that he found no **proof of her virginity**, this claim was not to be accepted at face value. The **father and mother** of the slandered wife were to call for a hearing with the **town elders at the gate** to clear her name.

22:16–19. When the city fathers gathered to hear the case, the offended father could plead on the basis of the slanderous husband's dislike of his daughter and its product, the slander of her reputation. As evidence, they were to **display the cloth before the elders of the town** that they regard as **proof** of her **virginity** before marriage. Presumably this cloth contained bloodstains that testified to a ruptured hymen.

If the elders found the parents' complaint valid, they were to **punish** the slanderer by fining him **a hundred shekels of silver**. This represented an enormous sum of money at the time, since we know that David purchased the threshing floor of Araunah some centuries later for only fifty shekels of silver (2 Sam. 24:24). Such a staggering fine would serve as a considerable deterrent to the man who was inclined to escape a marriage by making false assertions about his wife. Since the damage was done not only to the wife but to the family reputation, the fine was paid to **the girl's father**.

Not only was there a financial penalty involved, but the slanderer lost the option to divorce the wronged wife forever: **She shall continue to be his wife; he must not divorce her as long as he lives**. Although the man could not divorce his wife, there was no restriction in the text on her divorcing him if the situation called for it.

22:20–21. If the charge of premarital promiscuity was deemed **true** by the elders, the woman would suffer the penalty of death by stoning. This punishment was to be administered not at the usual location near the gate of the city but at **the door of her father's house**. Just as false charges damaged the father's reputation and enriched him, genuine guilt would be laid on his doorstep. Because she had **done a disgraceful thing in Israel by being promiscu-**

ous while still in her father's house, he would be touched by her guilt. The possibility of such penalties would have served to give pause to the young woman who was tempted to be wayward and ought to have given parents a sobering reason to exercise close supervision of their daughters.

22:22. While premarital promiscuity was a serious threat to the stability of marriage and family life in Israel, adultery was a more serious danger. The man who was **found sleeping with another man's wife** was guilty of a crime not only against her but also against the life of the community. For similar reasons, the woman also was guilty; and the sole form of relief available was execution, which would **purge the evil** not just from their names but **from Israel** itself. Infidelity in marriage strikes at the heart of fidelity in society. The environment that condones it will condone many other offenses as well. What improperly happens in private between consenting adults threatens the public life of the community at large.

22:23–24. In Israel betrothal was more a form of marriage than of engagement, and this arrangement could be ended only by divorce. **A virgin pledged to be married** was in the eyes of the law **another man's wife**. Her silence in the case of a sexual assault in a town was presumed to indicate consent. The man who violated her and the virgin herself in such a case were both guilty and were subject to the death penalty.

22:25–27. A similar crime committed **out in the country** might issue in a different outcome, however, since it involved rape rather than consent. In such a case, **only the man** was subject to execution. Rape was a crime of assault and violence, **like that of someone who attacks and murders his neighbor**. The remote location of the offense would provide a presumption of innocence on the girl's part, for even if she had **screamed, there was no one to rescue her**.

22:28–29. In the case of a **virgin** who was **not pledged**, rape was a crime punishable by a large fine (**fifty shekels of silver**) and by a loss of freedom. The guilty man was required to **marry** his victim, and at the same time he lost his normal prerogative of **divorce**. While this penalty seems to cause damage to the victim even more than the perpetrator, it is reasonable to suggest that a condition is implied here: "assuming her willingness to marry him and her parents' approval of the marriage." Such a condition would often have existed, since her violation would have marred her as a potential marriage partner in the eyes of other potential mates.

22:30. This verse addresses a special case concerning marriage to a stepmother, which was prohibited. The man's natural father is presumed to have died, leaving a wife behind. Marriage is ruled out on the grounds that it would be a stain on the father's memory and a show of disrespect: **he must not dishonor his father's bed**. Analogous Hebrew expressions are used elsewhere to refer to dishonorable actions of a sexual nature (cp. Deut. 27:20; Gen. 9:20–24).

> **MAIN IDEA REVIEW:** God's people must love one another in responsible ways, showing respect for life and property and for the purity that makes believers distinct from their neighbors.

III. CONCLUSION

Fractured Scriptures

Den Hart once published a list of ficticious Scripture verses in his irreverent magazine, *The Wittenberg Door*. Hart decided to rewrite certain popular memory verses in order to make them more realistic from the point of view of modern American Christians. The results make up in entertainment value what they lack in truth.

For example, there is the altered version of Romans 12:2: "Be not conformed to this world, but be transformed by the renewing of your Master-Card." Then there is the interchange contained in the revised version of Matthew 8:21, "Another man said to him, 'Lord, first let me go and bury my father.' And Jesus told him, 'Sure. No problem! I mean, I wouldn't want to inconvenience anyone.'"

Hart redesigned Matthew 18:15 according to the way things are often done: "If a brother sins against you, go and tell someone about it, but don't approach the brother himself. If he sins against you again, go and tell a whole bunch of people about it; if he sins against you again, leave the church and go somewhere else." Then there is the famous statement in Luke 18:22, "When Jesus heard this, He said to him, 'You still lack one thing: go, sell all you possess and give it away to the poor . . . ha, ha, ha, just kidding.'"

The rewritten version of Colossians 3:5 is also instructive: "Put to death, therefore, whatever belongs to your earthly nature: sexual immorality, impurity, lust, evil desires and the greed which is idolatry. Clothe yourselves therefore in successful business ventures, a good self-image, natural fibers, and a deep tan."

As Hart's revisions show, there is little public sentiment for the internal war against impurity. The results of such neglect can be devastating, however, because it is possible to appear pure without actually being so. Sooner or later the adulterations of the impure believer's inner life will emerge, and a public exposure will result with all its attendant disappointments.

PRINCIPLES

- The opposite of love is indifference to the genuine needs of others.
- God is concerned that Christians live consistent with their profession even in the seemingly small and insignificant areas of life.
- God wants believers to take an interest in the well-being of the society in which they live.
- Protection of human life can be costly; but so is the neglect of that protection.

APPLICATIONS

- Contemplate the world of nature to discover what it teaches about the Creator.
- Give impurity no point of leverage in your life by judging impure thoughts and confessing them.
- Be reluctant to express any opinion of people that could damage their reputation.
- Regard every opportunity to make a moral decision as a testing ground of your relationship to the Lord Jesus.

IV. LIFE APPLICATION

Misplaced Confidence

Scripture offers few more pertinent examples of the dangers of impurity than the life of Samson (Judg. 13–16). He began his ministry by repeated demonstrations of his great God-supplied strength and ended it in blindness and at the mercy of his enemies. By compromising with the world system in its Philistine form, he forfeited his divine protection.

God had used Samson, and he concluded that God would always use him—or even worse, that God needed him. As a result, he set himself up for an unpleasant awakening to the truth.

Up until the time of his involvement with Delilah, Samson experienced consistent victories. Every time he faced the Philistines, he defeated them. God was using him because he was available. In that way, at least, Samson was praiseworthy. However, he exhibited a misplaced confidence. He apparently concluded from his successes that God was endorsing his lifestyle and that moral purity didn't matter to the God of Israel.

A. J. Gordon, one of the founders of Gordon-Conwell Seminary, liked to tell of an experience he once had while on a walk. He was looking across a field at a house in the distance. Beside the house was what appeared to be a

Deuteronomy 22

man pumping furiously at an old style hand-operated water pump. As Gordon watched, the man continued to pump at a tremendous rate; he seemed absolutely tireless, pumping on and on, up and down, without ever slowing in the slightest.

It was such an astonishing sight that Gordon decided to approach it to get a closer look. As he drew near, he could see that the person at the pump was not a man at all, but a wooden figure painted to resemble a man. The arm that was pumping so rapidly was hinged at the elbow and the hand was wired to the pump handle. The water was pouring forth, but not because the figure was pumping it. It was an artesian well, and the water was pumping the man!

God does not want Christians to be pushed and pulled along by the prevailing opinion of the world. Godly people are not to yield, as Samson did, to the allurements of a system that sacrifices spiritual reality on the altar of pleasure.

V. PRAYER

Father, keep us alert to the dangers of compromise. Help us be people who would rather lose an arm than forfeit your approval of us. At the same time, keep us from pride in our godliness and give us sensitivity to the needs of others, that we may demonstrate your love to them. Amen.

VI. DEEPER DISCOVERIES

A. Proof of Virginity (22:17)

Parents of a slandered wife were expected to present evidence that would vindicate her at a public hearing: "'Here is the proof of my daughter's virginity' . . . her parents shall display the cloth before the elders of the town" (Deut. 22:17). The nature of this cloth is open to some dispute. It has been argued that the husband's accusation is that the wife is not menstruating, and that is taken as proof that she had been pregnant before the wedding. The cloth in question, according to this point of view, was an article of clothing containing menstrual bloodstains. Both this view and the one taken in the commentary suffer from the difficulty that if the husband knew of the existence of these items he would have been foolish to make the accusation. It might be, however, that the new wife had been instructed to provide such evidence to her parents just in case some such accusation should ever be made.

B. Dishonoring the Bed (22:30)

Israelite males were warned about taking a widowed stepmother, since the faithful man "must not dishonor his father's bed" (Deut. 22:30). The

Hebrew of this expression is literally, "he must not uncover the corner [or wing] of his father's garment." A few years later, Ruth would use similar language to say to Boaz, "I am Ruth your maid. So spread your covering over your maid, for you are a close relative" (Ruth 3:9 NASB). Although it is not immediately recognizable by modern eyes, this was nothing less than a proposal of marriage. The wings or corners of the garment represented the legal protection provided by a husband. In Deuteronomy 22:30, God was thus prohibiting the inauguration of a marriage of a stepmother to her stepson.

VII. TEACHING OUTLINE

A. INTRODUCTION

1. Lead Story: The Apology of Aristides
2. Context: Israel must be careful to protect life and to exhibit a commitment to truth without any mixture of error.
3. Transition: The people of God must consistently show regard for the lives of their neighbors while exhibiting confidence in God's truth. They must promote the preservation of life while at the same time protecting the purity of truth.

B. COMMENTARY

1. Promote the Preservation of Life (22:1–8)
2. Protect the Purity of Life (22:9–30)

C. CONCLUSION: MISPLACED CONFIDENCE

VIII. ISSUES FOR DISCUSSION

1. What are some examples of how the principles of verses 1–3 are violated in modern society?
2. What are some consequences of the modern tendency toward a blurring of the line between the sexes?
3. Can you think of some ways that Christians can make themselves distinctive in the modern world?
4. Why is a good reputation so important?

Deuteronomy 23

The Cutting Edge

I. **INTRODUCTION**
Holy Is as Holy Thinks

II. **COMMENTARY**
A verse-by-verse explanation of the chapter.

III. **CONCLUSION**
Grim Is Out
An overview of the principles and applications from the chapter.

IV. **LIFE APPLICATION**
Hidden Dangers
Melding the chapter to life.

V. **PRAYER**
Tying the chapter to life with God.

VI. **DEEPER DISCOVERIES**
Historical, geographical, and grammatical enrichment of the commentary.

VII. **TEACHING OUTLINE**
Suggested step-by-step group study of the chapter.

VIII. **ISSUES FOR DISCUSSION**
Zeroing the chapter in on daily life.

Quote

"How little people know who think that holiness is dull. When one meets the real thing... it is irresistible. If even ten percent of the world's population had it, would not the whole world be converted and happy before a year's end?"

C. S. Lewis

Deuteronomy 23

IN A NUTSHELL

Deuteronomy 23 describes what a holy life looks like in the mundane challenges of daily living. The people of God must be distinctive not only in their public worship but in their private practices and in their core values.

The Cutting Edge

I. INTRODUCTION

Holy Is as Holy Thinks

As January 1, 2000, approached, a significant portion of the Christian church was indistinguishable from the world at large in terms of the panic level. Various places advised believers to hoard cash and stockpile all the food they could. Some even suggested retreating into the mountains with our cash and food, taking guns and ammunition so we would be able to beat off the assaults that would come when people began to starve. It was a disgraceful testimony.

Instead of adopting a fortress mentality, the leading edge of the testimony of Christians should have been our generosity. We should have been acknowledging our openness to share what we had with others if hard times did come. After all, where would we be if Jesus Christ had taken the attitude that self-preservation was the goal of living?

Most surveys reveal that we Christians behave much like our unbelieving neighbors because we believe much the same way . . . and our beliefs are not being formed by our acquaintance with Scripture. For example, one survey asked people, "Who preached the Sermon on the Mount?" Most professing Christians didn't know. Some thought Jesus did, but about the same number thought the sermon was preached by Billy Graham. A number of churchgoers thought that it probably was preached by someone on horseback.

One public opinion question asked, "Does the statement, 'God helps those who help themselves' come from the Bible?" Among people who were regular church attenders, 60 percent thought it did. Interestingly, among people who did *not* attend church at all, only 53 percent believed the statement originated in Scripture. It may be that if we stayed home on Sundays, we might be better acquainted with the Scriptures.

While the last sentence was uttered with my tongue firmly planted in my cheek, it is no exaggeration to say that the modern church—especially in the West—has lost its cutting edge. God wants his people to be distinctive in their behavior and values and to draw their distinctiveness from a thorough acquaintance with his precepts as revealed in Scripture. If we are not holy people, we have little to say to the world.

Deuteronomy 23:1

II. COMMENTARY

The Cutting Edge

> **MAIN IDEA:** The people of God are to be holy in everything, from public worship to practices of hygiene, but especially in their core values.

A Distinctive in Public Worship (23:1–8)

> **SUPPORTING IDEA:** Israelites must gather in holy assemblies distinctive from the world in which they live.

23:1. God intended Israel's influence in the world to be enhanced by his nation's commitment to holiness. Although the term *holiness* has been twisted nearly out of recognition by its associations in the modern world, at its heart holiness means "distinctiveness." If Israel was not different from those nations around her, she would have little influence in attracting them to Yahweh, the source of her distinctiveness. Lines would have to be drawn between those who could and could not participate in Israel's public assemblies of worship and deliberation. Among the excluded were those who had been **emasculated by crushing or cutting**. They could not **enter the assembly of the LORD**.

The last term must be carefully defined. It is not coterminous with "the community of Israel," nor is it the equivalent of "those who can worship the Lord." *The assembly of the Lord* referred to those formal gatherings of Israel for festivals or times of national crisis. Outside of such events, the assembly of the Lord did not exist, although the nation certainly did. People who were physically deformed were always accepted as full members of the Israelite family under normal conditions. The lone exception was their ineligibility for service in the priesthood (Lev. 21:21).

23:2–3. People were also restricted from the assembly if they were descendants of a **forbidden marriage**. The term is not restricted to illegitimacy but referred as well to marriages between Israelites and those from pagan cultures and to the products of incest. **Even down to the tenth generation** was an idiom that meant "indefinitely" (the Hebrew text makes this explicit, adding the word "forever" to the end of v. 3; cp. NKJV).

As a case in point, people of **Ammonite or Moabite** descent were excluded. These two tribal peoples were the products of incestuous encounters between Lot and his two daughters (cp. Gen. 19:30–38).

23:4–6. If Ammon and Moab's improper origins were not problem enough, Moses explained, God also held them responsible for their failure to meet Israel **with bread and water** as they approached the Holy Land. Still worse, **they hired Balaam**, the mercenary false prophet, **to pronounce a curse**

on Israel. The fact that God **turned the curse into a blessing** did not relieve them of the guilt of their actions in his eyes. As individuals who might have been living inside the territorial confines of the promised land, they were excluded from participation in the national assembly of Israel, and the nation was **not to seek a treaty of friendship with them** in the future.

This prohibition, of course, says nothing about the spiritual condition of individuals of Ammonite or Moabite descent. Like Rahab from Jericho, they could be redeemed. Like Uriah of Hittite descent, they could display lives of great righteousness. Still, they could claim no part in Israel's national gatherings.

23:7–8. Restrictions against Edomites and Egyptians were less severe for historical reasons. The former were descended from Esau, Jacob's twin brother, and that family tie was not to be despised. Egyptians were given special consideration because Israel had **lived as an alien in his country**. Those descended from these two nations could **enter the assembly of the LORD** in the third generation.

B Distinctive in Private Practices (23:9–14)

SUPPORTING IDEA: *Impurity, whether moral or metaphorical, must be avoided by a holy people.*

23:9. Moses began and ended this brief section with statements of general principle—everything impure should be avoided by Israel. Israel could not expect victory in battle against their enemies unless they maintained their distinctiveness—even in a military camp.

23:10–11. The first of two specific examples is cited. A **nocturnal emission** was not a moral failure, but it had the potential to be a ceremonial one. Although the likelihood of its being known in the camp was small, that was beside the point. The Israelite soldier would know of his uncleanness and should take steps to cleanse himself of his impurity. Going **outside the camp** and staying there until nightfall would meet this objective. After washing himself, he could **return to the camp**. Uncleanness as described here was a ritual condition and implied no moral or spiritual fault.

23:12–13. Moses' second example of distinctiveness in hygiene had to do with the regular disposal of excrement. Since this would be a recurring issue in a military camp, Israel's soldiers must plan accordingly. They must first **designate a place outside the camp** for such purposes. Presumably, failure to use the designated area would defile the camp and would require ritual ablution, although that is not made explicit here.

A shovel was a part of the soldier's field gear, and it was used to **dig a hole** that would **cover up** the excrement.

Deuteronomy 23:14

23:14. This section on distinctiveness in hygienic practices concludes with the rationale for such precautions. The Lord himself would always be present in the camp of his people. While he was there **to protect and deliver** their enemies to them, he expected his people to acknowledge his presence in their midst, even by paying attention to such mundane functions. Failure to do so would be offensive to him, and soldiers soon to do battle would want to avoid the possibility that the Lord might **turn away** from his people because of the condition of their camp.

Bible students have been quick in the past to point out the health benefits of regular washing and the proper location of latrines as described here. It should be noted, however, that these considerations do not necessarily form the fundamental reasons for such practices. Many of the distinctions in the law of God are there solely because Yahweh so decreed it. Israel's observation of those laws would set them apart from the nations.

Ⓒ Distinctive in Personal Values (23:15–25)

SUPPORTING IDEA: *Israel must maintain holiness among the nations by the values the nation holds, particularly with regard to treatment of people within and outside the covenant community.*

23:15–16. The holiness of Israel was to go much deeper than the observance of bodily emissions and proper washings. They must, in fact, exhibit their distinctiveness especially in their treatment of the oppressed. They were slaves in Egypt, and Yahweh freed them. Therefore, they were to display his virtues by the way they treated a slave who had **taken refuge** with them. They should provide sanctuary to the fleeing slave and refuse to **hand him over to his master**. The slave was to be permitted to live among the people of Israel, where he would find sympathy and understanding. He was not to be oppressed but given freedom to live **wherever he likes and in whatever town he chooses**.

23:17–18. Holiness was to extend to matters of sexual behavior as well. Israel was to set itself apart from the Canaanites, who practiced cultic prostitution. Although prostitution across the board was regarded as abhorrent (cp. Lev. 19:29; 21:9; Deut. 22:21), to engage in the practice and justify it on the basis of worship took degradation to a different level.

The Hebrew term for **shrine prostitute** is *qadesha*, meaning "holy one." Although *holy* is not an adjective usually connected with prostitution in the modern world, the term does communicate the fundamental idea of holiness, which is *separation*. Shrine prostitutes were set aside or dedicated to the worship of the pagan god in question.

Israel was to stay clear of any such notion in connection with Yahweh. They were not to serve as prostitutes, either male or female, and they certainly were not to attempt to fulfill an obligation to God by paying it from **the earnings** they had gained in a way that the Lord detested.

23:19–20. Israel's core values must also include concern for the well-being of a **brother**. Israelites could not charge those of their own nation **interest** on loans, whether **on money or food or anything else. A foreigner** could be charged interest but not a fellow descendant of Jacob.

23:21–23. A vow was a promise made to God that was conditioned upon his providing a desired benefit. The worshiper would come to the tabernacle (or later the temple) and publicly proclaim, "If God will produce (the desired benefit), then I will donate (so many shekels) to the poor (or to some other cause)." All vows were voluntary and were made at the worshiper's discretion. Moses insisted here, however, that if an Israelite made **a vow to the Lord**, he should **not be slow to pay it**. Yahweh always collects what is vowed to him scrupulously and would **certainly demand** what was promised. No guilt is incurred on the part of the person who refrains from making a vow. However, the worshiper must commit himself to doing **whatever** his **lips utter**. An Israelite's word must be his bond at all times, whether the promise was made to the Lord or to a brother.

23:24–25. In Israel, necessity would provide certain freedoms that would normally have been violations of God's command against stealing. If a person entered a **neighbor's vineyard** and was hungry, he had the God-given right to **eat** what he could consume on the spot. He could not, however, **put any in a basket** as though the vineyard belonged to him. Similarly, he could pick his neighbor's corn to eat but not collect it as though it were his own.

> **MAIN IDEA REVIEW:** The people of God are to be holy in everything, from public worship to practices of hygiene but especially in their core values.

III. CONCLUSION

Grim Is Out

Many of us associate holiness with a kind of melancholy grimness. One passage that God used to explode this myth was the account of Israel's return from the Babylonian exile (Neh. 8:1–12). Ezra gathered the people and read from the law of God. As he was reading, the people's hearts ached so deeply from hearing the Scriptures that they began to weep. What happened next is illuminating:

Nehemiah, who was the governor, Ezra the priest and scribe, and the Levites who taught the people said to all the people, "This day is holy to the Lord your God; do not mourn nor weep." For all the people wept, when they heard the words of the Law. Then he said to them, "Go your way, eat the fat,

Deuteronomy 23

drink the sweet, and send portions to those for whom nothing is prepared; for this day is holy to our LORD. Do not sorrow, for the joy of the LORD is your strength." So the Levites quieted all the people, saying, "Be still, for the day is holy; do not be grieved" (Neh. 8:9–11 NKJV).

From God's point of view, holiness is the partner of joy, not sorrow. The closer we are to God, the more consistently we exhibit the joy of his character. To be at his right hand is to know the eternal pleasures that he supplies (cp. Ps. 16:11).

PRINCIPLES

- Sometimes believers are hampered in their public effectiveness by limitations that are no fault of their own.
- God is able to transform the hostile intentions of wicked people into blessings for his people.
- God is always near his people, but their sinful behavior may cause his presence to be grievous.
- Christians must allow no unclean thing to interfere with a harmonious relationship with Christ.

APPLICATIONS

- Consider the areas of your life that are not wholly consecrated to God and resolve to separate these areas to him.
- Confess your sins daily to God, and appeal to him for help in forsaking them.
- Stop rationalizing behavior that you know to be wrong.
- Always be a person of your word.

IV. LIFE APPLICATION

Hidden Dangers

A Polish girl named Marie Sklondowska once heard one of her favorite teachers say, "Some of you have stars at your fingertips." The encouragement, although given in a rather offhand fashion, made a strong impression on her. She decided to reach for those stars and enrolled in a science curriculum at the Sorbonne in Paris. There she distinguished herself as a student. She also fell in love with one of her professors, a young man named Pierre Curie. They were soon married and reaching for the stars together.

Their research was difficult, and their theories were the objects of scorn at times, but they pressed on. Just at the moment they were most discouraged, they walked into their laboratory one evening after dinner and noticed evaporation dishes glowing in the dark. They had discovered radium, and their names became famous the world over.

However, Madame Curie discovered that the handling of a powerful radioactive element such as radium yielded undesirable side effects. Soon she was suffering from burns. Years later, she contracted cancer that had been induced by her prolonged exposure to the element she discovered. That cancer eventually took her life.

Christians must make sure that their dreams have no unwanted side effects. Often hidden deep within our desires lie unseen dangers that can produce spiritual destruction (cp. Jas. 1:15). Spiritual wisdom requires that we exercise discernment to anticipate the pitfalls in what may appear to be a good thing.

V. PRAYER

Father, help us to cleanse ourselves from every defilement of flesh and spirit and present ourselves to you as clean instruments. May our offering of ourselves be free of pollution. Amen.

VI. DEEPER DISCOVERIES

A. Born of a Forbidden Marriage (23:2)

Moses insisted that a person who was "born of a forbidden marriage" could never enter the assembly of the Lord, nor could any of his offspring. Older translations use the word *bastard* as the translation of this Hebrew word, *mamzer*. The term is rare in biblical Hebrew, appearing only here and in Zechariah 9:6. It is difficult to be dogmatic about the meaning of the word, but the NIV translation seems a reasonable one, since it would also exclude people born through incestuous relationships and perhaps even those born to cult prostitutes (cp. vv. 17–18).

B. Do Not Seek a Treaty of Friendship (23:6)

Moses warned Israel against engaging in what would be called today normal diplomatic relations with Moab and Ammon. Verse 6 seems to contradict later revelation concerning forgiveness, since it insists, "Do not seek a treaty of friendship with them as long as you live." How does this relate to Jesus' teaching about loving one's enemies (Matt. 5:44)?

For one thing, the two commands do not operate in the same realm. Moses' command to Israel applied to national foreign policy, and it was implicitly directed at national leaders.

When Israelites found themselves in a relationship with Moabites, they were not required to behave boorishly or hatefully in order to fulfill

Deuteronomy 23

Deuteronomy 23:6. They could have behaved lovingly toward their Ammonite acquaintances.

Their national leaders, however, were not permitted to formalize treaties with Moabite or Ammonite national leaders. As idolatrous peoples, those nations had endangered Israel in the past and would again in the future. Subsequent events showed the wisdom of this restriction (cp. Judg. 10:7–11:33; 2 Sam. 10:1–9; 2 Kgs. 1:1; 3:4–27).

VII. TEACHING OUTLINE

A. INTRODUCTION

1. Lead Story: Holy Is as Holy Thinks
2. Context: Israel's neighbors must never be able to squeeze God's people into the mold of their pagan deities. In Israel's national distinctiveness lay not only national survival but God's favor as well.
3. Transition: The people of God must be set apart—distinctive from the surrounding nations. The nation must be holy in its public worship, private practices, and personal values.

B. COMMENTARY

1. Distinctive in Public Worship (23:1–8)
2. Distinctive in Private Practices (23:9–14)
3. Distinctive in Personal Values (23:15–25)

C. CONCLUSION: GRIM IS OUT

VIII. ISSUES FOR DISCUSSION

1. What advice would you give to a person who harbors bitterness toward God about his severe disabilities?
2. Can you think of occasions in which God has turned the evil intentions of others into good in your life?
3. How does God use your sufferings to benefit others?
4. Is it ever valid to dedicate a sinfully gained possession to the service of God?

Deuteronomy 24

Portrait of a Caring Society

- I. **INTRODUCTION**
  The Glue of Love

- II. **COMMENTARY**
  A verse-by-verse explanation of the chapter.

- III. **CONCLUSION**
  The Quality of Mercy
  An overview of the principles and applications from the chapter.

- IV. **LIFE APPLICATION**
  No Missed Calls
  Melding the chapter to life.

- V. **PRAYER**
  Tying the chapter to life with God.

- VI. **DEEPER DISCOVERIES**
  Historical, geographical, and grammatical enrichment of the commentary.

- VII. **TEACHING OUTLINE**
  Suggested step-by-step group study of the chapter.

- VIII. **ISSUES FOR DISCUSSION**
  Zeroing the chapter in on daily life.

Deuteronomy 24

Quote

"Act in such a way that you always treat humanity, whether in your own person or in the person of any other, never simply as a means but always also as an end."

Immanuel Kant

IN A NUTSHELL

Moses paints the portrait of a caring society in Deuteronomy 24—a society in which people respect one another's possessions and rights and care about people's feelings more than their own comforts.

Portrait of a Caring Society

I. INTRODUCTION

The Glue of Love

Three-year-old James was attending Sunday school for the first time. His teacher was telling the story of the events of Good Friday, and they made a powerful impression upon him. That evening during dinner he said, without any introductory remarks, "Jesus died on the cross."

His parents, who were Christians, were pleased to hear this pronouncement and used the occasion to explore how much he understood. His mother asked, "Why did Jesus die on the cross, James?"

The little guy thought for a moment and then said, "Because he couldn't get off." It was clear that the theological import of the crucifixion hadn't quite broken through in James's young mind.

Still, as his parents reflected on his answer, the more accurate it seemed to them in reality. Jesus was stuck to the cross, although not by the nails that pierced his wrists. His love for humanity held him there far more firmly than any physical restraints. Hatred may have sentenced him to death, but it was the love of Jesus that kept him on the cross. His was a self-imposed restraint, borne for the good of humanity and their eternal welfare.

In the same way, societal laws can force people to pay their taxes and refrain from physical violence, but the best means to produce a civil community is to have people love one another.

II. COMMENTARY

Portrait of a Caring Society

MAIN IDEA: *To create a genuinely caring society, citizens must respect the possessions and the innate dignity of their neighbors.*

A Respectful of the Possessions of Others (24:1–7)

SUPPORTING IDEA: *The people of God regard what belongs to others, whether a mate, property, or life itself, as inviolate and not subject to the whims of individuals.*

24:1–4. The NIV correctly follows the more recent analysis of these verses that recognizes verses 1–3 as a long and compound protasis ("if-clause"), with the apodosis ("then-clause") coming only in verse 4. These verses do not state the basis upon which a divorce may legally be obtained but instead regulate the behavior of a man who has already determined to divorce his wife. Moses recognized that a man might find **something indecent** in his wife that could cause him to want to divorce her. It is unlikely that *something indecent* is to be construed as an exact synonym for adultery for, as many have noted, the penalty for adultery was death.

The expression is open-ended because the emphasis here is not on the divorce but on what happens afterward. If divorce were chosen as the course of action, and the first husband formally dissolved the marriage by writing his wife a **certificate of divorce**, and she then married another, then the first husband could never remarry the woman, even if she was a widow, for **that would be detestable in the eyes of the LORD**.

The emphasis in this legislation was not on regulating the behavior of the wife but in restricting the right of a husband to treat his wife as a disposable property. He must be sure that he wanted to end the marriage the first time, because once his wife was gone **from his house** she was lost to him forever. To show disrespect for a former wife by maintaining a future interest in her as a mate would be to **bring sin upon the land** that God was giving Israel.

Jesus cited this passage when asked about the propriety of divorce but noted that in the original design of God, marriage was to be a permanent arrangement. What Moses commanded was a concession in recognition of the hardness of hearts of the people of Israel (Matt. 19:1–12).

24:5. In a caring society, people recognize that the normal rules and responsibilities from time to time will need to be set aside. Once such example is the case of **a man who has recently married**. The newlywed **must not be sent to war** or have other obligations to the community **laid on him** for the first **year** of marriage. Others would have to assume additional obligations, because the newly married man was **to be free to stay at home and bring happiness** to his bride.

24:6. Israel was permitted by God to take collateral to enforce payment of a debt, but certain items were off limits in this regard. No one could take a **pair of millstones . . . as security** because to do so would be the equivalent of **taking a man's livelihood** from him. These stones were worked in pairs. They consisted of a large base stone that remained stationary and a smaller upper millstone that was turned against it. Even the removal of the smaller stone would put a miller out of business, since the lower stone was useless by itself. In this way, God sought to clothe his command to love one's neighbor in practical garments. The term *livelihood* may also be translated as *life*. If that is the intent, the millstones in question would be smaller versions designed for the needs of an individual household.

24:7. Still more threatening to a caring society was the person who removed not a person's source of income but the person himself. One who was **caught kidnapping one of his brother Israelites** was subject to the death penalty. Whether his intent was to treat the captured individual **as a slave** or to sell him was irrelevant. Such a callous disregard for the value of another person was an **evil** that could not be tolerated.

B Respectful of the Dignity of Others (24:8–22)

SUPPORTING IDEA: *In a caring community, people regard the dignity of others as more important than acquisition of wealth.*

24:8–9. The dignity of fellow Israelites is encased in Moses' instructions concerning leprous diseases. The clue that links verse 8 with what follows in the connection to what the Lord did to Miriam along the way from Egypt. Numbers 12:1–15 describes how Miriam (the ringleader) and Aaron challenged Moses' authority. Miriam, for her part in this rebellion, was stricken with leprosy because of her resistance to divinely established authority. Although the command to deal cautiously in handling possible outbreaks of disease is important in itself, it also serves as the stage upon which the larger issue of authority is addressed. God will not deal gently with challenges to those whom he has placed in authority. Although Moses was meek (cp. Num. 12:3) about defending himself, God was not, and would not be in the future.

Therefore, the **Levites** were not to be challenged in diagnosing **cases of leprous diseases** (cp. Lev. 13–14). Once they had issued their findings according to what God had **commanded them**, their words were to be followed carefully (cp. Heb. 13:17).

24:10–13. Although one Israelite might make a loan to one of his neighbors, he was to respect the dignity of that debtor by not invading **his house** to demand the **pledge** of collateral. Instead, he was to **stay outside** and let the debtor **bring the pledge out** to the lender. By this instruction, Moses conveyed Yahweh's principle of living that gave higher priority to the feelings of a person than to the proper prerogatives of those with financial motives in mind.

Taking the point still further, in the case of a **poor** person, the collateral might be limited. If his pledge of repayment was something so vital as **his cloak**, it was to be received only symbolically and had to be returned **by sunset** so he could **sleep in it**. Such a regard for his condition would reap benefits of thanksgiving from the debtor and would be regarded as a righteous act by God.

24:14–15. Even the feelings of **a hired man** who was **poor and needy** were to be taken into account. It mattered little for purposes of this law whether the needy man was **a brother Israelite or an alien** living in the promised land. If he was owed **wages**, they were to be paid each day **before sunset**. His situation might be so desperate that he was counting on those wages, and if he failed to receive them he might cry to the Lord about the matter, leaving the one owing wages **guilty of sin**.

24:16. The worth of the person is especially emphasized by the commands of this verse. Each person was to bear responsibility for his own actions and not for the actions of another. **Fathers** were not to be executed because of the actions of their **children**, nor **children** because of the sins of **their fathers**. If there were actions that deserved death, **each** was to **die for his own sin** (see "Deeper Discoveries").

24:17–18. The lowest people on the social scale were **the alien, the fatherless,** and **the widow**, and God's defense of these dominates the last six verses of the chapter. People even in these categories were not to be deprived of justice. Nor were they to be taken advantage of. The **cloak** of an ordinary debtor might be taken briefly as collateral (cp. vv. 12–13), but even that was prohibited by those who had lent money to widows. It was Yahweh's purpose to create a sense of concern for the helpless in Israel, and Moses makes this explicit in verse 18. The Israelites are bidden to **remember** that they were once helpless **slaves in Egypt**. God had **redeemed** them from their sad condition, and they should be concerned for those who were defenseless.

24:19–22. God included a special item in this paragraph just to provide for the three groups mentioned in verse 17. When an Israelite was **harvesting** his **field**, he was not to take particular care to collect every sheaf. Occasional portions were to be left unharvested for the benefit of the poor. The same applied to the collection of **olives** and to the **grapes** of the vineyard.

By leaving the harvest unfinished, the caring Israelite could demonstrate his recognition of the importance of each person's dignity. A poor person could at least salvage something of his personal worth by gleaning in the fields of a neighbor rather than by going begging.

> **MAIN IDEA REVIEW:** To create a genuinely caring society, citizens must respect the possessions and the innate dignity of their neighbors.

III. CONCLUSION

The Quality of Mercy

Young Sally felt the weight of her responsibility the fateful day when her mother was ill. She wanted to do a good job relieving her mom of normal responsibilities so she could recover from her illness. Making sure that her mom was comfortable in the bedroom, Sally made her way to the kitchen. After straightening some things, she decided to make her mom a cup of tea, remembering that her mother had done so when her father had been sick.

She took the tea into her mother's bedroom, beaming with satisfaction at the accomplishment of the task. Her mother was effusive in her praise of her daughter and said proudly, "I didn't know you knew how to make tea."

"Yes, Mommy. I do. I boiled the water and tea leaves together just like you always do." Mom sipped her tea while listening attentively to her daughter's account. Then Sally explained, "I couldn't find the little strainer thing, though, so I used the fly swatter."

Her mom nearly choked. "You used the fly swatter to strain this tea?"

Sensing her mother's anxiety, Sally calmly comforted her by saying, "Don't worry, Mommy. I used the old fly swatter so I wouldn't mess up the new one."

At such times, a mom has to use all her self-control to realize that what is needed is not lessons in hygiene so much as an appreciation for the effort made by her daughter. Sensitive people do not sacrifice relationships on the altar of sound hygienic practices.

PRINCIPLES

- The health of marriage and the health of society are bound together; as one goes, so goes the other.
- The wise Christian will learn from the spiritual blunders of others.
- Equal justice under law is a spiritual as well as a civic principle.

APPLICATIONS

- Make allowances for the feelings of others as well as their physical or spiritual needs.
- Before criticizing others, remember your own spiritual history and how you have been guilty of similar offenses in the past.
- Love people and use things rather than loving things and using people.
- Acts of compassionate generosity are important, but it is wise to remember how such acts will be received before doing them.

IV. LIFE APPLICATION

No Missed Calls

Baseball umpire Bill Guthrie once gave a major league baseball player a lesson in respect. Almost from the first pitch, the catcher for the visiting team began to find fault with the umpire's calls. Guthrie took it patiently for three innings, but when the bottom of the fourth inning began with the same litany

Deuteronomy 24

of criticism, the umpire stopped the game. He walked around in front of the catcher and said, "Son, you've been a big help to me calling balls and strikes, and I appreciate it, but I think I've got the hang of it now. So I'm going to ask you to go to the clubhouse and show them how to take a shower."

God misses no calls when it comes to our behavior toward a neighbor. He keeps track of our actions and never forgets kindnesses done to others. Our role is to love the people around us and let God take responsibility for keeping track of the results.

V. PRAYER

Father, give us the grace to see life through the eyes of others. Help us to understand their motives and their yearnings, and to point them to you, the answer to every question. Amen.

VI. DEEPER DISCOVERIES

A. Another Man's Wife (24:2)

People sometimes assert that a second marriage that follows a groundless divorce is invalid, since the person who enters into it is still married to the original partner "in God's eyes." Deuteronomy 24:2 refutes that notion, noting that the divorced wife "after she leaves his house . . . becomes the wife of another man." Although a second marriage may be entered wrongly or even adulterously, it is still regarded as a marriage in the sight of God.

B. Fathers and Children (24:16)

Moses gave a fundamental ground of justice when he asserted, "Fathers shall not be put to death for their children, nor children put to death for their fathers; each is to die for his own sin" (Deut. 24:16). Some have found in this verse a contradiction of 2 Samuel 12:10, where David is told by God, "Now, therefore, the sword will never depart from your house, because you despised me and took the wife of Uriah the Hittite to be your own." The statement implies (and history bears out) that David's sins had far-reaching implications for his posterity.

Deuteronomy 24:16, however, is a principle of jurisprudence to be observed as the normal practice of Israelite courts. The judges in those courts could not render decisions with the omniscient insight of Yahweh himself, so they were bound to limit their application of the law to the people who were directly responsible.

In David's case, his children were not punished for his sins, but through their waywardness (and the consequent parental anguish) David was punished for his own. There is no suggestion in the narratives about David's subsequent family history that his children who behaved so badly were coerced into doing so.

VII. TEACHING OUTLINE

A. INTRODUCTION
1. Lead Story: The Glue of Love
2. Context: Moses calls on Israel to demonstrate love for neighbors in more than superficial ways.
3. Transition: In an increasingly impersonal world, God wants his people to develop insight about the feelings of other people and behave toward them with respect and understanding.

B. COMMENTARY
1. Respectful of the Possessions of Others (24:1–7)
2. Respectful of the Dignity of Others (24:8–22)

C. CONCLUSION: NO MISSED CALLS

VIII. ISSUES FOR DISCUSSION

1. Why do you think God exempted from military service men who were newlyweds?
2. Is there any connection between societal breakdown and individuals fleeing from personal responsibility?
3. How can a good memory become a spiritual asset?
4. Why do you think God includes accounts of spiritual blunders in the Bible?

Deuteronomy 25

No Muzzled Oxen

I. **INTRODUCTION**
The Weapon of Dying

II. **COMMENTARY**
A verse-by-verse explanation of the chapter.

III. **CONCLUSION**
Mountains in the Way

An overview of the principles and applications from the chapter.

IV. **LIFE APPLICATION**
Caring Hurts

Melding the chapter to life.

V. **PRAYER**
Tying the chapter to life with God.

VI. **DEEPER DISCOVERIES**
Historical, geographical, and grammatical enrichment of the commentary.

VII. **TEACHING OUTLINE**
Suggested step-by-step group study of the chapter.

VIII. **ISSUES FOR DISCUSSION**
Zeroing the chapter in on daily life.

Deuteronomy 25

> ## Quote
>
> *"The moral test of government is how that government treats those who are in the dawn of life, the children; those who are in the twilight of life, the elderly; and those who are in the shadows of life—the sick, the needy and the handicapped."*
>
> Hubert H. Humphrey

Deuteronomy 25

IN A NUTSHELL

God intended Israel to establish not only a just society but one that protected the rights of those who were vulnerable because of their weakness.

No Muzzled Oxen

I. INTRODUCTION

The Weapon of Dying

Joseph Tson pastored a church in Rumania during the era of Communist oppression. Because of his testimony, he was exiled from the country in 1981. When he decided it was time to return home and preach the gospel again, he knew he was taking a risk. He recalled Jesus' warning in Matthew 10:16, "I am sending you out like sheep among wolves. Therefore be as shrewd as snakes and as innocent as doves."

Since sheep amid wolves have no real likelihood of survival, Tson decided he would approach the resumption of his ministry with the full confidence that he would not survive. In his book *Pastoral Renewal,* he later wrote, "After our return, as I preached uninhibitedly, harassment and arrests came. One day during interrogation an officer threatened to kill me. Then I said, 'Sir, your supreme weapon is killing. My supreme weapon is dying. Sir, you know my sermons are all over the country on tapes now. If you kill me, I will be sprinkling them with my blood. Whoever listens to them after that will say, "I'd better listen. This man sealed it with his blood." They will speak ten times louder than before. So, go on and kill me. I win the supreme victory then.'"

His captor sent him home, causing him to reflect about the days before his exile: "For years I was a Christian who was cautious because I wanted to survive. I had accepted all the restrictions the authorities put on me because I wanted to live. Now I wanted to die, and they wouldn't oblige. Now I could do whatever I wanted in Rumania. For years I wanted to save my life, and I was losing it. Now that I wanted to lose it, I was winning it" (Tson, p. 44).

Tson's experience shows that the service of Christ is often paradoxical. Safety lies not in caution but in the realization that our life is Christ's to spend however he wishes. In our vulnerability we place ourselves squarely in his hands and in his purposes, the safest place of all. We also gain an appreciation for those around us who are weak and helpless.

II. COMMENTARY

No Muzzled Oxen

> **MAIN IDEA:** While humanly invented systems of justice concentrate on the punishment of the guilty, God's laws point toward helping the vulnerable while establishing justice.

Deuteronomy 25:1-3

▣ Protecting the Vulnerable (25:1-16)

SUPPORTING IDEA: *Those in society who are weak must be protected by those who are strong. The guilty criminal and even animals can look to Yahweh for protection.*

25:1-3. Hebrew law made no provision for imprisonment. While the cities of refuge (cp. Num. 35:6-34) were inconvenient, they did not inhibit life in any material way for the accused offender. Apart from fines and restitution, punishment for offenses in Israel sometimes involved corporal punishment, as outlined in this brief paragraph. Under God's covenant, men could not coerce others. If they had **a dispute**, they had **to take it to court and let judges decide the case**. Although the language of verse 1 suggests a civil matter, verse 2 implies that criminal offenses were to be decided by the same methods. If the judges determined that a man was **guilty** and that his behavior merited physical punishment, they were not to remove themselves but have the guilty person **lie down** and receive the flogging in the officials' **presence**.

The number of lashes was to be in keeping with the severity of the **crime**, but never **more than forty lashes**. Hebrew practice later reduced the number to thirty-nine for the sake of caution (see 2 Cor. 11:24). This restriction was only partly attributable to considerations of mercy: **If he is flogged more than that**, the offender **will be degraded in your eyes**. The innate worth and dignity of humanity was a line never to be crossed, in particular since the offender was a **brother**. Even criminals, in their vulnerability before an angry community, are covered by God's protection.

25:4. This protection extended even further. The **ox** upon whom life depended as he trod **out the grain** was not to be deprived of his necessary food. The Hebrew farmer was not to **muzzle** the ox as he did his work.

The apostle Paul quoted this verse twice and in similar contexts, justifying remuneration for those who do the work of ministry. In 1 Corinthians 9:9-11, he showed the applicability of verse 4 to realms of life that go beyond ancient Hebrew farming:

> It is written in the Law of Moses: "Do not muzzle an ox while it is treading out the grain." Is it about oxen that God is concerned? Surely he says this for us, doesn't he? Yes, this was written for us, because when the plowman plows and the thresher threshes, they ought to do so in the hope of sharing in the harvest. If we have sown spiritual seed among you, is it too much if we reap a material harvest from you?

The principle of protection for the vulnerable and needy should extend to other realms as well.

25:5–6. In this context of protecting the vulnerable, we find the so-called "law of levirate marriage" (from the Latin *levir*, "brother-in-law"). The practice was designed to protect the family that had no male heir to inherit the land. The law proposed a situation where **brothers** were **living together** (i.e., on contiguous plots of land), and one of them died **without a son**. In such a case, the man's **widow** could **not marry** an outsider and give her new husband title to property that had belonged to her first husband's family. Instead, she must become the wife of her husband's brother—at least until she could give birth to a male heir, who would keep the property in the family. The reference to fulfilling **the duty of a brother-in-law to her** is a euphemism for sexual relations. The son who was born would legally be the child of the dead brother, whose name would **not be blotted out from Israel**.

25:7–10. It followed from the purpose mentioned above that refusal to marry a brother's widow was a significant offense, showing disrespect to the widow and to the memory of the deceased. If the brother refused his duty, the widow could press charges before the town elders, and the man would have to declare his refusal publicly before a court of law (v. 8).

The primary leverage of the law in such a case was shame and humiliation. The **brother's widow** was to approach the offender **in the presence of the elders, take off one of his sandals, spit in his face**, and declare his reproach before all. The shame was to persist across future generations, for the offender's offspring would be known as **The Family of the Unsandaled**. Even as early as the time of Ruth, the application of this law seems to have been altered somewhat, although the account there (Ruth 3:10–4:10) does not precisely fit the conditions described in Deuteronomy 25:7–9.

25:11–12. These verses appear to lack any connection with the content of verses 7–10. However, both paragraphs define relationships involving two men and a woman, and both have a bearing upon the issue of Israelite descent. Verse 11 envisages a situation where two men were involved in a violent struggle and **the wife of one of them** attempted to come to the aid of her husband by grasping his opponent's **private parts**. The grasping in question was certainly with violent intent, and her action might render the man in question unable to produce children. Like the unwilling brother of verses 7–10, her behavior threatened Israel's future generations; therefore, the punishment for this offense was to **cut off her hand** with **no pity**.

25:13–16. The law of God also protected commercial transactions from dishonest dealing by prohibiting the use of **two differing weights** (**heavy** for buying and **light** for selling), and the use of **two differing measures** (for dry and liquid commodities). The presence of these items in one's bag or in one's house would carry with it the temptation to trade **dishonestly**.

Instead, the Israelite **must have accurate and honest weights and measures**, to keep from violating the tenth commandment and to insure long life

Deuteronomy 25:17–18

in the land that God was granting. The Lord **detests** such behavior, and he alone grants longevity.

B Punishing the Oppressor (25:17–19)

SUPPORTING IDEA: *God's concern for helpless and vulnerable people is coupled with a concern to punish those who oppress them. Among Israel's historical oppressors, none figures more prominently than the Amalekites.*

25:17–18. The **Amalekites**, when Israel was moving **out of Egypt**, intentionally targeted the **weary and worn out** and **all who were lagging behind** and **cut them off** (i.e., killed them). They preyed on the weak and vulnerable, demonstrating that **they had no fear of God**. Although the Amalekites lived in the remote regions east and south of the Dead Sea and were not residents of the promised land itself, God expected Israel to deal severely with them because of their cruelty.

25:19. Once the job of conquest was complete and Israel had **rest from all the enemies** in the land, God insisted that his people carry out his pronouncement of judgment against **Amalek**. This is the sole example of a people being singled out for judgment who did not constitute a barrier to the occupation of the land of Canaan. The extent of God's wrath against the Amalekites is suggested in the command that Israel should **blot out** not merely the people but the very **memory of Amalek from under heaven**. Although this assignment was burdensome, Israel must **not forget** that carrying out God's extermination order was their responsibility.

MAIN IDEA REVIEW: *While humanly invented systems of justice concentrate on the punishment of the guilty, God's laws point toward helping the vulnerable while establishing justice.*

III. CONCLUSION

Mountains in the Way

Haddon Robinson likes to tell the story of the person from Colorado who moved to Texas and built a new home. He placed in it an enormous picture window that gave a superb view of the west Texas range. He wrote a letter to friends back in Colorado and complained, "The only problem with my new picture window is that there is nothing to see."

At about the same time, a Texan moved to Colorado and, like his counterpart, constructed a new home with a large picture window that overlooked the Rocky Mountains. He, too, wrote a letter to the folks back home complaining, "The only problem is I can't see anything; the mountains are in the way."

People have a tendency to miss the obvious. Some visit a city and see the sights while missing the hurting people who live there. Others hear a person's critical words and overlook the cry for love and friendship in those words.

Prayer

Spiritual insight helps us see through the mountains to the valleys of human pain that lie beyond.

PRINCIPLES

- Individual believers are not to usurp the role of civil government and judge people who are offensive.
- Christians should be among those who speak loudest in defense of civil liberties and the protection of the weak.
- Some duties exist simply because we are part of a larger family or community.
- When shame is missing from corporate life, society quickly becomes uncivilized.

APPLICATIONS

- By the care with which you live your life, gain a reputation for honesty and integrity.
- Never be angry when someone tells you the truth about yourself, even if it hurts to hear it.
- Let your fear of God show in your concern for the poor and vulnerable.

IV. LIFE APPLICATION

Caring Hurts

A woman in a hospice facility realized she was dying, so she made a special request to her favorite nurse: "Will you hold me? I think if you hold me I can do this well."

The nurse climbed onto the bed and held the slender form until she passed into eternity. The chaplain of the facility, after later telling of the episode, was asked, "What about the nurse? What did it do to her?"

The chaplain replied that she had taken four days off to go to the mountains. She wanted to think and feel and decide whether she should come back to work again.

"She'll be back," he said. "You learn in a place like this that caring hurts—but when you really care, you offer something special—and become special yourself."

V. PRAYER

Father, give us compassionate eyes: to see needy people where they are and to take steps to help them, and to defend those who are without a defender. Amen.

Deuteronomy 25

VI. DEEPER DISCOVERIES

A. The Amalekites (25:17)

The Amalekites were the offspring of Eliphaz, son of Esau (Gen. 36:12). They were a nomadic and belligerent people that roamed the wastelands south and east of the Dead Sea. Although Israel was commanded not to let Amalek's cowardly actions go unpunished, this commission was neglected. Although others made some progress, nearly four hundred years would pass before David finally wiped out the Amalekites (2 Sam. 8:11–12).

B. Remember (25:17,19)

God's command to Israel to "remember" (v. 17) and "not forget" (v. 19) the murders of Amalek may strike casual readers of the Bible as a contradiction of the commands of the New Testament to forgive (cp. Matt. 6:12,15–16; Eph. 4:32; Col. 3:13). There is no indication in the text, however, that Israelites were to act out of spite or hatred in carrying out what was a judicial decree of God. Israel was not to *remember* in the sense of holding personal grudges. Their responsibility to remember was an act of obedience that they owed to Yahweh, in whose name they would be acting.

VII. TEACHING OUTLINE

A. INTRODUCTION
1. Lead Story: The Weapon of Dying
2. Context: In assuming responsibility for the vulnerable in the community, the people of God would best represent the heart of Yahweh in the world.
3. Transition: Christians who know Christ well are willing to suffer for the sake of those who are vulnerable, lost, and without hope in the world.

B. COMMENTARY
1. Protecting the Vulnerable (25:1–16)
2. Punishing the Oppressor (25:17–19)

C. CONCLUSION: CARING HURTS

VIII. ISSUES FOR DISCUSSION

1. What is the wisdom of dealing with crime by not imprisoning those who are found guilty of it?
2. What are the advantages of living in a society that recognizes the reality of shame?
3. Why might a man refuse to father a child in the name of his brother?
4. Does God forget the sins of a people when the generation that committed them dies?

Deuteronomy 26

His Persistent Presence

I. **INTRODUCTION**
They Never Failed

II. **COMMENTARY**
A verse-by-verse explanation of the chapter.

III. **CONCLUSION**
Through the Waters
An overview of the principles and applications from the chapter.

IV. **LIFE APPLICATION**
Even in the PGA
Melding the chapter to life.

V. **PRAYER**
Tying the chapter to life with God.

VI. **DEEPER DISCOVERIES**
Historical, geographical, and grammatical enrichment of the commentary.

VII. **TEACHING OUTLINE**
Suggested step-by-step group study of the chapter.

VIII. **ISSUES FOR DISCUSSION**
Zeroing the chapter in on daily life.

Deuteronomy 26

> ## Quote
>
> "Earth's crammed with heaven,
>
> And every common bush afire with God.
>
> And only he who sees takes off his shoes,
>
> The rest sit around and pick blackberries."
>
> Elizabeth Barrett Browning

IN A NUTSHELL

The faithfulness of God to his people in the past, according to Deuteronomy 26, will be matched by his exaltation of them in the future—provided they are faithful to his covenant.

His Persistent Presence

I. INTRODUCTION

They Never Failed

Early in 1856, the career of explorer and missionary David Livingstone seemed on the verge of ending violently. He was in the seventeenth year of his African explorations, looking for a route into the central part of the continent from its east coast. He had been receiving reports about possible attacks by hostile tribes for much of the trip, and his bearers were growing tense and uncertain. Every noise in the jungle pushed frayed nerves closer to the breaking point.

After reading in his Bible from Matthew one night, Livingstone began to write in his journal, all the while weighing the advisability of abandoning his search:

> January 14, 1856. Evening. Felt much turmoil of spirit in prospect of having all my plans for the welfare of this great region and this teeming population knocked on the head by savages tomorrow. But I read that Jesus said: "All power is given unto me in heaven and in earth. Go ye therefore, and teach all nations . . . and lo, I am with you alway, even unto the end of the world." It is the word of a gentleman of the most strict and sacred honour, so there's an end of it! I will not cross furtively tonight as I intended. Should such a man as I flee? Nay, verily, I shall take observations for latitude and longitude tonight, although they may be the last. I feel quite calm now, thank God!

Livingstone survived the trip and completed his maps and observations. Later, after returning to Scotland to receive an honorary doctorate from the University of Glasgow, he recalled the occasion and the words of Jesus in Matthew 28:20:

> Would you like me to tell you what supported me through all the years of exile among people whose language I could not understand, and whose attitude towards me was always uncertain and often hostile? It was this: "Lo, I am with you alway, even unto the end of the world!' On those words I staked everything, and they never failed!"

As Yahweh encouraged Israel by the promise of his presence and providential care, so the promise of Christ encourages believers to rely upon his power and faithfulness for their every need.

II. COMMENTARY

His Persistent Presence

MAIN IDEA: Israel's future blessing is connected with its faithfulness to the covenant; Yahweh has already demonstrated his faithfulness to his word.

A Confessing God's Faithfulness in the Past (26:1–11)

SUPPORTING IDEA: Worshipers of Yahweh should confess his faithfulness to them.

26:1–2. Chapter 26 brings to a close the formal stipulations of God's covenant expectations of Israel begun at Deuteronomy 12:1. Moses opened the chapter by anticipating the days ahead when the nation would enter and settle in the land that God was providing. The Israelite worshiper should plan to go to the place that the Lord would choose for his central sanctuary. He should bring with him **some of the firstfruits** of the land as an offering.

26:3–4. The worshiper was to **say to the priest** at the entry to the tabernacle or temple, **I declare today to the LORD your God that I have come to the land**. Although God commanded elsewhere a regular offering of the firstfruits of the land (cp. Exod. 23:19; 34:26), the words of this verse make it clear that this was a one-of-a-kind offering. The people of God were to recognize the wonders of being in the land in a settled way, and they should make both a tangible and verbal confession of its reality. The newly harvested produce was to be given to **the priest**, who was to **set it down in front of the altar of the LORD**.

26:5. The worshiping Israelites would then **declare** what could be considered a summary statement of faith: **My father was a wandering Aramean**. The last term could also be translated *Syrian*, since *Aram* was the Hebrew term that describes the region that is today known as Syria. The reference is to Jacob, who lived among his relatives in Aram-Naharaim, "Aram of the Two Rivers" in northwest Mesopotamia. The worshiper was to verbalize the contrast between the humble and nomadic character of the patriarch and condition of his offspring, who **became a great nation, powerful and numerous** after being in Egypt.

26:6–7. The greatness of Israel did not consist in their numbers, however, because **the Egyptians mistreated** them and made them **suffer**. Their greatness came from their connection with the Lord, to whom they **cried out** in their **misery**. Israel was now settled in the land not because of numerical strength but because of the fact that Yahweh **heard** them and **saw** their pathetic condition.

26:8–10a. Yahweh not only heard; he responded to Israel's cries, bringing them **out of Egypt with a mighty hand and an outstretched arm**. His compassionate purpose and the **miraculous signs and wonders** he gave translated into **great terror** on the part of Israel's Egyptian oppressors. Just as God had sworn to do, he would give his people **this land, a land flowing with milk and honey** (cp. Exod. 3:8,17).

While the preceding words were to be directed to the priest as a confession of Yahweh's goodness, the first portion of verse 10 finds the worshiper turning directly to the Lord. He was to say, **Now I bring the firstfruits of the soil, that you, O LORD, have given me.**

26:10b–11. The formal statement of confession was to be concluded by the worshiper's placing **the basket before** the altar of the Lord and bowing down. There is no contradiction between this statement and that of verse 4, since the confessor did not have direct access to the altar and would have needed the priest to serve as his mediator.

At the conclusion of this time of confession and worship, other portions of the harvest were to be shared among the worshiper, **the Levites and the aliens** among Israel so everyone could **rejoice** in the **good things** God had provided. Rejoicing is the handmaid of worship.

B Declaring the Worshiper's Faithfulness in the Present (26:12–15)

SUPPORTING IDEA: *The worshiper's expectation of God's blessing in the future is nurtured in the soil of his faithfulness to God's commandments.*

26:12. This paragraph specifies still another practice that would have to wait until the conquest of the promised land was complete. Every three years, in **the year of the tithe**, Israelites were to set aside a special portion of their produce to share with **the Levite, the alien, the fatherless and the widow**. This apparently was in addition to the annual tithe to support the work of the tabernacle (or later the temple; see the commentary on 14:27–29.) Although the regular annual tithe was for the support of the priesthood at the central sanctuary, this was a local tithe, designed to assist Levites who were living in towns scattered throughout the land. These four categories of people were to be able to enjoy life and **be satisfied** with Yahweh's provision for them just as others were.

26:13–14. The faithful Israelite would be able to say to God: **I have removed from my house the sacred portion** (i.e., the tithe) **and have given it** to the specified groups. He was to declare directly to the Lord the completeness of his obedience: **according to all you commanded**. This was not a claim of sinlessness, but of faithfulness in this critical area of loving one's neighbor.

Deuteronomy 26:15

The faithful believer could say in a general way, **I have not turned aside from your commands nor have I forgotten any of them.**

Part of obedience in such matters involved storing the sacred portion, and along the way many temptations might have tested the worshiper's determination to obey. An occasion that would provoke **mourning** might test his resolve. **While I was unclean** is probably more accurately translated "for any unclean use." The portion was sacred, thus none of it could be used for the ordinary meals of a household or be fed to animals. Nothing belonging to God could be offered **to the dead** in a flagrant violation of the covenant.

26:15. The worshiper who had behaved faithfully could appeal to God to **look down from heaven . . . and bless . . . Israel and the land.** Israel would not be blessed because their obedience merited it, but because obedience was the requirement of the covenant and because God had **promised** to bless them if they were faithful.

C Anticipating God's Faithfulness in the Future (26:16–19)

SUPPORTING IDEA: *Israel's promise to obey Yahweh will be more than matched by Yahweh's promise to exalt Israel in the future.*

26:16. The final paragraph of the chapter is also a summary of the entire stipulation section of Deuteronomy (chs. 12–26). **These decrees and laws** thus look back to the bulk of the book. But observing the letter of the law was not sufficient in itself. God intended that his people **carefully observe** what he had said with all their **heart** and with all their **soul.**

26:17. **You have declared** may refer to Exodus 24:7, where Israel declared, "We will do everything the LORD has said; we will obey." Or it may refer to a more recent similar declaration by the current generation of Israelites. They had said publicly that they intended to keep God's **decrees, commands and laws,** and now it was time to follow through on their promises.

26:18–19. The covenant was now sealed. Israel had declared that Yahweh was their God. The Lord had **declared this day** that he recognized them as **his people, his treasured possession.** As they obeyed, they could expect that just as God had promised, so he would perform, bringing them **fame and honor high above all the nations** of the earth.

MAIN IDEA REVIEW: *Israel's future blessing is connected with its faithfulness to the covenant; Yahweh has already demonstrated his faithfulness to his word.*

III. CONCLUSION

Through the Waters

Robert Morrison was the first Protestant missionary from England to the people of China. In 1807 he arrived in Canton as a representative of the London Missionary Society and quickly threw himself into a study of the language. Because he was so successful as a language scholar, he was hired by the British East India Company to serve as a translator and did so for about twenty-five years. The compensation he received enabled him to have time to do extensive written translations as well. He translated the Bible, a number of prayer books, hymnals, and many tracts into Chinese. He laid the foundation for others who would come later, although he saw only a handful of conversions through his own labors.

Through the challenges of his spiritual development and preparation for the field, he clung to the promise of Isaiah 43:2: "When you pass through the waters, I will be with you." In a letter to his father, he explained how he drew courage during a terrifying ocean voyage from his confidence in God's presence: "I mention these circumstances to excite thankfulness to God, who brought us safely through. I pleaded the promise, in its literal sense, 'When thou passest through the waters, I will be with thee,' and blessed by God, it was fulfilled."

That Bible-born confidence was to support Morrison many times over through the years. Trust in the promise of God is the key not only to weathering the perils of the present but to receiving eternal life itself. The triumphant believer who can avow with John the Baptist that "He who has received [Christ's] testimony has set his seal to this, that God is true" (John 3:33 NASB).

PRINCIPLES

- Every demonstration of God's faithfulness to us is an opportunity for us to testify of him to others.
- An enriched capacity for rejoicing is an expanded capacity for worship.
- Celebration is best done in the company of others who can rejoice with us over God's goodness.
- Before we can pray for God's blessing, we should ask ourselves if our disobedience could hinder his blessing.

Deuteronomy 26

APPLICATIONS

- Take the next opportunity you have to declare God's faithfulness to another person.
- Give God the beginning, not the dregs, of your income.
- Make sure your friends, relatives, and acquaintances know which side of the spiritual fence you are on.
- Make a list of ten to fifteen blessings in your life that you consider special gifts from God.

IV. LIFE APPLICATION

Even in the PGA

Tom Lehman became a Christian while in high school. After playing on his college golf team, he decided to try to make a living playing professionally. He managed to qualify for the PGA tour in 1991 when he won three tournaments on the Ben Hogan Tour and was voted player of the year.

Just as he was making a name for himself, Tom ran into a bump in the road. His doctor discovered polyps in his colon that were diagnosed as precancerous. Tom and his wife took God's promise to Joshua as their own during that difficult time: "Be strong and courageous. Do not be terrified; do not be discouraged, for the LORD your God will be with you wherever you go" (Josh. 1:9). After surgery, Tom was pronounced healthy and fit for the tour once again, and the next year he won the British Open. Giving tribute to the faithfulness of God, Tom said, "In every difficult situation, even on the golf course, I remember Joshua 1:9."

V. PRAYER

Father, let us be people who place our confidence in you. When others ask us for the reasons for our hope, give us a fearless confidence in you. Amen.

VI. DEEPER DISCOVERIES

A. To the Lord (26:13)

The normal rendering of the expression *to the Lord* is "before the Lord," and many translations render it just that way. However, the Hebrew preposition can mean nothing more than "to" on occasion, and since the words of the confession address the Lord directly, it is apparent that the NIV translation is accurate.

B. Holy Dwelling (26:15)

The prayer of the righteous Israelite was to be, "Look down from heaven, your holy dwelling place." The words after the comma appear here in Scripture for the first time. They are not intended as a denial of God's special presence in the tabernacle, nor a denial of his omnipresence. They simply recognize one of God's own descriptions for his place of residence and the fact that his holiness requires a separation from sinful humanity.

VII. TEACHING OUTLINE

A. INTRODUCTION

1. Lead Story: They Never Failed
2. Context: Israel could never point to an occasion in their history when Yahweh had failed to honor his promises. God's record of faithfulness was designed to help them over their challenges in the future.
3. Transition: Christians are to be people with long memories of God's faithfulness who face the future with hope and joy.

B. COMMENTARY

1. Confessing God's Faithfulness in the Past (26:1–11)
2. Declaring the Worshiper's Faithfulness in the Present (26:12–15)
3. Anticipating God's Faithfulness in the Future (26:16–19)

C. CONCLUSION: EVEN IN THE PGA

VIII. ISSUES FOR DISCUSSION

1. What is the most impressive testimony for Jesus Christ that you have ever heard?
2. What part does affliction play in shaping a person's testimony?
3. Why does rejoicing play so prominent role in worship in Scripture?
4. What has been the most personally encouraging example of God's faithfulness in your own life?

Deuteronomy 27

Coated Stones and Curses

- I. **INTRODUCTION**
  Spurgeon's Text

- II. **COMMENTARY**
  A verse-by-verse explanation of the chapter.

- III. **CONCLUSION**
  Values Matter
  An overview of the principles and applications from the chapter.

- IV. **LIFE APPLICATION**
  Bad for the Heart
  Melding the chapter to life.

- V. **PRAYER**
  Tying the chapter to life with God.

- VI. **DEEPER DISCOVERIES**
  Historical, geographical, and grammatical enrichment of the commentary.

- VII. **TEACHING OUTLINE**
  Suggested step-by-step group study of the chapter.

- VIII. **ISSUES FOR DISCUSSION**
  Zeroing the chapter in on daily life.

Deuteronomy 27

Quote

"Unless we know the difference between flowers and weeds, we are not fit to take care of a garden. It is not enough to have truth planted in our minds. We must learn and labor to keep the ground clear of thorns and briars, follies and perversities, which have a wicked propensity to choke the word of life."

Clyde Francis Lytle

IN A NUTSHELL

God desires that, even before their rebellion, his people understand the consequences of rebelling. Those consequences will serve as a deterrent to sin and encourage them to learn the truth and to put it into practice.

Coated Stones and Curses

I. INTRODUCTION

Spurgeon's Text

*F*ew people would have predicted that anything important would happen on that frigid Sunday morning in January of 1850 when Charles Haddon Spurgeon, then fifteen years of age, ducked into a church to get out of the snow. As might be expected, the crowd was sparse; not even the minister came. Speaking extemporaneously and from his limited education, a layman of the church simply read the text of Isaiah and made a few comments on each verse. He came to Isaiah 45:22, which says, "Look unto me, and be ye saved, all the ends of the earth: for I am God, and there is none else" (KJV). The preacher noted that obedience to this call did not require great ability, because anyone could look—even a child.

After about ten minutes of exposition, the preacher fixed his gaze on Spurgeon and said, "Young man, you look miserable, and you will always be miserable—in life and death—if you don't obey this text. You have nothing to do but look and live!"

Spurgeon looked to God and was indeed saved. Through Spurgeon's conversion, God used that humble substitute preacher, armed only with the words of Scripture, to produce tens of thousands of spiritual descendants and to validate the power of God's Word.

II. COMMENTARY

Coated Stones and Curses

> **MAIN IDEA:** Although Moses is soon to leave the scene, the law of God will remain. God's commandments, together with the sanctions for violating them, must be taught to future generations.

A The Teaching of the Covenant (27:1–13)

> **SUPPORTING IDEA:** The leaders of God's people are to use both visual and oral means to teach God's law to the people.

27:1–3. Now that the content of the covenant obligations had been specified (Deut. 12–26), that content must be reinforced and the penalties for violating it specified. For this purpose, **Moses** gathered to his side **the elders of Israel** and they **commanded** Israel to communicate the covenant to all the

Deuteronomy 27:4–6

people. The steps that were to be taken once Israel had **crossed the Jordan** were designed to ensure that the people knew what God expected of them.

The people were to construct a visual display of the **commands** they had heard. This display was to be made on **some large stones** that they were to **coat ... with plaster**. While Yahweh had given the Ten Commandments on stone tablets that were apparently engraved by his finger, this display was apparently to be painted on a white plastered background rather than carved. It is likely that the word **all** (v. 3) is hyperbolic, since the law's summary contained in the Ten Commandments would be enough to remind Israel of its covenant obligations (see "Deeper Discoveries"). Israel was also to be reminded that God had kept his side of the bargain, since they were entering **a land flowing with milk and honey**, just as he had **promised**.

27:4–6. Moses' instructions to **set up** the **stones on Mount Ebal** is apparently to be regarded as a further specification of the same process mentioned in verses 1–3 rather than to a second display of the law. In this way the content of the commandments would be visible to those who would gather there for a solemn covenant renewal celebration.

The centerpiece of this celebration was to be **an altar** that would be dedicated to Yahweh. This altar was not to be a permanent fixture of Israel's worship, since God would eventually choose a city to serve as the home of a central sanctuary (Deut. 12). As a legitimate temporary place of worship, however, it had to be constructed according to divine principles. It had to be made of stones that were free from human fashioning. No iron tool could be used in fashioning them. The Lord apparently intended Israel to understand that the only valid approach to him was to be made with gifts that he had provided: "It is by grace you have been saved, through faith—and this not from yourselves, it is the gift of God—not by works, so that no one can boast" (Eph. 2:8–9).

The stones of the altar were to be collected from the field. On the altar, Israel was to offer **burnt offerings**, sacrifices that would be consumed by fire in recognition of God's demand for a substitute for sinners.

27:7–8. Once the vertical dimension had been satisfied, then Israel could proceed to offer **fellowship offerings** on the altar. These were animals that were dressed and roasted with one portion being burned, a second becoming the property of the priests, and a third shared between the worshiper, his family, and his friends. They were to eat the offerings, **rejoicing in the presence of the LORD**. At the same time, the celebration was not to interfere with their first priority once inside the land: to **write very clearly all the words** of God's law on the specified **stones**.

27:9–10. So the nation would know that there were consequences for unfaithfulness to the covenant, **Moses** gathered beside him **the priests** to further solemnize the warnings. Since Israel had accepted the terms of the covenant (Deut. 26:16–17), they could now be called **the people of the LORD**. This required obedience to **his commands** in general, and in particular, obedience in the matter of formalizing the covenant sanctions, which constituted one of the **decrees** that Moses was giving **today**.

27:11–13. The people were to be divided into two groups. The first group would **stand on Mount Gerizim** and **bless the people**. It would consist of **Simeon, Levi, Judah, Issachar, Joseph and Benjamin**. The listing is noteworthy in that it actually consists of seven tribes enumerated under six headings, since Joseph consisted of two tribes, Ephraim and Manasseh. This was apparently necessary because it was important that Levi be included in this process. The priestly tribe might serve as mediators of Yahweh's worship system, but it was important that everyone realize that they were subject to the terms of the covenant just as their countrymen were.

The second group, consisting of **Reuben, Gad, Asher, Zebulun, Dan and Naphtali**, were to stand on **Mount Ebal** and express the **curses** of the covenant. In effect, the covenant ceremony would become a sort of antiphonal expression of the consequences of obedience (blessings) or disobedience (the curses).

B The Teeth of the Covenant (27:14–26)

SUPPORTING IDEA: *Israel would place themselves under the judgment of heaven if they should fail to obey Yahweh's law.*

27:14–15. Deuteronomy 27:14–26, unlike the more formalized list in Deuteronomy 28, does not specify the exact consequence of disobedience to each covenant violation. Instead, the list is selective in a very specific sense: the sins described in verses 14–26 are largely secretive in nature. That is, individual Israelites might violate these precepts without their actions becoming known by the community at large. The implication: God sees those who violate his covenant, and he can take his own steps to deal with offenders whether or not they are formally charged by the local government.

Instead of having **all the people** state the content of these items, they were to listen as **the Levites** repeated them, and then they were to add their own **Amen** at the conclusion of each. The first such affirmation concerned the person who would take action that struck at the heart of the covenant by carving an **image** or casting an **idol**. The folly of such behavior is seen in that the product of it, like a shelf or table, is **the work of the craftsman's hands**. That such an item could be set **up in secret** did not mean that it would go unnoticed by Yahweh.

27:16. Likewise cursed would be the man who dishonored **his father or his mother**. No particular action is specified here. The Hebrew verb here translated *dishonors* means "to make light of." The expression might refer to disrespect that emerges in one's speech. It certainly rebukes the attitude that Jesus would later condemn as seen in the tradition of the Pharisees:

Deuteronomy 27:17–19

You say that if a man says to his father or mother: "Whatever help you might otherwise have received from me is Corban" (that is, a gift devoted to God), then you no longer let him do anything for his father or mother. Thus you nullify the word of God by your tradition (Mark 7:11–13).

27:17–19. Other violations of the covenant included moving a **neighbor's boundary stone** and thus undermining the peace of the community for the sake of personal greed. The spirit of the second half of the Decalogue would certainly be transgressed by **the man** who led **the blind astray on the road**. People like the blind, **the alien, the fatherless or the widow** deserved the assistance, not the disregard, of the entire community. Although violence or neglect might go unseen by others, the God who sees human hearts was able to enforce the terms of the covenant.

27:20–23. The emphasis on privately committed sins is evident in this section on sexual misconduct. The first prohibition (v. 20) deals with a person who engages in sexual intercourse with **his father's wife**. The last expression might mean simply "his mother," but it more likely describes a stepmother, or even a widowed stepmother. The restriction was given not simply because incest was an act of rebellion against Yahweh but also because the person who violated it dishonored **his father's bed** (cp. Gen. 49:4 Deut. 22:30; 1 Chr. 5:1). Bestiality was prohibited (v. 21), as was incest, whether of **sister**, half-sister (v. 22), or **mother-in-law** (v. 23).

27:24–25. The theme of secretiveness is continued in the curse upon the man who would kill his neighbor **secretly**. There is no perfect crime within the covenant community, because Yahweh sees everything. Nor is anger a necessary ingredient in violating God's standards. The person who acted as a mercenary and accepted **a bribe to kill an innocent person** stood under the same curse as other abusers of the covenant.

27:26. The final verse of the chapter pronounced a summary malediction on all who did not **uphold the words** of God's **law by carrying them out**. The curses of this section of Deuteronomy reflect not some supposed belief in the magical power of words. Rather, they recognize the ability of the omnipresent God of the covenant to enforce his own legislation. Whether he would choose some kind of direct confrontation with covenant violators or would use providentially arranged circumstances to accomplish his purpose was quite irrelevant.

> **MAIN IDEA REVIEW:** Although Moses is soon to leave the scene, the law of God will remain. God's commandments, together with the sanctions for violating them, must be taught to future generations.

III. CONCLUSION

Values Matter

Since American culture has sought to marginalize or drive Christian faith from the public square, our culture has suffered accordingly. Since 1960, for example, the population in America has increased 41 percent. By contrast, violent crimes have increased 550 percent, more than thirteen times the increase in the population. Since that time, a sizable portion of our population has decided that they ought to be free to take possessions and pleasures at the expense of others.

Also since 1960, out-of-wedlock birth rates have increased nearly 500 percent, although the number of babies born during this period has remained nearly constant. We have seen sexual freedom become the byword of the period, but we have not managed to counteract the notion that philosophies of freedom, like all philosophies, have consequences.

Still another trend since 1960: the rate at which teenagers are taking their own lives has more than tripled. Suicide is now the second leading cause of death among adolescents. What is especially interesting is that in 1960 the typical suicide in America was an older, depressed male. That is no longer true. To quote one authority, "The [suicide] rate is rising most rapidly among younger males . . . who are not usually depressed but are angry, frustrated, resentful, often using drugs and unable to communicate their distress." Advocates of the prevailing view may tell others that Christianity has no place in modern America, but the sad statistics of our cultural life contradict them. If people will not love God, sooner or later they will stop loving their neighbors—and even themselves.

PRINCIPLES

- Hearing alone is less effective in learning God's truth than hearing combined with reading.
- The person who believes he must earn the right to go through the door of eternal life will miss the mark.
- Our identity as the people of God is marked primarily by our faithfulness in obedience to him.
- What we do in public determines our reputation; what we do in private determines our character.

APPLICATIONS

- Guard the content of your mind, keeping free of unhealthy influences.

Deuteronomy 27

- Judge evil tendencies while they are still thoughts, because spiritual health begins in the innermost person.
- Recognize that the wellspring of obedience is gratitude.
- Meditate on the connection between a successful public life and obedience to God's commandments.

IV. LIFE APPLICATION

Bad for the Heart

Not long ago the American Heart Association published in their periodical *Circulation* the results of an extensive investigation into the connection between anger and heart disease. Based on work done at the University of North Carolina, including the monitoring of thirteen thousand adults over a six-year period, researchers concluded that a person inclined to anger is about three times more likely to suffer a heart attack than one who approaches life more calmly. The ratio was confirmed even after scientists allowed for other risk factors such as high blood pressure, high cholesterol, smoking, and obesity.

A propensity to anger also carries with it certain intrinsic penalties in the realm of human relations. The angry person's friendships are always at risk. In the very first line of her book *The Kitchen God's Wife*, Amy Tan observes, "Whenever my mother talks to me, she begins the conversation as if we were already in the middle of an argument." Although there is such a thing as unsinful anger (cp. Eph. 4:26–27), people seldom exhibit it.

Those who desire to be good representatives of Jesus Christ must guard against becoming angry people—for their own sake, for the sake of those they love, and for the honor of their Savior.

V. PRAYER

Father, let our lives be free from the necessity of learning everything the hard way. Help us be wise and discerning, learning how to live from the truths of Scripture, the counsel of wise people, and the blunders of those who are foolish. Amen.

VI. DEEPER DISCOVERIES

A. The Words of This Law (27:3)

Although it is possible that the entire content of Deuteronomy (or at least the stipulations of the covenant in chs. 12–26) were written on stones in the promised land, it is more likely that the command of verse 3 was fulfilled by writing a summary of that law in the form of the Ten Commandments. A number of students of Deuteronomy have noticed that the content of chapters 12–26 serves to elaborate those commandments:

> Deuteronomy 12–13: An expansion of the first three commandments, concentrating on the exclusion of false gods and devotion to Yahweh.
>
> Deuteronomy 14:28–16:17: An elaboration of the fourth commandment and the holy rhythms of Israel's life.
>
> Deuteronomy 16:18–18:22: Like the fifth commandment with its emphasis on respect for parents, this section describes the proper attitude toward other authority figures: prophets, priests, and kings.
>
> Deuteronomy 19:1–21:9: An expansion of the principles of the sixth commandment, the prohibition of murder, especially at the beginning and end of this portion. The section also contains principles that elucidate the eighth, ninth, and tenth commandments.
>
> Deuteronomy 22:13–30: An elaboration of the seventh commandment and related sexual offenses.
>
> Deuteronomy 23–26: Enlargements upon the eighth and tenth commandments, and other miscellaneous laws.

The scheme is not exact, nor is it important that it should be. It is evident from a study of the sections, however, that Moses' exposition does serve as an echo and enlargement of the core content of the covenant, the Ten Commandments.

B. Mount Ebal and Mount Gerizim (27:12–13)

The two mountains, each about three thousand feet above sea level, frame a small valley in the heart of the Holy Land near the town of Shechem. It was near that community that Jacob bought a small parcel of ground from Hamor (Gen. 33:19). Ebal lay on the north side of the valley and Gerizim on the south. Josephus notes that on the latter mountain Sanballat constructed a temple and began the Samaritan priesthood. The woman of Samaria referred to Gerizim in her conversation with Jesus (John 4:20).

VII. TEACHING OUTLINE

A. INTRODUCTION
1. Lead Story: Spurgeon's Text
2. Context: Moses lays the groundwork for the continued teaching of the law of God in the years to come, both its content and the consequences for disobeying it.

Deuteronomy 27

3. Transition: By their faithfulness to the word of God, Christians should live lives characterized by blessings rather than curses.

B. COMMENTARY
1. The Teaching of the Covenant (27:1–13)
2. The Teeth of the Covenant (27:14–26)

C. CONCLUSION: BAD FOR THE HEART

VIII. ISSUES FOR DISCUSSION

1. How does God weave accountability for one's behavior into the fabric of life?
2. How did moving a landmark threaten the stability of Israelite society?
3. How does God's faithfulness to his promises encourage us to be obedient people?
4. Why do you think God combined a celebration with the construction of Israel's "covenant reminder" stones?

Deuteronomy 28

Decisions of Life and Death

I. **INTRODUCTION**
   The Devil Did It

II. **COMMENTARY**
   A verse-by-verse explanation of the chapter.

III. **CONCLUSION**
   Poor Prophets

   An overview of the principles and applications from the chapter.

IV. **LIFE APPLICATION**
   Reap a Destiny

   Melding the chapter to life.

V. **PRAYER**
   Tying the chapter to life with God.

VI. **DEEPER DISCOVERIES**
   Historical, geographical, and grammatical enrichment of the commentary.

VII. **TEACHING OUTLINE**
   Suggested step-by-step group study of the chapter.

VIII. **ISSUES FOR DISCUSSION**
   Zeroing the chapter in on daily life.

Deuteronomy 28

> ## Quote
>
> "True repentance hates the sin, and not merely the penalty; and it hates the sin most of all because it has discovered and felt God's love."
>
> William Mackergo Taylor

Deuteronomy 28

IN A NUTSHELL

God longs to bless his people, and he will do so as they remain faithful to his covenant. But if they rebel, he will bring affliction into their lives.

Decisions of Life and Death

I. INTRODUCTION

The Devil Did It

At an evangelical college in America, a guest lecturer from Europe, observing the Christian response to events, said, "I've noticed a very odd reaction. If something 'good' happens, you thank God. If something 'bad' happens, you suddenly blame the devil. Where is your recognition of the providence of God?"

The lecturer raised an intriguing question, and one that deserves an answer. C. S. Lewis surfaced the same issue some years ago when he wrote an essay on insecurity. In Shakespeare's play *Hamlet* the branch of a river tree breaks and Ophelia is drowned. Did Ophelia die because the branch broke or because Shakespeare wanted her to die at that point in the play? "Either—both—whichever you please," Lewis said. "The question is not a real alternative at all, once you have grasped that Shakespeare is making the whole play" (Lewis, p. 79).

The practical dualism that is so common among American Christians has a tendency to promote an uncomfortable dishonesty in Christian thinking. We may attribute painful events to the devil, but we get the uneasy feeling from time to time that we are kidding ourselves.

Dualism has nothing to do with Christianity. The biblical point of view is that nothing that happens lies outside the sovereign power of God. If something terrible takes place, God had the power to prevent it and—for good reasons that he usually does not share with us—chose not to. The biblical expression of this is found in the words of the psalmist: "Our God is in heaven; he does whatever pleases him" (Ps. 115:3).

God can and often does make our lives happy and peaceful, but he also has the ability to bring affliction into them. Even then he generally does so with a view to curbing our waywardness and bringing us back to himself. In Scripture he tells us his intentions in these matters, as he told Israel of old, so that we will choose the wise path and stay close to him.

II. COMMENTARY

Decisions of Life and Death

MAIN IDEA: *Moses places before Israel the two great options for the nation's future: obedience together with divine blessing, or disobedience and its accompanying miseries.*

A God's Blessings for Obedience (28:1–14)

SUPPORTING IDEA: *If Israel remains true to its national covenant, Yahweh will bless and exalt his people.*

28:1–2. Moses placed the option of obedience before Israel. If they would **fully obey** Yahweh, then they would be set **high above all the nations of the earth**. The other option, that of disobedience and cursings, will be set before them beginning in verse 15.

28:3–6. These verses describe the extent of Yahweh's blessing, described in a series of merisms (all-inclusive contrasts). Israel will know blessing everywhere: **in the city** and **in the country**; with their children, their **crops**, and their **livestock**. They will even be **blessed** in the kitchen.

28:7. In their obedience, the nation will find that they need not fear **enemies** from outside the land. When they go into battle against an aggressor, their opponents will **flee** from them in **seven** different directions and **will be defeated**.

28:8–10. The blessing of God would be a universal experience in Israel. It would include material prosperity (**barns**) as well as success in **everything** the nation attempted. In the process, Israel would begin to realize the purpose for which God was placing his people **in the land**. The Abrahamic covenant (Gen. 12:1–3), given six centuries before, included an **oath** to bless **all the peoples on earth** through the patriarch's offspring. By Israel's obedience and by God's affirmation of them **as his holy people**, the nation would become a universal blessing. Even those who were not brought under the provisions of genuine faith would **fear** Israel and would respect their unique position as God's people (cp. Prov. 16:7).

28:11–14. The blessing portion of this chapter concludes with a general exhortation and summary of the benefits that Israel could expect for covenant faithfulness. In its obedience Israel did not *earn* God's blessing. That blessing had begun with Yahweh's own initiative in singling out Abraham and the **forefathers**. Obedience was merely the condition that was necessary for the blessings to continue. Israel could look forward to **abundant prosperity** because of its connection with the patriarchs and because of God's grace.

That prosperity was connected closely with **the heavens**, which Yahweh would **open** so **rain** could fall on the land. Israel would be so wealthy that her people would **lend to many nations** instead of needing to **borrow** from them. The only real threats to this abundance lay in Israel's stubborn tendency to **turn aside from any of the commands** that God had given them and to embrace **other gods**.

B God's Cursings for Disobedience (28:15–68)

SUPPORTING IDEA: *If Israel rebels, however, God will discipline the nation severely.*

28:15–19. These verses form nearly exact negative correspondents of verses 1–6, with the word **not** inserted in verse 15 and **curses** for *blessings* throughout. Israel would experience reversals of fortune if the people turned away from the covenant.

28:20–24. The most obvious form in which God's disapproval would manifest itself was through nature. **Confusion and rebuke** would mark everything the Israelites attempted if they sought to do it with their backs to the Lord. They would experience **disease, fever, inflammation, heat,** and **drought**.

Instead of dripping rain to support crops, **the sky** would turn to **bronze**, and in turn the **ground** would be hard as **iron**. Instead of prosperity and plenty, Israel would know famine and hardship until they were **destroyed**. The latter term is not absolute, since God had already sworn otherwise. However, when Israel turned away from God, they were useless as instruments of his grace.

28:25–26. Instead of consistent victories, the armies of Israel would **be defeated** before their **enemies** if they rebelled. Israel's own military efforts are described in verse 25 in the same way that her enemies' were in verse 7. Instead of becoming a blessing to the nations, Israel would **become a thing of horror**. As they were defeated in battle, their **carcasses** would become carrion for vultures and carnivores, and the land would be so depleted of population that no one would be available **to frighten** such creatures **away**.

28:27–29. The Lord would not turn a blind eye to the follies of Israel if they forsook him. In his determination to turn their hearts back to him, he would **afflict** them with the same kind of **boils** that had come upon the land while they were slaves in **Egypt**. They would experience physical and mental sufferings if they persisted in their waywardness. Directionless and unsuccessful, they would become easy prey for their oppressors.

28:30–32. Nor would the nation's sufferings be limited to the physical realm. They would face gruesome disappointments—losing their wives to their enemies and building houses without being able to **live** in them. Their vineyards would yield **fruit** that would not be theirs to **enjoy.** They would suffer the loss of their livestock before their eyes and be helpless to do anything about it.

To cap the disaster, the Israelites would suffer even the loss of their children. Their **sons and daughters** would become slaves in foreign lands and they could do nothing but long for their return because they were so **powerless.**

28:33–37. If Israel should turn away from the Lord, invaders would overwhelm them and take what their **land and labor** would **produce. Cruel oppression** would be their lot, and the horrors of their experience would **drive** them **mad.** They would experience incurable physical afflictions **from the soles** of their **feet** to their **head.** Because of their rebellion, the Lord would **drive** them along with their **king** (in whom they would falsely place their trust) into **a nation unknown** to them. In Israel's history this warning was vindicated twice: once, when the Assyrians carried the Northern Kingdom (Israel) captive, and once when the Babylonians did so to the Southern Kingdom (Judah). Even there, worshiping **gods of wood and stone,** Israel would continue its stubbornness (only a small fraction of the exiles would return from Babylon). Instead of victory and prosperity, Israel's rebels would know **scorn and ridicule.**

28:38–42. Israel in rebellion would experience the terrible curse of disappointments. The nation would **sow much** but **harvest little** because of the **locusts. Vineyards** would receive the people's efforts, but they would not know the joys of harvest because of the **worms.** Their **olive trees** would suffer as well. Even their children would **go into captivity.**

The terrible feature of rebelling against Yahweh was that he could marshal all of nature's forces in disciplining those who were wayward. Indeed, this entire section of curses has both preventive and corrective purposes. The people of Israel were supposed to take stock of the awful possibilities before they made a choice to worship other gods. If they were already involved, they should interpret their afflictions for what they were—Yahweh's loving attempts to bring them to repentance.

28:43–46. Yet during these catastrophes, Yahweh would show that his afflictions were not broadcast but carefully discriminatory. Although the idol-worshiping Israelites would suffer because of their defection from the Lord, **the alien** who lived among them would become increasingly prosperous because of his faith in Yahweh. As aliens were increasing in prosperity, the native Israelites would **sink lower and lower.** The spiritually sensitive person would learn from this and turn back to the Lord.

Those who failed to grasp the import of Israel's miseries and who persisted in their unfaithfulness would be **destroyed.** The contrasts between prosperity and defeat would be so marked that they would be **a sign and a wonder . . . forever**.

28:47–48. The contrast between Israel's choices was stark indeed. During the time of prosperity, the Lord asked that they serve him joyfully and gladly. Because the nation refused, they would be forced to serve their enemies. Those enemies, unlike Yahweh, would not create an environment of prosperity for the people of God. Instead of a pleasant life of service to God, Israel would learn **hunger, thirst, nakedness**, and **dire poverty** through the **iron yoke** of divine discipline.

28:49–52. The ultimate form of this discipline would be a distant nation with customs unlike Israel's that would subject God's people to harsh treatment. They would **devour the young** of their **livestock** and their **crops**. They would plunder the fields, vineyards, and barns until Israel was **ruined**. When Israel refused to pay tribute, they would **lay siege** to her cities until the **fortified walls** of those cities collapsed.

Although it is natural to see this language as descriptive of the Babylonian invasions (particularly the third one in 586 B.C.), there is no reason to limit its application to that devastating judgment. The earlier invasion of the Northern Kingdom by the Assyrians in 722 B.C. could be foreseen here also, and the predictions were at least partially fulfilled by the invasion of Sennacherib in 701 B.C.

28:53–57. The worst effect of Israel's spiritual defection would not be the devastations of the enemy, however, but the damage done by Israelites to one another. The sieges to come would find mothers eating **the fruit of the womb**, the **flesh** of their own **sons and daughters**. When a man engaged in the same horror, he would prove so selfish that he would refuse to share his cannibalistic pleasure with other members of his household. Refined women would resort to eating **afterbirth** and even their own **children** because of the devastating famine in the cities.

28:58–59. The Lord insisted that his people **revere** his **glorious and awesome name**, and they could do that only by **carefully** obeying **all the words** of the law that Moses was giving. To do otherwise was to invite **fearful plagues** that would last from generation to generation, **harsh and prolonged disasters, and severe and lingering illnesses**.

28:60–62. Although Israel thought it had seen the last of **Egypt**, rebellion would **bring upon** them the **diseases** of that land of enslavement; indeed, **every kind of sickness and disaster**—even horrors **not recorded** in the book Moses was writing. Conditions would deteriorate so rapidly that Israel would experience a dramatic population decline because of their disobedience.

28:63–64. God warned that he would not observe two standards of morality—one for Israel and another for the pagan peoples who occupied the land. If he had **uprooted** the Canaanites for immoral behavior, he would do the same with his people. They would have to swallow the bitter draft of their own waywardness; they would **worship . . . gods of wood and stone** in far-away places.

The phrase in verse 63, **it will please him to ruin and destroy you,** does not mean that God found delight in the pain and destruction he would inflict, but that he continued to delight in Israel even as he administered this discipline. Another translation reads, "It shall come about that as the LORD delighted over you to prosper you, and multiply you, so the LORD will delight over you to make you perish and destroy you" (NASB).

28:65–68. God's disciplinary exile of his rebellious people would become a miserable experience. Among the oppressing **nations**, Israelites would find **no repose**, but instead **an anxious mind, eyes weary with longing, and a despairing heart**. They would **dread** every **day** yet long for the next. They would reach a low point when they would be sent **back** to **Egypt** and placed on sale as **slaves**. Their withered and emaciated condition would prove so unappealing, however, that **no one** would **buy** them.

> **MAIN IDEA REVIEW:** Moses places before Israel the two great options for the nation's future: obedience together with divine blessing or disobedience and its accompanying miseries.

III. CONCLUSION

Poor Prophets

Sophisticated modern experts often prove to be inaccurate prophets. For example, in 1949 an article in *Popular Mechanics* predicted the coming downsizing of computers: "Computers in the future may weigh no more than 1.5 tons." Building on that shaky foundation, Ken Olson, the founder of Digital Equipment Corporation, said in 1977, "There is no reason anyone would want a computer in their home."

A Yale University management professor once commented on a paper turned in by a student, "The concept is interesting and well-formed, but in order to earn better than a 'C,' the idea must be feasible." The paper was a proposal for an overnight delivery service, and the youthful author was Fred Smith, who went on to found Federal Express Corporation.

It takes no predictive ability at all, however, to be able to chart the course of the person who turns his back on God. More consequences are connected to this decision than to any other it is possible to make. Although the heartaches and difficulties that follow do not come from hostile intentions, they reflect the desperate seriousness of the struggle for the soul of a human being. As Moses would say, "See, I set before you today life and prosperity, death and destruction" (Deut. 30:15). The choice is ours.

PRINCIPLES

- The Lord longs to exalt his people as trophies of his work in them.
- Mental confusion can be the product of divine discipline.
- No amount of human willfulness can overcome God's determined love.
- While catastrophes do enter the lives of godly people, they attach themselves far more predictably to people who reject him.

APPLICATIONS

- Be more concerned about your holiness than about your happiness.
- Find your security in the promises and the holy character of God.
- Choose God's ways and success will find you.

IV. LIFE APPLICATION

Reap a Destiny

In his book *What My Parents Did Right,* musician Don Wyrtzen, son of evangelist Jack Wyrtzen, tells about a lesson he learned about honesty. The Wyrtzens were in New York City for one of Jack's evangelistic rallies. Don and a young friend decided to spend the day riding the subway—for free. Instead of purchasing tokens, they would duck underneath the turnstiles and board the trains. Don later bragged to his father about his "accomplishment."

Wyrtzen explained to his young charge that what he had done was wrong. He insisted that Don write a letter of apology to the New York City Port Authority and include in the letter the cost of the tickets he had not purchased. "Dad felt that being honest in little things was exceedingly important," Don explained. "He wasn't going to let an opportunity to teach me this slip by. I have been grateful for his tough lessons since." Jack was wise enough to subscribe to the triplet:

Sow an act, reap a habit.
Sow a habit, reap a character.
Sow a character, reap a destiny.

V. PRAYER

Father, grant us the wisdom to see that in the daily choices that we make we are forming our inner person. Help us maintain the integrity that ought to characterize all disciples of Jesus Christ. Amen.

VI. DEEPER DISCOVERIES

A. Come In . . . Go Out (28:6,19)

"When you come in, and . . . when you go out" is an example of a *merism*, a figure of speech that uses two extremes to convey the notion of "everything" or "at all times." Other examples: "From the least to the greatest" (Jer. 6:13); "When you lie down and when you get up" (Deut. 6:7; 11:19). "When you come in, and . . . when you go out" suggests "in everything you do." In Deuteronomy 31:2, it is associated with leadership ability (cp. also 1 Kgs. 3:7).

B. Destroyed (28:51,61)

As used in Deuteronomy 28, *destroyed* does not mean "obliterated" but "ruined with respect to purpose." Israel would have survivors from its rebellion, but the people would lose their capacity to serve as the vehicle for blessing the nations, the purpose God intended in setting them apart (Gen. 12:1–3).

VII. TEACHING OUTLINE

A. INTRODUCTION
1. Lead Story: The Devil Did It
2. Context: Moses places before Israel the two great options of life. As a people, they will have to decide which path they will take: the one that leads to life, or the one that leads to destruction.
3. Transition: Christians face the same issue. After conversion, there is a life to be lived. That life will be marked either by faithful obedience and its attendant joys, or by rebellion and its sorrows.

B. COMMENTARY
1. God's Blessings for Obedience (28:1–14)
2. God's Cursings for Disobedience (28:15–68)

C. CONCLUSION: REAP A DESTINY

VIII. ISSUES FOR DISCUSSION

1. Are all personal tragedies the products of rebellion?
2. How can God turn personal defeats into victories?
3. Why do you think the cursings in Deuteronomy 28 occupy four times the space of the blessings?

Deuteronomy 29

Eyes to See

I. INTRODUCTION
Tongue Sight

II. COMMENTARY
A verse-by-verse explanation of the chapter.

III. CONCLUSION
Looming Sorrows

An overview of the principles and applications from the chapter.

IV. LIFE APPLICATION
About Five Knots

Melding the chapter to life.

V. PRAYER
Tying the chapter to life with God.

VI. DEEPER DISCOVERIES
Historical, geographical, and grammatical enrichment of the commentary.

VII. TEACHING OUTLINE
Suggested step-by-step group study of the chapter.

VIII. ISSUES FOR DISCUSSION
Zeroing the chapter in on daily life.

Deuteronomy 29

> Quote
>
> *"When people stop believing in God, they do not believe in nothing. They believe in anything."*
>
> G. K. Chesterton

Deuteronomy 29

IN A NUTSHELL

God's past faithfulness and his ability to enforce the sanctions of his covenant argue for a heartfelt fidelity to his truth. Unfortunately, as Moses speaks, Israel seems spiritually dull.

Eyes to See

I. INTRODUCTION

Tongue Sight

*E*vangelist Robert Sumner tells in one of his books about a man in Kansas City who was terribly injured in an explosion. His face was badly burned, and he suffered the loss of his eyesight. The victim was a new Christian, and he told friends how his greatest point of sorrow after the accident came when he realized he would never be able to read the Bible again. The sadness was made worse since he had also lost both his hands and thus could not be taught Braille.

Then someone raised his hopes when they told him of a blind woman in England who had learned to read Braille with her lips. When he tried it, however, he was disappointed to discover that the nerve endings in his lips had been destroyed in the explosion. He noticed, however, that he could still feel the raised characters with his tongue. He was encouraged, so he began the long process of learning to differentiate the characters of the Braille alphabet with his tongue. At the time Sumner wrote his book, the man had read the entire Bible four times with his tongue.

Although the injured man had lost his eyesight, he had not come close to losing his spiritual sight. He was wise enough to know what was supremely valuable to him, and as a result he was able to resume a personal intake of the Word of God. His actions put to shame the untold thousands who can easily read the Scriptures but do not do so.

II. COMMENTARY

Eyes to See

MAIN IDEA: Moses calls for a wholehearted loyalty to Yahweh based on his faithfulness in the past and the consequences of failure to follow him.

A The Covenant History: Review (29:1–9)

SUPPORTING IDEA: In spite of Yahweh's past faithfulness, Israel still lacks spiritual insight. They need to recall how he protected them and provided for them so they can behave as his people in the future.

29:1. It is a matter of debate whether the phrase **these are the terms** looks backward to the content of chapter 28 and preceding or forward to the material of chapter 29. Arguments can be marshaled to support either position, but on balance it seems more likely to refer backward (the verse is actually 28:69 in the Hebrew Bible). Regardless, the terms given to the present generation **in Moab** represent a more specific elaboration of the covenant God had **made** forty years before with the Israelites at Mount **Horeb**.

29:2–4. Moses constructed a clever word play that built on the relationship between physical and spiritual sight. He first reminded Israel that their **eyes** had **seen** the **wonders** of God's work in Egypt, work that had touched **Pharaoh, all his officials,** and **all his land**. Their **own eyes** had viewed the spectacular and **miraculous signs** of Yahweh.

In spite of these visual feasts, however, in a deeper sense Israel still lacked **eyes** that saw or **ears** that heard the personal meaning and application of God's wonders. The nation still needed the Lord to give the people a **mind** that understood.

29:5–6. As testimony to the truth of the accusation in verse 4, Moses talked about the **forty years in the desert**. Israel wore on their backs and feet proof of Yahweh's faithfulness: **clothes** and **sandals** that **did not wear out**. Also, Israel had managed to survive without eating **bread** or drinking **wine**, since God had supplied the nation's food and drink through miraculous means. The Lord took such extraordinary measures so Israel **might know** that he was their God, yet they seemed not to grasp this fundamental issue.

29:7–8. If Israel's supernatural food and clothing were not enough, they need only recall that even after reaching the eastern side of the Jordan River they enjoyed remarkable victories over **Sihon king of Heshbon and Og king of Bashan**. Although God had not promised Israel those lands, they became the property of **the Reubenites, the Gadites and the half-tribe of Manasseh**. As in all his dealings with his people, the Lord had given them even more than he had promised. His character should have been evident, even to the most hardened among them.

29:9. Unfortunately, the goodness of Yahweh was still only a hazy notion in the minds of many of his people. They could, however, in spite of their stubbornness, **carefully follow the terms** of God's **covenant**. If they did, they would enjoy success **in everything** they undertook.

B The Covenant Relationship: Reinforcement (29:10–15)

SUPPORTING IDEA: *Israel must now renew the covenant with Yahweh, appreciating his faithfulness and presence as well as the impact their commitment will have on future generations.*

29:10–11. As Israel prepared to enter the land, they were, in effect, renewing the covenant between themselves and the Lord. The covenant affected everyone from the **leaders, elders,** and **officials** to the nation's families, including **wives** and **children,** and even the **aliens** living in the camps.

29:12–13. The nation, as Moses spoke, was gathered in a solemn assembly in order **to enter into a covenant with the LORD.** Although their lives in the future would be touched by what they did on this occasion, the Lord had taken the initiative in the relationship from the very beginning. Now he was **sealing** his commitment to the people of Israel **with an oath.** Even in this he was displaying his faithful character. He was renewing the covenant on the basis of what he had previously **promised** the people and because of a previous oath that **he swore** to the patriarchs **Abraham, Isaac and Jacob.**

29:14–15. The terms of the agreement would be binding not only on those **standing** east of the Jordan River as Moses spoke but also on their children and grandchildren, generations yet unborn. As a result, it was important that those who were agreeing to its terms should do so on the basis of understanding and devotion.

The Covenant Demand: Renunciation (29:16–21)

SUPPORTING IDEA: Although the nation will be confronted with enticements to cling to other gods, neither Israel as a whole nor any individual should yield to those temptations, since they will bring terrible punishments.

29:16–18. The central demand of the covenant was that Israel should cling solely to Yahweh their God. This should not prove overwhelming, because the Israelites could recall their previous exposure to the terrible idolatries of **Egypt,** and they could also remember the **detestable images and idols** of the countries they had passed through on the way to Canaan. They knew the depravities of those who worshiped gods of **wood and stone, of silver and gold.**

To keep themselves and their future generations from such practices, the people must make sure that no individual **man or woman** should be drawn **away** to such idolatry. Even worse, they must not permit a single **clan or tribe** among them to worship **the gods of those nations** they had passed through. Even a single person whose **heart** was drawn to idolatry could prove to be a **root** producing **bitter poison** that would destroy the whole nation of Israel. Because of past history, Moses was not optimistic about Israel's future course: "For I know how rebellious and stiff-necked you are. If you have been rebellious against the LORD while I am still alive and with you, how much more will you rebel after I die!" (Deut. 31:27).

29:19–21. Although Israel included hundreds of thousands of people, an individual **person** might hear **the words** of Yahweh's **oath** and conclude that it guaranteed his safety regardless of his behavior. If that person should **persist** in going his own sinful way, he would bring disaster on the whole nation—on the one who was attempting to obey (**the watered land**) and those who were not (**the dry**).

Such high-handed rebellion would bring stern reprisals from Yahweh. The Lord would **never be willing to forgive** such an individual. **His wrath and zeal** would **burn against** such a rebel and bring on him the **curses** that were part of the terms of the covenant. Eventually, the Lord would **blot out his name from under heaven**. In ways that were not specified, the Lord would single out such a person **from all the tribes of Israel for disaster**. This person could not rely on his inclusion in the covenant community for protection from the consequences of his waywardness.

D The Covenant Stakes: Reputation (29:22–29)

SUPPORTING IDEA: *The punishments that Yahweh will inflict for covenant disloyalty will prove a reproach upon Israel and will cause the nations to wonder why such horrors should have been inflicted upon them.*

29:22–23. The consequences of rebellion would affect the reputation of Israel **in later generations**. Even **foreigners** who came **from distant lands** would be able to see the **calamities** and **diseases** that had been visited on the promised land because of such conduct and covenant defection. Indeed, it would be hard to miss, since the land itself under such conditions would become no better than **a burning waste of salt and sulfur** with no vegetation growing on it. Canaan would resemble **the destruction of Sodom and Gomorrah** more than a land flowing with milk and honey.

29:24–26. So terrible would the condition of the land prove that even the pagan **nations** surrounding Canaan would ask, **Why has the Lord done this?** The **answer** to that question would be laid directly at the door of Israel: **because this people abandoned the covenant of the LORD**. Their guilt would be doubly dark in view of the fact that they had forsaken **the God of their fathers** who had **brought them out of Egypt**. Instead of returning love and devotion for Yahweh's own expressions of kindness, they would have turned to **other gods** with whom they had had no experience at all, idols that **he had not given them**.

29:27–28. The answer to the question of the nations concludes with a reference to the Lord's **anger**. What the nations would know of him would come in connection with his righteous indignation against the land of promise and his fulfillment of the **curses** connected with the covenant. God's character would be known to the pagans primarily in connection with the **wrath** that had **uprooted** Israel **from their land and thrust them into another land** as captives.

29:29. This verse can stand alone because of its differentiation between what God had disclosed and what he had kept hidden. However, in context these words address the puzzlement that would come when Israel found itself captive in a strange land. How could God's severe discipline be brought into line with his promise of future blessings and his oaths to the patriarchs? This was not a question that Yahweh was choosing to answer for the present. Such matters would remain a **secret**. All Israel needed to know at the moment was that the terms of the covenant, **the things revealed**, belonged to them and their children. God was urging them to follow **all the words** of the law.

> **MAIN IDEA REVIEW:** *Moses calls for a wholehearted loyalty to Yahweh based on his faithfulness in the past and the consequences of failure to follow him.*

III. CONCLUSION

Looming Sorrows

Remember the description of the prodigal son: "He came to his senses" (Luke 15:17)? The statement indicates that he had lost them somewhere along the way. Sin, which is action independent of the will of God, does that to us. Samson had a similar experience in his dealings with Delilah. He seemed to be a little slow mentally as she kept getting closer and closer to the knowledge of what made Samson unique. In her last seduction, Samson found himself walking around with a loom attached to his head as he defended himself against the Philistines (Judg. 16:14). One might suppose at that point he would be a little suspicious of his lover's designs. Unfortunately, he was not. When the Philistines later blinded him, they were only acting out what had already happened to him spiritually. His preference for fleshly pleasures over allegiance to Yahweh cost him dearly. Spiritual blindness dulls a person in every area of life.

PRINCIPLES

- Christians are to build their confidence in God from his acts of faithfulness to them in the past.
- The more we have seen God do for us, the greater is our responsibility to love and serve him faithfully.
- Man's heart is so dull that it requires a work of grace for him to gain spiritual insight.
- The choices we make today will affect not only us but our descendants.

APPLICATIONS

- Be grateful for God's work in your life.

Deuteronomy 29

- Turn God's faithfulness into a prayer, poem, or a letter to someone who needs encouragement.
- Expect God to honor his promises in Scripture.
- Rely on the faithful character of God when you face a crisis.

IV. LIFE APPLICATION

About Five Knots

Former *New York Times* drama critic Alexander Wollcott used to sit at the window of his apartment overlooking the East River and watch the boat traffic. A visitor to the apartment once asked, "How can you sit here by the hour watching one battered old tugboat after another chugging by at ten knots? That's pretty dull."

Wollcott explained: "It's not always tugboats. Every now and then a dead body floats by."

His guest was shocked: "A dead body? What's a dead body doing in the river?"

Wollcott shrugged and replied: "I can't say for sure, but my guess would be about five knots."

When God is left out of it, life can become incredibly dull. By contrast, new horizons and possibilities present themselves to those who can see spiritually. Jesus told his disciples, "Open your eyes and look at the fields! They are ripe for harvest" (John 4:35). Once spiritually dull eyes have been made to see, the world becomes a stage upon which God's purposes are acted out.

V. PRAYER

Father, help us to resist the enticements of a world gone astray and hold to you in love and loyalty. Help us to walk in the light so our spiritual vision will not be impaired. Amen.

VI. DEEPER DISCOVERIES

A. A Root That Produces "Bitter Poison" (29:18)

Literally, this expression means "poison and bitterness." The couplet may signify the root cause of idolatry as being a spirit of disloyalty. As long as a wayward spirit is present, there will always be a threat of defection from Yahweh. Or it could describe the individual person who, in his incomplete adherence to the Lord, becomes a poisonous plant in the congregation of Israel.

B. "Never Be Willing to Forgive Him" (29:20)

Sometimes these words are contrasted with the appealing statement of the apostle Peter: "The Lord is not slow in keeping his promise, as some understand slowness. He is patient with you, not wanting anyone to perish, but everyone to come to repentance" (2 Pet. 3:9). Based on this apparently divergent principle, critics like to suggest that the God of the Old Testament is a bloodthirsty monster, unlike the forgiving deity of the New Testament.

However, in neither Testament is God willing to forgive the person who is in a state of rebellion. A person in the condition described in verse 19 is not seeking forgiveness, nor is he entitled to it. Later in the same chapter of 2 Peter, the apostle describes those who twist Paul's letters: "[Paul] writes the same way in all his letters, speaking in them of these matters. His letters contain some things that are hard to understand, which ignorant and unstable people distort, as they do the other Scriptures, to their own destruction" (2 Pet. 3:16). In both testaments, the repentant and contrite person will always find mercy before the Lord (Pss. 34:18; 51:17).

VII. TEACHING OUTLINE

A. INTRODUCTION

1. Lead Story: Tongue Sight

2. Context: As Israel prepared to enter the land, they paused to renew their covenant with Yahweh. Since they could not hope to succeed without his help, Moses urged them to consider how faithfulness to the Lord would smooth their way in the perilous days ahead.

3. Transition: Christians, too, need the insight that God provides to see the connection between their own behavior and the way events unfold.

B. COMMENTARY

1. The Covenant History: Review (29:1–9)

2. The Covenant Relationship: Reinforcement (29:10–15)

3. The Covenant Demand: Renunciation (29:16–21)

4. The Covenant Stakes: Reputation (29:22–29)

C. CONCLUSION: ABOUT FIVE KNOTS

VIII. ISSUES FOR DISCUSSION

1. How does God differ in his treatment of faithful believers and neglectful believers?
2. When God brings difficulties into a believer's life because of unfaithful behavior, does this indicate that such calamities are the sign of divine discipline?
3. Since prosperity issues from obedience, are all prosperous people obedient?
4. Why did God swear an oath of faithfulness to Israel?

Deuteronomy 30

Choose Life

I. INTRODUCTION
A Telling Question

II. COMMENTARY
A verse-by-verse explanation of the chapter.

III. CONCLUSION
I Led Three Lives

An overview of the principles and applications from the chapter.

IV. LIFE APPLICATION
Develop the Passion

Melding the chapter to life.

V. PRAYER
Tying the chapter to life with God.

VI. DEEPER DISCOVERIES
Historical, geographical, and grammatical enrichment of the commentary.

VII. TEACHING OUTLINE
Suggested step-by-step group study of the chapter.

VIII. ISSUES FOR DISCUSSION
Zeroing the chapter in on daily life.

Deuteronomy 30

Quote

"Conversion is not a repairing of the old building; but it takes all down and erects a new structure. The sincere Christian is quite a new fabric—from the foundation to the top-stone all new."

Joseph Alleine

IN A NUTSHELL

Israel will have to suffer because of disobedience to the covenant, but God's purposes will ultimately be fulfilled. In Deuteronomy 30, Moses urges the people to choose life and spare themselves the miseries of an existence without a knowledge of God.

Choose Life

I. INTRODUCTION

A Telling Question

Many years ago in the city of St. Louis, an attorney visited a client—a Christian businessman—to discuss some matters of concern. Before the meeting ended, the lawyer's client somewhat hesitatingly said to him, "I've often wanted to ask you a question, but I've been afraid to do so."

"What do you want to know?" asked the lawyer.

The man replied, "I've often wondered why you're not a Christian."

The man hung his head. "I know enough about the Bible to realize that it says no drunkard can enter the kingdom of God; and you know my weakness!"

"You're avoiding my question," continued the client.

"Well, truthfully, I can't recall anyone ever asking me that before, or explaining how to become a Christian."

Picking up a Bible, the Christian businessman read several texts showing that everyone is under condemnation, and how Christ came to save the lost by dying on the cross for their sins. "By receiving him as your substitute and redeemer," he explained, "you can be forgiven. If you're willing to receive Jesus, let's pray together."

The lawyer was eager to receive God's gift. When it was his turn, he prayed, "O Lord, I am a slave to drink. One of your servants has shown me how to be saved. O God, forgive my sins and help me overcome the power of this terrible habit in my life."

That newly converted lawyer was C. I. Scofield, who later edited the reference Bible that bears his name. In time, with God's help, he did conquer his addiction, and he left a legacy of godliness and Bible teaching that blessed many lives. The church of Jesus Christ would have been immeasurably poorer had not his client taken the time to ask a simple question that day. Christians today, as Moses did in the plains opposite Jericho, can urge their friends and associates to choose a relationship with God as the core of their existence.

Deuteronomy 30:1-3

II. COMMENTARY

Choose Life

> **MAIN IDEA:** Although Israel is destined to suffer because of disobedience to the covenant, that will not be the end of the story. The nation's repentance will come when its heart is changed, and with that repentance will come restoration and prosperity.

A A Hopeful Future (30:1–10)

> **SUPPORTING IDEA:** Israel will return to Yahweh when her people take to heart the fulfilled warnings of the covenant.

30:1–3. In Deuteronomy 30, Moses finds himself in the paradoxical position of predicting the failure of Israel to observe the covenant he has been expounding. Instead of responding to his message, the nation would only get the point **when all the blessings and curses** came upon them. Because of their rebellion, they will be dispersed **among the nations** to meditate upon the loss of their special relationship with Yahweh. While they are scattered there, they will at some point regret their folly in rebelling and **return to the LORD**. They will do so enthusiastically, accepting everything Moses was telling them east of the Jordan River. At that time, the Lord will **restore their fortunes** and **have compassion** on them, unifying them once again in the land of their inheritance.

30:4–5. God's kind intentions toward his newly repentant people will not be limited to those in the promised land. Even if they find themselves **in the most distant land under the heavens**, the Lord will bring them back to Canaan. The land is described as **the land that belonged to your fathers**, the latter probably referring not to the patriarchs (who after all owned virtually nothing in the land) but those of the present generation and afterward, who will at that time be viewed as the fathers of the country. The restoration will, in fact, be greater than the original conquest, since God will ultimately make Israel **more prosperous and numerous** than they were when Moses spoke.

30:6. Such a restoration would come about only because of a dramatic change in the hearts of the people. As Moses observed in the previous chapter, the nation to whom he was speaking still had little inclination to know God (cp. 29:4). In the future, however, at a low point in their national life, when most are still outside the land, **God will circumcise** their **hearts** and incline them to **love him** completely. When that heart change takes place, and only then, will Israel truly begin to **live**.

30:7–8. Although the descendants of the twelve tribes by that time will have suffered cruel and inhuman treatment on the part of their **enemies**, God will place the **curses** not on Israel but on those who **hate and persecute** them. This remarkable reversal of history will give them hope and encouragement, and the people **will again obey the LORD and follow all his commands**.

30:9–10. These verses elaborate on the promised restoration and describe it as extending to Israel's **work**, family and **livestock** fertility, and to the **crops** of the land. Such wholesale prosperity will grow from the **delight** that the Lord will take in Israel as they **obey** his **commands and decrees**.

B A Hopeful Message (30:11–14)

SUPPORTING IDEA: *The conditions for a restored Israel are neither too remote to grasp nor too difficult to keep.*

30:11–13. The Lord's commands that will bring prosperity and a restored condition are not beyond Israel's reach. God's truth is **not up in heaven** where it cannot be known; it is revealed. Neither is his word **beyond the sea**, where it is impossible to see or hear. Because Moses had expounded the law, God's truth is fully accessible to all who desire to meditate upon it and obey it.

30:14. The word, in fact, was **very near** to all who were listening as Moses spoke. It could be understood and repeated by the **mouth** of all his hearers. It could be reflected upon in the **heart** and obeyed by all who cared to do so (cp. Rom. 10:6–8). This verse does not challenge the many statements elsewhere that the law of God is impossible to keep perfectly. Israel would not have to keep the law perfectly but only in a relative sense, to enjoy the blessings of the covenant. The Scriptures give examples of people who do just that: "He who keeps the law is a discerning son, but a companion of gluttons disgraces his father" (Prov. 28:7; cp. Luke 1:6).

C A Hopeful Choice (30:15–20)

SUPPORTING IDEA: *God offers Israel simple options: life remaining faithful to Yahweh or death for rebelling against him.*

30:15. Moses placed before Israel the two broad possibilities. Either they would choose **life and prosperity**, or they would decide on **death and destruction**. Death in this context did not suggest that unfaithful Israelites would die physically because of their failure to comply with the terms of the covenant, though physical death at some point was a certainty. Instead, the death in question is a form of existence that is hateful, miserable, and unproductive, such as that described by the apostle Paul: "The widow who lives for pleasure is dead even while she lives" (1 Tim. 5:6).

30:16. Real life consists of loving the Lord, letting **his ways** guide one's path and growing in his character. Those who chose this option would **live and increase** and would know the blessings of God **in the land**.

30:17–18. Those who allowed their hearts to be turned **away** from the Lord, however, would suffer the miseries of a tragic and unfulfilled existence. If they should **bow down to other gods and worship them**, they would find themselves headed for destruction. They would forfeit the possibility of living **long in the land**.

30:19–20. The covenant between God and Israel was to be a cosmic spectacle. **Heaven and earth** would serve as the **witnesses** if Israel should defect from her allegiance to Yahweh. In time he would have to call them to give testimony (cp. Isa. 1:2; Jer. 2:12–13). It was customary in Ancient Near Eastern suzerainty treaties to call on the gods to serve as observers and guarantors of the agreement, but of course Yahweh as the sole God of all things would never invoke the concern of pagan deities to ensure the observance of his covenant. *Heaven and earth* in this context may mean "those angels and people living in heaven and on earth."

Moses urged the people to **choose life**, noting that the Lord was their life. Those who lived without reference to the God of Israel were not living at all. They had adopted an agonizing form of protracted death as the mode of their existence.

> **MAIN IDEA REVIEW:** Although Israel is destined to suffer because of disobedience to the covenant, that will not be the end of the story. The nation's repentance will come when its heart is changed, and with that repentance will come restoration and prosperity.

III. CONCLUSION

I Led Three Lives

In his book *I Led Three Lives*, Herbert Philbrick tells how he was a spy for the Soviet Union, a counterspy for the FBI, and a private citizen who made a living as an advertising salesman. The book and the television series based on his life described how he rose to the top of the Communist Party in the United States as he simultaneously supplied intelligence information to the American government.

Herbert had always been a kind of halfhearted atheist, but his Communist handlers insisted that he continue to participate in church as part of his cover. One day, the message he heard at church broke through:

> One morning I was feeding my baby daughter. She was such a delight. I enjoyed every moment with her. Between bites of baby cereal, I got to looking at her tiny little ear in the sunlight coming through the kitchen window. Her ear was so beautifully formed. No

larger than the end of my thumb, yet amazingly complex and perfectly designed for the task of gathering sound.

As I gazed at her little ear, a voice in my head said, "Herbert, it takes more faith to believe in evolution than it does to believe in a creative God." By "a voice in my head," I don't mean the voice of an angel or anything, but it was as if a heretofore suppressed part of my rational mind broke free and began to reason with my more logical self. For the better part of a week I rethought everything I had believed about the origin of man and indeed the universe.

As I look back on that sunny morning feeding my daughter, I thank God for allowing me to know him in a personal way. I still believe in a "creator God," but he is much more than that to me now. It's kind of like reading a wonderful book and then discovering the author lives in the flat next door. You still treasure the book, but that is soon overshadowed as your friendship grows with the author. As you share a meal or watch a football game together, you become friends. Your relationship becomes much more than author and reader (Philbrick, p. 8).

As Moses said, the Lord is our life. We are not simply to follow a set of rules; we are to fall in love with a person. We are not just to subscribe to a list of principles but to attach ourselves in love and submission to the one who is ultimate greatness.

PRINCIPLES

- Conversion engages the mind as well as the emotions.
- Distance is no barrier to the love of God.
- A healthy relationship with God is built on the internal changes he brings about through Christ.
- A life that is lived without regard to God cannot be called living.

APPLICATIONS

- Learn life's important lessons from Scripture instead of the school of harsh experience.
- Thank God for the persistence of his love.
- Take the risk of asking your friends the questions that will bring their spiritual condition into the open.
- Be ready to give a testimony of God's work in your life.

Deuteronomy 30

IV. LIFE APPLICATION

Develop the Passion

Leighton Ford told of the need for passion for souls in his book *The Christian Persuader*, which includes the story of the time his little girl, Debbie Jean, was lost. His wife had left Debbie Jean and her four-year-old brother with Leighton while she went to the store. Suddenly Debbie Jean was nowhere to be found.

After making a few inquiries, Leighton discovered that a neighbor's child had seen her heading in the direction of her school, which was only a few hundred yards away; but Debbie Jean could not be found on the school grounds.

While his wife checked the shopping center across the street, Leighton went to the principal, and together they looked through the classrooms but without success. As they looked, Ford's mind recalled the terrible stories he had heard of little girls who had disappeared and were never heard from again. He began to walk up and down the street while calling her name. Half an hour later when he had all but reached the end of his rope, the little girl came around the corner of the school with a smile on her face, wondering why her dad's brow was so furrowed. Debbie Jean had gone to the candy store just beyond the school and had bumped into a friend who had invited her home.

Later, after a long and pointed discussion with his daughter, Leighton Ford meditated on the episode. During the seemingly endless two hours that his daughter was missing, nothing else mattered. In his study, important tasks lay neglected. He could think of only one thing: his lost little girl. He had only one prayer, and he prayed it a thousand times: *Oh God, help me find her.*

The church of Jesus Christ will never be what God intends it to be until we have that kind of passion for reaching out to the world beyond our walls. When we have the longing we need for lost people, we will discover that the necessary spiritual power has been there all along.

V. PRAYER

Father, give us a passion for the lost and a recognition that without your Spirit's work our efforts will accomplish nothing. Amen.

VI. DEEPER DISCOVERIES

A. Circumcise Your Heart (30:6)

These words form an apt description of a painful but necessary internal change. They also appear in Deuteronomy 10:16, where the "surgeon" is the individual Israelite: "Circumcise your hearts, therefore, and do not be stiff-necked any longer." There is no contradiction concerning the agent in this process. Before we can accomplish such spiritual surgery, we must be properly motivated, and that is the work of God. The internal spiritual change in Israel described in this verse has yet to happen.

VII. TEACHING OUTLINE

A. INTRODUCTION
1. Lead Story: A Telling Question
2. Context: Israel may have to touch bottom before finally realizing their need of a personal relationship with Yahweh. When he changes their hearts, they will return to him.
3. Transition: The Bible has a glorious and hopeful message of good news called the gospel. God does not ask for self-reformation but faith in his Son as the source of life.

B. COMMENTARY
1. A Hopeful Future (30:1–10)
2. A Hopeful Message (30:11–14)
3. A Hopeful Choice (30:15–20)

C. CONCLUSION: DEVELOP THE PASSION

VIII. ISSUES FOR DISCUSSION

1. In what ways have you, like Israel, had to learn spiritual lessons through hard experience?
2. What are some ways that faith in Christ produces life in the believer?
3. What were the biggest barriers to your coming to faith in Christ?
4. Why isn't the Christian faith simply keeping a list of rules?

Deuteronomy 31

Prelude to a Sad Song

I. **INTRODUCTION**
   Cessation of Hostilities

II. **COMMENTARY**
   A verse-by-verse explanation of the chapter.

III. **CONCLUSION**
   Changing Heads

   An overview of the principles and applications from the chapter.

IV. **LIFE APPLICATION**
   No Place to Be

   Melding the chapter to life.

V. **PRAYER**
   Tying the chapter to life with God.

VI. **DEEPER DISCOVERIES**
   Historical, geographical, and grammatical enrichment of the commentary.

VII. **TEACHING OUTLINE**
   Suggested step-by-step group study of the chapter.

VIII. **ISSUES FOR DISCUSSION**
   Zeroing the chapter in on daily life.

Deuteronomy 31

> **Quote**
>
> "Love thy God and love him only
> And thy breast will ne'er be lonely."
>
> Aubrey Thomas DeVere

IN A NUTSHELL

Aware of his impending death, Moses presents Joshua to the nation as his successor and predicts his nation's spiritual waywardness in years to come.

Prelude to a Sad Song

I. INTRODUCTION

Cessation of Hostilities

In 1974, after thirty years of personal warfare, Lieutenant Hiro Onoda finally surrendered. He was the last known Japanese soldier to cease hostilities after the surrender of Japan in 1945. He had lived on the jungle island of Lubang in the Philippines and continued his individual war for three decades, refusing to believe the radio reports of a homeland surrender. He had heard the appeals from Filipinos to end his war and had read the accounts in Japanese-language newspapers, but he didn't believe them, either. He went on hoping that the Japanese navy would return and assist him in recapturing Lubang for the emperor.

When Lieutenant Onoda walked out of the jungle, he did not create the peace; he merely began to benefit from it. Much like the unconverted sinner before God, he continued to wage a war he could not win by refusing to accept a victory won by someone else.

In Deuteronomy 31, Moses foresaw a long and terrible struggle between the people of Israel and their God. They would suffer terrible disasters and defeats until the day when they would turn away from false gods and return to God and accept the peace won for them by his love.

II. COMMENTARY

Prelude to a Sad Song

> **MAIN IDEA:** *Israel gains a new leader and a new and sorrowful national song as Moses prepares to end his ministry as covenant mediator.*

A The Preparation of the Leader (31:1–8)

> **SUPPORTING IDEA:** *Moses' days as Israel's leader were approaching their end; it was time to encourage the people and commission their new leader.*

31:1–2. His work as Yahweh's mediator now complete, Moses announced to his people that his life was approaching its end. He had lived for **a hundred and twenty years**, those years falling roughly into three periods: (1) forty in Egypt, (2) forty in Midian, and (3) forty leading Israel to the edge of the promised land. Since the covenant had been ratified, and the Lord had told

Deuteronomy 31:3–6

him that he could **not cross the Jordan**, he knew that his earthly end was at hand.

31:3–6. Israel's fate, however, did not depend on Moses or any human leader. The Lord God **himself** would lead his people into the **land** and **destroy** the **nations** who lived there. During the period of the conquest, **Joshua** would also be there to serve as their guide, as the Lord had already announced.

Because Yahweh was faithful, the inhabitants of the land would meet the same fate as **Sihon and Og, the kings of the Amorites**. When the defeats of those native armies were complete, however, Israel must **do to them all that** Moses had **commanded**. They must not shrink back from the unpleasant work of executing the remaining population, as Moses had explained to them in Deuteronomy 7:1–2.

Whether engaging in this task or taking on the opposing armies, however, Israel must **be strong and courageous**. Instead of being afraid or terrified because of the warlike Canaanites, they must turn their eyes on **the** LORD, who would be **with** them throughout the process. His presence would make all the difference, and they need not fear that he would ever **leave** or **forsake** them (cp. Heb. 13:5).

31:7–8. Moses turned to Joshua and commissioned him **in the presence of all Israel**. Like the people, Joshua would also need to **be strong and courageous**, since he would serve as general of the army and chief administrator in dividing the land **among them as their inheritance**. Joshua would be comforted by the remembrance that **the** LORD **himself** would also be with him. Fear and discouragement are the chief obstacles to any spiritual objective, and God's presence—known by faith—is the answer to both.

B The Preservation of the Lyrics (31:9–13)

SUPPORTING IDEA: At some point, both Moses and Joshua would be gone. To perpetuate the spiritual purposes of the nation, the Levites must read the law to the people every seven years.

31:9. After Moses and Joshua had passed off the scene and Israel was scattered throughout Canaan, the responsibility for the renewal of the commitment to the covenant would fall upon **the priests, the sons of Levi**, and upon **the elders of Israel**. They would have to reacquaint the people with the provisions of the **law** on a regular basis. The phrase **this law** often refers to the Pentateuch—the first five books of the Old Testament—but in this context it probably meant the covenant stipulations of Deuteronomy 5–26 (cp. 4:44–45; 29:21,29; 30:10; 32:46).

31:10–13. The mission of the priests would be to **read** God's covenant stipulations to Israel **every seven years, in the year for canceling debts** (cp. 15:1–2). This reading would take place in the fall at **the Feast of Tabernacles**, when all the people were assembled to worship the Lord and celebrate his faithfulness at harvest time. The reading would be observed at the place he would choose (cp. 12:1) as the central sanctuary of Israel. Each generation of **children** must **hear** God's law and **learn to fear** him.

C The Presentation of the Leader (31:14–23)

SUPPORTING IDEA: *The divine appointment of Joshua must be publicly recognized, especially in light of the people's coming defection.*

31:14–15. Moses' long tenure as leader of the people of God was soon to end. That made all the more important a public presentation of **Joshua** as the divinely appointed successor to **Moses**. To ensure God's approval of this appointment, the two men came and **presented themselves at the Tent of Meeting**. There the Lord appeared, as he had in the wilderness, in a **pillar of cloud** that **stood over the entrance to the Tent** and commissioned Joshua as the leader of Israel.

31:16–18. The departure of Moses was not to be a happy one. Instead of expressing confidence in the people, God had to tell his servant that the people would **soon prostitute themselves to the foreign gods of the land**. They would begin to violate **the covenant** almost before the ink was dry upon it.

Because Israel would forsake him, Yahweh would also **forsake them** (see "Deeper Discoveries"). Their defection would bring **disasters and difficulties** into their lives. These problems would be designed to awaken the people and cause them to wonder if their trials were connected with God's displeasure. The recognition of the connection between pains and prior behavior would be the first step on the road to repentance. God's tribulations are remedial rather than punitive.

31:19–20. The road to misery was so predictable that Moses was commissioned to write a song (Deut. 32:1–43) to commemorate it. This song would become a witness to Yahweh's faithfulness and Israel's disloyalty through the years. Israel's downward spiral would be made all the more bitter for taking place in a **land flowing with milk and honey**. Only after Israel began to **eat** its **fill and thrive** would the nation **turn to other gods**.

31:21–22. The value of singing as a worship practice lies in part in the way in which it facilitates memorization. In the years to come, **when . . . disasters and difficulties** plagued their national life, Israel would be unable to escape God's witness against them because the song of Moses would **not be forgotten** by the **descendants** of the original generation that entered the land. Its poignant reminders of God's faithfulness and Israel's treachery would make their guilt a present reality. The fact that God knew what the people were **disposed to do**, even before they did it, testifies to the strength of his love and the weakness of their loyalty to him.

Deuteronomy 31:23

31:23. The coming defection would be painful to Joshua, a man of proven character. God urged him to **be strong and courageous** in the face of Israel's fickle ways. Although he would not live to see the falling away of the coming generations, he would **bring the Israelites into the land as God promised**. As Moses had known Yahweh's constant presence, so would Joshua.

D The Prediction of Rebellion (31:24–30)

SUPPORTING IDEA: *Moses recognizes the fundamental waywardness of the hearts of his countrymen and predicts their rebellion in days to come.*

31:24–26. Moses concluded his ministry by placing **in a book the words of this law** (see commentary on v. 9) to serve **as a witness** against the waywardness of Israel. This book of the covenant he gave **to the Levites** for preservation alongside **the ark**. (The book is to be distinguished from the two tables of stone bearing the Ten Commandments that were placed *inside* the ark.)

31:27–30. The future of the nation would be darkened by the people's **rebellious and stiff-necked** nature. Moses had served as a brake on those tendencies, which would now become more evident after his death. Brief periods of loyalty would be followed by much longer periods of unfaithfulness. To counter these things, Moses gave orders to assemble **all the elders** of the tribes so he could **speak** words **in their hearing** that would later rebuke them in their defection.

Moses knew that the people of Israel would **become utterly corrupt** as they fell into the worship of idols that their own **hands** had **made**. In God's great love for them, he would permit **disaster** to fall upon them in his efforts to gain their attention. To ensure that these dangers would never be far from their minds, Moses composed and **recited** the words of a song that would characterize their troubled history.

MAIN IDEA REVIEW: *Israel gains a new leader and a new and sorrowful national song as Moses prepares to end his ministry as covenant mediator.*

III. CONCLUSION

Changing Heads

While leading a tour of the Bible lands some years ago, I was struck by the number of surviving Roman statues that were more or less intact except for a missing head. When I called the attention of the guide to this phenomenon, he explained that what I had seen was no accident. Carving an entire statue was expensive, and people on the fringes of the Roman Empire resented having to commission a fresh statue every time a new emperor came to power. So, to save money, they simply chopped off the head of the old statue and replaced it with a likeness of the new emperor's head.

Human leaders may seem far more alike than different, even leaders like Moses and Joshua. However, when it comes to ultimate leadership, God insists that our allegiance to him be exclusive and permanent. Although Moses was dying, God as the true leader of Israel was still alive. Yahweh would be there when Israel needed his provision and his protection. Christians are never to be in doubt about who is the head of the church and of every Christian's life. Jesus Christ alone occupies this place.

PRINCIPLES

- It is sometimes easier to trust God in a life-threatening battle than in the small challenges of daily life.
- Although spiritual growth puts our wills to the test, after the battle has been won, we recognize that the Lord is the true victor in the struggle.
- Only people of proven character should be placed in positions of spiritual leadership.
- No amount of temporal success can compensate for the loss of God's approval.

APPLICATIONS

- If you aspire to spiritual leadership, begin by being a good follower.
- Be courageous in your own spiritual environment. Be forthright but loving in identifying your attachment to Jesus Christ.
- When facing your next challenge, recall how God made you equal to previous tasks.
- Spend some time in the Word of God every day.

IV. LIFE APPLICATION

No Place to Be

One day God would send his wayward people into captivity in Babylon. There they would live in an environment dominated by what had caused them to be sent there in the first place: idolatry.

Deuteronomy 31

There are many people in church every Sunday who have been born into and raised in Christian homes. They came to know Christ at a young age. Their parents loved them enough to do what they could to keep them from stepping into some of the spiritual potholes they had stepped in. Young people like these have tremendous advantages, and that is as it should be.

But they also have to face a serious danger, too. They may assume that because they don't know what it is like to be a slave in a strange land and because they have grown up in an environment of spiritual freedom, "Babylon" isn't really all that terrible. After all, their parents or their grandparents or others before them came out of it.

But Babylon is an awful place, and it should be avoided at all costs. How much better off would God's people have been if they had never seen Babylon! Untold numbers of Israelites actually made their conversion to idolatry complete by being there. Most of the Israelites who went there never came back to their homeland.

So what are people converted as children supposed to do? How can they maintain a level of thanksgiving and joy in their salvation when they can hardly remember being unsaved? The answer is simple: they have to be wise enough to profit from the failures and blunders of others. They have to read the Scriptures, which are filled with accounts of people who failed and learned from failure. They must also read the "book" that is being written by people around them on a daily basis. They have to read life and see where leaving Jesus Christ out of their lives would lead. They have to profit from the miseries of people who have sought fame and fortune, found both, and discovered them to be empty and meaningless.

V. PRAYER

Father, keep us from looking for satisfaction in ways that are inconsistent with your truth. Thank you that you alone can satisfy our inner longings. Help us to find our rest and our satisfaction in you. Amen.

VI. DEEPER DISCOVERIES

A. Never Forsake You (31:6,17)

God promises not to forsake his people in battle in verse 6, and then promises that he will certainly forsake them if they give their hearts to false gods in verse 17. It seems clear from the combination of these two passages that the first statement contains an implied but unstated condition: "as long as I am your God." The blessings of the covenant, which included the presence of God at all times, did not apply to those who had broken the covenant.

VII. TEACHING OUTLINE

A. INTRODUCTION
1. Lead Story: Cessation of Hostilities
2. Context: Moses was soon to die. Before departing, he gathered the leaders of Israel together and urged them to recognize Joshua as their new leader. He would need their support, since the people had a tendency to turn away from Yahweh.
3. Transition: Just as Moses composed a song that would remind Israel of their wayward tendencies, so we need fresh reminders of our weaknesses.

B. COMMENTARY
1. The Preparation of the Leader (31:1–8)
2. The Preservation of the Lyrics (31:9–13)
3. The Presentation of the Leader (31:14–23)
4. The Prediction of Rebellion (31:24–29)

C. CONCLUSION: NO PLACE TO BE

VIII. ISSUES FOR DISCUSSION

1. How do yesterday's spiritual victories help us to face the next challenge?
2. What are some ways that we can keep God's Word fresh in our own thinking?
3. Have you observed wayward tendencies in your own heart? How do you address them?
4. Why is prostitution an apt figure of speech to express the defection of a believer to other gods?

Deuteronomy 32

What's Your Song?

I. **INTRODUCTION**
   Wonderful Things

II. **COMMENTARY**
   A verse-by-verse explanation of the chapter.

III. **CONCLUSION**
   What Kind of Song?
   An overview of the principles and applications from the chapter.

IV. **LIFE APPLICATION**
   The Sorrows of Mount Nebo
   Melding the chapter to life.

V. **PRAYER**
   Tying the chapter to life with God.

VI. **DEEPER DISCOVERIES**
   Historical, geographical, and grammatical enrichment of the commentary.

VII. **TEACHING OUTLINE**
   Suggested step-by-step group study of the chapter.

VIII. **ISSUES FOR DISCUSSION**
   Zeroing the chapter in on daily life.

Deuteronomy 32

Quote

"Grace binds you with far stronger cords than the cords of duty or obligation can bind you. Grace is free, but when once you take it you are bound forever to the Giver, and bound to catch the spirit of the Giver. Like produces like. Grace makes you gracious, the Giver makes you give."

E. Stanley Jones

IN A NUTSHELL

Moses teaches Israel a song that will remind them during their defections that Yahweh is gracious, faithful, and desirable above everything.

What's Your Song?

I. INTRODUCTION

Wonderful Things

In 1922, archaeologist Howard Carter was completing nearly fifteen years of digging in the famous Valley of the Kings in Egypt. He was hoping to find the royal tomb of Pharaoh Tutankhamen. Having found nothing after many months of searching, however, his days of digging were coming to an end; funding for the expedition was running out.

Then workers discovered sixteen steps leading into the ground. In the hope that the find might prove significant, thousands of baskets filled with rocks and sand were carried away. At the base of the steps, a door was found at the end of a long passageway. Carter gouged a small hole in the door and inserted a candle into the hole and peered in. As his eyes grew accustomed to the light, details emerged into his view, and he saw strange animals, statues, and everywhere, reflecting the light of the flickering candle, the glint of gold. He wrote, "For the moment, I was struck dumb with amazement."

A colleague asked, "Can you see anything?"

Carter's reply was, "Yes, wonderful things."

That attitude ought to reflect the heart of a believer who looks into the pages of Scripture in search of the truth about his Lord. In the Bible God has revealed the essential truths about himself for every believer. Here is found the pivotal truths about the waywardness of the human heart, the compassion of Jesus Christ, the atoning work of the cross, and God's loving heart toward sinners. Here the way of salvation and the keys to reclaiming a ruined life are revealed. However, only those with a conviction that the Bible contains such treasures will engage in the search.

II. COMMENTARY

What's Your Song?

MAIN IDEA: *In the light of Yahweh's greatness and faithfulness toward Israel, the people learn a song that will testify to them even in the dark days of wayward behavior.*

A The Song of Moses (32:1–43)

SUPPORTING IDEA: *Moses teaches Israel a song about Yahweh's faithfulness and their unfaithfulness.*

32:1–4. Although the **words** of Moses in his song were designed to testify against Israel's coming defections, the true subject of the song was the

greatness of our God. Once convicted of their sin, Israel would be brought back to God not by the failure of their idols but by the supreme faithfulness and beauty of **the Rock** of Israel, a **God who does no wrong.**

32:5–6. The song of Moses is set against a future day when Israel will defect to pagan gods, with a backdrop of its past unfaithfulness in the matter of the golden calf (cp. Exod. 32). In contrast to Yahweh's consistency, Israel **acted corruptly toward him**, exhibiting the traits of **a warped and crooked generation.**

32:7–9. The first step toward repentance would come when they remembered the days of old. Israel's possession of her **inheritance** was due to the **boundaries** Yahweh **set up** for the people. He took such an interest in them because he chose them as **his allotted inheritance.**

32:10–14. Israel became Yahweh's inheritance solely through his grace, because the nation could not commend itself to him through its own merit. God found Israel **in a desert land**, in **a barren and howling waste.** This appears to describe the people at Sinai after the miraculous events of the Red Sea. Even though God had delivered the people from slavery, they were little more than a helpless and disorganized mob until he began to shape them into a distinct people. In the manner of **an eagle** concerned for its **young**, the Lord **led** the infant people. They had not yet experienced the enticements of **foreign** gods.

From the barren wasteland of the Sinai, God protected Israel on its way into the Transjordan area, making the people **ride on the heights of the land.** God supernaturally provided for them, bringing them food and drink from **the rock** and providing them victories over the king of **Bashan** and entitlement to his property. Israel enjoyed **curds and milk from herd and flock** and the product of vineyards they had not planted. They knew his grace and favor every day.

32:15–18. And in response to Yahweh's kindnesses, what did Israel do? **Jeshurun** (an ironic title for Israel meaning "the upright one") **grew fat and kicked.** Instead of responding in love and gratitude, the nation **abandoned the God who made him and rejected the Rock his Savior.** By their attachment to pagan gods they **sacrificed to demons, deserted** the God of their fathers, and **forgot the God** who had given them **birth.** Although Israel had also turned to foreign gods at Moab (cp. Num. 25), the song anticipated worse days to come.

32:19–21a. Israel's defection caused the Lord to act in justice toward his **sons and daughters** and to hide his **face from them.** Because they proved to be **a perverse generation (children who are unfaithful)**, he determined to detach himself and **see what their end** would be. In violation of the covenant, Israel made Yahweh **jealous** by their devotion to **worthless idols.** His jealousy stemmed not from the imagined virtues of pagan deities, but from his recognition that Israel's actions insulted him and guaranteed that their lives would be filled with hardship.

32:21b-25. Israel's future defection would be remedied by using the technique of jealousy. Following the coming of Christ, Yahweh would **make them envious** by the Gentiles, those who were **not a people.** Until that happened, however, Yahweh's judgments would have to be experienced: the **fire** of his wrath, calamities, arrows, famine, deadly plague, wild beasts, and **vipers**. Even worse, **the sword** of foreign armies would **make them childless**, and **terror** would **reign** upon young and old, men and women alike.

32:26–30. Still, Yahweh would refuse to send total devastation upon Israel. Although he was tempted to **scatter them** and **blot out their memory**, he considered **the taunt of the enemy** and decided against it. That he should even have considered such judgment proved that Israel was **a nation without sense** or **discernment**. They had every advantage until the day **their Rock** sold them into misery because of their unfaithfulness.

32:31–35. The rejection of Israel would not be complete, however. Yahweh was not like the deities of the nations, as even their **enemies** had to **concede**. The vine or life force of the pagan idols was rooted in the soil of moral degradation and impotency and yielded the expected poisonous fruit. Just as Sodom and Gomorrah were overthrown in a moment, so pagan idols would be in the affection of Israel. God was keeping **in reserve** his purposes to eliminate the **deadly** competition for Israel's affection. In due time the **foot of the idols** would **slip** and the **day of disaster** would come **upon them**.

32:36–39. Yahweh's purposes for his own people were different, however. He would **judge** them with **compassion**. These acts of mercy would not come, however, until the time when he saw their strength was gone and their hope of rescue from idols had vanished. Then and only then he would taunt them by pointing to the impotency of the gods who **drank the wine** of Israel's **drink offerings**. When all Israel's confidence in such paganism was exhausted, Yahweh would convince them that **there is no god besides me**.

32:40–43. The song of Moses concluded with Yahweh taking a fresh oath of commitment to Israel. He lifted his **hand to heaven** to **declare** that he would **take vengeance** on his **adversaries**. The latter, in this case, refers to **enemy** nations that would enslave Israel. The heads of the enemy leaders would roll and Yahweh alone would be triumphant. As a result of this victory, the rest of the nations will be called on to **rejoice** with his people. He will take steps to restore **his land** and his **people** to his favor.

B The Sermon of Moses (32:44–47)

SUPPORTING IDEA: *Nothing is more important—indeed, more life-giving—than for Israel to internalize the words of Moses.*

32:44–45. The song, with the help of **Joshua son of Nun**, Moses **spoke** in the hearing of all Israel. It was not enough, of course, just to recite the content. Moses proceeded to apply its lessons to the Israelites.

32:46–47. The lawgiver insisted that his people **take to heart all the words** he had been declaring. Not only their fate but that of their **children** depended on how well they did. They were to **obey carefully all the words of this law** (this last expression probably refers to the covenant stipulations of Deut. 5–26). By carefully heeding them, Israel would **live long in the land**.

C The Sentence of Moses (32:48-52)

SUPPORTING IDEA: *Moses faces the consequences of his own rebellion, because God is no respecter of persons.*

32:48-50. The price that would be paid for flouting God's word would now be paid by **Moses** himself. On the day he finished the song, Moses was directed to **go up into the Abarim Range to Mount Nebo**. Moses would be allowed to **view Canaan** from a distance, and then he would **die and be gathered** to his people.

32:51-52. Moses would suffer this fate because he and his brother Aaron **broke faith** with God **in the presence of the Israelites** at the waters of **Meribah Kadesh** (cp. Num. 20). Their offense was not a wholesale rebellion but an act of impatience. Still, because spiritual leaders incur a stricter judgment (cp. Jas. 3:1), Moses would **see the land only from a distance**.

MAIN IDEA REVIEW: *In the light of Yahweh's greatness and faithfulness toward Israel, the people learn a song that will testify to them even in the dark days of wayward behavior.*

III. CONCLUSION

What Kind of Song?

We are taught in Scripture that God is infinite. His depths cannot be reached: "Oh, the depth of the riches of the wisdom and knowledge of God! How unsearchable his judgments, and his paths beyond tracing out!" (Rom. 11:33). Just because his judgments are unsearchable, however, is no reason not to search for them—or him. Moses told Israel that in the words he had spoken life could be found and enjoyed.

Becoming a Christian believer is crucial, but this is only the beginning of the process. Conversion gives you the spiritual equipment to pursue a quest that will last throughout your earthly life as well as eternity. Conversion puts you in the category of people who are able to seek God in earnest.

During an interview with a group of astronauts, the crew was asked, "What do you think is the single most important key to successful space travel?" One astronaut offered the following response: "The secret of traveling in space is to take your own atmosphere with you."

That is what it takes to seek God. You take your atmosphere (God's Word) with you wherever you go. You recognize that there is more of God to know, and you are determined to know all of him you can.

Moses was forced to write a sad song about the history of Israel's relationship with God. If someone wrote a song about your relationship with God, would it be sad or joyful?

Prayer

PRINCIPLES

- In a world of constant change, God alone is the Rock upon which to build a life.
- Although the world places a premium on the latest things, some realities are discovered by looking into the past.
- Many people find spiritual growth possible only when times are hard; prosperity tends to promote complacency.
- Demons lie behind much of the world's pagan worship systems.

APPLICATIONS

- Ask God to give you opportunities to share the blessings of his work in your life with a friend.
- Don't lose opportunities to see God at work in your life by being stubborn.
- Set your heart on learning God's Word.

IV. LIFE APPLICATION

The Sorrows of Mount Nebo

Many people have had to share Moses' sorrow from atop Mount Nebo, wistfully contemplating how things might have turned out differently. Moses forfeited the experience of entering the promised land because of a brief moment of anger. He let down his guard, and sin robbed him of an experience that might have been his.

It is far better to recognize that all of life is sacred. *Now* is the defining moment in every life. Legendary Green Bay Packers coach Vince Lombardi used to prepare his players for a game by telling them, "Every play *is* the football game. One missed tackle, one missed block, one dropped pass, and we never know how things might have turned out differently. You have to give effort on every play as though this one in particular will make all the difference."

We as Christians cannot regain tomorrow what we have lost through a brief moment of spiritual insanity or inattention today. We have to face each spiritual choice with alertness and spiritual vigor, for in that choice may be our lives. In the words of John Greenleaf Whittier, "For of all sad words of tongue or pen, the saddest are these, 'It might have been!'"

V. PRAYER

Father, thank you for your Word. Grant that I might treasure it for what it is—your love letter to me. Help me see its values, pursue its virtues, and love its author. Amen.

Deuteronomy 32

VI. DEEPER DISCOVERIES

A. My Anger (32:21–22)

The Hebrew term used here is literally, "my nostrils." Perhaps it reflects the fact that a person's nose turns red when he is angry. The figure is a common one in the Hebrew Bible, and it occurs about thirteen times in Deuteronomy.

B. You Broke Faith (32:51)

This Hebrew verb is used elsewhere of a wife's unfaithfulness to her husband: "If a man's wife goes astray and is unfaithful to him" (Num. 5:12). It also appears in the account of a misunderstanding between the tribes: "The whole assembly of the LORD says: 'How could you break faith with the God of Israel like this?'" (Josh. 22:16).

VII. TEACHING OUTLINE

A. INTRODUCTION
1. Lead Story: Wonderful Things
2. Context: Moses teaches Israel the words to a song that will describe their wayward inclinations. But the song will also bear witness of Yahweh's loving intentions toward his people.
3. Transition: Although God's heart is grieved when his children wander, he never stops loving them. They can avoid much sorrow, however, by their faithful obedience.

B. COMMENTARY
1. The Song of Moses (32:1–43)
2. The Sermon of Moses (32:44–47)
3. The Sentence of Moses (32:48–52)

C. CONCLUSION: THE SORROWS OF MOUNT NEBO

VIII. ISSUES FOR DISCUSSION

1. In what ways does God resemble a rock?
2. Why does prosperity often lead to spiritual neglect or rebellion?
3. Is jealousy always a sinful impulse? Why or why not?
4. Why would God decide to take an oath (v. 40)?

Deuteronomy 33

The Riches of His Grace

I. **INTRODUCTION**
The Constant Rooster

II. **COMMENTARY**
A verse-by-verse explanation of the chapter.

III. **CONCLUSION**
High-Tech Arachnid
An overview of the principles and applications from the chapter.

IV. **LIFE APPLICATION**
Sneering at Doctrine
Melding the chapter to life.

V. **PRAYER**
Tying the chapter to life with God.

VI. **DEEPER DISCOVERIES**
Historical, geographical, and grammatical enrichment of the commentary.

VII. **TEACHING OUTLINE**
Suggested step-by-step group study of the chapter.

VIII. **ISSUES FOR DISCUSSION**
Zeroing the chapter in on daily life.

Deuteronomy 33

> Quote
>
> "With the goodness of God to desire our highest welfare, the wisdom of God to plan it, and the power of God to achieve it, what do we lack?"
>
> A. W. Tozer

Deuteronomy 33

IN A NUTSHELL

*Even if Israel's inclinations are suspect, the nation itself will not be able to escape God's gracious intentions toward them.

The Riches of His Grace

I. INTRODUCTION

The Constant Rooster

The noted British preacher Charles Haddon Spurgeon was walking through the countryside with a friend. The two noticed a barn with a weather vane on the roof. Part of the metalwork of the weather vane proclaimed, "God Is Love." Spurgeon observed to his friend that he thought the weather vane was a poor location to enshrine such a sublime message. "After all," Spurgeon noted, "weather vanes are changeable, but God's love is constant."

His friend demurred: "I don't agree with you, Charles. You misunderstood the meaning. That sign is indicating a truth: regardless of which way the wind blows, God is love."

Israel was poised to enter the promised land and the nation would have to rely on God's constant love. As though to anticipate their uncertainty and timidity, Moses provided an encouraging rebuke, showing how God would bless Israel not because of the nation's infidelity but in spite of it.

II. COMMENTARY

The Riches of His Grace

MAIN IDEA: *Although the course of Israel's future will prove rocky, the nation belongs to God, and he will bless them.*

A Prologue to the Blessing of the Tribes of Israel (33:1–5)

SUPPORTING IDEA: *Moses praises Yahweh as the one who made Israel his own at Sinai.*

33:1. Although Moses had taught Israel a song that emphasized their fickleness and tendency to forsake Yahweh, the Book of Deuteronomy concludes positively with a series of blessings on the tribes of Israel. **Moses** is described as **the man of God**, a title often used as the designation for a prophet (Judg. 13:6,8; 1 Sam. 9:6; 1 Kgs. 12:22). Outside of this text, the expression is used of Moses only in Joshua 14:6 and in the heading of Psalm 90. Although Deuteronomy 33 contains the words of Moses, the third person often is used in the narrative, and it may be that Joshua or a designated scribe transcribed his words.

33:2–5. The Lord is praised for his dramatic and powerful appearance to Israel. God revealed himself at **Sinai** with **myriads of holy ones**. Such language normally describes angels (Ps. 89:5,7; Isa. 13:3; 1 Thess. 3:13), and that is likely the intent here. Although angels are not described in Exodus as present during the Sinai events, the New Testament affirms their involvement in the transmission of the law of God (cp. Gal. 3:19; Heb. 2:2). Those angels **bow down** at Yahweh's **feet** and **receive instruction**. **Moses** has now given **the law** to Israel as a prized **possession** so the nation's **people** might know him as well. Yahweh was related to Israel (**Jeshurun**; see comments on 32:15) as **king** at the time **the leaders** and **tribes** assembled at Sinai.

B Pronouncements of Blessing on the Tribes of Israel (33:6–25)

SUPPORTING IDEA: *Much in the manner of Jacob of old, and speaking as a prophet, Moses prays for and blesses the tribes of Israel.*

33:6. The order of blessings on the tribes does not follow the order of any of the other listings of the tribes. No two lists, in fact, follow the same order. (For the reason behind Simeon's omission, see "Deeper Discoveries.")

As in the case of Jacob's patriarchal blessing (cp. Gen. 49), however, **Reuben** the firstborn heads the list. Moses asks that Reuben **live** and multiply, something that was in jeopardy when Reuben engaged in fornication with Jacob's concubine Bilhah (cp. Gen. 49:4).

33:7. Moses prayed that **Judah**, the tribe that Jacob predicted would eventually rule (and the tribe from which the Lord Jesus descended), might be returned **to his people**. It is difficult to assign the answer to this prayer to a specific historical situation. Since Judah often led the tribes into battle (cp. Judg. 1:1–2), the prayer may cover multiple military situations, a view that is supported by the reference to **foes**.

33:8–9. Although **Levi** and Simeon had been combined in the blessing of Jacob (Gen. 49:5–7), by the time of Deuteronomy Levi had distinguished itself as a tribe. They were the caretakers of the holy things, including the **Thummim and Urim**, the "perfections and lights" that together formed a divinely given method of determining Yahweh's will (cp. Exod. 28:30; 1 Sam. 14:3,18; 23:9). Levi's **favored** position had come about **at the waters of Meribah** (cp. Exod. 17:1–7) when the Levites had set aside family loyalties (cp. v. 9) and had proven their faithfulness to the **covenant**, as they did again later in the episode of the golden calf (cp. Exod. 32:26–29).

33:10–11. The supreme mark of God's favor toward Levi, however, lay in his stewardship of the **precepts** of the Lord. These laws the Levites would teach and would also offer **incense** and **offerings** to God. Moses prayed for a skillful fulfillment of his responsibilities and for protection from Levi's **foes**.

33:12. The youngest of Jacob's offspring, **Benjamin** had known the secure protection of God through the unnerving events of the descent into Egypt (cp. Gen. 38–48). Moses prayed that Benjamin's descendants would likewise **rest secure** in God's future protection, much like a choice son riding upon or between a father's **shoulders**.

33:13–17. Again in this paragraph the tribes of **Ephraim** and **Manasseh** (cp. v. 17) are combined under the name of their father **Joseph**. Moses prayed for the prosperity of both tribes, asking God to provide **dew from heaven** and subterranean **waters** so the people might know his choicest **gifts of the earth**. In doing so, the people would recognize that they were receiving **the favor** of Yahweh, **him who dwelt in the burning bush** (cp. Exod. 3:1–3). In this the tribes would bask in the inherited glory of **Joseph . . . the prince among his brothers**. In his blessing, Moses reaffirmed the Jacobean preference for Ephraim (**ten thousands**) over Manasseh (**thousands**).

33:18–19. The two youngest sons of Leah, **Zebulun** and **Issachar**, are also treated together. They would inherit perhaps the choicest of Yahweh's land grants, comprising much of what was later called the Galilee, including the Valley of Jezreel, the nation's breadbasket. Moses predicted that they would **feast on the abundance of the seas**. The territory of Zebulon contains Israel's only natural harbor (at the modern city of Haifa), but the feasting in question could refer to goods gained by trade with seafaring nations, **treasures** exchanged for the tribes' abundant foodstuffs.

33:20–21. Yahweh is described here as **he who enlarges Gad's domain**. The tribe is described as one who lived east of the Jordan **like a lion, tearing at arm or head**. Gad's territory came from land that had belonged to Sihon and Og and was gained by conquest, and Gad **chose the best land for himself; the leader's portion**. When the two and one-half tribes asked for territory east of the Jordan River and outside the promised portion, their request was granted, with the stipulation that they fight until the other tribes had gained their property as well (cp. Num. 32:16–27). In this matter Gad **carried out the LORD's righteous will**.

33:22. The tribe of Dan is likened to **a lion's cub, springing out** of the territory **of Bashan**, apparently because of his martial vigor. The last location is used not because Dan settled there but because Bashan was a place where lion cubs were more commonly seen. Dan's territorial allotment lay in the extreme southwest portion of the promised land adjacent to the Philistines (Samson was a Danite).

33:23. The tribe of **Naphtali**, whose territory lay along the westward edge of **the lake** of Kinnereth or Galilee, is promised God's abundance and blessing.

33:24–25. Asher, whose name means **blessed**, would be **favored by his brothers** in the years to come. Asher's prosperity would be of such a magnitude that he could be lavish with such an expensive item as **oil**, which was

Deuteronomy 33:26–28

normally used in anointing the head (cp. Ps. 23:5; Matt. 6:17), not the **feet**. During the coming years Asher would know the security of **iron** and **bronze** bolted **gates** and **strength** adequate for each test.

C Praise and Blessing Concerning God and Israel (33:26–29)

SUPPORTING IDEA: *Moses exults in the generosity and power of Yahweh and pronounces the people blessed because of their association with him.*

33:26–28. Yahweh, **the God of Jeshurun**, is unique **in his majesty**. As **the eternal God** and the **refuge** of his people, his **everlasting arms** would support them against all their enemies. The coming battles against entrenched foes should hold no terrors for Israel, since God had determined that the people would be **secure in a land of grain and new wine**.

33:29. Contemplation of such divine excellencies caused Moses to rejoice in Israel's association with Yahweh, who had already proven himself **as a shield and helper**. Now Israel would see his **glorious sword** unsheathed as he went before them in battle against their **enemies**.

MAIN IDEA REVIEW: *Although the course of Israel's future will prove rocky, the nation belongs to God, and he will bless them.*

III. CONCLUSION

High-Tech Arachnid

The European water spider lives at the bottom of a lake, but it breathes air. This amazing creature does a somersault on the surface of the water, catches a bubble of air, holds it over the breathing holes in the middle of its body while it swims to the bottom of the lake, and spins a silk web among the seaweed. Then it ascends and brings down bubble after bubble until a little balloon of air is formed where it can live and eat and mate. Its brain is about the size of the head of a straight pin.

We properly draw a lesson from such astonishing technology about God's creative wonder, but we dare not miss an even more important point. If God takes such care to provide for spiders, how can we doubt that he will take care of his children? Yet many of us spend anxious nights worrying whether he will provide for our needs.

PRINCIPLES

- God's love does not depend on the current spiritual condition of those whom he loves.

- One of the greatest testimonials to God's love is his provision of his Word.
- Spiritual leadership ought to be given to those who have proven themselves under stress.
- The spiritual heritage of the godly lives on after they are gone.

APPLICATIONS

- Before panicking at some threat, ask God to give you a calmness that is born of trust in him.
- Look for an opportunity to teach God's covenant to someone who doesn't know him.
- Be satisfied with God's provision for you.
- In the future, develop a tendency toward gratitude rather than anxiety.

IV. LIFE APPLICATION

Sneering at Doctrine

Joseph Parker, the famous preacher of Victorian London, noted that the doctrines that men were inclined to dismiss as "old-fashioned" managed to create missionary societies and Sunday schools. They built orphanages, hospitals, and brought an end to the slave trade. The doctrines of historic Christianity gave children new value, mothers new hope, and fathers new accountability.

He wrote: "We cannot first sneer at the doctrine and then claim its infinite beneficence, nor can we borrow its socialism that we may quench its inspiration. Let us be very careful how we give up trees that have borne such fruit, and in whose leaves there has been such healing."

V. PRAYER

Father, your generosity overwhelms me; your constant goodness amazes me. Help me to turn this amazement into worship and your goodness into testimony. Amen.

VI. DEEPER DISCOVERIES

A. The Missing Tribe (33:6–25)

Simeon's name does not appear among the list of tribes who are blessed in this portion of Deuteronomy 33. This may be because the Simeonites were gradually assimilated into the territory of the tribe of Judah. They never sustained a distinct tribal territory except for certain cities in Judah (Josh 19:1–9). At least some of the tribe of Simeon did maintain their tribal identity, however: "Shimei [a descendant of Simeon] had sixteen sons and six daughters, but his brothers did not have many children; so their entire clan did not become as numerous as the people of Judah" (1 Chr. 4:27).

B. Thummim and Urim (33:8)

In every other occurrence of these two terms, the order is reversed. How the urim and thummim ("lights and perfections") were used to determine God's will remains a mystery. They formed part of the breastpiece of the high priest, which was in turn part of the ephod that was worn over his shoulders. (For the biblical description of the details of these items, see Exod. 28:6–30.)

VII. TEACHING OUTLINE

A. INTRODUCTION

1. Lead Story: The Constant Rooster
2. Context: Moses encourages the wayward people of God by blessing them as a whole and their individual tribes as well.
3. Transition: Man may break promise after promise, but God is constant and faithful to his affirmations of blessing.

B. COMMENTARY

1. Prologue to the Blessing of the Tribes of Israel (33:1–5)
2. Pronouncements of Blessing on the Tribes of Israel (33:6–25)
3. Praise and Blessing Concerning God and Israel (33:26–29)

C. CONCLUSION: SNEERING AT DOCTRINE

VIII. ISSUES FOR DISCUSSION

1. In what ways does the law of God benefit and distinguish people who possess it?
2. Outside of purely military conflict, how does God protect his people from their enemies?
3. In what ways is God a refuge to those who know him?

Deuteronomy 34

Epitaph for a Giant

- **I. INTRODUCTION**
  John Harper's Testimony

- **II. COMMENTARY**
  A verse-by-verse explanation of the chapter.

- **III. CONCLUSION**
  What's Your Epitaph?
  An overview of the principles and applications from the chapter.

- **IV. LIFE APPLICATION**
  Only Fourteen
  Melding the chapter to life.

- **V. PRAYER**
  Tying the chapter to life with God.

- **VI. DEEPER DISCOVERIES**
  Historical, geographical, and grammatical enrichment of the commentary.

- **VII. TEACHING OUTLINE**
  Suggested step-by-step group study of the chapter.

- **VIII. ISSUES FOR DISCUSSION**
  Zeroing the chapter in on daily life.

Deuteronomy 34

> **Quote**
>
> "Faith, mighty faith, the promise sees,
>
> And looks to that alone;
>
> Laughs at life's impossibilities,
>
> And cries, It shall be done!"
>
> Charles Wesley

IN A NUTSHELL

Moses dies, leaving behind the testimony of a profound knowledge of God and great spiritual usefulness.

Epitaph for a Giant

I. INTRODUCTION

John Harper's Testimony

In April 1912, John Harper boarded the *Titanic* along with his six-year-old daughter, Nana, as the first stage of a trip to Moody Church in Chicago where he was scheduled to be the guest preacher for the next three months. When the *Titanic* struck the iceberg, Harper made sure his daughter was placed into one of the lifeboats and then undertook what would be the last evangelistic work of his brief life. When the ship began to slip beneath the waters of the frigid Atlantic, hundreds of passengers jumped or fell into the water. Harper began to swim from one passenger to another, appealing to individuals to trust Christ.

Harper asked one young man who was sitting on a piece of floating debris, "Are you saved?"

"No," the man replied.

Harper then shouted the words of Acts 16:31: "Believe on the Lord Jesus Christ, and thou shalt be saved" (KJV). The man did not answer, and a moment later John Harper, teeth chattering in the frightful cold, moved away to talk to others.

Later the current brought the two men back together. Again Harper asked, "Are you saved?"

Once again, the young man answered in the negative.

With his last breath, Harper urged the man, "Believe on the Lord Jesus Christ, and thou shalt be saved." No one saw the evangelist after that. Although Harper never knew it, the young man had decided to respond to his last appeal. Not long afterward, the new convert was rescued by a lifeboat.

At a *Titanic* survivors meeting in Canada some years later, this man gave his testimony recounting how John Harper had led him to Jesus Christ. He explained, "I was John Harper's last convert."

Many Christians are merely treading water, waiting for their inevitable end. God wants us to be remembered for the way we made him known to a dying world.

Deuteronomy 34:1-3

II. COMMENTARY

Epitaph for a Giant

MAIN IDEA: *Although Moses was denied the privilege of entering the promised land, his uniqueness as a prophet and servant of God remained unparalleled for generations.*

A The Vision of Moses (34:1–4)

SUPPORTING IDEA: *Yahweh grants Moses a personal vision of the land of promise.*

34:1–3. In keeping with divine instructions, **Moses climbed Mount Nebo** from the **plains of Moab** where the tents of Israel were located. From this overlook he viewed **the whole land** with what must have been a mixture of satisfaction and disappointment. Although he had done well to bring Israel to the verge of what once seemed an impossible aspiration, he would not be sharing the joy of actually setting foot in the land because of his disobedience (cp. Num. 20).

The description of the land begins looking due north (**from Gilead to Dan**) and then swings westward to **Naphtali**, then steadily southward through **Ephraim and Manasseh, Judah,** and **the western** (Mediterranean) **sea**, ending with **the Negev** and **the Valley of Jericho**, elsewhere called the Arabah, southward. It should be remembered that the tribal designations are anachronistic, since the allotments to each tribe were made some years later. It seems highly likely that this chapter was written some years after the death of Moses, perhaps by Joshua in connection with the writing of the book that bears his name.

34:4. The promised land was not mere geography, however. It was the fulfillment of an **oath** that Yahweh had made beginning six centuries before to **Abraham**, then **Isaac**, and finally **Jacob**. This promise testified of God's faithfulness, and the importance of faithfulness on the part of those who claim allegiance to him. As one who had violated his commission to sanctify Yahweh in the eyes of the covenant community, Moses was able to **see** the land but not to **cross over into it**. Although many in the valley below him had done far worse, Moses was a leader, and God's standards for him were higher.

B The Death of Moses (34:5–8)

SUPPORTING IDEA: *The death and burial of Moses as well as his mourning period were appropriate for one so highly esteemed*

34:5–6. Although Moses apparently died there on Mount Nebo, he was not buried there. Instead, Yahweh personally cared (through the archangel

Michael; cp. Jude 9) for his body and **buried him** not on the mountain but in the valley opposite Beth Peor. The location was unknown at the time Deuteronomy 34 was written and remains so today. The wisdom of the secret depositing of the lawgiver's body is apparent. No shrine covers it and no pilgrimages are made to it. That would have pleased Moses, who lived not for the exaltation of himself but for the glorification of the one he served.

34:7. The death of Moses was not, however, the result a weakened or decrepit physical condition. Although he **was a hundred and twenty years old when he died**, his health was still good. **His eyes were not weak nor his strength gone.** Israel's entry into the land and his exclusion from it—in other words, the completion of his work—were the causes of his death.

34:8. In recognition of his status, the Israelites **grieved for Moses . . . thirty days**, as they had with Aaron (Num. 20:29). Such a proper time of **mourning** does not issue from a deficiency of hope in the resurrection but from a proper recognition of the loss of those who remain: "Godly men buried Stephen and mourned deeply for him" (Acts 8:2).

C The Testimony of Moses (34:9–12)

> **SUPPORTING IDEA:** Although Moses' work was assumed by a capable successor, he had no peer as a prophet and servant of God.

34:9. Part of finishing the work Moses had to do was providing for its continuation. That work was now transferred to the capable hands of **Joshua**, who **was filled with the spirit of wisdom** because of his ordination at the **hands** of Moses. Joshua did not receive new statutes and ordinances, but he urged Israel to do **what the LORD had commanded Moses**.

34:10–12. The failure of Moses to enter the land cast only a small shadow on an otherwise unique life. As the author of the chapter notes, **since his death no prophet had risen in Israel like Moses, whom the LORD knew face to face** (cp. Num. 12:6–7). He left a legacy of **miraculous signs and wonders** performed in Egypt and in the wilderness that were accomplished publicly, **in the sight of all Israel**.

> **MAIN IDEA REVIEW:** Although Moses was denied the privilege of entering the promised land, his uniqueness as a prophet and servant of God remained unparalleled for generations.

III. CONCLUSION

What's Your Epitaph?

The cynic Ambrose Bierce once defined an epitaph as "an inscription on a tomb, showing that virtues acquired by death have a retroactive effect." While

Deuteronomy 34

some evidence exists to support this jaded point of view, many gravestones yield fascinating information about deceased people or their survivors. A case in point is the epitaph of John Newton, author of the hymn "Amazing Grace." Written by the former slave trader several years before his death, it crystallizes how the man thought of himself: "John Newton, Clerk, once an infidel and libertine, was, by the rich mercy of our Lord and Saviour, Jesus Christ, preserved, restored, pardoned and appointed to preach the faith he had long labored to destroy."

Moses' epitaph was not written in stone but on the pages of Scripture and in the loving memory of believing people everywhere. When you are gone, what testimony will you leave behind?

PRINCIPLES

- God never forgets a promise.
- Our lives will last as long as God has something for us to do.
- Christians can mourn, but not as those who have no hope (cp. 1 Thess. 4:13).
- Training leaders is part of the work of discipling.

APPLICATIONS

- Never lose sight of the kingdom toward which you are headed.
- Don't allow yielding to sinful emotions to cost you and others possession of a full reward.
- If you aspire to leadership, place yourself under the hands of the writers of Scripture and learn wisdom.
- Point other people to the truth of Scripture, and they will follow you gladly.

IV. LIFE APPLICATION

Only Fourteen

Christine Tinling, former missionary to China, heard the story of an elderly leper who came to the door of the Foochow colony asking for a place to die. He had nothing—no money, no relatives, and almost no clothes. He wore only part of a burlap sack that he had converted into a loincloth.

The missionaries bound up his wounds, fed him, and gave him medical care. A local pastor came to visit the man and shared the good news of Christ with him. When the leper was asked if he would like to receive Jesus, he refused, explaining, "No, Jesus gave himself for me, but I have nothing to give him in return for a gift like that."

The pastor explained, "He wants no gift except yourself."

The leper continued to resist, saying, "How could he possibly want an ill-smelling, rotten old leper like me?"

Eventually, the light broke through and he became a Christian. As the new believer undertook the study of the Scriptures, he began to go from room to room, sharing the gospel with his fellow sufferers. He continued his evangelistic work until his feet became so diseased that he could no longer walk.

As he lay on his deathbed, the leper apologized to the missionaries for the feebleness of his spiritual efforts, explaining, "I only got fourteen." He had led fourteen of his fellow lepers to Christ!

That poor leper's effort puts the lie to many of our excuses. We have fewer obstacles and more opportunities, yet our spiritual bequests are often considerably smaller. When we stand before Jesus Christ to have our works examined, what gift will we present to him?

V. PRAYER

Father, thank you for giving us a place of testimony in the world. Help us to take our opportunities seriously and to become people who will be missed when we're gone. Amen.

VI. DEEPER DISCOVERIES

A. Pisgah (34:1)

The term *Pisgah* is often translated as a proper noun and the name of a place, but this is not the only option. The Hebrew noun means "ridge" or "range," and it may refer in this verse to the peak of the mountain ridge in Moab that runs along the Jordan River valley.

B. Dan (34:1)

This term is usually understood to refer to the city and area (formerly known as Laish; cp. Judg. 18:27) conquered by the Danites during the later period of the judges. However, that would have been off the expected route of Abraham in Genesis 14:14, and does not fit that well with the description here. It may be that Dan in this verse refers to an otherwise unknown town in the region of Gilead.

VII. TEACHING OUTLINE

A. INTRODUCTION

1. Lead Story: John Harper's Testimony

Deuteronomy 34

2. Context: Moses is given a view of the promised land and then dies. Although he is absent from Israel's national life, he leaves behind a unique and enduring testimony and influence.
3. Transition: Moses stands as an example of the difference one life can make. Christians who live well can exercise a profound influence upon others.

B. COMMENTARY
1. The Vision of Moses (34:1–4)
2. The Death of Moses (34:5–8)
3. The Testimony of Moses (34:9–12)

C. CONCLUSION: ONLY FOURTEEN

VIII. ISSUES FOR DISCUSSION

1. Why do you think God buried Moses where his body would never be found?
2. Do you think Christians generally hold healthy attitudes toward grieving for a lost loved one? Why or why not?
3. Why did God call attention to the spirit of *wisdom* that Joshua received? Why not power or some other benefit?
4. What do you think ran through Moses' mind as he viewed the promised land?

Bibliography

Aharoni, Yohann, and Michael Avi-Yonah. *The Macmillan Bible Atlas.* Rev. ed. New York: Macmillan Publishing Company, 1968.

Allen, Ron, and Gordon Borror. *Worship: Rediscovering the Missing Jewel.* Sisters, Oreg: Multnomah Publishers, 1982.

Aristides. *The Apology of Aristides.* Translated from the Greek and from the Syriac version in parallel columns by D. M. Kay. Online on March 31, 2002 at hhtp//www.ocf.org/Orthodox Page/reading/St. Pachomius/aristides.html.

Baly, Denis. *The Geography of the Bible.* New York: Harper & Row Publishers, 1957.

Beitzel, Barry J. *The Moody Atlas of Bible Lands.* Chicago: Moody Press, 1985.

Bright, John. *A History of Israel.* W. L. Jenkins, 1959. Third edition. Philadelphia: Westminster Press, 1981.

Bullinger, E. W. *Figures of Speech Used in the Bible.* Grand Rapids: Baker Book House, 1968 [reprint].

Campbell E. F. Jr., and D. N. Freedman. *The Biblical Archaeologist Reader 3.* Pittsburgh, 1955.

Childs, Brevard S. *Introduction to the Old Testament as Scripture.* Philadelphia: Fortress Press, 1979.

Cohen, A., ed. *The Soncino Chumash: The Five Books of Moses with Haphtaroth.* London: The Soncino Press, 1947.

Craige, Peter C. *The Book of Deuteronomy.* The New International Commentary on the Old Testament. Grand Rapids: William B. Eerdmans Publishing Company, 1976.

Driver, S. R. *A Critical and Exegetical Commentary on Deuteronomy.* International Critical Commentary. Edinburgh: T & T Clark, 1895.

Edersheim, Alfred. *Old Testament Biblical History.* Wilmington, Del.: Associated Publishers & Authors, n.d.

Ford, Leighton. *The Christian Persuader: The Urgency of Evangelism in Today's World.* Minneapolis, Minn.: WorldWide Publications, 1966, 1988.

Harrison R. K. *Introduction to the Old Testament: With a Comprehensive Review of Old Testament Studies and a Special Supplement on the Apocrypha.* Grand Rapids: William B. Eerdmans Publishing Company, 1969.

Keil, C. F., and F. Delitzsch. "The Fifth Book of Moses (Deuteronomy)." Vol. 1: *The Pentateuch: Three Volumes in One.* Translated by James Martin. Commentary on the Old Testament. 10 vols. N.d.; Reprint ed., Grand Rapids: Wm. B. Eerdmans Publishing Co., 1973.

Kline, M. G. *Treaty of the Great King: The Covenant Structure of Deuteronomy: Studies and Commentary.* Grand Rapids: Wm. B. Eerdmans Publishing Co., 1963.

Bibliography

―――. *The Structure of Biblical Authority.* Grand Rapids: Wm. B. Eerdmans Publishing Co., 1972.

Lewis, C. S. "The Laws of Nature." In *God in the Dock.* Grand Rapids: William B. Eerdmans Publishing Company, 1970.

McIntosh, Douglas. *The Golden Rule: Love Full Circle.* Review and Study Guide by James S. Bell Jr. Chicago: Moody Press, 1999.

―――. *The War Within You: Overcoming the Obstacles to Godly Character.* Chicago: Moody Press, 2001.

Merrill, Eugene H. *Kingdom of Priests: A History of Old Testament Israel.* Grand Rapids: Baker Book House, 1987.

―――. *Deuteronomy.* Vol. 4. The New American Commentary. Nashville: Broadman & Holman, Publishers.

Miller, Patrick D. *Deuteronomy.* Interpretation: A Bible Commentary for Teaching and Preaching. Louisville: John Knox Press, 1990.

Morgan, Robert J. *From This Verse.* Nashville: Thomas Nelson Publishers, 1998.

―――. *Real Stories for the Soul.* Nashville: Thomas Nelson Publishers, 2000.

―――. *More Real Stories for the Soul.* Nashville: Thomas Nelson Publishers, 2000.

Pfeiffer, Charles F., and Howard F. Vos. *The Wycliffe Historical Geography of Bible Lands.* Chicago: Moody Press, 1967.

Philbrick, Herbert A. *I Led Three Lives.* Quoted in *Illustration Digest* (November 1990–January 1991).

Sterrett, T. Norton. *How to Understand Your Bible.* Downers Grove, Ill.: InterVarsity Press, 1977.

Tan, Amy. *The Kitchen God's Wife.* Quoted in Raymond McHenry, "Anger." *In Other Words* [disk illustration service] (October 2000). Available by subscription from In Other Words, 6130 Barrington, Beaumont, TX 77706.

Tenney, Merrill C., ed. *The Zondervan Pictorial Encyclopedia of the Bible.* 5 vols. Grand Rapids: Zondervan Publishing House, 1975.

Thompson, J. A. *Deuteronomy: An Introduction and Commentary.* Vol. 5. The Tyndale Old Testament Commentaries. Downers Grove: InterVarsity Press, 1974.

Troeger, Thomas. *The Parable of Ten Preachers.* Nashville: Abingdon Press, 1992.

Tson, Joseph. *Pastoral Renewal.* Quoted in "Living Sacrifices." *Leadership,* 8, no. 4 (fall 1987).

Wood, Leon. *A Survey of Israel's History.* Grand Rapids: Zondervan Publishing House, 1970.

Wright, Christopher. *Deuteronomy.* New International Biblical Commentary. Peabody, Mass.: Hendrickson Publishers, 1996.

Glossary

Abib—The first month in the Hebrew calendar (March-April); also called Nisan.

acacia—A tree similar to the hawthorn, featuring gnarled branches and thorns, and possessing a close-grained, durable wood, which God commanded to be used in the construction of the tabernacle and the ark of the covenant.

adultery—A subcategory of *fornication,* the general term in Scripture for sexual sin. Adultery was committed when at least one partner in sexual activity was married to someone else. This term is often used figuratively in Scripture of the spiritual unfaithfulness of God's people.

alien—(also *stranger, foreigner*). When it translates the Hebrew word *ger,* the term refers to a person not of Israelite birth who lived among the Jewish people and engaged in the worship of Yahweh.

Ammonites—The descendants of Ammon, the incestuously conceived child of Lot. Ammonites were idolaters who lived in the region east of the Jordan River.

Amorites—Originally applied to the descendants of one of the sons of Canaan. Because they occupied the hill country, the term gradually broadened to include other ethnic groups in the hills. Sometimes the term is a rough synonym of "Canaanites."

anthropomorphism—A figure of speech in which God is described in terms of human physical attributes (e.g., "the arm of the Lord").

Arabah—The deep valley on the eastern side of Israel's central mountain ridge that contains the Dead Sea and the Jordan River valley.

Asherah pole—An image used in the worship of the Phoenician goddess who is often associated with Baal.

Ashtoreth—The Canaanite goddess usually pictured as the consort of Baal.

atonement—The covering of sin by the application of an atoning sacrifice, normally the blood of a substitute. On Israel's Day of Atonement, the high priest sprinkled the people with the blood of a sacrificial goat.

avenger of blood—The near male kinsman of a homicide victim whose responsibility it was to execute the guilty offender.

Baal—A term meaning "lord." This word was ccasionally used of Yahweh in the Hebrew Bible until its use was co-opted by the followers of a Sidonian deity by that name.

Bashan—A rich highland region lying east of the Sea of Kinnereth (Galilee). Today Bashan is largely included in the area known as the "Golan Heights."

blasphemy—An abusive verbal accusation, especially when directed against God.

booth—A temporary shelter or "tabernacle." At the Feast of Booths or Tabernacles Israelites erected such temporary structures to remind them of their sojourn in the wilderness.

Canaan—One of the sons of Ham, whose name became attached to the land occupied by his descendants; the promised land.

carrion—The carcasses of animals that have died of disease or old age. Carrion was forbidden as food to Israel.

cities of refuge—Six cities, three on either side of the Jordan River valley, to which a person could flee for justice when he had inadvertently caused the death of another.

clean—A ceremonial rather than a moral category.

conquest—The period during which Israel drove the Canaanites from the promised land, roughly covering the time between the death of Moses (about 1406 B.C.) and the death of

Glossary

Joshua (about 1390 B.C.). In reality, the conquest lingered on for an additional three centuries.

covenant—A formal agreement between two parties about their future relations. A covenant involved a pledge of fidelity and well-defined sanctions for violating the pledge.

cubit—A linear unit of measure roughly equivalent to the distance between the elbow and the tip of the middle finger. In modern terms, a cubit is approximately 17.6 inches.

divination—The process of using the occult to predict the future. Often this was done through the interpretation of the lines on the liver of a sacrificial animal.

Documentary Hypothesis—The (discredited) notion that the Pentateuch was not the literary product of Moses but of a clever forger who blended several divergent traditions into the religion of Israel.

Ebal—A mountain in central Palestine lying just south of Mount Gerizim which was the site of the reading of the curses for violations of God's covenant.

elders—The senior officials of an Israelite tribe or town. During the wanderings of Israel, leaders of the twelve tribes served as elders of the whole nation.

euphemism—A figure of speech in which an acceptable expression is substituted for a more direct or objectionable expression (e.g., Deut. 32:50, "gathered to your people" = "buried").

Edom—The rocky region south and east of the Dead Sea, inhabited in Old Testament times by the descendants of Esau, who was also known as Edom ("Red").

fornication—The broadest biblical word for sexual sin.

gates—The location in ancient cities that included administrative headquarters, markets, and law courts.

Gerizim—The mountain in central Palestine that was just north of Mount Ebal and served as the location for the reading of the blessings for covenant obedience.

Gilead—The region east of the Jordan River and north of Ammon which was famous for its spices and aromatic gums.

high place—A site occupied by altars of worship. When Israel invaded Canaan, these were normally associated with pagan deities. As time passed, they were co-opted into the worship of Yahweh, although God intended for them to be destroyed once Jerusalem was established as his worship center.

hyperbole—A figure of speech in which the speaker or writer uses an intentional exaggeration for effect (e.g., "walls up to the sky," Deut. 9:1).

intercession—The process of appealing to an authority (especially to God) on behalf of others

inheritance—The land of Canaan, or the individual Israelite's portion of that land. The concept serves in the New Testament as a picture of the believer's rewards.

judges—Regional governors or deliverers raised up by Yahweh to restore Israel to fellowship after a period of idolatry. Although the judges did serve a judicial function, they were also executives and administrators.

Kinnereth—The Old Testament name for Galilee. The word means "harp," suggested by the shape of the Lake of Galilee.

leaven—An agent (yeast being the prime example) that causes bread to rise.

Levites—The tribe in Israel that was assigned responsibility for managing the worship of the nation. It included the priests (all descendants of Aaron) as well as those who managed the physical arrangements of the altar and tabernacle (or later, the temple).

mediator—A "go-between." In the context of the covenant, Moses was the mediator between Israel and Yahweh.

mercy seat—The flat surface on the lid of the ark of the covenant. The blood of a sacrifice was placed on the mercy seat on Israel's Day of Atonement.

Glossary

metaphor—A figure of speech that equates two entities in order to emphasize some quality in one of them (e.g., "The Lord is my Shepherd").

Moab—The incestuously conceived brother of Ammon and son of Lot. Moab's descendants, the Moabites, lived east of the Jordan River valley.

murder—To kill in a calculated and malicious way for vengeance or personal advantage. Murder was carefully differentiated in divine law from manslaughter, which was often accidental or impulsive.

nation—In the Bible, a group of people united by a common culture, often through kinship and/or language. A nation could consist of only a few hundred people in some cases.

Nisan—The first month in the Hebrew calendar (March-April); also called Abib.

Negev—The arid and rocky southern portion of the Holy Land that extends to the Gulf of Aqaba.

Palestine—A geographical term that is often used in biblical scholarship as a rough equivalent of "the promised land." Ironically, the word is derived from the name of Israel's ancient enemies, the Philistines.

patriarchs—The ethnic fathers of Israel, especially Abraham, Isaac, and Jacob.

Pentateuch—The five books of Moses: Genesis, Exodus, Leviticus, Numbers, and Deuteronomy.

postmodernism—The view that truth cannot be determined, but only exists as an instrument of power by those in authority.

priests—In Israel, the subdivision of the family of Levi (those descended from Aaron) assigned to present gifts at God's altar and manage the holy articles of worship.

redeem—To buy back or purchase an animal or human who has been designated for sacrifice.

Sabbath—The seventh day of the week; the day of rest in the Israelite economy.

shekel—The primary coin of Israel's economy, made up of twenty *gerahs*, or two *bekas*.

Shekinah—A Hebrew word meaning "that which dwells," often used of the *Shekinah* glory, the visible manifestation of Yahweh that often was present at the tabernacle of Israel. The glory of God was typically seen as a cloud during the day or as a pillar of fire by night.

Shema—A Hebrew imperative meaning "Hear!" that is used in Deuteronomy 6:4, the centerpiece of Deuteronomy and the core declaration of Israel's faith.

Shephelah—The foothills connecting Israel's central mountain ridge on the west with the coastal plain.

simile—A figure of speech in which one person or thing is compared to another (e.g., "like a devouring fire," Deut. 9:3).

Suzerain—The superior king in a suzerain-vassal relationship. In the covenant with Israel, Yahweh is the great king and the one who dictates the terms of the relationship.

tabernacle—A tent; in particular, the tent that served as the place where Yahweh met with Israel. The tabernacle served as a portable shrine until Israel was established in the land, when its ministries were localized in Jerusalem. Its function was eventually replaced by the Solomonic temple.

theophany—The description of a divine appearance, often using dramatic language and hyperbole (see Deut. 33:2–5).

torah—The Hebrew word usually rendered "law" or "teaching." Sometimes *torah* is used as a synonym for the Pentateuch, since these books contain the law of God given through Moses.

transcendence—The quality of God that separates him from his creation; his majesty or "otherness."

Transjordan—Literally, "across the Jordan," the region lying east of Canaan, across the Jordan River from the land of promise.

Glossary

vassal—The subservient entity in a suzerain-vassal relationship. In God's covenant, Israel was the vassal.

Yahweh—The usual way of spelling the Old Testament's personal name for God. Only the consonants (YHWH) are preserved in the Hebrew text, so no certainty attaches to this rendering.